In the Shadows
of Victory

In the Shadows of Victory

RENDEZVOUS WITH DESTINY

*Three Bestselling Novels
Complete in One Volume*

Rhineland Inheritance
~

Gibraltar Passage
~

Sahara Crosswind

T. DAVIS BUNN

Inspirational Press • New York

Previously published in three separate volumes:

6/98 Gen fund 25⁰⁰

RHINELAND INHERITANCE, copyright © 1993 by T. Davis Bunn
GIBRALTAR PASSAGE © 1994 by T. Davis Bunn
SAHARA CROSSWIND © 1994 by T. Davis Bunn

These stories are entirely creations of the author's imagination. No parallel between any persons, living or dead, is intended.

Jacket illustration by Joe Nordstrom.

First Inspirational Press edition published in 1998.

Inspirational Press
A division of BBS Publishing Corporation
386 Park Avenue South
New York, NY 10016

Inspirational Press is a registered trademark of BBS Publishing Corporation.

Published by arrangement with Bethany House Publishers,
A Ministry of Bethany Fellowship, Inc.

Library of Congress Catalog Card Number: 97-77411
ISBN: 0-88486-195-3

Printed in the United States of America.

Contents

I
Rhineland Inheritance

~

This book is dedicated to

Gil Morris

For the friendship
And the challenge.

Prologue

The Former Third Reich of National Socialist Germany

October 1945

JAKE KNEW SOMETHING big was in the air the moment he closed the door in his fiancée's face.

Maybe he knew before. Maybe that was what gave him the strength to leave her photograph taped to the back of his locker. Six months had passed since she had written about her new lover. Yet the tattered photo had remained with him through two more postings and the end of the war. But no more.

Captain Jake Burnes set his cap at the proper angle, hefted his worldly belongings, and marched out to meet his future.

The future stood waiting for him in the form of a new-old buddy, Captain Sam Marshall, head of the local MP garrison. The war had taught both men the trick of making friends fast, then losing them even faster.

"Need a hand?"

"Thanks, I can manage," Jake replied. "I decided to lighten the load."

"Come again?"

"Never mind." Jake started off toward the camp's main gate. To his left sprawled one of the Allies' internment camps, full to overflowing both with former German soldiers and the never-ending stream of refugees.

Marshall swung in beside him, matching Jake's stride with the unconscious habit borne on a thousand parade grounds. "Got a jeep waiting for you up at the gate."

Jake hid his gratitude behind pretended surprise. "This the normal treatment for somebody who's just been kicked off base?"

"Just thought a buddy might need a lift, is all," Marshall replied. "And maybe a little escort duty."

"You what?"

"You've made some enemies around here," Marshall said.

Jake's shoulders bounced once in a humorless laugh. "Tell me something I don't already know."

They walked on in silence for a time before Marshall said, "Got my marching orders this morning. Along with all my men."

That stopped him. "Connors can't be meaning to send all of you home at once."

"That's where you're wrong," Marshall replied. "The good colonel's decided to get rid of all my men. And me. Next week."

"He plans to guard the camp with those untrained gorillas of his?" Jake glanced over the fence to where one of the newly arrived MPs walked in bored guard duty. The man was built like a full-grown bull, all shoulders and swagger.

"That's what it looks like." Marshall's eyes followed Jake's. "Another dozen piled in this morning. Drawn from every division in Europe, by the sounds of it. None of them ever pulled MP duty in their lives. Only time they ever saw a stockade was when they were inside."

Jake shook his head. "Doesn't make sense, sending his only experienced men home all at once like that."

"There's a lot around here that doesn't make any sense," Marshall replied. "And more every day."

"Such as?"

"Heard some of them talking last night, filling in the new boys. Work details, from the sounds of it. Nothing to do with any guard duty I've ever heard of." Marshall watched the sentry make another pass. "Sounded like a bunch of bandits making ready for the big heist."

"Then you must have heard wrong," Jake said flatly. "That whole camp doesn't have two plug nickels to rub together."

"Maybe," Marshall said doubtfully. "They kept saying something about orders direct from Colonel Connors. Strange to see a commanding officer take such interest in new MPs."

Jake resumed walking. "Yeah, well, if I don't ever hear that name again, it'll be too soon."

"They were talking about you, too," Marshall went on. "What I heard made me think you might stay healthier if I were to see you off base."

"Why would they bother with me?" Jake returned the sentry officer's laconic salute. "I'm history."

"Ever wonder why Connors would be so eager to get rid of his best officer? Not to mention the only man on his staff who speaks passable German."

Jake hefted his duffle bag into the back of the jeep. "Maybe he's got somebody else in mind for the job."

"Seems like a lot of trouble to go through over a grudge," Marshall persisted.

"I gave up trying to figure the colonel out a long time ago." Jake started to climb in; then something made him hesitate. He turned back around, and spotted a young kid watching through the wires.

The boy was no more than twelve or thirteen, but nonetheless wore the ragged remnants of a uniform. They had come across a lot of such child-warriors in the war's last days. In his frantic final effort, Hitler had sent out whole battalions of the very young and very old. Most had received no training whatsoever. Many had not even been armed.

Jake saw a pair of dark eyes stare at him with the fathomless depths of one without hope. He had seen too many young eyes carry such expressions as he had trudged and fought his way through the war. Still, the gaze tugged at his heart. It always did.

For some reason he could not explain, Jake lifted his hand in farewell.

The boy remained still as stone for a time, then suddenly thrust both arms out through the wire. Fingers clawed the air, reaching for Jake, begging for what he could not give. The boy's face became a mask of soundless pleading.

"Hey!" An MP with the battered face of a long-time boxer lumbered over. "Back behind the wire!"

Long before the MP reached him, the boy spun and fled into the camp.

Jake stood and watched the vacant space where the boy had been, and wondered why after two years of active duty he still could not stop hurting for the kids. He shrugged it away as best he could, climbed into the jeep, and said, "Let's go."

Chapter One

*T*O JAKE, this new colonel seemed a good joe—at least, as far as any superior officer could be. "Captain Jake Burnes, right?"

"Yessir, reporting for duty."

"Take a load off, Captain." Colonel Beecham buried his nose back in Jake's file. "Let's see. Left Officer Training School in October '42, got to the front just in time for the push up through Italy. In the meantime you've earned yourself a silver star, a bronze star, a purple heart, and a string of medals from here to Okinawa. What'd you do, son, decide it was your own private war?"

"Never much liked sitting around, sir."

"No, it doesn't sound like it." He flipped over another page. "Don't see any mention of you speaking French."

"Not a word, sir."

"So they assigned you as liaison for incoming French troops." The colonel snorted. "Another example of army logic."

"Temporary liaison, sir," Jake corrected.

"That so?" Colonel Beecham searched the file. "When are you due for release, Captain?"

"Seven weeks, sir. Just before Christmas."

The colonel squinted down an invisible rifle barrel at Burnes. "They assigned me a liaison officer who doesn't know a word of French and is going home in seven weeks?"

"Looks that way, sir."

"Whose feathers did you ruffle, Captain? General Eisenhower's?"

"Nossir. Only Colonel Connors', sir."

"Only." A glimmer of humor appeared in the steely gaze. "That must be Cut-Throat Connors, isn't that what they call him?"

"I wouldn't know, sir."

"I hear he'd sell his soul and mortgage his own mother for a star on his shoulder. What'd you do, son?"

"Nothing really, sir. Just a difference of opinion."

"Come on, Captain. Cut to the chase. Sure as gunfire in a battle zone, there's not a friend of Connors in sight. Let's hear it."

Jake decided the colonel really meant it. "I was responsible for a section of the Oberkirch internment camp."

"I know that. So?"

"Just before I arrived they'd had a couple of suicides among the former German soldiers. The officer whose place I took spoke some German and managed to get some of the men to talk with him. Seems like they'd been growing despondent over what was waiting for them outside—cities pretty much destroyed, no food, less work, chaos everywhere. The officer started looking around for some way to improve morale, and decided to train a couple of squads in touch football." Jake shrugged. "Since I speak German, he asked me to take over where he left off."

"Connors is awful proud of his football team, isn't he."

"Yessir."

Colonel Connors was responsible for security in the region north of Offenburg. It was well known that he was constantly scouting for football material, and any enlisted man who made his team won an MP billet and an extra stripe.

"What'd he do, challenge your German boys to a game? Put a couple of side bets down?"

"More than a couple," Burnes replied. "From what I heard, sir."

"And then your boys went out and whupped his pride and joy." The smile finally surfaced. "Wish I'd been there to see that."

"It was some game, sir," Burnes said with evident satisfaction.

"Worth getting stuck with a bunch of foreigners for your last posting?"

Burnes shrugged. "Can't be worse than guarding ten thousand defeated German soldiers."

Colonel Beecham settled back in his chair. "So you speak some German. How much is some?"

"I guess I can get around pretty well, sir. I was studying it before I got called up."

"Maybe you'll be of some use, after all. I've got quite a few bilinguals in French and English, but almost no German speakers. Just a chaplain who's almost never here and a young lady who's already too busy by half. Any chance of you changing your mind, maybe signing on for another tour?"

"None at all," Jake replied flatly. "Sir."

"It's like that, is it? You got somebody waiting for you back home?"

"Not anymore," Jake replied bitterly.

"She dear-johned you?"

"Six months ago, sir." The letter had simply said, don't come back expecting to find things like they used to be, because what used to be isn't there anymore. "Guess she got tired of waiting."

"Family?"

"Not anymore," Jake repeated, more softly this time.

The colonel's leathery features creased with concern. "While you were over here?"

Jake nodded. "Both at once. They had an automobile accident."

The letter had been waiting for him when his platoon had marched into Rome. The fact that he hadn't slept for three days had partly numbed the pain. The letter had been written by their elderly next-door neighbor and family friend. Snowstorm. Icy road. Oncoming truck. His dad had not made it to the hospital. His mother had died two days later in her sleep. No apparent injuries, the doctors couldn't explain it. Jake was sad but not sorry. His mother would have been lost without his father around.

"Tough," the colonel said, and clearly meant it. "What about brothers or sisters?"

"One brother," Jake said, telling the rest in a weary voice. "He was leading a mortar squad on D-Day. They were coming off the boat ramp onto the beach at Normandy. A German '88 round hit the ramp and took out the whole squad."

The colonel said softly, "I lost a son on the beaches."

Both men gazed at a spot somewhere between them for a moment of pained and silent remembering. The colonel was the first to speak again. "Sounds as if the only family you've got left is the army."

If you could call a group that had tried its level best to get him killed for two solid years a family. "Guess that's about it, sir."

"Well, we'll see if we can't bring you around to our way of thinking. We've got seven weeks to soften you up." Colonel Beecham leaned back and hefted a pair of size thirteens onto the corner of his desk. "Am I to assume that Colonel Connors did a thorough job of briefing you on your new responsibilities?"

"All I know," Jake replied, "is that right now I'm sitting in a squad room in what I hope is Badenburg. Sir."

"Okay, here's the scoop. As you may know, the Allies are in the process of splitting Germany into four sections, each to be governed by a different occupying force. France has been given responsibility for two portions extending out from their border. One of the sections is right here, the other is up on the other side of Karlsruhe.

"For the past few months, the French have been too busy taking care of business at home to worry much about this region, so we've been holding the fort for them. Sort of, anyway. Temporary measures tend not to hold too well in the army. But that's almost over now. The French are due in here the week after Christmas. The only American base that will remain in this area is Karlsruhe, which is where we are planning to consolidate. There and Stuttgart and Pforzheim, which remain in the American zone. Are you with me?"

"So far, yessir."

"Right." Without turning around, Beecham pointed toward the map on the wall behind him. "That red line you see there is the border between France and Germany. That's our responsibility. The place is like a sieve right now. We've got upwards of a thousand refugees pouring through there every night. I don't know where they're hoping to go, 'cause the French sure don't want them. Now that it's getting cold, the morning patrols are coming across bodies. It's a bad business, Captain. We didn't fight this dang war to have civilians dying in the bushes. Not in my area. The way I see it, we've got a responsibility to these people. If the war's over, then it's over, and we've got to start treating them like the human beings they are. Have you got any problems with that?"

"None at all, sir."

"Okay. Now, I've got seventeen hundred men under my command right now, but like all these places around here, we're losing them fast. The border area isn't as high up on the brass's list of priorities as I think it should be. As far as they're concerned, if these Eastern European refugees want to keep running until they drop, that's their business. But not for me. Nossir. They need to be properly cared for in the camps until we can get some kind of permanent billet sorted out. Am I getting through?"

"Loud and clear, sir."

"As I said, there's an American contingent up here at Karlsruhe. They're supposed to be helping out, at least until the French are settled in and up to snuff. But they're so tied up trying to find space for all the incoming personnel and equipment, they're busier than a one-legged man in a polka contest."

The colonel pointed a finger the size of a large-caliber gun barrel directly at Jake's chest. "That's your job, son. I want a concerted effort by all the military in this region, both those here now and those coming in, to help us close that border. Think you can do that?"

"I'll sure give it a try, sir."

"Good man. Our responsibility runs all the way from Karlsruhe right down to the Swiss border below Mulhouse. Almost exactly one hundred miles, a lot of which is heavily forested. What isn't covered in woodland, well, this war has made to look like something dragged up from hell."

"A tough job," Burnes said.

"An impossible job, with the men I've got right now," Beecham corrected. Which means it is positively vital that you get the other forces to help us out."

"From the sound of your voice I guess they're not all that interested."

"Some are, some aren't. Some of our commanders are still too busy fighting an enemy that has already surrendered to worry about civilian casualties. Others just don't care."

"There are men like that in every army, sir."

"Tell me about it," Beecham agreed wearily. "So your job, Captain, is to make them care."

"Yessir," Burnes said, rising to his feet.

"One more thing." The colonel's tone turned cold. "You're going to hear about it soon enough, so I might as well be the one to tell you. There's a lot of scuttlebutt going around just now about Nazi treasure. You know the SS used Badenburg as a sort of private resort."

"I've heard the same stories as everybody else, sir."

"So you've probably heard the tales about them burying everything from the Mongol diamond to Cleopatra's throne in the hills around here." The colonel rose to his feet. "I'm not going to waste my breath by ordering you not to go treasure hunting, Captain. But if I ever find out you've been in derelict of duty because of some fairy tale about the lost kingdom of Nod, or hear you've been out gallivanting on army time, I'll personally have your hide. You reading me, Captain?"

"Loud and clear, sir."

"You'll be working with a Captain Servais, who used to be with the Fighting Free French. Good man. Served with the Americans for a time. Highly decorated. You two should get along fine."

"I'm sure we will, sir."

"I've got a woman on my staff who was seconded from the new government staffers arriving in Berlin. Her name is Anders—Sally Anders. They sent her here to act as liaison with the incoming French forces. Quite a dynamo. She's off somewhere in the city just now, but any paperwork you need doing or red tape that gets in your way, she's your gal."

"I'll give it my best shot, sir."

"That's what I like to hear." The colonel's attention was already caught by something else on his desk. "Have Sergeant Morrows show you to your billet. Dismissed."

The colonel's office was in staff headquarters, which was situated in what appeared to be the only intact building on the road leading to town. It had formerly been a large manor house, and its ornate brick and iron fencing was now topped off with military-issue barbed wire. The great iron gates had been replaced by a guardhouse and standard checkpoint crossbar. The large formal grounds were now sectioned off into smaller self-contained units for stores, motor pool, staff quarters, infirmary, and parade ground.

The main base was a mile farther up the road running away from town, and had clearly been designed for a much larger contingent than the one which now occupied it. The camp was built on a hill overlooking the ruins of Badenburg. The ground had been cleared from the dense forest that surrounded them on all sides. Fresh-cut tree stumps, some of them as broad as six feet across, jutted from the snow-covered ground between the huts. Rutted tracks frozen to iron hardness ran in long straight army lines between the rows of billets. The Quonsets lumped across the hilltop like rows of metal measles.

Sergeant Morrows drove Jake across the frozen, rutted ground. He stopped before a Quonset, distinct from its neighbors only by the number painted on its side. Beecham's aide was a heavy-set sergeant who slid and cursed his way over the icy earth toward the entrance. "It ain't supposed to turn this cold for another three months, so they say. Guess we're in for one hard winter. You ever seen anything like this freeze, Captain?"

"I came up via Italy," Jake replied. "Never had much time for cold weather."

"Italy, huh. Fought with Patton?"

"So they say."

"Yeah, I never had much time for the high brass myself." Morrow's grin exposed a great expanse of yellow. "You liberate many of those signorinas yourself, Captain?"

Burnes shook his head. The colonel's aide was a man to keep as an ally. If possible. "The stories never tell you about how all the signorinas have fathers," Jake replied. "Or how all the fathers have shotguns."

"Yeah? Well, you won't have that trouble around here." The sergeant leered and shouldered the door open. "This is your billet, Captain. The whole barracks for the two of you. And look who's here. Captain Servais, this is your new teammate, Captain Burnes, late of Patton's army."

The man rolled from his bunk in the fluid motion of one accustomed to coming instantly awake. The man walked forward with the cautious gaze of someone who had learned in life-and-death struggles to measure all partners with great care. "Captain Burnes, did I hear that correctly?"

"You speak English," Jake said, accepting the man's iron-hard grip. "You don't know what a relief that is."

"Captain Burnes here don't have no French, but he speaks the local Kraut lingo," Morrows drawled. "Well, I'll leave you gents to get acquainted. Anything you need, Captain, and all that." Morrows turned and stomped away.

Jake watched Morrows' broad back retreating. When the door closed, he turned to find Servais watching him with a knowing gaze. "Sergeant Morrows has the ability to find anything, anywhere, anytime."

"I figured the colonel wasn't keeping him around for his charm," Jake said.

"Put the sergeant down in the middle of Antarctica, and in thirty minutes he'd have enough gear to equip an entire platoon," Servais said, motioning toward the hut's murky depths. "Will you take coffee? I don't have anything stronger, I'm afraid."

"Coffee's fine," Burnes replied, following Servais between bunks of rusted springs and rolled-up mattresses. "I can't get over how well you speak English. You sound almost American."

"I spent my summers as a waiter serving tourists on the French Riviera, starting when I was twelve," Servais explained, placing a battered pot on a small gas burner. "I soon discovered that the English gave better tips if I could speak to them. Then during the war I spent some time with American troops."

"Free French?" Burnes asked, dropping his gear beside a bunk.

Servais nodded. He filled a mug with coffee and handed it over. "Condensed milk there on the table beside you."

"Thanks." Burnes poured in some milk and took a noisy sip. "I heard some good things about the FFF. Never had a chance to see for myself."

"Where did you serve?"

"Italy, mostly," Burnes replied. "I walked every road from Salerno to Milan, or so it felt at the time. How about you?"

"North Africa, then here." Servais glanced at the medals decorating Jake's uniform. "I take it the pretty ribbons were not earned from the backseat of a command jeep."

"Not all of them, anyway." Jake motioned toward a dress jacket hanging from a nail in the wall, its array of medals glimmering in the glare of the single overhead bulb. "Looks like you carry your own set of stories."

Servais had the sort of strong, ugly face that many women would find irresistible—all jutting angles and craggy folds. His nose was a great lump jutting above a full mouth, his eyes black and piercing. He was not a big man, standing well short of six feet and slender to the point of appearing permanently hungry. But he carried himself with the solid assurance of one well used to his own strength. "What do you call yourself?"

"Jake. What about you?"

"Pierre." Servais glanced at his watch. "I'm scheduled for a patrol. But first I have to go by and pick up orders at HQ. You could change into fatigues and join me, if you like."

As with most army jeeps, the canvas top had long since worn out, there was no heat, and the exhaust puffed through holes in the flooring, nearly choking them every time Servais slowed down. Which he seldom did.

"I'm splitting my men up so the ones with field experience outnumber the newcomers two to one," Pierre shouted over the whining motor. "I don't know how long that will last, if they keep sending in new recruits as fast as they are now."

As far as Burnes could see, the only good thing about Pierre's driving was that he hit the bumps so hard it lifted Jake's backside off the seat and kept him from freezing solid to the cracked leather padding. "You survived the war just to die now?" Jake asked, keeping a white-knuckled grip on the jeep's rattling frame.

"A lot of my soldiers are just barely eighteen," Pierre went on. "They come from the newly liberated provinces, and they want to show their patriotism by acting tough toward the defeated Germans. I need the soldiers who actually experienced the war to keep them in line. The problem is, my best men are leaving. Their time is up and they're being discharged. Either that, or they are being rounded up and sent to Indochina. I don't know how I'm going to be able to handle the new ones without them."

The jeep did a four-wheel skid around an icy corner, almost wrapped itself around a tree, caught hold of the road at the last possible moment, and barreled on. Burnes shouted, "It's amazing you ever survived to fight the Germans."

Pierre slowed marginally. "These new soldiers are just kids. Full of anger and spite. Some of them feel like cowards because they weren't old enough to prove themselves. Most claim to have been in the underground. Some probably were. All of them are dangerous. To themselves and the Germans."

Staff Headquarters, and Colonel Beecham's office, was located in one of the few intact houses on the southwestern side of Badenburg. After turning in his duty rosters, Pierre took the time to show Burnes around. The officers' mess was located in what had probably once been a grand ballroom, although the chandelier had long since been dislodged by a bomb. A few links from the heavy chain still dangled from the ceiling. Directly underneath, the shattered flooring had been hastily relaid with stone. It was hard to find wood these days, as the locals were stealing anything they could find to warm their homes.

Jake was still looking at the ornamental frieze encircling the ceiling when they rounded the corner, which was why he walked directly into one of the most beautiful women he had seen in two long years. She backed up a step, set her cap in place, said, "You're straightforward, soldier. I'll have to give you that."

Jake stammered up an, "I'm sorry, ma'am. I didn't—"

"Apologies accepted. I wasn't looking either." She was lithe and tall, with auburn hair piled and pinned beneath the cap. Her eyes were the color of smoke from a winter's fire. "Are you supposed to be shepherding this poor lost lamb around, Pierre?"

"Captain Burnes is quite capable of looking after himself," Pierre replied. "How are you, Sally?"

"Busy. You'll have to excuse me." She stepped between them. "Nice to have met you, Captain, I suppose."

The two men watched Sally as she walked down the corridor and out of sight. Jake realized he had been holding his breath. He straightened and asked, "Who was that *that*?"

"Sally Anders." Pierre's eyes had not shifted from the point where Sally had disappeared from view. "Also known as the Ice Queen. Late of Ottawa. Secretary to the general staff."

"Married?"

"Her fiancé was lost at sea. North Atlantic convoy duty." Pierre shook his head. "My friend, if I'd had someone like that waiting for me at home, I would have learned to walk on water."

The three platoons were drawn up under a gray sky that threatened to blanket them with yet more snow. Pierre's orders were given from the hood of the jeep. Jake Burnes understood not a word. Yet his lack of French could not keep him from observing the casual hold which Pierre maintained over the power of command. The troops listened carefully to his clipped sentences. He lightened them with a joke that brought smiles to most faces. He gathered them together and made them feel a part of something larger. Jake did not need to know the words to understand what was happening. He was watching a leader.

Pierre jumped from the jeep, said in English, "There's been a lot of movement down the southern stretch. I thought I'd take them myself today. Care to come along?"

Jake understood that he was being tested. He knew that it would jeopardize their work together if he pointed out that this excursion was not part of his duty roster. "Whatever you say."

Pierre placed a grizzled Belgian sergeant-major on point and two hard-eyed corporals as back sentries, and ordered them to move out. They were soon tramping along paths that were invisible under their mantle of snow, trusting their sergeant's experience to take them out and bring them back.

The pace was hard. The ground was broken, with invisible traps for the unwary beneath the white covering. They moved in a silence disturbed only by grunts and heavy breathing.

Every mile or so they would come upon a guardpost, usually invisible until they were almost upon it, any roughness from the recent construction hidden under winter's blanket. A half-frozen man would crawl down from his tree house, stamp up and down, slapping feeling back into his body, and make a shivering report. A new man would be assigned to shinny up the tree ladder. Once in place, the squad would be again under way.

They had been going long enough for Jake to work up a fair lather when the ground exploded at his feet. This time there was no bomb; only a young deer that had taken shelter in a steep-sided levee. The deer bounded upward, throwing up a glorious blast of snow, then disappeared into the woods.

Jake leaned against a tree, slowing his breath and letting the weakness drain from his legs. Around him the men laughed with relief. Jake smiled at chatter he did not hear, and recalled his last injury, when a land mine had exploded less than a dozen feet away. The point man had hit the trip wire, and had simply vanished. Jake had caught a sliver of shrapnel across his forehead, slicing him open clean to the bone. There had been more blood than damage, and after a couple dozen stitches and one night in the mobile infirmary, Jake had been sent back to his squad.

As he stood and gathered himself, Jake glimpsed something moving rapidly to one side of his field of vision.

"There!" he shouted, then was up and after the running figure.

The man raced through the trees in great leaps that lifted him clear of the clinging snow. Jake felt the air pumping in and out of his lungs as he pounded after him. The man was carrying a dark sack, that much Jake could see in his fleeting glimpses as he chased him through the woods. Twice the sack caught in low branches, each time granting Jake a breath's span to close the gap. Behind him he heard whistles and shouts and crashing sounds, but he had no time to look around. No time for anything but the challenge of the chase.

Then the shot blazed out and smacked the tree beside him, throwing a cloud of snow into his eyes. Jake's war-trained reactions reasserted themselves. He was down and rolling, then crouched and searching, pistol in hand without knowing how it had come free from the holster.

Pierre crawled up beside him, breathless. "Did you see where the shot came from?"

Jake made a vague gesture forward and to the right. "Somewhere up there."

Pierre motioned for two soldiers to head over, the others to fan out. Then forward. Careful, now. Cautious. But as fast as possible.

They caught the man's tracks and followed them until it began to snow. Dusk was gathering, the men were cold, the quarry had vanished. Somewhere up ahead, the Rhine River marked the border with France, but without proper night gear they would find it by falling in.

Pierre was preparing to turn them around. But Jake wanted to press on. Had to. Someone had shot at him. Wasn't the war over?

Then in the last light of fading day, Jake caught a glint in the snow ahead. Cautiously he approached, bent over, and with wet woolen mittens pulled it from the ground. The sight was so incongruous he stared at it for a dozen breaths before realizing what he had.

"What is—" Pierre came up close enough to see. He stopped cold, whispering, "Nom de Dieu!"

"Gold," Jake whispered. And it was. A solid gold cross, as heavy as his pistol, attached to a thick gold chain and studded with gemstones. "Gold."

Chapter Two

"**Y**OUR FIRST DAY on the job," Colonel Beecham said, bristling. "What happens? First you run down the best secretary in the Sixth Army right outside my door."

"Sir, I can—"

"Then you hook up with this French johnny, go gallivanting out in the woods in the exact opposite direction from where your responsibilities lie."

"I can explain, if you'll just—"

"Then you start an international border incident by leading an entire squad right smack dab into the middle of an ambush."

"—let me tell you—"

"And windup the day by picking a treasure out of the snow and getting the wind up of the entire division."

"Please listen to my side of the—"

"Not to mention the rumors you've stirred up. The last thing I heard, it was a treasure chest so big it took fifteen pachyderms to cart it home. Don't ask me where you found fifteen grown elephants in the middle of the Black Forest. Left over from Hannibal's crossing, I suppose." Frosty eyes riveted him to the far wall. "Well? What've you got planned for this evening. An invasion of China?"

"Nossir," Jake surrendered.

"Glad to hear it. Did you bring that good-for-nothing malcontent Servais with you?"

"He's just outside, sir."

"Bring him in."

Jake hastened to the small annex one door down from the colonel's office, where he found Pierre leaning over Sally Anders' desk. Pierre straightened from his position and wiped the smile off his face as he caught sight of Jake's pallor. He followed Jake back to the colonel's office, marched smartly through the doorway, saluted, and announced, "Captain Pierre Servais, reporting as ordered, sir!"

"Cut the malarkey, Servais," Beecham snapped. "I've got about as much time for you as I do for your friend here. Now what were you doing out on patrol?"

"Checking out some new men, sir."

"Don't you have sergeants for that work?"

"Not really, sir." Servais turned serious. "I lost four just this week on postings back home. And the requests for men to be promoted to fill their places haven't been granted yet."

"Who's got the paper work?"

"Sir, I believe—"

"Morrows!" the colonel bellowed.

"Sir!" The corpulent sergeant appeared with a speed only possible for someone dedicated to listening through keyholes.

"Find out where the promotion papers for Servais' men are. And if there's any holdup, tell whoever's responsible that I've been meaning to find volunteers to test our new paper parachutes."

"Right away, sir."

"Okay, now listen up, you two." Beecham swivelled around and glared at them. "For your information, the war's over and they've stopped pinning medals on anybody who moves. If either of you two yahoos tries another end run like this, I'll use you as tent pegs! Understand?"

"Yessir," they said in unison.

"Now, where's the contraband?"

"With Morrows, sir."

"Good grief, man." Beecham was genuinely exasperated. "You don't have the brains the good Lord gave a gnat, do you?"

"Yessir, I mean, nossir."

"Leaving gold with Morrows is like asking a rabbit to take care of some lettuce for you. Sally!"

The auburn head appeared in the doorway. "You rang?"

The colonel's voice softened. "Be a sweetheart and go chase up our good sergeant. Tell him I expect to have the cross on my desk, chain and jewels intact, or I'll personally stake him out for tank target practice."

"Only if you give me first shot," Sally replied, and left. Jake thought he had caught a glimmer of sympathy as she glanced his way, then decided it was just his imagination.

"All right, listen up, you two. Your responsibilities are to liaise with the Americans and the incoming French. This does not include skipping out for a light fling in the snow after lunch. Nor has anybody told you to pretend there are Nazis behind every bush and go marching off to war in the woods. Is that clear?"

"Yessir."

"Don't let me hear about any such collision courses from either of you, not ever again. I hate to lose good officers. Now get out of my sight."

"How are we supposed to liaise with troops if we can't go out in the field with them," Burnes grumbled.

Servais, his elbows propped on the bar and his head down almost level with his glass, gave a restricted little shrug. "Send them love letters, maybe."

Jake swiped a hand over his head. "I thought for a minute there I was going to get scalped."

"That's why they call him Smoke Beecham."

"As in, where there's Beecham there's fire?"

Servais shook his head. "As in, dragon's breath. After Beecham passes, all that's left is a tiny puff of smoke."

"He seemed nice enough when I first talked with him."

"The colonel must have wanted something," Servais mused.

"He did."

"Like what?"

"He wants me to stay on. Or so I thought this afternoon."

Servais straightened. "Speak of the dragon himself."

Jake rose from his slouch just in time to hear the gravelly, "Evening, boys. Give me the usual, Tom."

"Yessir, Colonel."

"Can I buy you soldiers a round?"

"Thank you, no thank you, sir," they said together, still at attention.

"Forget the parade ground razzmatazz for a minute and come join me in the corner," he ordered, and walked over to the far table. Reluctantly they picked up their glasses and joined him. "Siddown. That's it. Sure you won't take up my offer?"

"I'm fine, thank you, sir."

"Well, maybe later." Beecham's easy-going manner carried no suggestion of the earlier roasting. "All right. We've got maybe fifteen minutes before the crowd arrives. Tell me what you think about your little forest run."

"Colonel," Jake looked positively pained at having to go through it again. "I'd just as soon——"

"Listen to me, gentlemen," Beecham said, leaning up close to them. "That little speech wasn't meant for you. Well, not entirely. I've got to make sure you keep your priorities straight. But what I had to make plain to my staff was that I won't put up with any bozos turning into treasure hounds."

"It wasn't anything like that at all, sir," Jake protested.

"I know that, son," Beecham said kindly. "I knew it as soon as I heard you'd left the cross with Morrows. That was a mistake, though. Big mistake. I thought I'd have to use a tire wrench and some dynamite to pry his grubby little mitts loose."

Beecham leaned back and waited for the bartender to set down his drink. "Thanks, Tom."

"Welcome, Colonel."

"Morrows' not the only greedy little so-and-so on the base," the colonel continued. "And that's our problem. There's no harm in telling you the truth. Not now, anyway. As long as I can rely on you both to keep your traps shut about it."

"I think I'll have that drink after all," Jake said.

"Tom! Bring over a couple of whatever they were having, will you?"

"Right away, sir."

"Rumor has it that the Nazis had a big stash of treasure around here somewhere," the colonel said quietly. "It wouldn't surprise me, since the SS used this city as their personal country club. Nor does it astonish me that we haven't found anything. Have you been into Badenburg yet?"

Jake shook his head. "I've just been in Germany a little over a month, sir. The only town I've seen is Oberkirch."

"That's not much more than a village," Beecham replied. "And not too badly hit, if I recall. Son, Badenburg ain't no more."

"Bad," Servais confirmed quietly. "Very, very bad."

"Supposedly there are over thirty thousand people living in the ruins," Beecham continued. "Personally I just don't see how. There doesn't appear to be three bricks standing together. Not enough shelter to keep a dog dry. But you'll see it for yourself soon enough, I suppose. Karlsruhe's supposed to be as bad, though I haven't seen it for myself."

"Worse," Servais said softly. "Same ruins, more people."

"What I'm trying to say, gentlemen, is we've got more important things to do than go traipsing off into the countryside looking for lost treasure. Now, I'm pretty sure I can count on you two to keep your heads over this. But I *know* the same can't be said for a lot of the others on my staff. Do you follow?"

"Yessir."

"They had to hear me come down on you two, and come down hard. It was the only hope I had of keeping order." Beecham grimaced. "The problem isn't restricted to the

lower ranks. My aching back, I wish it was. Word has it
that the general in charge of the Frieburg area has got three
squads doing nothing but scouring the area for Nazi loot.
I'm not in the finger-pointing business. But my problem's
the opposite. I've been given an impossible duty, and only a
quarter of the men I need to do it with. As long as this
situation continues I'm going to come down hard on anybody who doesn't have his nose to the grindstone."

Beecham took a long swallow. "But that doesn't mean
you boys can't continue looking around as long as it's on
your own time. And as long as you keep it quiet."

Jake permitted himself the first smile of the evening.
"Quiet as church mice in slippers, sir."

"Right. Now tell me what happened."

Interrupting each other in turns, they related the events
of the afternoon. When they had finished, Beecham sat lost
in thought for a time, then asked, "So you think it was two
men?"

"Not at first," Jake replied. "The shot came from the
direction he was running in. But the more I think about it,
the more I'm sure he didn't have time to turn and aim."

"It couldn't have been just a lucky shot?"

"Maybe," Jake said doubtfully. "But I don't think so."

"As hard as he was running," Servais added, "it would be
tough to hit anything without taking a couple of breaths to
quiet down."

"So it really was an ambush," Beecham mused.

"I figure more like a last line of defense," Jake said. "If he
gets in trouble he runs toward somebody stationed at a
certain point—"

"Who shoots down my men," Beecham growled. "I don't
like it. Not one bit."

"Jake's not sure he was actually shooting to hit," Servais
interjected.

"What's this?"

"Just a hunch, sir," Jake replied. "But it was a high-caliber bullet, I'd know the sound of that shot anywhere."

"Sniper?"

"That was my guess. Pierre's men didn't find a second set of footprints. It would have been hard to miss them in fresh snow. I figure maybe he was stationed in a blind, and in our haste to follow the running guy, we missed the obvious."

"Not so obvious at all, Captain," Beecham said approvingly. "So he bought his man a few seconds of time with a well-aimed miss."

"Enough time for him to evade us," Servais said. "And it would have been no more than another escaped black marketeer, except for the cross."

"The cross, yes," Beecham agreed. "How do you think he lost it?"

"I saw the sack catch on branches a couple of times," Jake said. "That's how I got up as close to him as I did."

"Close enough to see him clearly?"

Jake shook his head. "I only know he had to be a young man to run that fast. Dark hair. Gray sweater and pants, or at least that's how they looked in the light. Never saw his face."

"So the cross fell from a hole in his sack."

"Unless someone else dropped it," Servais offered.

"That's possible," Beecham replied. "But doubtful. If this is an established routine, they might use the same track. But for a man fleeing to run directly over the same piece of ground as the last man in the snow, at dusk . . ." Beecham shook his head. "It's extremely doubtful."

Beecham tasted his drink and looked up. "How trustworthy is this sergeant-major of yours, Servais?"

"An excellent man, sir. One of the best."

"So leave him and his squad on patrol duty in that area for a while. Let's wait and see if they spot anything more."

"Should I warn him to look out for anything in particular?"

Beecham gave a humorless smile. "Given the circumstances, Captain, I seriously doubt if your men will be caught napping in that area for a long time to come. Just make sure you ask him about footprints."

"Yessir."

"Sir," Jake said. "Could I ask what is going to happen to the cross?"

"Why, soldier, are you getting money hungry all of a sudden?"

"Nossir, well, that is—"

Beecham waved the matter aside. "They've got forms for such things now. And routines."

"I can imagine," Servais said. "Bye-bye cross."

"One of two things will happen," Beecham went on. "They'll put up notices, and if anybody comes forth and shows a legitimate claim to it, then back it goes."

"Which is unlikely," Jake said.

"In the extreme, son. Unlikely in the extreme. If it's Nazi loot, which would be my guess, then for all we know it came off the neck of the bishop of Cairo, or Persia, or the back side of Tibet. Anyway, there'll be a little wait, then the assessors will make an evaluation and give you a reward."

"Buy us off," Pierre translated.

"The reward is about a tenth of the estimated value, the last I heard. Which ought to be something. To keep the peace, I'd advise you to take a third of it and split it among your men."

"That's a good idea, sir," Jake said, recognizing an order when he heard one.

"The paper work will take six months or thereabouts, maybe longer. By that time your boys'll be scattered to the wind. Be sure and get everybody's home address, Servais."

"Yessir, I'll see to it tomorrow."

As the colonel rose to his feet he clapped Jake on the shoulder, leaned over, and said, "A word to the wise, soldiers. Sit with your back to the wall from now on. You're going to be a lightning rod for every jerk suffering from an acute case of greed."

"But all we found was the cross," Burnes protested. "And you have that now."

"You know that and I know that," Beecham answered. "But the boys slavering over these rumors are going to wonder."

"About what," Servais demanded. "Sir."

"About whether or not you two didn't pull this one out of the ground because it had already been seen by the squad, then neatly kick a pile of snow over the rest."

"What rest? There wasn't anything—"

Beecham held up a hand. "There doesn't have to be. They only need to think there is. Or might be. Even one chance in a million will be enough to have them gathering like a pack of wolves after a kill."

Beecham straightened up. "You both should take anything of value you have in your room, give it to Sally, and let her lock it in the company safe. And as I said, guard your backs."

At the sound of other voices echoing down the hall from the Officers' Club, they rose to their feet with one accord. Servais led Jake out and down the side stairs and over to where his jeep was parked. No word was spoken. None was necessary. They weren't ready to face the prying eyes and probing tongues just yet. The colonel's warning was too fresh.

Pierre barreled along the road back to the main camp at what Jake considered kamikaze speed. So when they rounded the curve and saw a mobile checkpoint right in front of them, it was too late to stop.

Pierre scattered the MPs like so many white-topped bowling pins, and only missed ramming through the barrier by doing a four-wheel spin that carried them within inches of the MPs' jeep.

In the momentary stillness following their icy halt, Jake recognized a few faces among the soldiers picking themselves off the ground. He only had time to whisper, "Trouble."

"You know them?" Servais murmured back.

"Unfortunately."

"Well, well, well." The MP closest to the jeep was a tough-looking sergeant, about as pliant as a tank barrier. "Hey, boys, look who we've got here."

A voice from the darkness said, "If it ain't our old friend Captain Turncoat Burnes."

"Out in the dark all by hisself," said another shadow. "Except for another dang foreigner. Not German, though. Whassa matter, Captain Turncoat, did the Krauts at the camp get tired of playing your games?"

"You boys been playing much football lately?" Jake asked quietly.

"Here and there, Captain. Here and there. We missed having you around for a rematch, though. Ain't that right, boys? Pity how the camp league was disbanded all of a sudden like that. But I guess you knew all about that, huh, Captain Turncoat."

"No," Jake replied quietly. "I hadn't heard."

"Musta happened the day you left. Yeah, we and the boys were just talking about how tragic it was you had to leave us all of a sudden like that."

"Compliments of your friend," Jake said. "Colonel Connors."

"Yeah, well, he might be our friend, Captain Turncoat, but he sure ain't yours." The sergeant's gaze shifted. "That your Frenchie driver? Whoever he is, he just about made meat pies outta my men."

"The name is *Captain* Servais to you, Sergeant."

"Hey, boys, get a load of how the Frenchie here parlays the lingo." The gaze remained settled on Servais. "As for trying to pull rank, Frenchie, it's after curfew, nobody's out, and we're miles from the base. Which means there ain't a soul to hear you squeal when my boys take you out back and give you and Captain Turncoat here a little driving lesson. Compliments of the house." Dark eyes gleamed in the lantern's glow. "That is, unless you boys got something real nice to tell us."

"What are you talking about," Servais demanded.

"He means the cross," Jake explained. "News travels fast around here."

"That kind of news sure does," the sergeant replied.

"There isn't any more treasure out there," Jake replied flatly.

"Now that's a real pity," the MP said. " 'Cause my boys are real eager to get on with the driving lesson, and I can't hardly see any other way to keep them under control."

The barrel-chested sergeant took a step back and joined the solid phalanx of men surrounding the jeep. "Now are you boys gonna come quietly, or do we start our lesson in safe road habits right here?"

Jake stiffened for the lunge, but before he could do more, Servais was up and moving faster than Jake thought possible.

Instead of rushing the men who were directly beside his door and thus prepared, Pierre leapt up and over the windshield. He raced down the hood, screaming like a banshee, and crashed into the two startled men in front of the jeep. A pair of blows that were little more than a blur, perfectly aimed for the point where jaws joined necks, and the men went down like felled trees.

The small man vanished into the darkness, still screaming.

"After him!" the sergeant yelled.

But as the circle began to break up, before there was a leader or a clear sense of direction, Servais was back, still yelling. He leapt up so high his body rose above the head of the first attacker, so high he kicked *down* on the man's head. Touching earth, he spun like a top and planted a flying boot alongside the second man's face. He met the oncoming fourth with hands like blades. In two strokes he stood over another body.

Jake broke his own stillness with two bounding strides, quickly covering the distance between himself and the sergeant, and put all his speed and weight into flattening the man's nose. The sergeant howled, grabbing his face with both hands.

Then a baton landed on Jake's shoulder, and the ground rushed up to meet him.

He caught sight of Pierre falling beneath a trio of baton-wielding MPs, and was tensing his body in anticipation of the next blow when headlights came up from the other side of the barrier and shone full upon the tableau.

The door to the saloon car opened and shut. A pair of light-stepping shoes approached. Nobody moved. Everyone was as frozen as the night.

A woman's voice rang out, "What's going on here?"

The voice was answered by silence, save for some heavy breathing and a few soft groans. "You, Sergeant!" Sally Anders' fury rang in the crisp air. "I'm speaking to you! What's the meaning of this?"

The big man rose from his crouch, attempting with one hand to stem the red tide flowing from his nose. His voice was clogged and his face pale in the headlight's beams. "They were resisting arrest, ma'am."

"That's absolute rubbish and you know it. I've heard all about your football game, Sergeant. As has Colonel Beecham, in whose jurisdiction you're now standing, and who is waiting impatiently for the urgent papers I'm delivering."

The sergeant pointed over to where Servais lay prostrate on the snow-covered ground. "Ma'am, that Frenchman was driving like a lunatic. Almost mowed me and my men down."

"No doubt a safer tactic than being stopped and mobbed by you thugs," she snapped back. "Now if you want to carry on a grudge match one-on-one, Sergeant, that's your business. But a vendetta with twenty against two will not only cost you your stripes, but earn you passage home in the brig." Her voice was an angry lash. "Do I make myself clear?"

"Yes, ma'am," the sergeant muttered.

"Now back off. All of you! Captain Burnes, are you able to drive?"

Jake lifted himself with difficulty, his shoulder throbbing. "I think so, ma'am."

"Some of you men lift Captain Servais into the jeep. Move!"

"I'm all right," the Frenchman said in a slurred voice, struggling to his feet.

"Have your men lift this barrier. Now, Sergeant! I haven't got all night." Sally started toward her car, then spun back and snapped, "And if there is one more incident, if just one hair on either of these officers' heads gets mussed in any way, by anybody, at any time, I will report to Colonel Beecham that I witnessed a bunch of MPs assault a pair of superior officers. He will then personally see to it that each one of you spends the next few years where you belong—in a hole!"

After Sally's door slammed shut, there was a moment's silence, then, "Whattawe do, Sarge?"

"What the lady said," he replied dully. "Open the gate."

"But, Sarge—"

"Just do it!"

Jake eased himself behind the wheel and started the motor. When the sergeant stepped forward, Jake faced him squarely and said, "You and your boys never could play football."

The big man tasted bile. "We'll get you yet, Turncoat."

"Doubtful, doubtful," Jake replied, ramming the gears home. "Brawn doesn't make up for lack of brains. Not on the field, and not in life."

They followed Sally's car back to staff HQ in silence, enjoying the feel of the wind, the sense of ease between them, even the aches of their bodies. They were alive! The thrill of combat was one never to be forgotten, never sought, but when there, it was incomparable. Alive!

Sally drew up in front of the HQ building, got out and waited for them to stop. In the jeep's headlights Jake realized that the woman's face was wet with tears. He turned off the motor and jumped out, instantly solicitous. But she cut his gesture short. "You two are nothing more than a pair of animals!"

The onslaught was so unexpected he had no defense. "I—what?"

"Haven't you had enough of war?" Her shrill voice split the night. "How long will it take for you to see the evil behind all this violence?"

"Wait. They were the ones who—"

"I don't *care*!" she screeched. "All I want is for it to *stop*! I thought you were different. Caring enough to help the

German soldiers regain some self-respect, build up morale, but you're no different from all the rest of them! You can't fight the Germans anymore, all the fight's been beaten out of them. So now you've got to find somebody else to fight."

"That's not it at all," he protested, taking a step forward.

"Yes it is, and don't you dare come near me! Those men out there are supposed to be on the same side as you! And what were you two doing? Going after them like the combat soldiers you are! Go look at yourself in the mirror, soldier. Aren't you just spoiling for another fight? That's all you're really good for, isn't it? Isn't it?" Sally turned and fled into the quarters.

Jake watched her depart, then turned back and slumped into the jeep. Servais eyed him with a jaundiced air and said through bloody lips, "If I were you, my friend, I believe I would cross her off my list."

Chapter Three

*T*WO DAYS AFTER the night attack, Jake Burnes entered the central Karlsruhe HQ to the sound of applause.

The Karlsruhe army staff was split into a dozen different segments, as no building large enough to house everyone had survived the war. The main headquarters was contained in a requisitioned two-story office complex which had somehow escaped unscathed, while its neighboring factory had been reduced to a two-acre dust heap.

Staff housing was a routine problem, causing the same set of predicaments throughout all Germany. As 1945 gave way to 1946, there were over a million American soldiers struggling to police their segment of a destroyed nation, and waiting with growing impatience for orders to be shipped home.

No longer was there the unifying goal of victory. Victory was theirs. The time of celebration had passed. The horrors of discovering the concentration camps were behind them. The Nuremberg Trials had begun. A new routine was being established, that of victor ruling over the vanquished.

Four nations had substantial forces occupying Germany—France, Britain, Russia, and the United States. A number of others were also represented, from Greece to Denmark, Belgium to Australia, South Africa to Canada.

The Four Powers gathered and argued continually. Stalin was proving almost impossible to deal with. His demands rankled more and more each day. Even as far away as Karlsruhe, on the other side of the country from the gathering Soviet troops, people were on edge whenever Stalin's name was mentioned.

But the biggest practical problems were unrelated to the high-level diplomacy. The infighting among the tightly concentrated forces around each base was ferocious. Command posts had to be split up and spread out across cities and regions, roads were scarred and pitted, and working telephones were as rare as fresh eggs.

Finding allies for any undertaking, especially one as peripheral as joining another nation's forces to help guard a border no longer under attack, was essential. Liaison jobs had to be handled like nitroglycerine.

Knowing all this added mightily to Jake's surprise over the reception he and Pierre received.

As Jake let the door shut behind Servais, he turned to find the cluster of officers clapping and whistling for the pair of them. They exchanged astonished glances as a man with major's pips walked up with hand outstretched. "Major Dan Hobbs. Let me be the first to congratulate the men who took Connors' gorillas down a peg."

Jake accepted the hand, but quickly confessed, "Actually, it was the lady who saved the day."

"Yeah, we're taking up a collection to send the Ice Queen a wreath." The major grinned. "Tell me you didn't have the whole thing timed."

"We didn't have the whole thing timed," Jake agreed.

"Then somebody's fairy godmother was working extra hard that night." Major Hobbs clapped Jake on the back, said, "Come on into my office, gentlemen."

Once his door was closed, the major said, "Connors is making himself an impressive list of enemies."

"I didn't know he was so well known," Jake said.

"How long have you been in these parts?"

"Just over a month," Jake replied. "Transferred up from Italy."

"So you arrive, get together a squad of prisoners and whip Connors' pride and joy from here to Moscow."

"I sort of inherited the team," Jake explained.

"Then you dig up the first whiff of treasure—"

"Like you said," Servais said to Jake. "News travels fast in these parts."

"And then proceed to whip his goons a second time."

"It came close to being the other way around," Jake pointed out. "How did you hear about it?"

"One of my men was up at Badenburg and caught sight of the Ice Queen laying you two out in front of HQ. So did Colonel Beecham. Colonel Beecham ordered her to tell him what happened, as she wasn't all that eager to have it spread around. My man overheard the story." Major Hobbs grinned. "Man, I wish I'd been there to help you guys out."

"We could have used it, sir."

"Skip the sirs, it's just us turkeys here anyway. You know Connors is scouring the forces stationed around here, trying to dig out all the toughest guys?"

"I guess that news missed us."

"Yeah. He's putting together a rough crew. Sort of his own private army. The other MP officers around here can't stand him. They won't allow Connors' boys even to set foot into their territory. That's why he agreed to play touch football with your team. Nobody else'll touch them with a ten-foot pole."

"They were big," Jake said. "But they were dumb. It wasn't that hard to out-think them on the field."

"So I heard." The major's good cheer clouded over. "We're hearing some rumors that they've worked over some people. Way outside the line of duty. Nothing proven. Just stuff passed down the road."

The idea burned a hole in his gut. "I thought the war was over."

"Yeah, that's what I heard too." Major Hobbs' gaze turned sharp. "I've even been wondering if there might not be more than bullies at work here."

"I don't follow you."

The major focused on Servais. "You've been around here for a while, haven't you, Captain?"

"Almost six months, sir. Since just after VE-day."

"Had you ever seen a roadblock at that point before?"

Slowly Servais shook his head, knitting his brow in concentration. "Now that you mention it, nossir. Nowhere near it."

"Strange place to set one up," Major Hobbs went on. "Out in the middle of nowhere, forest around on every side, only traffic that time of night probably between the base and headquarters down the hill. Makes you wonder."

"Do you think they set up an ambush for us?"

"You said it, not me, soldier." The major played it casual. "Just the same, I'd watch my step if I were you."

"That's exactly what Colonel Beecham told us."

"Yeah, there's no water on the colonel's back. If he said something like that to me, I'd pay attention. Now, what was it I could do for you gents?"

Jake explained his official mission. "We'd like to ask you to assign men to patrol the border as far as Wissembourg to the north and Rastatt to the south."

Major Hobbs stood and walked over to the large map on his side wall. After a moment's inspection, he said, "We're talking about a forty-mile stretch, give or take a dogtrot."

"That's about it, yessir."

"I guess I've got no problem with that." The major came back and sat down. "I'll have to run it by the brass, but I doubt they'll object. There's a lot of respect for Beecham around these parts. What are we supposed to be on the lookout for, anyway?"

"Displaced people, escaped POWs—"

"Guys carrying sacks of treasure on their backs," the major added.

"Does everybody know about that?"

"Well, I couldn't tell you for sure, but my guess is that by now they're discussing it at the White House. Sure as little green apples it's festering in the brain of every one of my men."

"It was just one cross," Jake objected.

"This time," Major Hobbs observed. "Goodness only knows what might pop up next time, am I right?"

"I suppose so," Jake said glumly.

"Well, don't you worry, Captain. I'll make it perfectly clear that the first soldier of mine who turns trigger happy with the scent of treasure goes home in handcuffs."

"Hello, soldier." Sally Anders seemed neither pleased nor displeased to see him. "What brings you here?"

Turning his cap over in his hands, Jake entered her small cubbyhole. That she merited a private office was the clearest possible indication of her prestige. Her desk was piled high with forms, official-looking documents, and buff-colored envelopes marked Priority. "I don't know whether to say thank you or I'm sorry."

"Why, soldier, are you feeling guilty about something?"

"You saved our lives back there," Jake said. "And for that I'm grateful."

"I don't know about your lives," Sally replied. "But I did save you from a beating."

"Those goons wouldn't have stopped until we were a couple of bloody pulps."

She made round eyes. "Those nice men? Do you really think so?"

"This is hard enough, Miss Anders. Could you maybe hold the jokes until I'm through?"

"Sorry." She folded her hands over the papers nearest her. "Proceed, soldier."

He took a breath. "I'm not saying I agree with what you said out there on the street. But I want to tell you how sorry I am that I—"

"Neither did the colonel," Sally interrupted. "Agree, I mean. He got the story out of me in the end, you know. I never was able to stand up to him in a fight. He was pretty angry that I hadn't let him kick the colonel and his men from here to Cincinnati. But he did call Connors this morning and give him a good roasting. He told the colonel the only thing which saved him was that I refused to testify against his boys so long as you two remained intact. I think you should be safe."

Jake remained silent, his eyes on his hat.

"Oh, I'm sorry. I interrupted your groveling," Sally said, all mock sympathy. "Do go on, Captain."

"You're going to make this as tough as you can, aren't you."

"No reason not to. You're too big to turn across my knee, and a piece of my mind won't help things a bit. Might as well make you squirm."

Burnes started for the door.

"Jake!"

Reluctantly he turned back. Sally said quietly, "You really shouldn't give in so easily, soldier."

It was Jake's turn to show surprise. "Ma'am, if you think I'm giving in, you've got another thing coming. This is what we combat soldiers call a strategic withdrawal."

Sally inspected him for a long moment, then came to some internal decision of her own. "Have you got your jeep?"

"Right outside. Why?"

She rose from her chair. "Take me into town, will you? There's something I'd like you to see."

"Sure."

She pointed to a group of burlap sacks piled in one corner. "Give me a hand with those."

Jake walked over and hefted one. "What's in them?"

"Contraband, soldier. Don't ask so many questions."

They made the trip in silence, Jake because he was too wary of being shot down again, and Sally because she seemed to prefer her own company. Directions were passed on with the minimum of words or a simple hand movement.

Their route took them down what had once undoubtedly been a major thoroughfare, now a broad strip of cracked and pitted pavement bordered on both sides by rubble. The surroundings were as gray as the sky.

Not a single building was intact. As far as Jake could see, the world was filled with single walls jutting like crumbling fingers toward an uncaring sky. All open spaces were filled with bricks and mortar and the refuse of war. A thick layer of dust covered everything.

. The people they passed seldom looked their way. Attention was almost always focused downward, as though no one cared to see much of their world. There were a few bicycles, but most people straggled aimlessly by on foot. The only cars they passed bore military markings. On almost every street corner a man stood with a sign saying in German, "I must eat. I will do any work. Please help me."

At several crossings, gangs of street kids materialized from thin air and chased after them, calling out for candy, cigarettes, chocolate, or just calling. Jake had seen this kind of thing in the smaller village where he had been stationed before, but had never grown accustomed to it. Every child he saw appeared to be begging. And here there were so many of them. All skin and bones and ragged clothing. And eyes. Haunting eyes big as saucers and old as war itself.

They stopped in front of what probably had been a prestigious apartment block, now a flattened heap with two intact walls and a free-standing chimney. Jake could see a few pictures, washed-out wallpaper, and water-stained curtains hanging from the interior of destroyed apartments.

He parked as Sally directed and followed her down a set of stairs into what had previously been a neighborhood bomb shelter. The door of the low building was marked with a broad painted cross. From the interior rose the sound of children chattering and playing.

On the bottom step Jake hesitated, his forehead creased in thought. Sally turned around. "What's the matter, soldier? Afraid of a few kids?"

Jake shook his head, unable to figure out what had surprised him so. He followed her into what appeared to be a crudely painted fairy tale kingdom. The walls were decorated with bright sketches of stories done with an amateur's hand—Jesus on the Mount, walking on the water, calming the storm, healing the leper, gathering the little children. In the far corner stood a makeshift communal kitchen. Beside it stretched a long table with benches. The ceiling was oppressively low. Without the wall murals the chambers would have been grim.

"Jake, I'd like you to meet Chaplain Buddy Fox."

"Any friend of Sally's is a friend of mine, Captain." The chaplain was a small man with sandy hair and a voice as gentle as his eyes. "Welcome to my little crèche."

Jake snapped his fingers and declared, "Laughter."

"I beg your pardon?"

"Laughter. I've been trying to figure out what it was about this place. It's the first time I've heard laughter off the base since," he tried to remember and was sobered by the realization. "Since I arrived in Germany."

"That's the chaplain's doing," Sally said quietly.

"I'm afraid we don't have much in the way of refreshments, Captain. The children devour everything just as fast as it arrives."

"Cookie's sent you some more supplies," Sally said. "We'd better get them out of the jeep before somebody makes them disappear."

They went back upstairs and pulled out the sacks from the back of the jeep. Chaplain Fox peered into the first one and said, "Please tell Cookie how very grateful I am," he said softly. "And the colonel, of course. Without them—"

"They know," Sally said. "We all do."

"This is a wonderful place," Jake said as they returned to the shelter. Eager little hands reached out for the sacks, but not with the imploring, demanding, frantic plea that met him everywhere he went outside. Here it was a game. "Really wonderful."

"Why, thank you, Captain. Here, just bring the sacks back to the pantry, will you? The only way I can ensure that we make our supplies last is to lock them up. I have no idea how children normally are at this age, but these are eternally hungry."

The several dozen kids all appeared to be under six. The youngest were still in diapers, gathered on a pair of stained mattresses by one side wall, watched over by a trio of young girls involved in some intricate hand game. A gray-haired matron sat on the floor surrounded by children, keeping them quiet with stories. Another woman watched over some children playing with battered building blocks and a few other toys. As the sacks were set down and the storehouse door relocked, the women's gazes remained fastened intently on Chaplain Fox.

Jake looked down at the children. "Whose are these?"

"Buddy's," Sally replied. "Chaplain Fox's."

"Well, there are several local people who help out," said the chaplain. "We have worked out a series of shifts, and pay what we can from these stores. No one really has enough to eat, you know. Many such women are quite happy to work for food, and we need as much help as we can afford. I still have my divisional duties, of course. But everybody helps as they can. Some with food, others with blankets, a few with chocolates and cigarettes and other things I can use for money. And then Sally and Colonel Beecham help with everything possible, from medicines to stores to paint for these murals."

"I mean," Jake said, "whose kids *are* these?"

"Nobody's," Sally replied.

"God's," Chaplain Fox corrected. "As are we all."

"I'm beginning to believe you," Sally said. "Sometimes, anyway."

"Nothing on earth could give me greater pleasure to hear," he said.

Jake asked, "Are all of these orphans?"

"A few of them, but not too many," Chaplain Fox replied. "Not anymore. Orphans are being gathered by church organizations, the young ones anyway. No, these are the unwanted."

"Kids kicked out of their homes," Sally explained. "The ones left to fend for themselves. They fall through the cracks of officialdom, because their parents are still drawing rations for them and legally, at least, they still have a home."

"They're just left on the streets?"

"Or in trash cans," Reverend Fox replied, smiling sadly. "Or at train stations. Or on rubble heaps. Some the local gangs bring in, now that they know we are here."

The chaplain caught sight of Jake's expression. "Do not be too harsh on the parents, Captain," he said. "Some are genuinely good people who have come to realize that under the present circumstances, they have no way of bringing in enough to keep their entire family alive. So one must be sacrificed for the good of all. Sometimes it is the youngest, sometimes the one who causes the most trouble, sometimes a sickly child, or one who appears to be a little slower than the others."

"This is awful," Jake murmured.

"This is war," Chaplain Fox replied. "This is why we need God. Here. Everywhere." He smiled at Sally. "And the grace of friends like this dear lady."

"You supply the love," Sally replied. "I'll see what I can do about the grub."

"God supplies the love," Fox countered gently. "And the healing. If you look, I wager you'll find there is quite enough of both left over for you."

Sally turned toward a group of a dozen or so young girls who had been quietly waiting for her attention. She squatted down and was swiftly enveloped by small arms and questioning voices.

Reverend Fox brought Jake back around. "You are Sally's friend?"

"I'd like to be," Jake replied.

"She needs a friend," he said, inspecting Jake with clear eyes. "Come with me, would you?"

Jake followed him back out into the cold winter air. "She's got walls high as the Matterhorn."

"Yes, she has." Buddy Fox offered a smile. "Just the sort of challenge for a strong man like yourself, I'm sure. Are you married, Captain?"

"No."

"Girl back home?"

"Not anymore."

"Ah. A casualty of war." He motioned toward someone behind Jake. "There goes yet another casualty, one I see much too often these days."

Jake spun, caught sight of a gang of young teenagers flitting around a corner and vanishing. "They're outcasts too?"

"Almost all children of that age are left to fend for themselves, at least to some degree," he replied. "Most of them have no fathers. Fathers are a rare commodity in Germany these days. Whole adult men of any age are, for that matter. An entire generation is growing up void of role models and direction, Captain. If only I had a division of strong and caring men like you. I just might be able to reach them."

As Sally came through the doors and up the stairs toward them, Jake asked, "Do you have any contact with these kids?"

"With several of the local neighborhood gangs, yes, as a matter of fact, I do. We offer them meals two afternoons a week. It is both a peacekeeping measure, and a way of learning who they are. Many of them are growing up like wild tomcats, constantly on the prowl, sleeping where and when they can."

"For some of them," Sally said, "the only kind words they ever hear are the ones Buddy speaks to them."

"If only there were some way to fill their empty days," the pastor said worriedly. "If only I could give them a *purpose*. They need that as much as they need more food."

Jake was about to express his sympathy over the plight of the young Germans when he was suddenly struck by an idea. He stood there, his mouth open, wondering how on earth anything could feel so *right*.

"Is anything the matter?"

He gathered himself, shook his head. "Let me go check on something," he said. "Maybe I can give you a hand with the kids."

Chapter Four

"*Y*OU WANT ME to do *what?*"

The colonel's roar echoed through the open door, stopping all typewriters, footsteps, and conversations within hearing range. Jake pleaded, "It's just a gimmick, sir."

"It's absolute madness, is what it is!"

"I'm not looking for results, sir," Jake persisted. "I'm just trying to give them something constructive to do with their time."

"You call running loose on the streets constructive?" The colonel's voice was loud enough to shake the windows three doors down. "This is what my liaison proposes is the best use of his time? Maybe I need to remind you, mister, that I could always make you officer in charge of the spud detail!"

"They're already running loose, Colonel," Jake replied as Beecham stomped over and slammed the door. "And as far as I heard, they live pretty much full time on the streets as it is."

Colonel Beecham walked back around his desk. "You've got to stop doing this to me, Burnes."

"Doing what, sir?"

"Putting me in a position where I should blow my stack. It's bad for my blood pressure." Beecham slumped back into his chair with a sigh. "You ought to know better than to come in and propose such a scheme in full earshot of everyone."

"I guess I wasn't thinking, sir," Jake replied, not understanding at all.

"No, that's one thing I'll agree with right off the bat. Maybe nobody heard you. Then again, maybe Morrows had some urgent filing that left him loitering just outside my doorway as usual. You know how it is. Anything to do with treasure, and this whole place threatens to come apart at the seams."

"I'm sorry, sir. It's just—"

"I know. I know." A glint of humor appeared in that steely gaze. "Buddy's got you hooked too, has he?"

"Sir?"

"Buddy Fox. The chaplain. He's gotten under your skin, has he?"

Jake nodded slowly, and confessed, "I heard them laugh."

"Yeah, that hit me below the belt too. Never knew I could get so much pleasure out of such a simple sound. Or miss it as much as I did when it was gone." Beecham fiddled with his pen, then gave an abrupt nod and said, "Okay, son. How much do you need?"

Jake's hopes soared. "As much as Stores can spare, I guess, sir."

"Well, you sure can't bring them here and have Cookie dole out the leftovers. Not unless you want to make us a laughing stock from here to Berlin."

"I can't?" Cookie already spooned out leftovers at the outside gate every evening to the people waiting there. They were always waiting, and there was never enough.

"Good grief, son. Did you really think you could line up a dozen young kids out there day after day and not have the word leak out? No, strike that. Word is bound to get out anyway. But can you imagine what they'd be calling us if we lined them up here?"

"It's more than a dozen, sir," Jake interjected.

"Even worse. The Burnes Blarney Brigade. Or maybe Beecham's Best. How'd you like to hear that every time you turned around?"

"I guess I hadn't thought it out, sir."

"Don't get me wrong, Captain. Your idea has merit. Anything that might help some of these kids needs to be taken seriously. But we've got to present it in a way people can accept. Do you understand?"

Jake nodded. "Just another hand across the waters."

"Now you're thinking. All we're doing is helping to feed a few of the older kids. Nothing more, nothing less. Everything clsc stays bctwccn us."

"And Captain Servais," Jakc addcd.

"And thc chaplain and Sally. Those two wouldn't give Connors and his goons the time of day. But around everyone else except them, lips are to stay permanently zipped tight."

"Mum's the word, sir."

"You just make sure those kids understand they're not to take any risks."

"From the looks of things, just being alive out there is risky," Jake replied.

"No additional risk, then." The gaze showed grudging approval, but all Beecham said was, "Still bucking for another medal, aren't you?"

"Nossir, that's not it at all," Jake answered, rising to his feet. "As you said, Colonel, I'm just trying to feed some hungry kids."

Captain Servais was still out on patrol. Jake stopped by the supplies division, known far and wide simply as Stores, then drove back into town alone.

When he walked through the crèche door, the first person he saw was Sally. "What are you doing here?"

"That's what I like about you, soldier," she replied, hands on hips. "You really know how to make a girl feel welcome."

"Is the chaplain around?"

"Why, hello, Captain." Chaplain Fox stepped out from behind a curtained alcove. "What can I do for you?"

"Cookie asked me to drop off some supplies," he said, hesitant to discuss the real reason behind his visit.

"Why, thank you, Captain, but we're not scheduled for another shipment until Thursday."

"We'd better get outside while there's still something to unload," Sally reminded them.

As they left the crèche, Jake said softly to the chaplain, "I need to talk with you. Privately."

"Just take that satchel on back to the storeroom, dear," Chaplain Fox said. He waited until she walked back down the stairs, then asked Jake, "What's on your mind, Captain?"

As swiftly as he could, Jake outlined his plan. The chaplain inspected Jake with a new appreciation.

There was a scraping sound. Jake turned around and discovered that Sally had remained standing on the bottom step. "I thought you were taking the things inside."

"Don't get hot, soldier," Sally said mildly. "I think it's a good idea."

"You do?"

"So do I," the chaplain told him. "There should be no difficulty increasing our meals to the children from two to five times a week. We pay our cooks with food, you know. I'm sure they would be happy to take on the extra work."

"You shouldn't call them children," Sally said, her eyes still on Jake.

"No," Chaplain Fox agreed. "I suppose I'm looking at the size of their underfed bodies, not the depth of their experience. They've packed a lifetime into a few short years. Some of them, several lifetimes."

"I don't know how long the support can last," Jake warned, thinking of his own impending departure.

"Anything that will help these young people stay alive and out of harm's way through the winter must be taken seriously, Captain."

"Call me Jake."

"Thank you, Jake. Yes, in times like these, seeing to the needs of today are as far as anyone can afford to look."

"So you think it will work?"

"It's not what I think, but whether they will accept it that is important." The chaplain hefted two bulky sacks. "Let's get these stores inside and go find out."

Jake picked his way across a stretch of shattered pavement as treacherous as river ice cracked by spring thaws. Over one million tons of bombs had been dropped on German cities by Allied planes during the last few months of the war. Few buildings were left intact, and inner city roads were treacherous in the extreme, especially now with their covering of frozen snow and slush.

Civilians walked and slid and stumbled wearily across the uneven sea of snow and ice and dirt. Those with bicycles pushed them along, not letting go for an instant— with the scarcity of transport, bicyclists lived under the constant burden of envy and the threat of theft. Nobody met Jake's eyes. Wherever he looked, eyes dropped immediately to the ground. But he felt their gaze on him always, everywhere.

They crossed a plaza whose once majestic central cafe was now a three-sided empty hulk. They were surrounded by windowless buildings whose empty eyes stared in dark and silent sorrow. From time to time Jake caught sight of families huddled within. Their only protection from the bitter weather was an occasional rag or blanket tacked over a hole. Wood was too precious as fuel to be used for boarding over the buildings' wounds.

"Whatever you see," the chaplain told Jake as they walked, "don't let the children sense your reaction."

"Why not?" Jake watched a group of elderly people being directed by a loud-mouthed overseer. They sifted through the ruins of a collapsed building, collecting bricks. These were piled into wheelbarrows and rolled to a corner of the square where the oldest women squatted and hammered off the clinging cement. The bricks were then loaded onto a single waiting truck. Everyone moved in the slow motion of the almost starving.

"I'm not sure," Chaplain Fox replied. "They just hate being looked at. Maybe they expect you to be disgusted as others have been. Maybe they want a reason to dislike you. Maybe it's shame. Maybe it's despair. I have simply found it best not to notice how they are forced to live."

He led Jake through a building entrance that had been tripled in size by a direct hit. The bomb had taken out the floor, revealing a deep basement far below. A beam too heavy to steal had been laid across the pit. Jake could see how at night the beam was dragged back and secured with wire cable, offering a wartime sense of security. Jake followed the chaplain across, his hands out and wavering.

The building's single intact chamber was redolent of cocoa. Chaplain Fox halloed through the makeshift entrance cover, then said to Jake, "This used to be one of the city's finest chocolate factories. It specialized in handmade pralines. That is why these children are able to claim it for their own. Two other families used to live here, but in their hunger the odor almost drove them mad. It has not been any better for the children. Since they moved in, I have had to take three of them to the hospital after they ate dirt which had collected the scent. Still, I suppose it is better than sleeping out-of-doors."

The tattered burlap curtain was thrown back, revealing a sunken-cheeked youngster of perhaps fifteen. He peered at the chaplain with undisguised hostility, then turned and shouted back into the chamber, *"Es ist der Pfarrer und ein Fremder."* It's the priest and a stranger.

"Lass denn rein," came back the reply.

Jake stepped gingerly into the gloomy depths. The only light came from a smoldering cooking fire and from around the burlap hanging over the single window. Better dark than freezing, he supposed. The room was marginally warmer than the outside.

Fox's German was surprisingly good. "Where is Karl? I have someone he needs to meet."

"The only person I'll ever need to meet is the devil, Pfarrer," a voice sounded from the gloom. "Isn't that where you say I'm headed?"

"I pray not," the pastor replied, untouched by the unseen man-child's anger. "This friend has an offer for you."

"Your friend, not mine," Karl scoffed. "Tell him we take whatever we want, with or without his offers."

"This one you'll like," Jake said for himself, pleased that he had managed to speak in a flat, unconcerned tone. He ignored Fox's startled glance at the sound of his German. "It'll give you something besides dirt to fill your bellies with."

"So, so. An invader who knows the mother tongue." A tall lanky youth, skinny to the point of emaciation, stepped from the shadows. "What do you have that could interest me, *Fremder*? Chocolates? Cigarettes? Where is it? In your pockets? Yes? You like me to search them for you?"

Jake stood his ground. He met the young man's hostility with a flat gaze. "You've got spunk, I'll give you that much."

"You'll give me nothing," he spat. "You'll give me death. That's what you'd like, yes? To see us all just curl up and die."

"Food," Jake replied. "Three times a week. Hot. Fresh. Add that to the two meals the chaplain is already giving you and there's a chance you might survive this winter after all."

The anger faltered momentarily. "You lie, *Fremder*."

"That is something I will try never to do," Jake said solemnly. "I will even start with truth. There is a chance this will only last for five weeks. But five weeks is better than nothing."

Other boys and girls emerged from the dimness, coalescing into wasted rag-draped shapes that appeared to be little more than hollows and eyes. Their eyes were huge. Great, dissipated eyes, large as saucers, that stared unblinking at Jake. Food.

"Hot meals," Jake repeated. "And something else you need to make life worthwhile. Something else you need almost as much as a home."

"What is that, *Fremder*?" But without the resentment this time.

Jake looked straight at the young German, and replied, "Hope."

"You want us to do your searching for you, is that right?"

Jake sat on a stone across from Karl, surrounded by silently listening wraiths. It was hard to tell the girls from boys, and not simply because of the dim light. Emaciation had stripped their bodies of muscle and feminine contours, and turned all faces into almost identical sets of hard lines and deep hollows. "There will be two groups," Jake said, explaining the plan he had outlined to the chaplain. "While your gang looks for smugglers, the others will search for some place large enough for a hidden hoard of treasure."

"Who is in this other group?" Karl demanded, turning to the chaplain. "The Crypts?"

Fox nodded in the affirmative, explaining to Jake in English, "The other gang I work with lives in an abandoned cemetery. Well, abandoned is not the right word. Stuffed to the gills and then left alone is more like it. They found an old mausoleum, broke in and stripped it bare, and are living there now."

"In my chambers the only language spoken will be my language," Karl insisted.

"Of course," Fox said. "It was a slip. Forgive me."

The unexpected courtesy stopped the youngster. Jake recalled Sally's comment that the only source of kindness for these children was the chaplain. Jake said, "What I need from you is your help in finding the people shipping the treasure across the border. I suppose it would be possible for your gang to search out information for me?"

Karl puffed out his gaunt chest. "We go where we like, when we please. We hear and see and know everything."

Jake rose to his feet. "Then it sounds like I've come to the right place."

"One moment, *Fremder*." Karl remained seated on his little rock throne, the room's single chair covered with several layers of sacking for comfort. "Why should we tell you anything? Why not just keep it all for ourselves?"

"Where would you go with treasure?" Jake countered. "Who could you trust to pay you anything, give you anything except a knife across your neck?"

There was a murmur of agreement through the room. It was the only time anyone else had spoken since their arrival. "And we can trust you?" Karl asked suspiciously.

"I bring you food," Jake pointed out. "And you know the chaplain's an honest man."

"I trust him to do as he says," the chaplain affirmed. "I think you should as well."

"We will discuss your offer, *Fremder*," Karl declared.

"Then come for a meal tonight," Fox replied. "Thinking is easier with a full belly."

On their way to the cemetery, Jake confessed, "I don't see how you can deal with this on a daily basis."

Fox made his way around an ice-encrusted bomb pit. "I just put my trust in the Lord and go where I feel called."

"But doesn't it get to you?"

"Of course it does. But I can't let it crush me. I wouldn't be able to do my job."

"I don't understand how you do it."

"There is sorrow everywhere, Jake. Everywhere and always. A man has three choices—any man, chaplain or otherwise. He can let it overwhelm him, and if he does, it will drive him around the bend. We've both seen cases of that, haven't we?"

"Too many," Jake confessed.

"Yes, that is the tragic nature of war. The product of war is ruin, of cities and of lives. Peace is only a by-product. A wish. A goal. That is why war must always remain an instrument of last resort for any civilized nation. But where was I?"

"Choice number two."

"Yes. The second alternative when faced with the agony of war is to lock yourself away. This the majority choose to do. Nowadays we are seeing thousands of men who simply refuse to leave the base except when on duty. Others do leave, but all they allow themselves to see is their hunger—for sex, for drink, for some gratification or another. Still others see nothing but their own hate. They remain blinded at will, and view their own pain and anger as justification for a nation's suffering."

"Are they wrong?"

"I try not to judge anyone, Jake. But I think their lives are misery. They remain imprisoned within themselves. God holds the key, of course. With forgiveness. With love. With compassion. And with healing. But only if they ask for it. And to ask they have to recognize their internal prison for what it is. That I see as my job, to be a mirror for anyone struggling to look with honesty. To help them see the lies they tell themselves for what they are."

They detoured around a building that had slipped from its destroyed foundations and created a hillock in the middle of the road. When they reached the other side, Jake asked, "And the third?"

"The third choice is to learn to take each day as it comes, and to do what you can with what you have. This means learning that you cannot avoid seeing the suffering of others, which is hard. Extremely hard. I would imagine that it would be impossible to do this without the strength of God in your heart. At least a believer can respond to this suffering with prayer. But the key is to learn to do with what you have, Jake. That is the central issue. Do not see yourself as a failure because you can't touch all who suffer. Recognize that universal healing can only come through Jesus Christ, and accept your assigned task. Then do all you can with everything you've been given."

Chapter Five

*T*HEY RETURNED FROM from the second meeting to find Sally Anders still at the crèche. Jake walked through the door and was met with the cocked head, the hands on hip, the blunt, "Well?"

"Well what?"

"Don't be obtuse, soldier. How did it go?"

Chaplain Fox answered for him. "It went splendidly. I do believe they have taken to both Jake and his idea."

Jake fumbled about with his cap, bent over to stroke the cheek of a passing little girl. Finally he glanced back at Sally. She watched him with a small smile playing across her lips. "You may invite me out to dinner, Captain Burnes," she said. "If you like."

"I like very much," he said.

"I know a little place not far from here. A farmhouse. Probably the only decent restaurant for miles. You can pay with dollars, chocolate, cigarettes, booze, or food."

"Sally, I think you should know I didn't do this for you. Well, not entirely. That is—"

"I know, I know," she said, reaching for his arm. "That's why I accept."

Jake pushed open the crèche door, waved a farewell to the smiling chaplain, said, "Step into my Rolls, and let me take you away from all this."

"If only you could, soldier," Sally said, mounting the stairs. "If only you really could."

They climbed a hill out of the city, passed through deep forest as darkness descended, then came over a crest and entered a clearing that stretched out for what seemed like miles. A cluster of farm buildings offered the only sign of life. The farmhouse was a vast structure, rising among a series of stables and barns that covered over an acre. Lit by lanterns and warmed by a sweet-scented wood fire, the farmhouse was the first sign of coziness Jake had seen in months.

"This is terrific," he said, taking his place at the end of a long farm-style trestle table. "How did you find it?"

"Being one of the few American women around means I field all kinds of offers," Sally replied, settling herself across from Jake. "You should know that, soldier."

Seven long tables filled what once had been a great family hall. Antlers and old blunderbusses decorated the high smoke-stained walls. The farmer and his wife, serious middle-aged folk, cooked and served with the help of a pair of shy country girls. The clientele was mixed. A few German civilian officials who had the power to obtain curfew passes sat in shiny suits beside women decked out in hats dating back to the thirties. They spoke in low whispers and avoided the eyes of everyone else. Most of the others were American officers from surrounding garrisons. Some escorted local girls. Those without female company sat in inebriated clusters and eyed the others with envy.

Sally's beauty drew a lot of stares. The candlelight flickered with gentle fingers across her face, deepening the glow in her eyes, softening her features. It even seemed to gentle her voice. "There's no menu," Sally explained as the host walked over and set two pewter mugs and a tall clay jug in front of them. "Homemade brew to drink, and whatever dish they have."

"*Schweine Roladen mit getrokene Pfifferlingen und Knödeln,*" the host said abruptly, "*Zwei Dollarn pro Kopf.*"

"I only got the first couple of words of that," Sally admitted.

"*Ist gut, wir nehmen zwei Portionen,*" Jake said for them both, then translated when he had left, "Pork loins rolled and stuffed with smoked ham. Pfifferlingen are mountain mushrooms, sort of nutty tasting. A lot of country people pick them in the fall and hang them out to dry. Knödeln are big potato dumplings."

Sally shrugged out of her jacket, a stiff affair meant to copy a uniform's uncompromising lines. Underneath she wore a starched white blouse which accented the delicate curves of her body. Her hair was pinned back, but enough had escaped to fall in abundant auburn disarray around her shoulders. "Where did you learn your German?"

"I was studying at the university when I was called up," he said by rote, then stopped himself. "That's not exactly true."

She leaned across the table. "Are we going to be truthful tonight, soldier? Sounds dangerous."

He ignored the jibe. "My brother was already in the infantry. Nothing was ever said about it, I guess there was no need to. After I finished my second year at university, I enlisted. That's just how things were. The last thing my dad told me was, be a good soldier. I was brought up to obey my parents. I did as I was told."

"Where are you from?"

"A small town nobody ever heard of. Sauderton. Pennsylvania. Dutch country. Solid people. Hard-working. Bedrock of the nation type of folk. The kind who go where they're told and do what they're told to do."

She inspected his face, and said, "Are you looking forward to going back?"

Slowly Jake shook his head. No.

"Why not? The decorated war hero coming home to a grateful nation. They'll have a parade for you, Jake. Make all kinds of speeches."

"Parades come to an end," Jake replied quietly, his eyes fixed on the fire. "Speeches go where all hot air goes."

"Why don't you want to go home?" Sally pressed.

"I'm just kind of lost, I suppose," he said quietly. "Here or there doesn't seem to matter so much, when 'there' is no longer the place I left behind. People and places change, I stay the same." He turned to face her. "Lost here, lost there, what's the difference?"

For some reason his words had stripped her bare. It took a while for her to gather herself, then she asked, "What is it you're after?"

"I don't know," he sighed. "Things just seemed a lot clearer in the war. Everything came down to one basic rule—knock out the enemy. That was the only way to survive."

"Weren't you scared?"

"I lived with fear all the time," he replied. "Every time we were about to go into action, I used to get such a sick feeling in my stomach until the first shot was fired. Then all that mattered was surviving. Keeping myself and my troops alive, and bringing the boys home."

"And so now you miss it."

"No," he stated flatly. "That's not it at all. I know some guys do, and I can understand them. I really can. But that's not the way I feel."

"What is it, then?"

He wrinkled his forehead in concentration. "What I did stood for something. I fought for what I believed in. There was a clear pattern to life. That much about it felt good. I was doing something with meaning. Now it's gone. All gone. I guess I just need something to believe in."

Sally filled their two cups, lifted her own, and said, "Here's to all the yesterdays, soldier. Wherever they've gone."

"To yesterday," he agreed.

"I want it all back. All of it. I'd trade my life for one day of how it used to be." She set down her cup and said softly, "I can't work out how it's supposed to be now."

"I can't either," he agreed.

Their meal was served, two steaming platters piled high with solid country cooking, German style. They ate in silence, gathering themselves, recovering from the shock of honesty.

Eventually she set her fork down with a contented sigh. "I didn't know how tired I was of army food, or how much I needed that meal, soldier. Thank you."

Jake nodded. "Will you do me a favor?"

"Depends."

"Stop calling me soldier."

The look of mock surprise returned. "All this time and I didn't notice? Excuse me, sailor. I didn't catch the cut of your uniform."

"Not sailor, either," he persisted. "Jake. Just Jake. It's my name."

"Okay, Just Jake. From now on, Just Jake, that's all you'll hear."

"Why do you make a mocking joke out of everything?"

"It's my last line of defense," she said, her tone brittle. "Don't knock it down. Please. It's not much, but it's all this girl's got left."

He searched her face and said quietly, "Tell me about your fiancé."

Her eyes became open wounds. Her mouth worked, but for a moment she could manage no sound. Then, "Why?"

"Because I want to know. Because I feel his presence with us here."

"No you don't," she said shakily. "What you feel is his absence. He is not here. I wish he were, but he's not."

"Tell me," Jake pressed.

She turned away from him and looked out beyond their table, beyond the farmhouse wall and the darkened forest and the dusty tumble-down city and the war-torn country, to a place and a time that was no more. Jake let her be, content to sit and watch her search the unseen distance, and wonder if a woman would ever love him that much. Or if he would ever deserve such a love.

She turned back and said with strength and a kind of fervor, "He was a great man, Jake. Not a good man. A *great* man. The hardest thing I've ever had to do in my whole life is forgive God for letting him die. Sometimes I can, and sometimes it's just beyond me. I mean—" She stopped and took a couple of harsh breaths. "The world needs men like him, Jake."

"Tell me about him," Jake asked, because it seemed now that she wanted the question asked. It tore at him more than he thought possible to encounter this love for another man in her voice and her eyes. But still he asked.

"Strong," Sally replied, smiling with a tenderness that washed over him, making it hard not to stand and rush over and crush her to his chest.

"Strong in body and strong in spirit," Sally went on, unaware of the effect she was having. "He was a leader. Not born that way, but made that way through his faith. All the credit for his life he gave to God." Sally looked at him, but saw him not. "I've never met a strong man who could be so humble. I admired him. I admired him as much as I loved him."

"And you loved him a great deal," he said softly.

"More than my own life," she said, her voice trembling. "More than . . . More than I thought it was possible to love and lose and survive. But I did. Lose him and survive the loss. For the longest while I didn't think I would. He taught me to see God as somebody alive. That was an incredible gift, his ability to make the unseen seem within reach. And now that he's gone, I can't find that invisible strength when I need it most."

"But you've made it."

"In a way. I almost didn't, though. I almost accepted the fact that this old body would keep right on ticking for another fifty years or so, but the life would be gone. Dead and dried up and blown away."

"What changed your mind?"

"The children," she replied simply. "Seeing others who hadn't ever had the chance to live and love at all suffer a hell as bad or worse than my own. It woke me up, Jake. It made me realize that I had a purpose too. It gave a meaning to what was left of my life. But I had to make a choice. I could either drown in my sorrow and watch my soul die, or I could struggle back to the surface and survive. Or try to.

And I did. But I didn't do it for me. I would never have had the strength to do it for myself. I did it for them."

She toyed with her cup, her eyes downcast. Jake waited quietly. At that moment, he would have been willing to wait for her all his life, and still count himself lucky. Then she said softly, "If only I could find my way back to what he taught me about the Invisible, maybe I could count my life as worth living again." She looked at him. "Do you think it might happen?"

"I don't know," Jake replied quietly. "I've never been much of a believing man myself."

"He would have liked you, Jake," she said, the tender smile returning. "He used to say that strength wed with wisdom was God's most underrated gift."

"I don't think of myself as particularly strong," Jake countered. "And I don't rank high in wisdom."

But she chose not to hear. "It's so easy to talk about God when I think of him," she mused aloud. "And so hard otherwise. I wish I could understand why."

Chapter Six

*T*HE NEXT MORNING, Servais was ebullient over Jake's scheme. "A masterpiece," he declared. "A stroke of genius."

"Just trying to feed a few kids," Jake said.

"Nonsense. You wait and see, my friend. This will benefit not only your young charges but us as well."

"They don't have a chance in a million of finding treasure, and you know it," Jake protested.

"I was not speaking of the treasure," Pierre answered. "Not just, anyway."

"What do you mean?"

"Let us wait and see," he replied. "Come. This is an important meeting today, and we must not be late."

The incoming French forces had established an initial base of operations next to the Rhine. The great river began high in the Swiss Alps, ran up through Germany, and ended its twelve-hundred-mile journey off the Dutch coast. It also formed the border between France and Germany from Basel to Karlsruhe, a distance of some one hundred miles. To the west of this border lay the province of Alsace, over which the Germans and French had fought for more than two hundred years. To the east loomed the Black Forest foothills. The river jinked and curved and split and tumbled over drops. The skeletal remains of bombed-out bridges grew giant icicles and stood as silent memorials to the recent war.

As Pierre set his customary blistering pace down the rutted road, he filled Jake in on the situation confronting the local French patrols. Boats were being intercepted nightly. The vessels were usually loaded to the gunnels with contraband or displaced aliens. These would-be immigrants wandered throughout Europe, in search of a better life. Their final destination remained unclear. Anywhere was better than the bombed wastelands of Eastern Europe, now occupied and stripped to the bone by Soviet troops. Most of these refugees were half-starved and feverish and on their last legs. When stopped they made no protest. They had long since reached a point where they continued moving only because there was no place where they could stand still.

When Jake and Pierre arrived at the camp, they found the tragedy of these displaced persons mirrored in the deep furrows creasing Major Gilbert's features. His office was built on a rise overlooking a massive internment camp, which used the Rhine's sweeping expanse as one natural boundary. Through the windows Jake could see tall wooden guardhouses rising every several hundred meters along the river. Guards watched over the flowing waters twenty-four hours a day. Jake was unimpressed. He saw with a soldier's eye, and noted how difficult it would be to police the undulating terrain with its many curves and crevices. No doubt a score of boats got through for every one caught.

The discussion between Servais and Gilbert was in French. Jake did little besides sit and look attentive. But he could tell Servais was getting nowhere. The major repeatedly shook his head, barked a reply, and flung an arm toward the large-scale map pinned to his wall. The response was clear. Until more troops arrived, the major was doing the best he could.

Pierre sighed in defeat, paused, then launched into a gentler assault. This time the major softened. And softened further still. Dark eyes turned in Jake's direction. The ma-

jor tut-tutted in time to Pierre's words. Jake struggled not
to squirm under the major's gaze, and wished he knew
what was going on.

"*Les pauvres garçons,*" the major said when Servais had
finished his tale. "*Et les filles. Les filles!*"

"I informed the major about your little project," Servais
murmured in an aside.

Jake nodded, concealed his alarm, and said conversationally, "If Colonel Beecham hears about this he's going to
roast us both over a slow fire."

The major launched into a hand-waving exposition, full
of sighs and headshakes and liquid gazes into the distance.
"The major has three children around that age," Servais
translated. "It breaks his heart to think of what those hundreds of children must be suffering."

"Strike that," Jake said. "It's fifty kids at the outside."

Pierre gave his head a minute shake. "I found it necessary to employ a bit of literary license."

"Meaning?"

Pierre shrugged. "I lied."

But the major was already up and moving for the door,
ushering them along with urgent gestures. Reluctantly Jake
allowed himself to be led down a well-worn path toward a
trio of warehouses lining one side of the camp. As he
walked, Jake glanced over the wire barrier and into the internment camp. His look was returned by a thousand
watchful, silent gazes. Bearded men. Kerchiefed women
and girls. Boys in oversized caps and ill-fitting clothes. All
with a vague sense of alienness that marked them as Eastern Europeans. All with a stillness borne on pleas so intense that no words spoken to a stranger could hold them.
At the warehouse entrance Jake returned the guard's salute,
and entered behind Pierre and the major. Inside he found
organized pandemonium.

At their end, supplies from a pair of trucks with red
crosses stencilled on sides and back were being unloaded by
jostling, sweating, shouting men. In the middle section a
group ran to and fro, all carrying clipboards and pens, all
pointing and shouting and counting and waving frantically

for attention. Farther back, yet another group sectioned big piles of clothing and supplies into much smaller piles, tied them with string, and shoved them on—all the while sweating and screaming and pointing and grabbing for more of this or that. At the very far end, a calm group passed on the little tied parcels to a seemingly endless line of waiting refugees. With each package went a few kind words in a language most of the refugees did not understand. Jake thought the entire scene looked extremely French.

The major immediately leapt into a swearing match with the two truck drivers. The pair gave as good as they got, at least in the beginning. But gradually they were whittled down to sulking submission. When the major turned away, the drivers retreated behind stinking French cigarettes and serious scowls.

"The major regrets he can only offer us the use of these two trucks," Servais translated, wearing a lopsided grin.

"For what?" Jake demanded.

"My friend," Servais said around his rictus grin, "I would strongly advise you to bow and give solemn thanks."

Major Gilbert wheeled about and paraded down the aisle, throwing grandiose gestures at the wealth stacked up around him. Pierre hustled alongside, dragging Jake with him, and translating, "All this has been entrusted to me for those in need. Inside or outside the wire, what does it matter? I feel I can trust you to give to those whose life might depend upon the giving. This trust is a rare and precious thing, and one which should be built upon."

Jake protested, "What about the refugees? Don't they need this stuff?"

The major stopped, and replied solemnly through Pierre, "My detainees are being seen to. They are receiving clothes and food and medicine and shelter. The greatest of their needs, however, is not to be answered by what you see here. They need a home. They need freedom. They need a regime where they do not have to live in fear of the knock on their door. They need a country where the sky does not rain death."

Gilbert gave a magnificent shrug. "Alas, these things I cannot offer. So I feed the bodies, and hope that someone will arrive soon with a way to feed their souls."

Moments later, Jake and Pierre were in the jeep on their way back to base, followed by their convoy of two borrowed trucks. "How could you do a thing like that?" Jake demanded.

Servais was all innocence. "Like what?"

"Make the major think I was playing Pied Piper to a townful of kids."

"Amazing what a desperate man is capable of," Servais replied. "Until I hit on that, I was afraid the only way I could crack his armor was with a mortar shell." For a change, Servais was keeping his speed down to a level that did not leave Jake gritting his teeth and hanging on for dear life. The pair of trucks grinding along behind were incapable of faster speed, loaded as heavily as they were.

"Only now it's gone from three dozen kids to three hundred," Jake complained. "I could throttle you."

"I would advise you not to try, my friend."

"Yeah, I saw what you did to Connors' goons. What was that?"

In North Africa, I fought with a man from Thailand. A Frenchman by birth, but he had lived most of his life in Indochina. He taught me."

"It's impressive to watch."

"For a while we weren't sure they were going to let us fight in the war," Pierre said. "De Gaulle was always arguing, arguing, and for the longest time all we did was sit around and try to gather news of what was happening. The waiting was terrible."

"I've never been any good at that either," Jake said. "Waiting."

"So he offered to teach me," Pierre continued. "Which helped pass the time. It was not easy to learn."

"It doesn't look easy. As a matter of fact, it looks on the wrong side of impossible."

"That is my specialty," Pierre replied. "Doing the impossible."

"Great," Jake said, stretching out as much as the jeep's cramped confines would allow. "Then we'll just let you be the one to sell the colonel on this."

Colonel Beecham scowled as they appeared in the doorway to his office. "Not you two again."

"Promising," Jake murmured. "Very promising."

Pierre began, "Sir, we have had—"

"Don't stand out there like a couple of bellboys," the colonel snapped. "Come in and shut the door."

"Yessir." Pierre scowled at Jake's barely repressed grin as he turned to shut the door behind them. Keeping himself rigidly erect, he started over, "Sir, we—"

"Keep it short and sweet, mister," the colonel barked. "And whatever it is that you're aiming to work up toward, the answer is no. I've got too much going on to get involved with whatever fun and games you two have thought up now."

Jake covered himself with a discreet cough.

"Sir," Pierre persevered, "we have received the support of the French garrison commander, Major Gilbert, for our children's relief project."

"So?" The colonel's attention was already being drawn back to the papers littering his desk.

"I, ah, believe Chaplain Fox is a little short of storage space just now," Pierre said delicately.

"So go see Stores," Beecham said. "Why are you bothering me with this?"

"Yessir." Jake spoke for the first time. Before Pierre could open his mouth again, Jake grabbed him by the shoulder and spun him around. "Thank you, sir. Sorry to have troubled you, sir."

But before they could get out the door, Beecham said, "Just a minute."

"Almost home free," Jake murmured.

"Come back in here and shut that door." When they had done so, Colonel Beecham demanded, "Exactly what kind of support are we talking about here?"

"We're not quite sure, sir," Pierre replied.

"Not sure? Not sure of what?"

"Well, you see, sir, the major got sort of impatient when they were loading the second truck, and sort of took over himself. After that, they just threw in whatever they grabbed first."

Colonel Beecham leaned away from his desk and said quietly, "Second what?"

"Truck, sir." Pierre motioned lamely toward the unseen front of the building. "Parked just outside, sir."

"You have two *truckloads* of supplies?"

"Yessir."

"Whose life did you mortgage for that payload, mister?"

"Nobody's, sir. You see, the major has three children—"

"Stop right there," Beecham snapped. "I am absolutely positive I don't want to hear any more of this. Just tell me one thing, mister. Is any of this payload stolen?"

"Nossir."

"Contraband?"

"Not a bit of it, sir."

"You haven't passed off a paymaster's chit?"

"We didn't have to sign anything, sir."

"Sort of manna from heaven, is that what you're trying to tell me?"

"I suppose you might put it that way, sir."

"Get out of here, both of you. And if you know what's good for you, you'll steer clear of me for the next few days. You hear what I'm saying?"

"Loud and clear, yessir."

"Scram."

They swept through the door at lightning speed, closed it softly, breathing a silent sigh of relief. Then they caught a hint of noise from behind the colonel's closed door. It sounded like a chuckle. Jake formed a question with his eyes. Pierre frowned and shook his head in reply. Not possible.

*   *   *

In the hallway, Jake said, "I'm thinking."

"Don't make yourself feverish," Pierre warned.

"I'm thinking we could use some reinforcements for breaking into Stores," Jake said.

Pierre considered the idea. "Sally?"

Jake nodded. "Come on, let's see if she's around."

On the way down the hall, Pierre asked, "Where were you until after curfew last night?"

"Don't ask."

"Sally?"

"I told you, don't ask." They walked on in silence, then Jake said, "She was right, you know."

"About what?"

"About us wanting to turn that little confrontation the other night into a battle. We didn't even try to work out a peace."

To his surprise, Pierre did not contradict him. "That is the trouble with women, my friend. They are often right. Too often for their own good." He inspected the man walking alongside him. "You like her, yes?"

"Very much," Jake confessed. "Maybe too much."

"Yes, I am liking her too. She is not only beautiful but smart enough not to be trapped by her own beauty. That is a rare trait, my friend. Very rare."

"She also has walls a hundred miles high."

"Ah, but every wall must have a door." Pierre grinned. "The question is, which one of us has the key?"

Sally was both there and available to help. She gave no sign to Jake that anything had taken place between them the night before, and treated Pierre's suave banter with polite disdain.

The trucks, however, brought a rise. When she had walked around them both, peered into the open flaps, smiled a greeting to the still disgruntled drivers, she walked back over and asked, "So who did you kill?"

"It's a gift," Jake said.

"The first of many," Pierre boasted.

Jake cast him a dark glance and said, "The silver-tongued devil here to my right told a French major that I was taking responsibility for the safety of several hundred kids."

"Well," Sally declared, "we can't make the gallant captain into a liar, can we?"

"What do you mean by that?"

"Let's find a place to stow these riches, then go have a talk with the chaplain." Sally climbed onto the running board of the first truck and pointed it forward and around the corner.

Stores was contained within its own private compound, and protected by its own guard contingent. Assignment to guard duty within Stores was one of the most fought-after postings in all Germany. Which Stores did not matter. Each was a gold mine of opportunity. Even the lowliest of privates assigned to Stores possessed an air of smug sleekness. Access to Stores meant a ready supply of trading goods, and in the broken-down economy of war-torn Germany, anything could be had for a price. Anything at all.

The Stores major was a banker in uniform, and wore an expression that remained constantly on the verge of saying no. He was singularly unimpressed with Sally's request for help. "Much as I'd like to help you, Miss Anders, I'm afraid storing your items here is absolutely out of the question."

"It's just for a couple of days, Frank. For goodness' sake, you're bound to have some corner you're not using."

"That's not the point. We simply can't set this sort of precedent. You're a bright girl, I'm sure you understand what I'm saying. We're talking about principle here."

Sally leaned across the desk, her eyes flashing. "I'll give you principle, you pompous stuffed shirt. I've got sixteen loads of goods on requisition right now, just waiting for the colonel's signature. It's a shame the paper work is about to get buried. For about ten years."

"You can't do that," the major protested.

"You just watch me." She held his gaze long enough to drive the point home. "Now please march outside and find us a nice, dry corner. And keep it well separated from any of your own stuff. If I catch any of your sticky-fingered mutts nosing around our goods, I'll make sure your next shipment of cigarettes winds up in Siberia."

While the goods were being unloaded, Sally went off and returned with two able-looking enlisted men, and posted them on either side of the supplies. She also made a hand-lettered sign and pinned it to the first stack of boxes. The sign read, "If you're found here tonight, you'll be found here in the morning."

"What's all this?" Jake demanded.

"Insurance." She turned to her two men, raised a finger, and said in a stern voice, "If anybody comes within fifteen paces, you are ordered to shoot."

"Sure thing, Miss Anders," said one of the men with a grin.

"I'll arrange for you to get some extra time off once we've got all this squared away," Jake promised.

"No problem, Captain."

"Yeah, sir," the other agreed. "We think it's great the way you're helping these kids."

Jake shot Sally a glance. She shrugged. "What can I say? Word gets around."

"Come on," Pierre said. "Let's go find the chaplain."

They drove back to the base, found Chaplain Fox in his office, and explained the situation to him. But he refused to take charge. "You seem to be doing a fine job on your own," he said.

"We haven't done anything but scare up a few supplies," Jake protested. "You have the contact with the kids."

"You have just as much influence with them as I do," he replied. "The colonel has been after me for shirking my base duties. I am afraid, my friends, that this is one ball you will have to run with yourselves."

Once they were all back outside his office, Jake asked, "What do we do now?"

Sally was already putting on her coat. "Do what the chaplain says, what else? Let's go scare us up some kids."

*   *   *

Jake managed to find his way back to the destroyed chocolate factory. Even though the gang had already received its first free meal, the greeting was no warmer than the last time. "What do you want, *Fremder*? We don't have anything for you yet."

"That's not why I'm here," Jake replied quietly. There was a fiercely pathetic air about the place. An air of defeat and impending death made their bravado all the more tragic. He worked at keeping his face blank.

"Brought a few of your little friends around?" Karl demanded. "Take them for a visit to your own private zoo?"

Servais stepped forward. "Perhaps I can help."

"No!" Karl shouted. "Here you will speak the mother tongue and nothing else!"

"My friend speaks no German," Jake said.

"Then he can leave! Him and the female too. We want nothing to do with you, *Fremder*, not you, not your friends, not your pity."

But Servais was not to be put off. He murmured, "Pep talk."

"I—" Jake stopped. "What?"

"Follow my lead," Servais said swiftly, then stomped to the center of the room, threw his hands up in a dramatic gesture, and roared out a torrent of words. In French. Which Jake did not understand at all.

The boys and girls watched him open-mouthed. When Pierre paused for breath, Karl asked, "What is he saying?"

"He, ah, he is speaking of the future," Jake managed. He was saved by another deluge of words from Servais, who had adopted the regal manner of a general addressing his troops, and did it well. So well, in fact, that even Jake found himself drawing up a little straighter.

When Pierre stopped the next time, Jake was ready. "The French officer has taken time from his extremely busy schedule to come and personally pass on very important information," he translated. "He wishes you to know that your bravery in the face of enormous difficulties has been brought to the attention of the highest authorities."

Servais was off again, using the enormous voice of one accustomed to speaking to a division drawn up for formal inspection. It held the youngsters spellbound. At the next pause, Jake continued. "We come to you with a new mission. One which is dangerous, but which we are sure you are up to. If we did not have confidence in you, we would not have selected you for such a vital task."

Again the hair-raising torrent, and then from Jake, "We want you to make contact with every gang in the center city. Tell them we wish to speak with all of them. Do not tell them of your investigation. First they must be judged as worthy. Have them and all their members gather at the staff headquarters on the outskirts of town—do you know where it is?"

"We know," Karl replied, now without rancor. Doubtful but curious. Caught up and listening.

"Tell them that whether or not they are chosen, all will be rewarded just for appearing. Including yourselves. Especially yourselves. They are to come tomorrow at dawn, just after curfew has been lifted."

Jake caught Pierre with a sideways glance, and the Frenchman stopped his verbal onslaught in midstream. "It is a perilous assignment, but one worthy of your skills." Jake waited, then asked, "Do you agree?"

There was a long pause, then, "We will do it."

Chapter Seven

$\mathcal{D}$AWN CAME RELUCTANTLY. The sun remained hidden behind a motionless veil of frozen mist. It coated every surface with a fuzzy winter's scrawl, a written warning of the four harsh months yet to come. The little group of men that Jake, Pierre and Sally had gathered stomped around, blowing into mittened hands and speculating in muted tones about whether the kids were going to show.

A sixth sense must have alerted them, because Jake could detect no change to the frozen dawn. Whatever the reason, all sound died away as though on signal, all eyes turned to search the gathering light.

With the scarcest of sounds, gray-faced wraiths began to emerge from the freezing fog. They walked with the evident fear of mongrels not sure whether a cuff and a kick awaited them. Yet they came. It was one thing to run alongside a passing train or jeep or truck or marching convoy, to beg with words and gestures, to meet the conquering soldiers on turf they knew and understood; it was another thing altogether to walk toward a place that before had meant only beatings or shots fired in the dark. Yet they came. They stumbled from cold and from hunger, they tripped on the tattered footwear that scuffed and slapped softly with each step. Yet they came.

Still the gathered men could not move. It was a confrontation that no one was ready for, no matter what they might have been told. Here was war, the small faces said in silent agony. Here was the reality of battle. Here was the hidden cost of the fighting as armies struggled against each other. Here was need.

"Welcome," Sally's voice rang out clear and bell-like in the silence. "Don't be afraid. We want to help you."

She reached with frantic hands for something, anything, to hold out, and came up with chocolate bars. She reached out with them and said in her hesitant German, "Look. For you."

Into this frozen tableau they came, slowly, fearfully, with suspicion battling hunger on their faces. Finally a scarred and dirty hand was close enough to reach out and take trembling hold of Sally's offering. Then another, and another, and another still.

As the number of scrawny hands reaching up toward Sally increased, the first ray of sunlight forced its way through the fog. Its unexpected power startled them all. Eyes squinted, hands were lifted to shield faces, and in that moment the soldiers were suddenly able to move, to act, to serve. The scene sprang to hectic life.

Pierre took charge of the handouts. Each youngster received chocolate, tins of food, soap, a blanket, an item of warm clothing. Those with rags stuffed with newspapers tied up around scrawny ankles received shoes. Each gang received a bucket, a pot, a portable cookstove, a handful of utensils. Each child heard words spoken with warmth. It mattered little that few soldiers spoke German, and fewer children understood English. What was important were the smiles accompanying the words; a few children even managed to smile back.

The men found it less and less possible to meet the eyes of the soldiers with whom they worked. There was too much emotion in the moment, too much being brought up, too much on the surface exposed for all to see. Gazes were limited to those across the line, those who waited and searched with the frank honesty of the young and the injured, those who spoke so much without saying a word.

Sally was seated on a pair of stacked cases, writing at a table made from two crates. Each gang identified their leader. Carefully Sally took down the name, after explaining over and over and over that no, she did not work with the dreaded police, and no, the information would be given to no one else. She wanted it only for sending out more supplies. Still the leaders would only give their first names. Sally accepted this condition, taking only what they would willingly give. When they saw that she was not ordering, not threatening, not insisting they answer or give back all this newfound wealth, most of them gave her everything she wanted.

Where was each gang's headquarters? In a cemetery; a bombed-out school; a bomb shelter; a cellar; a ruined bus. How many members? Ten; thirty; seven; four dozen. Did any have families with lodgings where they could have food and perhaps shelter in the worst weather? A few did, most did not. Identity cards? Almost none. To the authorities they did not exist. They were not part of the flimsy official structures, and therefore were simply not expected to survive. How old was the gang's youngest member? Fourteen; nine; twelve; seven; six; five; four.

Jake stood just beyond the fence of the supply center, assembling and addressing one gang at a time. Carefully he explained that he needed their help in an investigation. But whether or not they decided to help, they could keep the gifts. And if possible there would be more. And they were to take no risks, or no more than they were already taking. But yes, he needed their help. They could go where he could not. They could hear what his ears were deaf to. They could see into places closed to him and his men.

As he spoke, Jake caught sight of a change taking place in some of the youths—not all, but some. Their eyes caught a glimmer of something. Interest. The first shred of excitement. A shadow of pride. They were *needed*.

The process consumed more time than anyone expected. No matter how many children they dealt with, there were always more. The sun gathered strength and burned away the remaining mist, leaving the gathering in full view of all the soldiers arriving for duty. Groups gathered and clustered and pointed and stared. Eventually the Stores major came out from his office to order his men back to work, but before his words were out, he too was riveted by the sight.

And still they came. Holding back until the soldier keeping order motioned for each new gang to move forward. Not really believing it was all happening, even when the gentle words had been spoken and the wares settled into their open grasp. Their eyes searched everything with fear and hunger and pain, and seared the souls of everyone who turned their way.

Jake finished with one group and motioned the next one over, only to turn and find a thoroughly uncomfortable Stores major standing by his elbow. The man harrumphed a few times, shuffled his feet, then said, "How are your supplies holding out, Captain?"

"I've been a little busy, sir—"

"Getting low," Pierre called over. "Very low."

"That's what I thought. Let me see," he stammered, "that is, well, perhaps I might be able to find a few extra items around."

Sally filled Jake's astonished silence with, "Whatever you can spare, Frank, I'm sure would be most helpful. We appreciate it."

"Very much," Jake managed.

"Good. Then I won't be a moment." The major scurried off, barking for his men to follow. In a matter of seconds a steady stream of soldiers pushing trolleys loaded to the limit were headed their way.

Jake had scarcely begun with the next gang when a familiar voice stilled the entire procedure. "Is this your doing, Captain?"

"Tenhut!" shouted a voice about five minutes too late.

Jake snapped to attention with all the other soldiers. Suddenly the children were in a state of tense readiness for flight. "Yessir, I guess it is, sir."

Colonel Beecham cast a frosty gaze over the proceedings. "How much longer do you expect to be?"

"We're processing them as fast as we can, sir."

"See that you do, Captain. We can't have these kids blocking military traffic."

"Yessir, fast as we can, sir."

Beecham scanned the scene a moment longer, then tapped his cap and said, "Carry on, then."

"Yessir, thank you, sir."

Jake permitted himself a breath once the colonel had moved off. He returned his attention to the kids. They seemed to be watching him differently. As he finished with that group and started with the next, Jake tried to identify the change. Somehow the arrival of the colonel, his words, his salute, and his departure had validated Jake's mission. They listened more carefully, believed him more readily. He found them repeating questions less, no longer expecting some hidden price. The colonel had appeared and approved. They were being recruited for something *real*.

Another half hour, and the last of the gangs had been brought forward, their arms filled, their details taken, their mission stated. Jake watched them disappear into the distance with a sense of numb fatigue.

"A miracle," said a gentle voice behind him. "One of the most incredible miracles I have witnessed in this entire war."

Jake did not need to turn around to know who spoke. "You were drafted as the contact point," he told the chaplain. "It appears that every gang in the city knows who you are."

"Seven hundred and thirty-six," Sally announced triumphantly as she walked up beside him. "Fifty-nine gangs in all."

"And we ran out of our own supplies right at four hundred," Servais said, drawing up alongside. "The rest came from Stores."

"A modern-day version of the loaves and fishes," Chaplain Fox said. "This is a day for signs and wonders."

"Ah, excuse me," a stranger said, walking up to the group. "Could I ask who is in charge here?"

Chaplain Fox pointed at Jake's chest. "He is."

"I'm Dr. Weaver. Harry Weaver. I'm a surgeon at the local base hospital. A couple of my colleagues and I were down here for a conference this morning, and, well, we were wondering if perhaps we might be able to help with your project." He motioned toward where the last of the departing children were vanishing down the road. "We thought we might be able to vaccinate them, maybe set up a clinic or do rounds for a couple of days, something like that."

"Signs and wonders," Chaplain Fox repeated. He patted Jake on the shoulder, said, "You heard the colonel, Jake. Carry on."

Chapter Eight

$\mathcal{P}$IERRE AND JAKE drove south to Oberkirch, too overcome by the morning's events to speak. They traveled in silence, their senses open and filled by the surrounding countryside. The day had turned bright and crisp, the air scented by the forest and farmland through which they passed.

Military traffic was heavy, but mostly headed in the opposite direction. The Americans were either consolidating their men and equipment into the region around Karlsruhe or moving it farther east, in anticipation of the French army's arrival.

The base was a hive of activity. Platoons were being lined up and marched into waiting trucks. Piles of equipment were checked and sorted and loaded. Men marched and shouted and whistled and gestured wildly, competing with the din of a hundred revving truck and tank engines.

The staff headquarters was set in a relatively quiet alcove, separated from the main garrison grounds by a grove of trees. Jake and Pierre were halfway down the walkway when, from the top of the HQ stairway, an all-too-familiar voice stopped their progress.

"Well, well, well." Colonel Charles Connors had a reed-thin voice that adapted well to his air of perpetual disapproval. "Could this truly be the famous Captain Burnes?"

Jake snapped to attention, his eyes straight ahead. "Morning, sir."

"Yes, I do believe it is." Connors walked down three steps, pausing on the next to last so as to be able to look Jake straight in the eye. "What a pleasure it is to see you again, Captain."

"Thank you, sir."

Connors had an undersized body encased in a blanket of lard. His thinning strands of hair were Brylcreamed and laid across his skull in a vague attempt to hide his widening bald spot. He had no chin to speak of. His eyes were a pair of pale blue marbles. His nose was a sparrow's beak, barely substantial enough to support his eyeglasses. His mustache was pencil-thin and quivered as he spoke.

"It appears that I shall be seeing more of you than either of us expected, Captain."

"Happy to hear that, sir," Jake ground out.

"Yes, I'm sure you will be interested to hear that my authority to maintain law and order has been extended to include the region around Badenburg. That is, until the French arrive, of course." The blue eyes glinted. "Which means I shall be required to keep a very close watch over you, Captain."

"Then I'll certainly know where to turn if I ever have a question about right and wrong, sir."

The colonel reddened, subsided, and turned to Servais. "And who do we have here?"

Pierre snapped to attention. "Captain Servais, sir."

"Ah, yes. The gallant Frenchman who almost cost me half a guard detail."

"The road was very icy, sir."

"Yes, what a pity. Well, Captain, I would advise you to choose your companions with greater care. Captain Burnes here is what we could class in our army as a bad influence." Connors cast a disparaging eye down the front of Jake's uniform. "There are all sorts of ways for a man without scruples to gain a chestful of medals."

"Sir, I resent—"

"Dismissed, Captain," Connors snapped. Then, as they turned away, he continued. "Oh, by the way, I'm sorry to be the one to tell you, Captain. My men were forced to arrest several of your former team for inciting a riot in the camp the other evening. In any case, they got into a fight among themselves during the night. Several of them required hospitalization, I'm afraid. It appears that this football idea was not quite the morale booster that you and others made it out to be. The Germans are enemy soldiers and must be treated as such."

"You mean your animals waded into a bunch of helpless prisoners and took them apart," Jake said bitterly.

"I shall pretend that I did not hear that wild and careless accusation," the colonel said with pleasure. "And you watch your step, Captain. You can rest assured that I certainly will."

Once they had completed their official business, their return journey was held to a slow, dusty crawl. An endless line of trucks, armored personnel carriers, battle tanks, and heavy-equipment conveyors filled the road. Pierre waited until they had placed several hours between them and Oberkirch before asking Jake, "So who is this Connors, anyway?"

"Connors is a product of what I call the limousine school of war," Jake replied. "He went directly from OCS to a posting in Washington, and weaseled his way up the ladder from behind the safety of a desk."

"There are officers of this caliber in every corps," Pierre replied.

"Yeah, so I've heard. Connors is a special case, though. He's managed to make quite a name for himself. I was amazed at how many people were eager to give me the lowdown on him when I arrived in Germany."

"What brought him over from Washington?"

"Oh, he sort of resigned himself to the fact that Major Connors would never become General Connors unless he accepted an overseas posting. There was a problem, though."

Pierre made the sound of a clucking hen.

"Give the man a cigar," Jake confirmed. "Connors values his own skin above everything else, and his own comfort a close second."

"I can think of several French officers who are close relations of our dear colonel," Pierre mused. "Birds of a feather, you might say."

"With great care and after much deliberation," Jake continued, "Connors selected a posting to the general staff of the Sixth Army. He waited until the Germans looked pretty well whipped, but not to the point where they were ready to roll over and play dead. The staff headquarters was being moved every week or so, as the front rolled on across Belgium and into Germany. Connors figured he wouldn't have much trouble finding a deep, dark hole if the Germans ever tried to attack."

"Something went wrong," Pierre guessed.

Jake nodded. "Connors failed to take into account the command mentality of the Sixth Army's chief, General George Patton. Patton hates these pencil pushers almost as much as I do."

"As *we* do, mon Capitaine," Pierre corrected. "Don't leave me out of this."

"Right. So according to scuttlebutt, what followed then were the six most harrowing months of Connors' life. He survived—"

"Alas," Pierre interjected. "While too many good men went down."

"And he gained his colonel's wings," Jake went on. "But he also gained a reputation among the battle-hardened officers."

"One with the fragrance of sun-ripened Gorgonzola," Pierre suggested.

"Something like that. So instead of being posted to Nuremberg or Berlin or another of the great centers of postwar activity, Connors found himself relegated to this backwater near the French border."

"Not the place where one might be expected to have the chance to gain a general's star." Pierre shook his head. "What a pity."

"Rumor has it," Jake replied, "that his commanding officer told him he had almost as much chance of making general as the porcupine did of becoming America's favorite house pet."

"A bitter pill," Pierre said.

"So when I arrived in Oberkirch, I found the gallant colonel busy gathering a company of toughs in MP uniforms. Why, nobody could figure out, but there were a lot of ideas floating around. The one I liked best was that the general's straight talk had turned Colonel Connors into a certified loon."

Sally Anders put it more succinctly that evening over dinner. "Connors is a toad," she declared.

Jake feigned shock. "You're speaking of a superior officer."

"A great hairy toad," she insisted.

"Toads don't have hair," Pierre pointed out.

"This one does," she countered.

"Not that much," Jake said.

"And warts," Sally went on. "I bet he even catches flies with his tongue."

They ate together in the Officers' Mess because Sally had refused to dine with either of them alone, although both had invited her. Jake had even asked twice. Her reply was, you make too good a team to have it broken up fighting over a woman.

Pierre said, "I still don't understand why Connors went after you that way."

"All this fuss over a football game," Jake agreed.

"It doesn't have anything to do with the game," Sally replied. "Not directly, anyway."

"I don't understand."

"You gave people something they've been looking for," Sally explained. "A good reason to laugh at Connors. A group of half-starved German POWs beat Connors' prize

battalion at their own game, and did it because they used
strategy instead of strength. You punctured the balloon of
his dignity, Jake. You showed him for the pompous idiot he
is. And he hates you for it."

"How do you know Connors so well?" Pierre asked.

"Jake isn't the only one Connors has bulldozed. We've
got several here on our staff who are still nursing wounds."

"We have?"

"Anybody who's seen as a threat to Connors' ambitions
is given the chopping block as soon as possible." Sally
smiled at Jake. "Given the level of your diplomatic skills,
soldier, I'm surprised you lasted as long as you did."

"You should have heard Connors today," Pierre said, and
related the episode on the HQ front steps.

"That man is a menace in uniform," Sally declared.

"You won't find much argument with us on that point,"
Jake said.

"I can't believe he'd do such a thing to innocent men,"
she fumed. "You're going to have to do something, Jake."

He nodded. "I've been thinking about that."

"And watch your step. You're taking care of a lot right
now. Don't forget yourself." She lit up. "No, wait; I've got
an idea."

"Suddenly there's a dangerous light in your eyes," Jake
said anxiously.

Sally leaned conspiratorially across the table. "Do we
agree that Connors shouldn't be allowed to get away with
this?"

"Sure, but—"

"No buts," she said sharply. "Did you know that the
man's in love with his jeep?"

"He is?" Pierre asked.

"Sure," Jake replied. "Everybody who's ever served with
Connors knows about that jeep. He keeps it in a special
shed just outside the Oberkirch camp. Every day he man-
ages to catch some poor enlisted man doing something
wrong, just so he can order him to wash and wax it."

Pierre's eyes widened. "Wax a jeep?"

"It's the truth, I promise," Jake said. "Had these little throw rugs on the floor, made us scrape off our boots before getting in. Crazy."

"Okay, okay," Sally interrupted. "We already know the man's a maniac. Now what I suggest is we hit him where it hurts."

"The question is," Jake countered. "How much is it going to hurt us?"

"Not at all if we're careful." Sally was on her feet. "You two go get into your dirtiest fatigues. Meet me back here in an hour."

"Where are you going?"

"I've got to see a friend in Stores."

Chapter Nine

THE NEXT DAY, Jake tried to still his queasy stomach as he knocked on Colonel Beecham's door. He found some comfort in the greenish, pasty shade of Servais' face. When the muffled voice thundered from within, Jake swallowed once, turned the handle, and entered.

Beecham's weary expression deepened when they came into view. "Not you two," he groaned. "What do you want now?"

"You sent for us, sir," Jake pointed out.

"Impossible. The only reason I'd do that would be to hand you a pair of postings to Antarctica."

"Does that mean we're dismissed, sir?"

"No, you're here, so I might as well get to the bottom of this." He inspected the two men. "What are you doing in dress uniforms?"

"Our fatigues were, ah, stained, sir."

"Well, go over to Stores and draw out some more. I can't have my men marching around looking like a pair of parade-ground heroes." The colonel shuffled through his papers until he found one. "I've got a requisition order from Stores here. Do you know anything about it?"

Jake and Pierre exchanged baffled glances. "We haven't asked for anything, sir."

"Not you directly. It's from some doctor or other. Le'see, he wants syringes, inoculations for everything from typhus to the yellow peril, and enough other stuff to outfit a field hospital." Beecham lowered the page. "Does this have something to do with those kids?"

"I guess it might, sir."

"You guess." Beecham snorted. "Are you trying to steal my doctors, son?"

"Nossir, nothing like that. They just asked if they could help out."

"I'll bet." He studied the paper a moment longer, then scrawled his signature and thrust it forward. "Have Miss Anders try to sell the idea to the local Red Cross. But if they kick up a fuss, tell Stores I said it was okay."

"Yessir. Thank you, sir."

"And Burnes."

"Sir?"

"Don't bother me again. Not today. Not this week. Not for a month or so. Not if you value your hide. It's time for you and your sidekick to vanish from my sight."

"We'll make like the wind, sir," Jake promised.

"That'll be the day," Colonel Beecham said. "Oh, one more thing. Do either of you know anything about how Colonel Connors' jeep received a complimentary paint job last night?"

Jake found it difficult to keep his gaze straight, his voice level. Very difficult. "Nossir."

"Canary yellow, if I understand it correctly."

"News to me, sir."

"The perpetrators apparently attached a feather-duster to the rear bumper." Colonel Beecham found it necessary to frown fiercely over the news. "They painted large chickens in flight on either door. And wrote 'Property of the Chicken Colonel' across the front."

"Can't imagine who would do such a thing," Jake replied.

"Funny," Beecham said in a low voice. "I could come up with several dozen names right off the top of my head.

Which is exactly what I told Connors when he called me this morning and accused you two of doing the dirty deed."

To that Jake made no reply.

"All right, make yourselves scarce." Beecham dropped his eyes back to his papers. "Permanently."

Once back in the hallway, Pierre observed, "Our colonel is looking weary."

"Exhausted," Jake replied. "Utterly exhausted."

"We must try not to bother him further," Servais said.

"I'll explain the situation to Sally," Jake offered.

Pierre smiled. "Come, my friend. Let us go and tell her together. I no longer feel I can trust you alone with her."

But it was Sally who found them, a wide-eyed, fearful Sally who ran up and cried breathlessly, "You've both got to come with me at once."

"What's wrong?"

Sally had already turned on her heel and headed for the door. "There's no time to lose!" she called back. "Hurry!"

She asked them to stop by the hospital for a fourth passenger, Dr. Harry Weaver. The young man came racing down the stairs as soon as the jeep pulled up, black bag in hand. "I'm due in surgery in two hours," he said, climbing on board. "We'll have to hurry."

"Would somebody mind telling me what's going on?" Jake asked.

"To the chocolate factory," Sally cried. "Step on it!"

Pierre was sufficiently caught up in the urgency to throw caution to the winds. Conversation was impossible. All three passengers were kept busy simply trying to stay in the bouncing jeep.

They pulled up in front of the gang's ruined building to find Chaplain Fox waiting by the door. He waved them to a stop, his customary smile gone, his eyes grave with concern. As soon as the doctor alighted, Fox took one arm and led him forward, leaving the others to find their own way.

The stench hit Jake before he was over the entrance plank. The odor was so strong it was a physical shock. He forced himself onward, reached the doorway to the gang's single room, then stopped.

The doctor bent over an inert body. Jake immediately recognized Karl, the young leader. The boy moaned softly, struggling to move. He was restrained by the chaplain, who leaned over him, murmuring gently in his ear. Beside Karl, two bodies were stretched out, another boy and a girl. The smell from them, too, was a solid force, so strong it was difficult to breathe in the room.

"What is it?" Jake managed.

"It's just as I feared," the doctor replied, rocking back on his haunches. "We have been receiving reports from other regions, but this is the first confirmed case in this area. It's not surprising, of course. It tends to attack the young, the weak, the unprotected."

"What does," Jake demanded.

The doctor gave a sigh of resignation. "Cholera. Also known as the plague."

Chapter Ten

*T*HERE WAS NEVER enough time. There was never enough of anything. Jake moved in a constant, wearying blur, his mind always filled with all that remained undone.

No one assigned him the duty. Jake did not question how or why he shouldered these tasks. He simply did what was required. He had to. It was only later that he wondered at his unquestioning response to a call he had never heard. Not with his mind, anyway.

The first crisis arrived soon after they loaded the four inert youngsters into the jeep, and he and the doctor careened off to the local Red Cross clinic. The chaplain, Sally, and Servais stayed behind, heading off in different directions to do a rapid survey of the other gang hideouts.

Jake and Harry Weaver were met at the hospital by another staunch member of the No Brigade, a large doctor in starched whites. "Just a minute there, Captain," he said sternly as they came rushing up the stairs with Karl and another of the boys in their arms. "Where on earth do you think you're going?"

"This boy needs medical attention," Jake snapped. "There are two more in the same condition out in the jeep. Could you ask two of your staff to give us a hand?"

"Not so fast, not so fast." The doctor moved to block Jake's forward progress. "Where are these kids' papers?"

"They have no papers."

"Then this is out of the question," the doctor insisted. "This clinic is specifically designated to assist the citizens of this town only. And only those citizens whose papers are in order. As it is, my staff and I are stretched to the limit. The absolute limit. You will simply have to cart this boy and his friends off elsewhere."

"Wait," Harry Weaver began. "I am—"

"Hold it, Harry," Jake said, his voice ominously low. "Let me handle this one."

As gently as he could, Jake lowered Karl's limp body to the floor. He then turned, grabbed the clinic doctor by his lapels, lifted him clear off the floor, and in two swift steps slammed him up against the side wall.

"Now look here," the doctor said, his voice up two full octaves.

"No, Doc," Jake snarled back, his face a scarce three inches from the doctor's nose. "You look real good. You search that small mind of yours and make dead certain there's not some other clause you might have missed." He slammed the heavy man back against the wall like an oversized puppet. The doctor let out a high-pitched squeak. "You better *hope* there's something you've forgotten, Doc." Another slam. Another squeak. "That is, unless you'd like me to show you just how thin you can be stretched."

The doctor drew a breath with difficulty and managed to gasp, "Well, now, I think we might be able to do something."

Jake let the man drop, and wiped his hands on his coat. "Four beds," he commanded. "More when we need them. Or I'll be back."

"Really, Captain," the doctor said, collecting himself. "There's no need for threats."

"That was no threat, Doc" Jake replied, stooping down to lift Karl up again. "That was nothing but cold hard fact. Now let's see those beds."

*   *   *

Death became his enemy, shortages his greatest foe. Jake fought with the same single-minded purpose that had brought him and his men through other earlier battles. He fought with all that he had at his disposal, accepting help from whichever quarter it might come. He fought with the desperate determination of a commander who knew that preserving the lives of his men was his most sacred responsibility.

The chaplain, Sally Anders, and Pierre Servais were Jake's chief lieutenants. But there was never any question of who was in charge. There was no time to question it. Nor was there any need. Jake simply shouldered the burden and charged.

The change was mirrored in others. Children who had never learned to obey anyone or anything were gradually coming to follow instructions instantly and to the letter. At least they did so when the commands came from Jake. Pierre, since he spoke no German, became supplies driver and chauffeur extraordinaire.

Chambers that had harbored sick children were swept and scrubbed for the first time since the war's end. Proper latrines were dug. The chaplain took over the rubble heap next door to the crèche; with the help of some of the children he cleared a space, erected a shelter, and started an indoor-outdoor kitchen where the gangs could come and sit on dry ground and eat a decent hot meal at least once a day.

And of course, all of this meant that Jake had to scrounge for even more supplies.

Help began arriving from the strangest sources. Mornings would often begin to the sound of growling truck motors, staffed by men he did now know, coming from bases as far away as Stuttgart and Heilbronn, sent by officers he had never met. Each frantic day he would pass soldiers, speak with them, issue orders, alert them to a new outbreak or a point of urgent need, then hurry on, only to wonder afterward who he had just addressed.

Perhaps the greatest surprise was when the big-bellied, cigar-chewing Sergeant Morrows turned up at Jake's quarters late one evening. "What say, Captain."

"Sergeant." Jake assumed the sergeant was bringing a reprimand from the colonel for having shirked his duties, but he was too tired to care. He scrubbed a fatigue-numbed face with his towel, and slumped down on his bed.

The sergeant scuffed his boots on the doorjamb and said, "Quite a little operation you've got going here."

Jake closed his eyes with a long, deep sigh. The problem with such nights was that while his body begged for sleep, his mind had lost its ability to slow down.

"Me and the boys, well, we've been talking." Morrows seemed to be finding his speech hard going, but he plugged on. "See, the thing is, sir, my specialty in the war was sort of being able to find things."

Jake rolled his head on the pillow and opened one eye.

"Not steal, you understand. Nothing like that. Just sort of find them. And, well, like I said, me and the boys were just talking, and—"

"Disinfectant," Jake said.

"We, ah, what was that, sir?"

"We need disinfectant," Jake repeated. "Urgently. Gallons of it. Enough to scrub down the floors and walls of maybe a hundred rooms."

"Disinfectant. Right." From a pocket the sergeant produced a grubby envelope and a two-inch stub of a pencil. "Twenty gallons ought to do it? How about brushes and buckets?"

"Transport," Jake said wearily to the ceiling. "We're having problems getting the kids to the hospital, and the doctors to the kids, and the kids to the feeding center, and supplies everywhere."

"Don't see much problem there," Morrows said, scribbling busily. "One of my buddies runs the mechanics over at the motor pool. Either the commander lets them have some time off or he'll have to try to drive around on four flat tires."

"And drivers," Jake said. "And more strong backs. And building materials. We've got to make these rooms where they're living dry. And warm."

"Blankets and bedding too, right?" Morrows seemed undaunted by the growing list. "How about more clothes?"

"And food," Jake said. "Those kids eat more than a brigade coming out of battle. There's never enough food."

"You leave it with me, Captain. And get yourself some rest. You look done in." Morrows closed the door and stomped off.

Jake closed his eyes, sighed again, and rolled over on his side. Maybe tonight would be different.

Just when it appeared that they were almost on top of the most urgent needs, Jake was blindsided once again. And from the most unexpected direction.

He stopped by the kitchen to make certain Chaplain Fox had enough food and fuel for the day, before working through the Matterhorn of paper work accumulating on his desk. But while Jake was talking to the chaplain, a voice behind him said, *"Entschüldigen Sie mir, bitte, Herr Kapitän."*

Jake turned to find a woman wrapped in rags. A young girl stood by her feet, clutching onto her skirt, and peering fearfully up at Jake. Another child was in the woman's arms, a boy of perhaps four or five. Painfully thin. And inert. Jake did not need to look closer. Not anymore. The smell lingering around the boy was all the information he needed.

"You must take him to the Red Cross center," Jake told the woman. "Immediately."

"Please, Herr Kapitän," she said, her eyes brimming with tears. "My name is Friedrichs. I am a poor woman. My husband was a Nazi. SS. They see me and read my papers and they spit on me. But my boy, my only boy, he is sick. He is dying. Please, please, I beg you, a poor weak woman who has nothing and no one. I hear what you do for the children. All the city hears. Please help me, Captain. Save my boy from death."

Jake started to turn to the chaplain, only to be stopped by the most unexpected of sounds. Under his breath, the chaplain was singing. *Singing.* Jake sighed and shook his head. He reached for the boy.

"I will do what I can," Jake told her.

At that the woman broke down completely.

"You and your daughter must stay and eat with us," he said. "And we will try to find some warmer clothes for you." Jake started for the jeep. "And disinfectant for your home. You must take care that you and the other children do not also become ill."

After that, the sad little lines began to form each day long before Jake arrived. The women refused to speak with anyone save the captain. They would relinquish their children to no one but the captain. Jake began to arrive at the feeding station earlier and earlier, knowing that even an hour in the fierce winter weather would be enough to doom the weakest of the children. And still they were there before he arrived.

New squads were formed to hand out clothing, disinfectant, brushes and pails to each family. They came and deposited their precious, stinking bundles and were sent on their way weeping with pathetic thanks. Addresses were recorded. Notices were printed up in German, so that neighbors could be warned. Jake made the signs as official as possible, *ordering* the cowed populace to take no measure against the families with sickness, *ordering* the neighbors to come in for disinfectant and blankets and food, *ordering* them to take every possible measure to keep their families healthy, *ordering* them to report any sign of illness as soon as it appeared.

But despite their best efforts, the cholera spread. Surely not as quickly as it would otherwise have done, maybe not as rapidly as in other regions. But Jake did not afford himself the luxury of a yardstick. All he saw was the growing number of kids sick and on the borderland of death. And some over the border.

Grudgingly, the clinic gave them an entire ward, which they swiftly filled with so many mattresses that doctors and nurses and volunteers had to pick their way between them gingerly. Even so, it was not enough.

Finally, a delegation headed by Jake approached Colonel Beecham. The colonel replied that he could not go against explicit orders and allow civilians into the military hospital, especially those suffering from a highly contagious disease. But he then ordered a pair of heated Quonset huts, formerly used as warehouse space for kitchen perishables, to be given over to the relief effort. In less than a week, both were filled with moaning, crying, wailing, and sometimes dying children.

The extra space was enough. Barely, but enough.

Slowly, so gradually that at first no one was willing to believe it, the tide turned.

The number of incoming children began to drop. Then drop farther still. Then diminish to a trickle. And those in care began to improve—most of them, anyway.

The exhausted worry lines that had creased the faces of those who had given of their time and energy and love began to disappear. Smiles reemerged. People who had taken part in the effort found themselves bonded together in the joy of shared achievement, of having given without heed to self or selfish gain. Without self-congratulations, they felt a kind of pride. And for some, their efforts brought a healing of their own internal wounds. They could not have said why, nor where it came from. Yet these war-scarred men and women found themselves walking taller, their own burdens somehow lightened. They discovered that by helping the helpless, they too had been gifted the invisible hand of peace.

Even Jake managed a few nights of uninterrupted sleep.

Chapter Eleven

*J*AKE HIMSELF DECIDED they might actually have rounded the corner the day he took Karl home.

The boy was sunken-eyed and silent as the jeep wound its way through littered, bomb-pitted streets. But when they pulled up in front of the chocolate factory, Karl announced in German, "I will find what you are seeking."

It took a moment for Jake to realize what Karl was talking about. The last thing on his mind for weeks had been the possibility of unearthing lost Nazi treasure. "Have your team look all you want," Jake replied. "But you concentrate on getting well."

"Yes, I get well, so I can work for you," Karl replied. "But others will not do this work. Me. I work. And not just look. I *find*."

Jake understood him perfectly. "You don't owe me anything."

"No, nothing at all, just life. Is my life not worth something, Captain?"

Jake found himself admiring the boy's spirit. "You're going to be okay."

As he lifted himself from the jeep, Karl's eyes burned with renewed determination. He nodded once to Jake. "I find."

* * *

That afternoon Jake and Pierre returned to their liaison duties with heavy hearts. After weeks of neglect, they could only expect to find their fledgling border patrols in total disarray. Not to mention the state of their personal contacts with the chain of command.

Yet when they stopped at the main gate of the Karlsruhe base, the guard threw them a parade-ground salute and motioned for the gate to be swung open.

"Captain Burnes and Captain Servais to see Major Hobbs," Jake said, eyeing the open gate.

"Sure, sir. I know you. I brought a truck down your way a couple of weeks ago." The corporal motioned them forward. "You know the way, sir."

"Ah," Jake hesitated. "Maybe you'd better call ahead, soldier. Major Hobbs isn't expecting us."

"No problem, sir," the corporal replied. "I'm sure he'll be happy to see you."

Jake glanced at Pierre, but found only a mirror for his own confusion. He turned back. "You are?"

"Oh, yessir. Matter of fact, the major's started his own project to help the kids around here. I'm involved. It's great being able to do something for them, isn't it, sir?"

"Yes," Jake murmured. "Yes, I suppose it is."

"I'll call the major and let him know you're on your way, Captain. And thanks. You've been a real inspiration to a lot of us around here. Other bases, too, from the sound of things." He snapped out another salute, and waved them on through.

Once beyond the gate, Jake asked, "Did I hear what I thought I heard?"

Pierre shook his head. "My friend, I shall reserve judgment on that one."

Major Hobbs met them with a wry smile. "Do you have any idea how tough you've made it for guys like me?"

"Sir?"

"Oh, drop the sirs and siddown, both of you." Hobbs settled back in his chair, cranked it back, and propped up his feet. "I mean, if I'm going to be the model to my men that the general's always going on about, I now have to live up to the examples of Captains Jake Burnes and Pierre Servais. Did I get your name right, Captain?"

"Close enough," Pierre said distractedly.

"The general?" Jake asked dully.

"You'd think you two had found the end of the rainbow, the way Command's been going on recently." Despite his words, the major did not appear the least bit put out. "Yeah, Colonel Beecham's report must have really caught their attention."

"Colonel Beecham wrote a report to Command?" Jake asked.

"Hard to believe, I admit. Seeing the pair of you sitting there so dog-tired you can barely talk, I have trouble understanding what all the hullabaloo is about. But the colonel obviously disagreed. Had some nice things to say about you two. Haven't seen it myself, but from what I hear he really laid it on thick."

"He didn't tell us about any report," Jake said.

"No?"

"Not a word," Pierre confirmed.

Hobbs did not bother to hide his grin. "Probably figured a pair of swollen heads would just get in the way. But there you are. The brass are talking about the little miracle you've worked. Burnes and Servais, those're the words of the month."

"We didn't work any miracle," Jake protested weakly.

"It's not enough that I've got to spend all my free time prying goods loose from Stores, so I can send it down to you guys," Hobbs went on. "Nossir. Now I've got to go out and get my own hands dirty."

"This is the first we've heard about any of this," Jake stammered. "We just came up to find out how the patrols—"

"Oh, that's all taken care of," the major said with a wave of his hand. "I've got two full platoons assigned to it round the clock. Border's not tight as a corked jug, mind you, not by a long shot. But we're bringing in our share of would-be smugglers and refugees. Enough to make you two shine in your own reports."

"That's good news," Pierre said, as stunned as Jake. "Very good."

"Yeah, had to cover you boys while you were out making the world healthy and safe for democracy." The grin broadened. "Interesting how I still don't lack for patrol duty volunteers, seeing as how it's cold as the backside of beyond out there. I guess the treasure hounds are still hungry, even though they haven't come across any pack trains of diamond-studded gold bars or whatever you guys stumbled over."

"A cross," Jake corrected. "Just one cross."

"Just, the man says. Anyway, I got patrol volunteers running outta my ears."

"This is, well . . ." Jake turned to Pierre for help.

"Incredible," Servais finished for him. "We are deeply grateful."

"Glad to hear it." Major Hobbs dropped his feet to the floor with a resounding thump. "Seeing as how you two are now in my debt, I'd like you gents to come give my boys a little pep talk."

"A what?"

"Lay it all out. Describe what needs to be done and how to go about doing it. Cholera's appeared in three districts of this town already. The cellar kids are supposed to be dropping like flies. We heard you got it pretty much licked down your way. Is that right?"

"It appears so," Pierre replied. "But it's too early to tell for sure."

"Well, at this stage we're ready to try anything. So how about you two coming back tomorrow around eighteen-hundred hours, and telling my boys where to start and what to do next."

"I'm not much of a speaker," Jake protested.

The major waved it aside. "We asked for volunteers the day before yesterday, and got more offers than we can handle. They've heard about what you've been doing, I guess from the guys trucking down supplies, and now everybody and his cousin wants to get on the bandwagon. We'll use today to get the word out to be ready in time for your talk tomorrow. Okay?"

"I suppose—"

"Great. Anyway, it'll give you a chance to polish your act before laying it on for the general staff." The major was on his feet, hand outstretched. "Sure is good to know I can count on you guys."

Jake dropped Servais off at the headquarters building in Badenburg and headed toward the center of town. He found Chaplain Fox surrounded by helpers at the feeding station, preparing the day's meal. They had long since found it necessary to declare the lot off limits until the chaplain had blessed the meal and serving had begun; as a result, a crowd was already gathering just outside the lot's perimeters. If he had not been so distracted, Jake would have taken great comfort from the fact that a few of the kids had actually had enough energy to start a game of tag down the street.

Jake pulled the chaplain over to one side and told him about all the fuss being made over the relief effort. He finished with the complaint, "I'm not a hero. I don't even *feel* like a hero."

"Not many honest people do, Jake."

"What's that supposed to mean?"

"Most heroics are built on tragedy," Chaplain Fox replied. "And most heroes do not act alone. If a man is honest with himself, he can take little pleasure in gaining from someone else's misery. And he will always feel uncomfortable if people make him into a symbol for the noble actions of many."

Jake kicked at a loose stone, sending it spinning across the rubble-strewn lot. "So what is the answer?"

"Allow God to use you for His glory, not for your own," he answered simply. "When your moment of honor comes, remember David's prayer. Who am I, David asks of God, that you would call me by name? And what have I done that causes you to give such greatness to your servant's house?" The chaplain paused to smile at the little girl whose mother was tending the cooking fire, then continued. "Here at the moment when David is being crowned king of all Israel, he humbles himself before God and declares himself a *servant*. That to me is the only sane way to approach recognition and honor. To dedicate it to the Lord and seek to do His will."

Jake was still mulling over the chaplain's words when a voice behind him called out, "Excuse me please, Herr Kapitän."

He turned and saw Frau Friedrichs, the first woman who had brought her sick child to him. The memory of most faces were blurred by hurry and fatigue. But as she had been the first, Jake recognized her immediately. He walked over and asked in German, "How is your son?"

"Weak," she replied, her voice long since drained of all emotion. It was as flat and as hollow as her features. "Very weak. But he lives."

Jake nodded. He had seen too many of the children hanging on by the slenderest of threads. Too many. "Is he taking any food?"

"Your priest gives me what he can," she replied. "I make a soup. He drinks some when he wakes up."

He noted the darkened rings surrounding her sunken eyes, the hollowed cheeks. "Then he should live."

She nodded. "You are a good man. You did all you could."

"Not enough," Jake replied. The wound of seeing so many little bodies buried was with him still. "And your daughter?"

"She is well, thanks to you and your men. And thanks to your orders to clean and disinfect, only one other child in the block was ill. And because of your signs, the neighbors don't scream for us to leave anymore, to get out from our home, when we have no place else to go."

"For this I am glad," Jake replied quietly.

The woman dredged up the faintest hint of a smile. "When one has nothing, even the smallest bit of hope is very big, is that not so, Herr Kapitän?"

Suddenly Jake was struck by the thought that there was an entire city of mothers just like this one in Karlsruhe, all terrified by the thought of their children being snatched away by death. He stepped back, as if physically assaulted by the enormity of the crisis, pressed by the multiplied sorrow and the burden of all the pleas for help.

"Captain?"

In this moment of clarity, Jake no longer saw just this one scarred and exhausted woman. He saw a whole nation in desperate need. He saw all those who extended their hands in the terror of a dark and lonely room, with no one to help, no one to call upon, and knew he had to go. There was no choice. "Yes," he said softly.

"The children," Frau Friedrichs continued. "The children of the street, they tell me you seek Nazi treasure."

Jake focused on her with difficulty. "I am not—"

"I wish to help you, Captain," she went on. "I and many others. Others who have some hope today because of you and your men."

"It is not necessary," Jake protested. "You have enough to do just caring for your family."

"For me, yes, it is necessary." The woman straightened herself with visible effort. "My husband was a Nazi. But he and all he stood for is gone. Gone. Gone to the graveyard of tragic error. It is finished, thank God. It is finished."

"Yes," Jake agreed, and could only admire her strength.

"He never spoke of treasure. But I know of others who heard things. I will ask. I will search papers. And whatever I find is yours."

"Thank you," Jake said solemnly. "You shall receive your share of whatever is brought to me."

The news brought the faintest glimmer to her weary eyes. "Perhaps I should refuse, but I cannot. I shall accept anything you give, but not for me."

"For your children," Jake said, nodding. "I understand."

"You should know something, Captain," the woman continued. "Others are searching."

"I have heard."

"Men with white helmets and white sticks," she told him. "Men who have evil eyes and voices."

The news rocked him. "Connors?" he asked of no one in particular.

"They do not offer anything in return," she went on. "They do not bring kindness. They come in danger, and they wreak havoc. If they are against you, Herr Kapitän, then you must take care. Great care. I fear they are friends to no one but themselves."

Sally found him wandering around headquarters a few hours later. "You look lost, soldier."

"I was looking for Pierre. Sort of, anyway."

She searched his face, said, "What's wrong, Jake?"

He looked around to make sure no one else was within range, then said quietly, "I just had an indication that Connors might be hunting for Nazi treasure."

"So?"

"You don't find that surprising?"

"If you hang around these halls long enough, you'll be surprised at the things you can pick up." A group of officers exited noisily from a conference room. Sally grasped his arm and steered him away. "You've got to admit it makes sense."

"What does?"

"Come on, Jake. Connors may be a hazard, but he's no fool."

"He's not?"

"No, he isn't, and you know it. He probably had some treasure-hunting scheme festering in that little mind of his when he started collecting that gang of hooligans."

"It makes sense," he said slowly.

"Sure it does. You stick with Sally, soldier. She'll take care of you."

"But I never figured Connors for a money-grubber."

"Connors likes his own comfort, but I doubt that money is behind all this activity. What Connors wants most is power." She popped into her office and came out shrugging on her coat. "I've been cooped up in here all day. Mind taking a lady for a walk?"

"Not at all."

"There's a general in Freiburg who's gained a reputation for wanting to crown his career by unearthing a major Nazi hoard," Sally continued. "It's my guess that Connors has linked up with him, in return for a promise of those little stars for his shoulder pads."

Jake pushed through the door, returned the guard's salute, and declared to Sally, "The day Connors gets his promotion is the day I hang up my hat."

"You and me both, soldier. But for the next fifteen minutes, let's pretend Connors and all the rest don't exist, okay? I mean, a weary woman can take only so much of the world."

"Fine with me," Jake said, turning with her to follow the road away from town.

They walked in silence for a time, passing through a growth of tall trees before emerging into a pasture-like clearing. Sally took a breath. "Back home, this is what we'd call a big sky," she said, her face suddenly open and relaxed, her skin lit by the day's waning light.

Clouds scuttled high overhead and down along the horizon, cloaking a winterland scene back-lit by the late afternoon sun. "Sure is a good day to be alive," Jake said.

"And healthy," she added. Then more quietly, "I've missed you, Jake."

"I've missed *you*—very much."

"You've been too busy to miss anybody."

"Not you," he replied. "Not ever."

Her look softened. "I'm proud of what you did. Very, very proud."

"I'm not sure who it was behind the doing," he confessed.

"What's that supposed to mean?"

Jake struggled for a moment, wanting to share his thoughts, but not sure he could, even with himself. "It just didn't make any sense."

"It made all the sense in the world," Sally corrected.

"Wait, let me try to explain. Logically, I mean. None of this was any of my business." He stopped and turned toward her. "But I've never felt so sure of anything in my whole life, Sally. Can you make any sense out of that?"

She looked up at him. "And you said you weren't a believing man."

"I'm not." He stopped, then admitted, "Or at least I wasn't. I'm not so sure about anything anymore. And the chaplain said some things to me this afternoon that . . . "

Sally nodded slowly. "I know," she assured him. "That man has a way of making it all seem so clear. So *possible*."

"What he's suggesting suddenly seems the most sensible thing in the whole world," Jake agreed.

"Who knows," she said, taking his arm. "Maybe it is, and we're just slow to find out."

Chapter Twelve

"*I*'LL FLIP YOU for it," Jake offered as they entered the Karlsruhe base the following evening.

"No need, my friend," Pierre replied. "You have already been volunteered."

"This is worse than going into battle," Jake groaned.

Pierre nodded. "I agree. In battle all they do is shoot you. There is no telling what the high command will do if you mess this one up."

Jake glared at his friend. "Thanks a lot."

"Something slow, I would imagine," Pierre suggested. "Undoubtedly very painful."

Jake pointed to where Major Hobbs was motioning them over. "I think he means us."

"I happen to have a blindfold in my pocket if you think it would help," Pierre offered, and wheeled the jeep into place.

"Glad to see you boys," the major said in greeting. "We've got quite a crowd in there."

Jake gave a soft moan.

"Something wrong with our man?"

"A touch of indigestion," Pierre assured him. "Nothing serious."

"Oh. Right. Okay, here's the plan. I'll stand up and make just a couple of remarks—you know, pave the way for the main action. Then I'll introduce you, and you get on with the show."

Jake wiped clammy hands down his pantlegs.

"We've talked it over," the major continued. "And we don't think there's any need for you to go into great detail. We can handle that ourselves. What we need from you is a little pep talk, something to inspire them to get out there and work."

"That's what Jake is best at," Pierre offered. "Inspiration."

"Great, just great. Exactly what I wanted to hear." The major clapped Jake on the shoulder. "Okay, let's get this show on the road."

The several hundred men and women crowded together transformed the hall into a smoky din. Jake shook hands with a variety of officers, nodded greetings, stood while introductions were being made, yet heard not a word of what was said. Someone led him up onto the stage and directed him into a rickety folding chair. Jake sat and watched as the major approached the podium and called for order. He half listened as the major entertained the group with a few jokes. Then the major turned and pointed toward him. Applause swept through the hall. Jake knew it was time.

He found it to be just like the moment before combat. As soon as it started, his nerves quieted down. Jake stood and walked forward to the podium, shook the major's hand, waited for the applause to die. And somehow he knew what he needed to say. The words had long been there, just waiting for an opportunity like this to be spoken.

"You will all find your own reasons for doing this," Jake began. "Or you will quit. There is no glory in this work. There aren't any medals. Nobody is waiting to pat you on the back and say what a great job you have done. And what you are going to find when you get out there is not pretty. As a matter of fact, it is about as ugly and disgusting as it comes. So if you are not able to find something in yourselves to keep you going, you'd better get out. All I can tell you is what worked for me."

A hush gathered, a stillness from a deeper place of listening and understanding. The room became so quiet Jake could hear the occasional foot sliding across the polished floor. "Any one of you who has been in combat knows what it is like to take a village, or a hill, or a river, or whatever the objective might be. When it's over, you're bone-tired, more exhausted than you ever thought possible. Maybe you just saw a couple of your friends take a hit. Maybe you came close enough yourself to death to still have the feel of it lingering around you. So there you are. You sprawl out, maybe grab a quiet smoke and a cup of java. And what happens? Out of nowhere comes this cluster of little kids.

"Your first reaction is, go away. But you're probably too dog-tired even to say the words. So the kids hang around, just out of reach, and they stare at you. All rags and dirt and limbs as thin as little sticks."

Here and there in the room, heads began nodding as Jake intoned scenes and memories. "Then you move on," Jake continued. "It's strange what you remember from all that just happened. After coming that close to death, you'd expect the most vivid recollections to be of the battle. But that is not the way it works, at least not for me. No, what I remember most clearly is how big those kids' eyes looked. I used to think that all the war and suffering they had seen somehow opened their eyes to twice their normal size." Jake shook his head. "All I have to do is close my own eyes, and their faces are still there, still staring back at me.

"So what happens now? We won the war, right? We will be going home soon, at least most of us will. I am, and let me tell you, I am counting the days." Jake waited through the quiet chuckles, then said, "But those faces are still with me, just as I described them. All those kids, in every place I left behind.

"When this problem surfaced down in the town by my own base, I decided that maybe it would be a good idea if I could try to do a little something for just *one* kid. In just *one* town—before I went away and left all the ruin and destruction behind me. Before it was too late."

He stopped and waited for a moment, then finished, "I know those faces will still be with me until the day I die. But at least now, right there alongside them, will be these other faces. Some with smiles, even. Faces of a few people who might have a little more chance to make something of their lives because of what some of us did, or tried to do. And that is what is most important—that we *tried*. We tried to give them back a little hope."

Chapter Thirteen

*W*HEN THE BASE at Offenburg asked him to come down and give the same talk two nights later, Jake was less bothered. At least, until Sally Anders insisted on coming along.

"No how, no way," he declared, and tried to turn away.

But Sally was not having it. "You may consider it an order, soldier. You are taking me along, and that's final."

"Over my dead body."

"That can be arranged," she snapped. "Jake, who brought you to meet the kids in the first place?"

"I forget."

"Well, you best just unforget, mister. I'm calling in my chips."

"The only way I get through this is because I'm talking to a bunch of strangers," he pleaded.

"Then you can just consider me one of them," she retorted. "That should be easy enough, as scarce as you've been these past few weeks."

"Sally, you know how overwhelmed I—"

"So here's your perfect opportunity to make up for lost time." She batted her eyelashes. "Look at it this way. How often does an attractive girl throw herself at you?"

In the end it was all right. Once up on the podium, Jake had no room to think of anything else. The pressure to tell what was in his heart was just too strong.

Afterward, Sally waited while the commanding officers gathered and shook his hand and offered compliments. Her gaze never left his face, not even when Pierre tried to capture her attention. For that moment, that hour, she was his.

Without asking, Jake ushered Sally into the backseat of the jeep, clambered in beside her, then said to Servais, "Home, James."

Pierre surveyed the pair, his eyes dark and unreadable. Then he said, "I suppose it is time for the white flag."

"Don't be silly," she told him, but her voice lacked conviction, and her eyes were still on Jake. "I sat up front with you for the trip here. Turn about is fair play."

Pierre nodded, his expression blank. "Your mouth says one thing," he replied, "your eyes another, ma chérie." Then before Sally could respond, he gunned the motor and started off.

They sped back under a star-streaked sky. The trees were dark guardians lining the road; their sharp spears jutted upward, granting a sense of safety to the surrounding night. Sally shifted from time to time, drawing closer to Jake. Jake took heady draughts of the biting air, and felt that here, this moment, his life might truly begin anew.

Pierre drove with a chauffeur's precision, his eyes ever forward. He spoke not a word. Jake resisted the urge to reach out and pat Pierre's shoulder and offer words of friendship. Now was a time for Sally. She leaned against his chest, she filled his world.

Then they rounded the final corner before entering the city's outskirts, and the peace was shattered.

It was not a full-control checkpoint. Just a trio of white-streaked MP jeeps set at point, with a series of striped barrels rolled in front and their tops set alight. Spread out around the barrels were a dozen or more white-helmeted soldiers.

"Hang on!" Pierre shouted, simultaneously hitting the brakes and spinning the wheel violently.

The jeep almost went over. It careened up on two wheels, teetered, then slammed back and did a grandiose four-wheel skid into the right-hand pair of barrels. They missed the MPs stationed there only because the men flung themselves out of harm's way.

While Jake was still frozen in the protective position he had taken across Sally, Pierre jumped from the seat. "Come on, move it, move it!"

Jake's muscles obeyed the urgency in Pierre's voice. He lifted a visibly shaken Sally up and out of the jeep. Before her feet were even in contact with the earth, Pierre grabbed her and sped toward the closest shadows. Jake was immediately after them.

The MPs' stunned stillness was shattered by a violent, "After them!"

Tree limbs whipped Jake's face and snatched at his uniform, as if trying to hold him until the assailants could catch up. He fought with an animal's panic strength, struggling to keep up with the racing Servais.

"Through the trees! Over here!"

Thundering feet crashed through the brush behind them, adding speed to their flight. Sally's breath was a series of high-pitched gasps. Jake barely missed slamming into a tree he saw only at the last possible moment. Then came the unmistakable crackling sound of gunfire. Jake dropped, rolled, was up and running again, even before the sound had finished its echoing refrain.

Pierre jinked and weaved, crossed over a rutted track, and slid down the embankment on the other side, dragging Sally after him. Jake followed close on their heels, his breath a thunder in his ears. Pierre struggled up a rise; Jake moved in to take Sally's other arm and help lift her up the steep hillock.

At the top there was danger—a clearing without cover. From the other side, figures bounded out of the shadows, struggling through the high snow toward them. Jake was baffled. Panting hard, he dropped to his knees beside Pierre, wondering how their pursuers could have made it up and around them so fast. No, that wasn't possible, he could still hear the shouts and curses following them through the woods behind. Then who—

"Halt!" A voice carried strong and clear across the snow-covered pasture. "Who goes there?"

Behind them the other voices cut off as though sliced with a knife, and Jake knew a blessed rush of relief. "Captains Burnes and Servais. Who are you?"

"Captain Burnes? Is that really you, sir?" A shadow approached at a run; the moonlight revealed the fresh-faced squad leader from one of their own incoming border patrols. "Captain Servais? And who—Miss Anders? What are you folks doing out here?"

"Do us a favor, Corporal," Servais said, his breath coming in quick snatches. "Walk us back to the main road, will you?"

All three of them were shaky on their feet as they trekked back toward civilization, Sally most of all. She had been trying to run in low-heeled pumps. Jake and Pierre were not much better off, their dress shoes hardly made for open-field running over snow and ice. The soldiers were solicitous, and accepted their account of an attack by a band of raiders with genuine alarm.

When they reached the edge of the road, the corporal motioned to them to stay back, as they were weaponless. He and two of his men crept forward and disappeared. A few moments later they returned. "Looks like they scampered, sir."

Jake and the others emerged onto the road to find only their jeep still remaining. The corporal walked over to it and whistled softly. "Come take a look at this, sir."

They had not been satisfied to slash all four tires. The windshield and headlights were shattered. The seats had been hacked to ribbons with a sharp-bladed knife.

"Never seen anything like this," the corporal said. "Crazy how they'd destroy something as valuable as a jeep and not take it off as loot."

"The whole thing's crazy," Jake muttered.

"You can say that again, sir. Never heard of a band attacking military personnel before. Well, maybe we ought to walk you folks on back to the base. Somebody from the motor pool can come get your jeep. Sure doesn't look like it's moving from here on its own steam."

They gathered in Sally's office once the squad had been thanked and sent off. Sally vanished and reappeared with blankets and steaming mugs of coffee. They sat and sipped in silence for a few moments before Jake asked Pierre, "Why did you run?"

"It was automatic," he said succinctly. "I didn't think about it."

"Smart, all the same."

Pierre nodded. "A roving band of Connors' goons sets up a roadblock on the only highway leading back from Offenburg, five hours after curfew. What does that tell you?"

"But it doesn't prove anything," Sally protested.

"No," Pierre conceded. "Not that alone."

"What else is there?"

"The fact that they weren't there when we returned," Jake replied. "If it had been a legitimate checkpoint, they would have stayed around to arrest us. They had ample reason after Pierre gave them another sample of his driving skills."

Pierre looked up from his two-handed grip on the mug. "What were they after? That is what I cannot understand."

"The jeep?" Sally offered. "Do you think Connors is still carrying a grudge about that, even when he doesn't know for sure it was us?"

"He knows," Jake countered. "He may lack the proof, but he knows all the same."

"Maybe, but I do not think so," Pierre replied. "Something in my gut says the man would not go to all this trouble over one jeep."

"But what else could it be?" Jake demanded. "What could a couple of border liaison officers have that would rile a man like that?"

They sought the answers in silence, sipping the potent brew and gathering strength from the companionship for quite a while. Finally Sally set down her mug, stood, and rubbed a sore back. "Well, soldiers, this woman is off to bed."

Jake was instantly on his feet. "I'll walk you back."

"No need, but thank you." She smiled at Pierre. "Good-night, gallant driver."

"Bonne nuit," he murmured, his eyes on his friend. "Sleep well."

"I intend to." She allowed Jake to follow her down the hall, but at the back door leading to the staff's sleeping quarters, she stopped him with a firm, "It's been great, Jake. Thank you for letting me come along."

He inspected her face and said quietly, "That's it?"

"The trip to dreamland was captivating," she admitted. "But I had a rude awakening to reality on the road home."

"That wasn't reality, Sally," Jake protested. "This is."

For once, her sharp wit deserted her. She dropped her eyes and sighed, "If only . . ."

"If only what," he pressed.

She raised her gaze and said flatly, "Nothing, soldier."

"If you don't tell me, how am I supposed to know?"

"Maybe you aren't," she replied, more gently this time. "Good-night, Jake. Go get some sleep."

Chapter Fourteen

*J*AKE ROSE THE next morning wrapped in the mantle of gloom he had carried to bed the night before. He grunted his responses to Pierre's chatter, and pondered over the pain in his heart. While shaving he gave his face a careful scrutiny, trying to view it as Sally might. What he saw did not leave him reassured.

His face had been hardened by war. There were a few lines, mostly around the eyes and mouth. But not many, not enough to define his features. No, the war had *hardened* him. His chin was drawn like a hatchet, his nose a blade that split his face. The old parting he used to have in his hair was gone; instead, he drew the hair straight back, accenting the aggressive thrust to his jaw. His eyes were direct and cautious. And hard. Hard as the rest of him.

Jake sighed, wiped off the remaining lather, and turned away. A face only a mother could love.

They arrived at staff headquarters just as Sally came tripping down the stairs, half in and half out of her coat. At the sight of her, Jake's heart sped, and his mind sought frantically for something, anything, to change the way things were.

But Sally barely noticed him. She clambered over Jake and spilled into the jeep's backseat, yelling out, "To the hospital! Hurry!"

Jake hung on for dear life as Pierre raced back out the entrance drive and up toward a nearby farmhouse which was now doing duty as the military clinic. He risked a backward glance and asked, "What's going on?"

"They've got him," she said, but quickly interrupted herself to pound on Pierre's shoulder. "Stop!" She pointed to a running figure.

Harry Weaver was racing down the road toward them, looking as harried as Sally and just as grim. He leapt into the backseat. "Have you heard anything more?"

"No," Sally replied.

"About what?" Jake asked.

"Who's got whom?" Pierre demanded.

"Just go!" Sally yelled.

"Where?" Jake and Pierre managed in one voice.

"The stockade!" Sally almost lost control at that point, but with an effort drew herself back from the edge. "They've locked up Buddy Fox. And they hurt him!"

Pierre required no further goading. Jake doubted seriously whether all four tires ever hit the road simultaneously from that point on until they halted before the garrison's makeshift prison.

The stockade occupied the lower portion of what had once been a bank—the only section still intact after a bomb had done away with the upper four floors as neatly as a barber giving a crew cut. The gaping holes where once tall windows had stood were now sectioned off with cross-iron bars over their lower halves and boards closing off the tops.

A squad of MPs with white batons at the ready were gathered in front of the building. At the front and center stood the same sergeant who had led the checkpoint guard patrol.

Sally did not wait for Jake to alight. As the jeep rolled to a stop, she jumped out and stomped over, ready to do battle once more.

"Let him out," she snapped.

"Can't do that, Miss Anders," the sergeant replied, his eyes on Jake. "Orders."

"You want orders? Okay. Fine." She drew a letter from her pocket, whipped it open, thrust it in the MP's face. "I assume you can read."

The MP shifted his baton, thrusting it under his left arm, and accepted the paper. He kept his eyes on Jake. "How you doing there, Captain?"

"Morning, Sergeant," Jake replied. "How's the nose?"

The sergeant flushed and dropped his eyes to the paper, holding the moment as long as he could.

"Well?" Sally snapped.

"Yeah," the sergeant drawled. "That chaplain created a disturbance downtown. Had this mob crawling all over everywhere. You wouldn't expect a chaplain to incite a riot like that, now, would you?"

"Is that what you call trying to feed starving kids, inciting a riot?" Jake asked.

The sergeant's cold gaze rose back to meet Jake's. "Couldn't hardly get down the street, there were so many people. You know there's an ordinance against gatherings of more than half a dozen Krauts in one place without a permit. You *should* anyway. You being a liaison officer and all."

"That paper in your hand," Sally said, almost dancing with rage, "says that the chaplain has express permission to carry on his work, whatever it might require. It also states that you are *ordered* to release Chaplain Fox to my custody *immediately*. It is signed by Colonel Beecham, commanding officer of this garrison."

"Shame the chaplain had to go and put up such a fuss when we tried to arrest him," the sergeant went on. "Guess it's like Colonel Connors said. He's been hanging around people who've been a bad influence on him."

"Just get the man," Jake ordered.

"Go spring the chaplain, Jenkins," the sergeant said to one of his men.

"Sure, Sarge."

The sergeant's gaze never shifted from Jake. "Heard you had a little trouble with your jeep the other night, Captain."

"Nothing serious," Jake replied, his voice carrying a cutting edge. "Just a bunch of local roughs. You know the type. Cowards that cut and run at the first sight of a real fight."

Fury blazed in the sergeant's eyes, but before he could respond Jenkins came back through the door. He supported a battered Chaplain Fox by one arm. Sally gasped and raced up the stairs with Dr. Weaver.

She put her arms around the chaplain. "Can you make it down the steps?"

"They destroyed my kitchen," the chaplain moaned, allowing her and the doctor to take almost all his weight. "They tore it all apart and stole all my supplies."

"Must be talking about that mob," the sergeant said. "Didn't hardly have enough men to keep order down there."

"Here, Doc," the soldier said. "Lemmee give you a hand."

"You keep your filthy mitts to yourself," she snapped. "Come on, Buddy. It's all over."

"Not yet, it ain't," the sergeant said. "But it soon will be."

Jake helped them settle the chaplain into the passenger's seat. When everyone else was in, he jumped on the running board. "Let's go."

As they drove away, the sergeant waved his baton in the air and called, "Y'all come back now, y'hear?"

"I just don't understand it," the chaplain mumbled through bruised and swollen lips. "What reason could they possibly have for attacking me?"

"Scum like that don't need a reason," Sally said, wrapping a bandage around his forehead.

"Yes, they do," Jake said.

"Now just raise up your other arm," Harry Weaver said, and pressed down on his chest. "Does that hurt?"

"No, ah, there. Yes, there."

"Okay, can you take a breath for me?" He fitted the stethoscope back into his ears, listened carefully, and said, "Again."

Dr. Weaver dropped the instrument back down around his neck. "All right, you can lower your arm." He took a step back. "I'm afraid you have two cracked ribs. But your jaw is not broken as I first thought, and although there are a number of visible contusions, there is no sign of internal injury."

"Thank you, my dear," Chaplain Fox said to Sally as she tucked in the loose end of the bandage. Then to the doctor, "What does all that mean?"

"You should get better fairly quickly," he replied. "And should require no further treatment, except that I'd like to strap those ribs. And see you again in a few days, just to check your progress."

"So when can I go back to work?"

"In a few days. A week at the outside. That is, if you promise to take it easy and let these ribs heal properly."

"I'm not so sure going back there is such a good idea," Jake said slowly.

"Close the feeding station?" Sally was shocked. "Give in to those animals? What on earth for?"

"That's just it," Jake complained. "I can't figure out what this is all about. And whatever you think, Sally, this was done for a reason."

"I agree," Pierre said, speaking up for the first time since they had left the stockade. "And I don't think it was the chaplain they were after."

"But the children," Chaplain Fox protested to Dr. Weaver. "If I can't, who will look after the children?"

Sally kept her gaze on Pierre. "So who was it they wanted?"

"Your friend and mine," Pierre replied, "Captain Burnes."

"Me?"

"You."

"But why?" Sally demanded.

"I've been thinking about that," Pierre replied. "And I think I might have an answer. Might, you understand. This is just a guess."

"Sally, my dear," the chaplain began, but was shushed by her gentle pressure on his shoulder.

Sally said to Pierre, "Go on."

"Consider their attack the other night," Pierre said. "We assumed it was revenge for Connors' jeep."

Harry Weaver produced his first smile of the day. "That was you guys?"

Sally ignored him. "So what else could it have been?"

"The next time you plan something like that," Harry Weaver persisted, "be sure and count me in."

"Something else took place at the same time," Pierre went on. "Something Jake happened to mention in passing, which neither of us thought very important. He talked with a young man of the streets, and also with the widow of a former SS officer. And both promised to help Jake in his quest."

"The treasure?" Jake looked astonished. "But you and I both know we're looking for a needle in a haystack the size of a city."

"Not so fast," Pierre said.

"Even if there was any real chance, that rag-tag bunch don't have a hope of finding it. They've hardly got the strength to tie their own shoelaces, much less hunt for hidden treasure." Jake shook his head. "We don't even know if it really exists. Maybe it's all a myth."

"Let him finish, Jake," Sally ordered.

"Not a myth," Pierre countered. "Not all of it. We have a cross to prove that."

"Or at least the army has," Jake muttered.

"Jake," Sally snapped.

"What if there *were* a treasure," Pierre persevered. "What if our charming friend Colonel Connors knew it existed in this area, and thought he was closing in on it?"

"Then all of a sudden up pops Jake, with this crowd of Germans all throwing up dust and covering the same terrain," Sally added. "People Connors has no control over, people who wouldn't give him the time of day. The man would throw a size-twelve fit."

"And go after the ringleader with a vengeance," Pierre agreed.

Jake looked from one to the other, then declared, "You two are out of your tiny minds."

"Then come up with something better," Pierre challenged.

"Strike that," Sally said, rising from the bedside. "It's time to have a chat with Colonel Beecham."

"You can't bring the colonel in on something like this," Jake protested.

"You just watch me, soldier." Sally pointed toward the chaplain. "Take a good look at what those beasts did to Buddy, then tell me what I can and can't do."

"But we don't know anything for sure."

"We know enough," Sally replied. "Now, are you two coming, or do I have to go in there alone?"

"We're coming," Servais said, standing.

"Pierre," Jake moaned.

"Get up, Jake."

"But the colonel, you heard—"

"On your feet, soldier," Sally ordered.

"Wait," Chaplain Fox called out.

Sally turned back to the bed and said gently, "I'll go and see to your children, I promise. Each and every day."

"I know you will, Sally. And I am eternally grateful." He painfully raised himself up on one arm and said to Jake and Pierre with all the force he could muster, "No violence. If you resort to their tactics, then they have won. No matter what the outcome, they have won."

When Beecham heard what had happened to the chaplain, his jaw clamped and his eyes flashed. He remained stern throughout Pierre's account of their trouble at the crossroads and his subsequent guesswork. Jake sat squirming, convinced that once Pierre had finished, the colonel would extract the truth about Connors' jeep.

Instead, Beecham said, "Some rumors have been drifting around that back you up."

Sally sat up straighter. "What have you heard?"

"What I'm about to tell you is strictly off the record, do you understand?"

The three of them nodded.

Beecham focused on Jake. "Do you remember what I once told you about the general-turned-treasure-hound?"

"Yessir. Isn't he posted somewhere around Freiburg?"

"That's the one. Name's Slade. Up for retirement soon. Word has it that he wants to ride out of here in a blaze of glory."

"And Connors is his man," Sally finished for him. "Just as we thought."

"That's not certain," Beecham warned. "But what I can confirm is that Connors now has some hefty protection. Slade has taken Connors under his wing and given him a free hand to do pretty much as he pleases. I called Slade's office as soon as I heard about this set-to with you folks the other night, and got the brush-off from some snot-nosed Ivy League lieutenant." Beecham was obviously still burning at the memory of this encounter. "Last night I also heard that Slade is trying to get his authority extended to cover this area."

"That means the treasure must be located around here!"

"It means that Slade *might* think something *might* be in these parts," Beecham corrected. "If there really is any, which I'm still not certain about."

"What about the cross?" Sally countered.

"One cross is one cross, not a mountain of gold. But yes, I'm willing to admit that there is at least a chance you are right."

"A big chance," Sally said triumphantly.

"A *dangerous* one," Beecham amended. "If there really is a hunt going on around here, and Connors and Slade both know they're racing against the clock, you can bet your life they'll deal savagely with any ground-level opposition." He glanced at his calendar and went on. "The handover to the French is scheduled for early next month. After that, this will be French-controlled territory, and anything they find will be as far out of Slade's reach as the dark side of the moon."

"So do we tell the kids to hold off the search?" Jake asked.

"You can't do that," Sally protested. "What if Connors does find something?"

"He might anyway," Jake pointed out. "He's got a big organization behind him."

"But you've got contacts closer to the ground," Sally argued.

"You've seen Connors' tactics," Jake replied. "How would you feel if somebody was seriously hurt?"

"The kids will just have to be very careful," Sally said. "And they will. Because you're going to keep an eye on them."

"I think she's right," Colonel Beecham said. "As long as they proceed with extreme caution, I think it should be all right to let them see what they can find. I would hate like the dickens for Connors to end up with a lever to elevate himself to general."

"So would I," Jake agreed.

"Talk to them, Captain," Beecham directed. "If they understand the danger and agree to go ahead carefully, good. If not, call it off. It's your shot either way."

Once they had been dismissed, Jake headed straight for the exit. Sally caught up with him. "Where are you going?"

"I want to see if there's anything around the feeding station that can be salvaged."

"Wait, I'm coming with you. I need to check on the crèche."

"Not so fast," Pierre said. "None of us should go anywhere alone. If any one of us needs to go somewhere, we take an escort. Extreme caution starts with us."

"Agreed," Sally said.

"That's fine with me," Jake murmured, his eyes on Sally.

"All right, then. Let's go."

When they pulled up in front of the crèche, a great crowd of youngsters was milling about the street in front of the feeding station. Jake climbed from the jeep and said glumly, "I guess I'd better go break the news."

"Maybe we can work out something by tomorrow," Sally said hopefully. "A cold meal or something."

Pierre stood on the jeep's running board and searched the crowd. "What are those soldiers doing over there?"

"And those trucks," Sally added, pointing to a pair of green canvas tops beyond the gathering.

Just then a voice bellowed out, "All right, all right! Nobody gets nothing until we see some order around here. Corporal!"

"Yeah, Sarge?"

"You and a coupla men line these jokers up."

"I thought you told me to keep a lookout for the creeps in white hats."

"So line 'em up and keep looking. What are you, some kinda moron?"

"No, but I don't speak the lingo."

"Then, use your hands. They got eyes, don't they?"

Jake looked at a wide-eyed Sally. "What's going on?"

"Isn't that Sergeant Morrows?" she asked him.

"Food," Pierre announced, sniffing the wind. "Somebody is definitely cooking something."

They plowed through the mob, crossed the rubble heap, and came upon a sweating Sergeant Morrows with three frantic helpers. When the sergeant saw them he straightened and said, "Say, it's about time—I mean, glad you could get here, sirs. Hey, Miss Anders. Sure could use some help with these kids."

"What's going on here, Sergeant?"

"We heard what they did to the chaplain, sir. Me and some of the boys, we decided we couldn't let the kids go hungry."

One of the soldiers helping Morrows asked, "How's the chaplain, sir?"

"Dr. Weaver says he's going to be okay," Jake replied. He pointed at the gleaming new kettles and stands, the heaps of produce, the shiny steel platters and other equipment and asked, "Where did all this come from?"

"Turned out Stores had some stuff lying around they didn't need." Morrows caught the glint in Jake's eye and protested, "It ain't stolen, sir. Honest. Everybody's real hot over what they done to the chaplain."

"Sarge was turning stuff away," his assistant offered. "Volunteers too. Everybody wanted to get in on the act."

"Put a dozen or so guys spread out in front and back, in case the goons show up again," Morrows said. "I sorta hope they do."

Pierre put up a warning finger. "No violence, the chaplain said."

"There ain't gonna be no violence unless they come looking for it," Morrows replied. "And if they do, it won't last long. Sir."

"Why do you think they did it?" Sally probed.

"Goons is goons, ma'am," Morrows replied. "That's all the reason they need."

Sally nodded her satisfaction to Jake and said, "Looks like everything is under control here, soldier. I'll be in the crèche if you need me."

"I'll help out here," Pierre said to Jake. "Now would be a good time for you to spread the word."

Jake nodded, turned to Morrows, and said something he had never imagined he could say to this man. "You're a good friend, Morrows. To me and to the kids."

"Shoot, sir," Morrows replied, reddening. "It's a pleasure. Never knew anything so easy could mean so much."

Chapter Fifteen

$\mathcal{B}$Y THE NEXT DAY, word had spread through the garrison that the MPs who raided the feeding station had actually been after Jake and Pierre. Reinforcements had poured in. A guard routine had been set up for both the feeding station and the crèche. At Sally's insistence, another jeep had been requisitioned from motor pool, and a pair of brawny PFCs followed Jake and Pierre wherever they went.

When they stopped in front of the crèche that afternoon on their way to a meeting in Freudenstadt, Pierre told him, "You go ahead, my friend. I'll wait out here."

"What is this?"

Pierre shrugged. "Only a fool continues fighting after the battle is lost. Sally has chosen the victor."

"If she has," Jake declared, "she hasn't told me about it."

"Give her time," Pierre said. "If either of us stands a chance, it's you."

Jake walked down the stairs and pushed through the crèche door. Sally was kneeling in a corner of the room, so involved with a trio of young girls that she did not notice his arrival.

On her face was the same look of unguarded tenderness she had had when speaking of her dead fiancé. A flame rose unbidden within Jake, one so strong it threatened to turn his heart to cinders. There was no defense against this fire. Nowhere to run, no way to escape, not without pushing this woman from his life entirely. And that he could not do. Not even with logic whispering endlessly in his mind, she is not for you, not for you, not for you.

Jake watched her, wanted her, and wondered if there was even a chance, the slenderest of threads, that he might take the place of a man who was no more.

He feared her answer as he feared the pain of having her catch sight of him, and watching the tender expression disappear. As quietly as he could, Jake started back out the door.

"Jake?"

Reluctantly he turned back. Sally was already standing and walking forward, smiling and happy to see him. At the sight of her shining eyes, he felt as if a knife were being turned in his stomach.

"Are you off for your talk?" she asked. "Where do you have to go?"

"Freudenstadt."

"I wish I could hear you speak again," she said with real feeling. "But three of the kids are not well, and Harry promised to stop by later."

"I understand," he said quietly.

She searched his face. "What's the matter, Jake?"

The simple fact of her calling him by his name was almost too much to bear. He inspected the ground at his feet and said softly, "I have to go."

She didn't answer. Her silence lifted his gaze. He found her watching him with the stillness of a frightened forest creature. Jake did not stop to think, or wonder, or hope. His desire was too great.

He bent and kissed her.

A chorus of high-pitched giggles separated them. Sally managed a shaky smile. "We've got company."

Jake nodded, not trusting his voice just then. He caressed her cheek, then turned and left the crèche.

Later that evening Jake knocked on the door of the chaplain's room. "Mind a little company?"

"Good grief, no. Come in, Jake, come in." The chaplain beckoned Jake forward. "How on earth they expect me to sleep so much is beyond me."

"I can't stay long," Jake said, drawing up a chair. "Pierre's waiting for me downstairs."

"Nothing could help pass the time better than a chance to be of use to somebody," Chaplain Fox said. "What's on your mind?"

Jake recounted the discussion with Colonel Beecham and the others. "I'm beginning to think there really may be something to all this. And it's got me wondering. I kept thinking about all those kids, and what they've got to look forward to, growing up in a place like this."

But Chaplain Fox did not reply directly. Instead, he watched Jake for a long moment. "Is that the only thing that's bothering you?" he asked.

Jake sighed and examined his hands in his lap. He shook his head.

"Is it Sally?"

A nod this time.

"Do you love her, Jake?"

Another nod.

The chaplain leaned back and said to the ceiling, "Sally is a wonderful girl. She has so much going for her—gorgeous looks, a wonderful smile, brains, a good heart."

"I know," Jake said quietly.

"But she still has not come to terms with her past, Jake. You know that as well as I do. She holds on to her pain, and do you know why?"

"She's still in love with him," Jake replied.

"Of course she is. She will love him until the day she dies. But that doesn't mean that she has to stop living, not unless she chooses to."

"Are you sure you should be telling me this?" Jake asked.

"Sally and I have often spoken this way. I'm quite sure she would agree to my sharing it with you, and if not, then it's my fault, not yours. No, our dear Sally is frightened,

Jake. She has loved and lost, and the pain has seared her deeply. I believe that she sees in you the opportunity to love again, and is terrified."

"Scared of me? I'd never do anything to hurt her."

"Not willingly, no. But you're a strong man, Jake. A man of action. A man of power. She is both attracted to you and desperately afraid that you will take some risk, make some wild and dangerous step that will take you away from her." He watched Jake's reaction. "Do you see what I am saying?"

Jake nodded slowly. "She pushes me away so completely that I think maybe it would be better for both of us if I stopped trying."

"Safer, perhaps, but not better. Not for her, in any case. I have no fear for you, Jake. None at all. You will weather this storm. But Sally may not. Beneath that rough exterior is a sad and lonely young woman. I think she needs you, Jake. More than she realizes."

"I wish it were true."

"I'm fairly certain that it is," Chaplain Fox replied. "I fear that if she succeeds in pushing you away, she will return home and find what she thinks she needs. A safe man, one who never takes any risks whatsoever. Someone who always wears a hat when it's raining, who does everything by the book, who wants nothing more than to live a life of domestic tranquility. Sally is not that sort of girl, no matter how much she might try to convince herself otherwise. You've seen how she is, Jake. You know. She would be smothered by such an existence. Something of the nervous beauty we both admire in her would be extinguished. I fear the fire and depth within Sally would simply fade away."

Jake ran his hands over his face. "I wish I knew what to do."

"Be strong," Chaplain Fox replied. "Do you have a Bible?"

"Somewhere."

"I suggest you take it out and read it. Study the words of other wise men, men of strength who also loved God. Read about men and women who found the ability to withstand adversity by placing their trust in Him. Start with Proverbs, then the first book of Kings, some of the Psalms, the gospel of John, then the letter to the Romans."

"And then report back to you in the morning, right?"

Chaplain Fox smiled. "Ask the Lord to guide you. Not to gain what you want, though. You need to understand from the very outset, Jake, that He is not some bellboy, at your beck and call. Ask Him to *guide* you. Ask Him to show you how you can serve Him and so come to know your full potential, your true destiny. For that glorious completeness can only come to those who have given their lives to Christ."

"That's a big step," he murmured.

"The fact that you see it that way is a good sign," Chaplain Fox replied. "Whether or not this will bring the answer you hope for, I cannot say. That will depend on Sally's own reaction, and whether or not she, too, is willing to look honestly at herself. But whatever happens, Jake, you will know peace. That I can promise you from the depths of my own experience. You will know peace, and you will know the certainty of His glorious presence in your life."

Chapter Sixteen

JAKE DID NOT like mornings. Given the choice, he would have preferred to begin his days around noon. A slow, gradual rise to consciousness, followed by a cup of good strong coffee taken on the back stoop. Preferably alone. Jake saw no earthly reason to include other people too soon. His motor took a while to warm up.

Which was why, when the soldier standing guard duty pounded on their door, Jake could only manage a moan.

"Captain Burnes. Sorry to bother you, but you've got visitors, sir."

To Jake's befuddled mind, the soldier did not sound sorry at all. In fact, it sounded distinctly as if he had spent much of the night searching for just such an excuse to go out and bother somebody. After all, if he had to stay awake for guard duty, why should anybody else have a decent night's sleep?

Jake groped around, then realized that his gun was in his locker. Too far to lunge.

"Sir, are you there?"

Jake tasted the roof of his mouth and wondered why it had the distinct flavor of boot leather. He croaked, "Tell 'em to come back in the morning."

"It is morning, sir."

"Wha' time is it?"

"Just gone five, sir."

Jake groaned again.

"Sir, it's some kids. I think you'll want to see them."

Jake found the strength to open one eye. He sought out Pierre's bunk. No help there. Gentle snores emanated from beneath his friend's blanket. "You got any java in the guardhouse?"

"Just the dregs, sir. The pot's been cooking all night. It'll look like tar and taste like, well, I personally wouldn't give it to my dog, sir."

"Sounds about right," Jake said, fumbling for his pants. "Go get me a cup."

The corporal came trotting back just as Jake pushed through the door. "Here you go, sir. Don't say I didn't warn you."

Jake took a slug, and shuddered as the tarry black liquid slid down and lit a fire in his belly. "This had better be good, Corporal."

"Sir, these kids showed up about an hour ago," the corporal replied, scampering alongside Jake. "I recognized a couple of them from the infirmary—I put in some hours helping out there. I was afraid if they stood out there much longer we'd have to put them back in there again. I tried to shoo them off, but they'd just back off a pace and say, 'Kapitän Burnes.' Like that. I don't speak Kraut, so there wasn't a whole lot else I could find out."

"How many are there?"

"Three up by the gate, some more back by the treeline, I'd guess somewhere around two dozen." The corporal cast him a worried glance. "Hope I did right, waking you up, sir."

"You did fine, Corporal." Jake handed him the empty cup as they rounded the corner and arrived at the main gates.

The camp was enveloped by the utter dark of night's final hour, save for the searchlights reaching from each guard tower. The lights flanking the main gates were trained on a trio of boys wrapped in blankets and oversized greatcoats and stomping their feet to ward off the heavy chill.

"All right, Corporal," Jake said. "Open the gates."

"Sir, Sergeant Morrows explicitly ordered us not to allow either you or Captain Servais to go anywhere outside the camp without an armed escort." When he saw that Jake was about to protest, he pleaded, "Please, sir. If Sarge hears I let you go out there alone he'll have me on spud detail from now 'til kingdom come."

"All right, soldier," Jake relented. "Just stay back a few steps. These boys are very—" He searched for the right word, but could only come up with, "shy."

At the sound of Jake's voice, Karl had become fully alert. When the gates were pulled back and Jake walked through, he said, "Tell them to redirect those blasted lights."

"But, sir—"

"Play them out beyond us," Jake commanded. "And don't worry. With those kids in the trees nobody is about to sneak up on us."

"Okay, sir," he said doubtfully, and called to the watch-towers.

The proximity of the light made the darkness even more complete. Karl moved farther away from the corporal, and motioned for Jake to follow. When the soldier started along behind him, Jake ordered, "Stay where you are, Corporal."

"But, sir—"

"That's an order, soldier."

"Yessir." Resigned, he stepped back.

The other two boys moved up alongside, effectively blocking Karl and Jake from view. Karl cast a furtive glance around, then announced quietly in German, "I have been busy, Captain."

"Call me Jake," he replied, thinking that anything was better than *Fremder*. "And you shouldn't be out here. You'll just make yourself sick again."

"No more sickness. I become strong. Every day I am better."

Jake inspected the boy's face in the spotlight's reflected glare. "You look better. Not well, but better. You still have to take care of yourself."

"I take care. Just as you say, Captain. I take great care."

"Jake," he corrected.

Karl pointed to the soldiers behind them and demanded, "Those men, they also call you Jake?"

"Captain or sir," Jake relented.

"So. I take great care, Captain. And I do as I say."

"You've heard something?"

"I hear much, Captain. Hear much, see much, learn much." Karl's eyes darted once more around the camp and the encircling trees. Then he bent and opened his blanket. A dull glint of yellow flashed from around his neck. "And do more, Captain. Much more. I do what I say. I *find*."

"Captain Burnes," Colonel Beecham intoned, once Jake had completed his report, "I don't know whether to have you decorated or taken outside and shot."

"Maybe you should do both," Pierre murmured.

"The same holds true for you, Captain Servais."

"I slept through the entire incident, Colonel."

"That's no excuse," the colonel barked. "And as for you, Miss Anders, either you wipe that silly smirk off your face or I'll string you up alongside these two."

"Aye, aye, sir," Sally agreed. "Smirk dead and buried."

Colonel Beecham scowled at the coil of gold rope piled in the center of his desk. "Now what on earth am I to do with this?"

Jake began, "My advice, sir—"

"When I want your advice I'll ask for it, Captain. No, belay that. When I ask for your advice, I order you not to give it."

"Yessir."

The necklace was of woven red and yellow gold thread. Each hollow in its carefully knotted length was filled with a blood-red ruby. The total weight exceeded half a pound.

"Did the boys say whether there was any more where this came from?"

Jake remained silent as ordered.

"Watch yourself, Captain. You are about a hairsbreadth from a firsthand look at the hereafter."

"Sir," Jake replied, "I really don't see how we can refuse Karl's offer."

"You don't, eh."

"Nossir."

"All right, then." The colonel picked up the coil and let it cascade though his grasp. "Run it by me one more time."

"Karl says he has found the man who runs the smuggling ring. He and his gang managed to get this from him—don't ask me how. All he would tell me is that the shadows of this city are his friends. Anyway, Karl wants to be paid for the information. Part will go directly to him and his gang, and part to the other gangs that have helped out. The chaplain and I are supposed to dispense the funds."

"How much?" The colonel groaned.

"Ten thousand dollars."

"Good grief! Why not make it ten million? I'd have just about as much chance finding it."

"Yessir, I told him that," Jake replied calmly. "Karl will wait until the goods have been collected by our men—if we give our word that he will receive either the money or half of everything we gain from the arrests. The choice is ours, not his."

Colonel Beecham stared at him from beneath grizzled brows. "That boy is willing to trust us?"

"Not us," Pierre corrected. "He trusts Jake, and only Jake."

"What about this idea of spreading the dough around all the other kids?"

"I wondered about that too, sir," Jake replied. "It appears that during his stint in the hospital, Karl started growing a conscience."

"He's always had one," Sally countered. "He's finally found somebody to use as an example."

"All right," Beecham said. "I've got meetings scheduled with the brass in Frankfurt this afternoon. The plane's due here in two hours. I'll try this out on them and see what they say."

"Quietly, please, sir," Jake asked.

"A big amen to that," Sally agreed. "Make sure they understand this has to be kept quiet. There'd be a real explosion if Connors were to catch wind of this."

"Leave it with me. Connors isn't the only one with allies in the top brass. I'll do my utmost to make sure this thing stays under wraps." He looked at Jake and said, "Burnes, I'm leaving you in charge."

"Me, sir?"

"I know, I know, it's against my better judgment too. But O'Reilly is coming with me, and Saunders is still laid up." Major O'Reilly was the colonel's second in command. Captain Saunders, head of administration, was down with inflammation of an old chest wound.

"Sir, I'll try—"

"Spare me," the colonel growled. "Just try and keep the base intact. Do you think that's within your power?"

"Yessir, I'm certain of it, sir."

"We'll see." Beecham looked doubtful. "I keep asking myself how much damage one man can make in one day. But I've learned not to underestimate you, Burnes."

"Thank you, sir. I guess."

Jake took to carrying the little pocket New Testament around with him, pulling it out and glancing through it when he had a free moment. Most of it seemed to be just a jumble of old words, incomprehensible sayings, and strange commands that did not seem to have much to do with any problem he faced. But he drew comfort from the act of reading, not so much at the time, but afterward. There was a different flavor to the hours of that day, despite the fact that he felt like a blind man when the Book was in his hands.

That afternoon Sally found him bent over the text in the infirmary's cramped waiting room. "What have you got there, soldier?"

"Nothing," he said, embarrassed. He jammed it back into his pocket and buttoned down the flap. "The chaplain's asleep."

"Not anymore. I just went up to see him. I walked right by you, but you were so caught up you didn't notice me."

"That's not possible."

"How easily they forget." She pointed at his pocket. "What is it?"

"Nothing, Sally. Just a Bible."

"Just, the man says. Is this the chaplain's idea?"

"Who else's?"

"You'd better watch it, soldier. You've got all the makings of a great man."

Jake glanced around the room. "Who are you talking to, Sally?"

"I'm talking to you," she said. "Do you know what we are, Jake Burnes?"

"Misguided fools?" he suggested. "Poor lost souls?"

She stepped up close to him and said, "We are friends."

"I'm happy for that," Jake said quietly. "But I can't help wishing for more."

"Don't look down on friendship," she countered. "Most people go through their whole lives without one true friend of the other sex."

Jake thought about that and then said what came naturally to his mind. "Seems to me friendship would be a nice way to start something deeper."

She pulled away from him. "That's the problem with wisdom. Sometimes it comes out with the very last thing you want to hear." She started for the door. "I'm off to sort through some papers. Go see the chaplain, soldier. Tell him I said to watch it with the wisdom. You've got too much of it already."

"That woman certainly needs a friend," Chaplain Fox said, after Jake had told him of their conversation. "Friendship is such a serious responsibility, though, I sometimes wonder whether people would accept the challenge if they really knew what they were letting themselves in for."

Jake inspected the man resting comfortably in the elevated bed. There seemed to be a marked improvement in his condition since the day before. A number of his bruises were more pronounced today, but his entire demeanor had been helped by the night's rest. "I've met some strange ducks in this war, Chaplain. But I do believe you take the cake."

Fox smiled. "I once heard an old pastor describe himself as nothing more than a simple truth-teller. That is the ideal I set for my life. Just to tell people the truth."

"What if they don't want to hear it?"

"Sometimes what people object to isn't so much the truth itself as the way it's communicated," Chaplain Fox replied. "I believe God does not use the From-On-High routine with us very often, because being talked down to makes the message much harder to swallow. No, instead He uses plain, simple folk like you and me. And He tells us to be humble in everything we do and say. So I find a lot of people willing to listen to me. They may disagree, but that is their choice. At least I have done my bit."

"Maybe God uses you as His errand boy," Jake said. "But I doubt if He's gotten all that much out of me."

"Oh, I don't know." The clear gaze rested on him. "Take care of your new friend, will you, Jake?"

"I'll try," he said without conviction. "I don't know whether she'll let me."

"Just live up to your own responsibilities, and learn to give the rest to God's care." The chaplain turned his face toward the ceiling. "If you'll excuse me, I think perhaps I'll rest a little now. All this truth-telling is exhausting."

Sally found Jake later that afternoon checking preparations at the feeding station. "Beecham's come through again, soldier."

"He's back already?"

"Next thing to it," she replied, waving a yellow paper. "Take a look at this."

Jake wiped greasy hands on his apron, accepted the cable, and read, "Held over here. Tell Burnes he has green light. Proceed with caution. Wolves about. Beecham."

"That's it, then," Jake said, feeling the familiar old precombat adrenaline rush.

Sally was watching him. "I assume you read the closing lines."

"I'll take care, Sally. I promise."

Her gaze turned flat, opaque. "Yeah. Right," she said. "Tell me another one, soldier. You can hardly wait for the chance to go marching into battle."

"I am going to take care," Jake repeated, putting as much feeling into it as he could. "For you as much as for me."

The hardness melted away, exposing the wounds of another time. "Oh, Jake," she sighed. "Why do you have to say those things."

"You know why," he replied. "Now go tell Pierre to join me. He's playing Papa in the crèche."

Sally searched his face and started to say something, then stopped, wheeled around, and scrambled across the rubble heap. Jake watched with a hungry heart as she left.

"That's some dame, sir," Sergeant Morrows said, stirring a steaming cauldron nearby. He was grinning from ear to ear as he voiced the words.

"Hand that ladle to somebody else and come over here, Sergeant."

"Aw, hey, I didn't mean anything by that, sir. Can't you take a joke?"

Jake turned on his heel and stomped out of range. Sergeant Morrows followed reluctantly. He stopped a pace away and protested, "Honest, sir—"

"As far as anybody else is concerned I am chewing you out," Jake said softly. "So keep your face screwed up."

Morrows ducked his head, kicked at a stone, said, "Yessir."

"I believe I can trust you, Sergeant."

"I'd like to think so, sir."

"Can you find another dozen or so men who know how to button up their lips and keep them that way?"

"As many as you like, sir."

"We're going on a raiding party, Sergeant. As soon as it's dark." Jake glanced at his watch. "That gives you less than two hours to round them up and get them ready."

Morrows looked as if he had just sucked the juice from an overripe lemon, but nothing could hide the gleam in his eye. "Is it to do with the treasure, sir?"

"Could be, Sergeant." Jake scratched his face to maintain the scowl. "This has got to be on the QT, Sergeant. Strictly confidential. The colonel knows about it. He's given go-ahead. The danger doesn't come from him."

"I understand perfectly, sir." Morrows was having trouble restraining himself. "Where's the rendezvous point?"

"At the lay-by between HQ and the main camp. In ninety minutes."

"We'll be there, sir. Armed and ready for the dance."

"Go to it, then." Jake spotted Pierre and waved him over. "Servais and I have got to see our contact."

Sergeant Morrows snapped to attention and bellowed out, "Sir, yessir! It won't happen again, sir!"

"Ninety minutes, Sergeant," Jake said quietly. "Be on time."

Chapter Seventeen

KARL POINTED THROUGH the blackness to a single glowing window. "He is in there."

They were gathered on a city street reduced to heaps of rubble by the allied bombardment. They huddled in what had once been someone's basement, now a hole partially filled with the remains of the house that had stood overhead. The building across the street had fared better. The walls appeared to be intact, and the window they watched held signs of great wealth in war-ravaged Germany—glass panes and curtains.

Jake turned to Sergeant Morrows and said in a muted voice, "Have your men fan out. You take the rear detail, circle around, and make sure every possible avenue of escape is covered."

Morrows squinted into the darkness, measuring the ground with an experienced eye, and said, "Fifteen minutes max."

"The signal to move will be a whistle. Remember, we want this man alive. Nobody is to shoot unless the other side shoots first."

"I've spelled it out personal to the men, sir."

Jake spent another moment going over everything in his mind once more. Then he said, "All right. Get going."

Sergeant Morrows rose from his crouch, gave the signal. They started forward in utter stealth. But the rubble beneath their feet was loose; as one soldier scrambled out, a rock went ricocheting down to the bottom, where it hit against a piece of roofing, then splashed into a puddle with a noise that seemed to shatter the night.

Each man froze where he was. All eyes remained on the window.

A second crack of light appeared as the door of the dwelling opened. A figure came into view, silhouetted by the interior lighting. He stood and looked straight at them. Jake resisted the urge to duck, to move, to hide.

Then the impossible happened.

A rasping man's voice spoke at a level barely above a whisper, yet loud enough to be heard clearly in the freezing quiet. *"Bitte kommen Sie vorwärts, Herr Kapitän Burnes.* I have been expecting you."

"I knew it was you because the other hunters would not have stopped at only one item," the man continued on in German, his voice strangely hoarse.

"I was told you had so much treasure stuffed in your chests that you'd never notice if one piece was gone," Jake countered. He sat alone in a cluttered parlor. His men surrounded the building. Everywhere Jake looked there were signs of wealth, relative to the rest of the German nation that winter evening—four solid walls, a dry chamber, the remains of a meal on a simple wooden table, a fire in the grate.

"Ah, there the mistake was made," came the whispered reply. "My training stressed thoroughness in all things, Herr Kapitän."

The man limped to one corner and hefted a high-caliber rifle equipped with a sniper's scope. "You should understand that."

"You shot at me in the forest," Jake said.

"Wrong, Captain. I shot at a tree. If I had shot at you we would not be speaking together now."

The right side of the man's lower face and much of his neck had been scooped out, as though someone had attacked it with a giant razor-sharp spoon. He swallowed with difficulty, and spoke only with great effort. Jake pointed at the wound and asked, "Where did you pick that up?"

"On the eastern front," he exhaled. "I was proving to be quite a bother, so the Russians moved up their artillery and opened fire."

"You're lucky to be here."

"In more ways than one, Captain. When the rout began, and the Nazi army was forced to retreat across frozen tundra with nothing to eat for days on end, I was safely back in my beloved Badenburg, settled in a comfortable hospital bed."

"So how did you get into the treasure-smuggling game?"

"There were almost no able-bodied men available toward the end of the war," he replied. "Even the severely wounded like me were forced into service. Not in uniform, however. No. I became servant to one of the ranking SS officers."

"I'm beginning to get the picture."

"There were many Nazi leaders who had holiday residences here, or hunting lodges just outside of town. It was expected of them, you see. This was the gathering point for the Nazi elite."

"And you came to know them all."

"Many of them, yes. A servant is able to see much, especially when he has so clearly given his all to the Fatherland." Slack facial muscles pulled together in a parody of a smile. "And when he can be trusted to remain silent."

"So you knew where they hid their treasure," Jake said.

"Not so fast, Captain. Not so fast. There is more to this than you realize."

"But there is treasure."

Again the rictal smile. "Indeed there is."

"Where?"

"Just over our heads. Some of it, anyway."

Jake resisted an urge to search the ceiling. "Why didn't you just cut and run?"

"Your patrols have become too thorough, Captain. My three best men are now sitting in various jails, charged with smuggling."

"They were caught on the way back in from dropping off their treasures in France," Jake guessed, and pointed with his chin to the half-finished meal. "Probably carrying contraband to make your lives here easier."

"Thank heaven for such minor miracles, yes?" He walked toward the wall cabinet, his left foot scraping across the floor. "A glass of schnapps?"

"I don't think we're going to be around long enough for that, thanks." Jake inspected the man. "So you knew I was coming and didn't run. You've got to admit, that sounds a little strange."

"Not if you knew what I know, Captain."

"Which is?"

"I shall come to that in a moment." He filled two glasses and handed one over. "Please."

Jake accepted the drink and set it down beside him. "Your moment's up."

"The American way, straight to the point, yes?" The man stomped over and sat facing Jake. "Very well, Captain. What I have upstairs is only the tip of the iceberg."

"What are you saying?"

"Personal effects some of the officers were in too much of a hurry to take with them." He gave another death's-head grin. "Or maybe their destination did not permit it."

"So you searched through their things and rounded up this little trove?"

"A few paintings which survived the bombardment, some decorative items they simply had to have on display, jewels intended for some fair neck or hand or ear." The man leaned forward. "But there is yet another stash, Captain. One which I have been unable to tap. Their savings, so to speak. Not what found its way to the government's own hoards. No. What I speak of are the precious items they chose to keep for themselves."

"And you know where all these things are buried."

"I do."

"And you want something in exchange."

"Naturally."

Jake thought it over. "What is your name?"

"Konrad," he replied, giving a small, seated bow. "Jurgen Konrad, at your service."

"So what's the deal, Herr Konrad?"

"There is so much treasure hidden away, Captain. So much you cannot even begin to imagine."

"So?"

"I am tired of running, Captain," Konrad replied. "I lost my youth in the war. I only want the conqueror's permission to live in peace. To have papers. And enough money to enjoy this freedom. I will give you the hidden treasure, Captain, if you will allow me to keep the small trinkets I have upstairs for myself."

"Some loose change for your remaining years."

"Compared to what remains concealed," Konrad replied, "these are mere trifles."

"You know I can't agree to anything like that without authorization."

"Of course. You will naturally have to take me into custody until an agreement can be reached."

"And the treasure upstairs," Jake added. "Do you really trust me that much?"

"The entire town speaks of Captain Jake Burnes. I know you through what I have heard."

"You don't know a thing about me," Jake contradicted.

"I know you are a man of honor," Konrad replied. "Under the circumstances, it is all that matters."

Chapter Eighteen

*J*AKE CALLED PIERRE and Sally into Colonel Beecham's office that evening. Sitting there surrounded by the
colonel's things gave them a reassuring sense of being under his direction. Since receiving the cable, they had heard
nothing. Sally's urgent entreaties over the telephone had
yielded no response. Colonel Beecham was not available.
Period.

"At least our German's safe," Jake offered. They had
stashed the man upstairs in one attic cubbyhole, the treasure in another. A pair of soldiers stood guard in the hall
outside, another on the next floor's landing, still more in
pairs outside. "Never had so many soldiers volunteer for
guard duty."

"Do you really think Connors and his men were that
near to closing in?" Sally asked.

Jake shrugged. "Herr Konrad thought so, and right now,
that's what matters."

"What do you mean?"

"I want him to feel that we are honoring his trust in us,"
Jake explained.

"Honest Jake the treasure dealer. You take the cake, soldier."

"He's put his life and fortune in our hands," Jake protested. "We owe him that much."

"It was a good idea to post the lookout by his residence," Servais told them. "We'll know soon enough if Konrad had reason to fear the MPs."

"Make sure those boys are relieved every couple of hours," Jake told him. "It's too cold a night for them to stand still any longer than that."

"Aye, aye, sir."

Jake looked chagrined. "Did I sound too much like the colonel?"

Pierre shrugged. "Somebody has to be in charge until Beecham returns. If that German soldier upstairs will trust you with his life, why shouldn't I?"

"Thanks, Pierre," Jake said quietly.

"I wonder how much that treasure upstairs is worth," Sally mused.

"Hard to say," Pierre answered. "The war has depressed prices tremendously. But I would still say enough for a man to live a very long and comfortable life."

In the old man's attic there had been six paintings, two of them fire-blackened but still recognizable as the work of masters. Three massive Persian silk carpets, far too bulky to smuggle out. A pair of silver and crystal candelabras. And four locker-size chests full to the brim with jewelry.

"I thought Morrows was going to burst a gut when he pried off that first lid," Jake recalled.

"I didn't know anybody's eyes could get that big," Sally agreed, rising to her feet with a yawn. "Well, I'm either going back to bed or sacking out on the floor right here."

"I'll walk you back," Jake offered, and when she did not object, followed her from the room.

They walked the short distance in silence. At the doorway to her billet, she turned and offered a sleepy smile. "Why don't you come up and see me sometime, soldier."

"I wish you meant that," Jake replied in a subdued voice.

The smile and the fatigue slipped away. "Give it time, Jake. Maybe it will happen."

"I hope so."

"I know you do." Softly now. "Dear Jake. Look at how tall you've grown."

"I'm the same height I always was."

"So tall," she repeated. "You positively tower over the other men around here."

"And still I'm not good enough for you," he said with a trace of bitterness.

"Don't say that," she said, but without anger. "Don't ever say that."

"I'll never be able to fill a dead man's shoes, will I?"

"That's not the point, Jake." She gave him a wounded look. "Can you tell me why life has to be so hard?"

"I wish I knew," Jake said, aching for her. Despite the fear and pleading in her eyes, he started toward her. But he drew back when he heard the sound of running feet thundering down the back hallway of the HQ.

Jake turned around. An instant later Pierre slammed back the door. "Red alert, Jake. Let's move out!"

"They hit Konrad's house about three quarters of an hour ago," Pierre said, hustling Jake back into the colonel's office. "When they found the place empty, they went totally berserk."

"Connors' men?" Jake nodded to Morrows, who was standing back waiting anxiously in the outer office. "Come on in, Sergeant."

"Thank you, sir."

"Who else?" Pierre motioned to the two men waiting inside. Both snapped to attention at Jake's entry. "Simpkins and Vance, the soldiers on duty when it happened."

"At ease, men." Reluctantly Jake moved behind the colonel's desk and sat down, making room for the rest. "Colonel Beecham is in Frankfurt," he explained. "He left me in charge during his absence." To his surprise, no one batted an eye at the news.

"Tell him," Servais ordered.

"Sir, we were heads down in the ditch like you ordered. All of a sudden these two trucks and maybe four jeeps—"

"Just the ones we could see," Vance interrupted. "But we could hear shouts and stuff from the road in back. Especially after."

"Right. So out they pile—"

"All MPs?" Jake demanded.

"Yessir. That is, all of them had on the white helmets and bands."

"Go on."

"So out they come on the bounce, like I said. And they hit the house six ways from Sunday, breaking down the door, shining lights everywhere, shattering windows, and poking their rifles in—"

"Just like this gangster film I saw back in the States," Vance offered.

Simpkins turned his way. "Who's telling this story, you or me?"

"You're doing fine, soldier," Jake said. "Carry on."

"Right, sir. So then there's this shout from inside, 'He's not here.' And somebody from outside called back, 'And the loot?' And the guy inside shouted, 'Gone!' Then, sir, this guy outside, he just goes bananas. Stomping around, cursing, screaming to wake the dead—"

"Woulda made a drill sergeant blush," Vance added. "Mentioned your name a few times. I'd just as soon not tell you what he said."

"That's all right, Simpkins," Jake said mildly. "I can imagine."

"Yessir. So then he sends the ones who speak Kraut to question everybody in all the surrounding buildings, to see if maybe anybody saw anything. And the other guys started combing the area. We couldn't get out any sooner, sir. They were all around us."

"We can thank our lucky stars there ain't no streetlights, sir," Vance agreed. "Two of them guys almost stepped on my toes, they was so close."

"Yeah, sir, we just hunkered down in the pit there and waited them out."

"And listened."

"Sir, you can't imagine the noise. I mean, people wailing and moaning and carrying on up and down the street, all these MPs shouting and cursing. I doubt most of the Krauts had any idea what was going on."

"They didn't have to," Jake said grimly. "Being awakened in the middle of the night like that probably reminded them of their worst nightmare."

"Yessir, I guess so. Anyway, these guys stick around a while, then all start coming back to that one who's still kicking up a storm around the jeep. We didn't wait to see what happened next. Soon as they were back on the other side of the street, we hightailed it outta there."

"Good work, you two. Better get yourselves some shut-eye."

"Yessir. Thank you, sir."

"Morrows, think maybe you could get Cookie out of bed?"

"No problem, sir."

"Ask him to make a couple of big pots of coffee, maybe some soup would be better, and a big box of sandwiches. Have your men take them over to the neighborhood the MPs just terrorized. Does anybody in your squad speak German?"

"Don't think so, sir."

Jake took out a piece of paper, scribbled furiously and handed it over. "Have them show this around the street. My guess is, half the neighborhood will still be up talking about it, now that the danger's over. Tell them to show the paper to everybody. It basically just apologizes for the disturbance."

"A good idea, Jake," Pierre murmured.

"Yessir, sure is," Morrows agreed, inspecting the paper. "A little PR at a time like this couldn't hurt anybody."

"I just want them to understand that we are sorry the MPs got out of line." Jake looked at Sally standing in the doorway. "Would you mind putting off your sleep for just a little while longer, and see if you can find Beecham for us?"

She spun on her heel and was gone without a word.

Jake looked at Pierre. "You'd better tell the guard detail to be on full alert."

Pierre was on his feet. "I'll send another squad up to the base as well."

"Good thinking," Jake agreed, and rose. "I guess it's time I had a little talk with our friend upstairs."

The German listened in watchful silence as Jake related the developments. "You see," he rasped, when Jake was finished, "I was right after all."

"They won't stop now," Jake said.

"You know my conditions," the man replied in his throaty whisper. "The only reason I spoke to you at all was to obtain my request."

"How much have you already shipped across the border," Jake demanded.

The man hesitated, then replied, "About as much as what you have here. Perhaps a little more. But not much. And there were three other partners to take care of."

"This isn't all the treasure you've collected, is it?"

Konrad became very still, his eyes blank.

"You didn't collect everything in one place," Jake persisted. "And I imagine there are several bombed-out mansions you haven't gotten around to looting yet. You probably hit the ones that were the least damaged, with the largest caches of valuables and in the most accessible places. It must be hard-going, trying to sift through all that rubble in the dark. Especially now that all but one of your partners are sitting in a jail somewhere."

The man remained mute.

"I thought so," Jake said. "You're trapped, aren't you?"

"Almost as trapped as you, Captain," Jurgen Konrad replied.

"I know where you could pick up some more partners fast," Jake continued. "Partners who can run fast, dig for hours on end, even crawl in and out of upstairs windows without being caught."

The gaze flickered. "You cannot be serious."

"Partners you can trust," Jake continued. "If they gave you their word, you could trust them with your very life. I would."

"Then you are a very simple man, Captain."

Jake shook his head. "I have worked with them. I have come to know them well."

"As well as any human being can know an animal."

"They are not animals," Jake said sharply. "They are survivors. Their way of life has been shaped by events beyond their control. They have faced difficulties that should have killed them, and yet they survived."

The German searched Jake's face and gave his head a slight shake. "This is so strange."

"What is?"

"You really do care for these cellar children, don't you, Captain?"

"They are worthy of your trust. And they will help you."

"Very well, Captain," came the rasped reply. "I will think over your words."

Jake nodded. "As to this other matter—"

"It exists," Konrad insisted. "The treasure is there."

"It's unlikely to be there for long," Jake pointed out.

"I understand your concern," Konrad replied. "But my demands must be met."

"Perhaps others know of this treasure," Jake pressed.

"Few ever knew of it," Konrad whispered. "And even fewer still came through alive."

"If one did, there may be others," Jake went on. "Any moment now, the MPs may stumble upon someone ready to tell the tale."

"Why are you speaking to me like this, Captain?" Konrad demanded. "You do not strike me as one who is greedy for treasure."

"I want nothing for myself," Jake asserted.

"Then why do you not simply agree to my demands and let us get on with it?"

"Because I do not have the authority," Jake confessed. "And my superior officer is not here."

"Contact him, then."

"I have tried. I am trying. I cannot find him."

"And this concerns you."

"Very much," Jake said grimly.

"You think others may be responsible for his disappearance?"

"I don't know what to think."

Konrad sipped from his water jug, making loud swallowing sounds that were painful in Jake's ears. He set down the jug and breathed heavily, as though the effort of drinking had exhausted him. Then he said, "What is it you want?"

"I have promised to reward my young German helpers," Jake said. "I need to take their payment from your hoard, to ensure that whatever happens they are properly compensated."

"A man of his word," the German said. "I was right to trust you, Captain."

"The soldiers who are working on this project also have a right to expect something," Jake continued.

"How much do you want?"

Jake thought it over and decided, "Everything we have taken from your attic and secured here."

"Impossible."

"You keep everything else."

"And if I am unable to travel to France to collect the proceeds from what has already been sold? Or retrieve anything more for myself here? You see the condition the war has left me in. I would be signing my own death warrant." Konrad shook his head. "The carpets, perhaps."

"Not enough," Jake replied. "A full chest. That is the least I need."

Konrad thought for a moment, then asked, "What about my papers?"

Jake thought it over, and decided that if he was going out on a limb so far, he might as well start sawing away. "I will go down and have them issued immediately."

"Also," Konrad went on, "you must have my partners released from your jails. Give me pen and paper so that I may write down their names."

"I can ask," Jake replied, fishing in his shirt pocket. "And I will. But I cannot order it. The officer in charge may be willing to do it as a special favor. But I can't promise anything."

Konrad considered this. "You will do this immediately?"

"I will write the letters tonight," Jake replied. "And send the couriers off at first light."

The German inspected him carefully. "You are taking a risk, yes?"

"This entire episode will probably cost me my rank," Jake replied soberly. "Maybe earn me a tour of duty behind bars."

"Then why do you do this?"

"I have my reasons," Jake said, rising to his feet. "When can I have your answer?"

"In the morning," Konrad replied. "I shall think about your request and tell you my decision in the morning. Perhaps your colonel will have come back by then."

"Perhaps," Jake said, unconvinced.

"You think he has run away and left you with all the risks?"

"No," Jake replied, definite for the first time that night. "Colonel Beecham is a good man."

"He may be, Captain," Konrad said, stretching out on his mattress. "But my trust lies in you. Good-night."

Jake marched back downstairs, stopped by Sally's door, and asked, "Any word?"

"He seems to have vanished from the face of the earth," Sally replied. She ran tired hands through her hair. "It's as if he had never even existed."

"Go get some sleep," he told her.

"What about you?" she responded. "You look ready to join the ranks of the walking wounded."

"That was an order," he said.

"Well, in that case—" She groaned her way to her feet, patting his arm as she passed on the way to the door. "Good-night, Commander."

"I'm just a simple soldier," Jake corrected.

"Not anymore," she replied. "Try to get some rest, Jake. From the looks of things, tomorrow is going to be a long day."

But when at last he was bedded down in the HQ's visiting officers' quarters, Jake found himself unable to calm his mind. As he rolled restlessly back and forth, he heard Pierre's voice calling softly through the darkness, "Are you asleep?"

"No."

"Worried about the treasure?"

Jake shook his head, then realized that Pierre could not see him. "No."

"What, then?"

"Sally," he confessed.

"I suppose I should be jealous," Pierre said. "I confess that I am not."

"Girl back home?"

"There was, back when the war began. But I lost her."

"Sorry to hear that," Jake said, and recalled his own loss.

"When I think of her, which I try to do as seldom as possible, it is with great regret."

"I know what you mean."

"Yes, I believe you. Perhaps that is why I can speak with you, that and the cloak of darkness which surrounds us. It hides my shame from the world."

"Shame over what?"

"It is said that some people are destined to love only once. I fear that I am not only such a man, but, I also loved the wrong woman. A lovely lady, truly beautiful. Half French, half Moroccan. But also treacherous. It still pains me deeply to think of her. Perhaps it always will."

"I know it's hard to believe," Jake said, and laced his fingers behind his head. "But you'll get over it. I did."

Pierre was silent for a moment, then said, "I marvel at you sometimes, my friend."

"Me? Why?"

"Because you *care.*" Pierre's bed creaked as he shifted around. "You have seen the worst of war and still you are alive inside. How have you managed this?"

"I don't know that I have," Jake replied quietly.

"You have, my friend. I see it in your eyes. I see it in the way you look at Sally. I see it when you are with the children. I have no doubts. None."

"Sometimes," Jake said slowly, "I remember . . . things."

"Ah, yes. Things. I have memories like these as well." The springs squeaked beneath Pierre as he raised himself up on one elbow. The white of his T-shirt and the dog tags hanging around his neck glinted in the faint light coming through their window. "I was seventeen when the Nazis invaded my country and made a laughingstock of the French army. I have never felt such helplessness as I did in those days, glued to the wireless, unable to do anything but cry and curse as Petain announced his capitulation to the Boche."

"Where were you raised?" Jake asked.

"Montpellier. West of Marseille. I ran away from home four days later. I caught a freighter to Algiers with a hundred other boys, all of us fired by the rumor that De Gaulle was gathering an expeditionary force to return and liberate my country."

"Did you have any brothers and sisters?"

"One brother. We were twins. He remained behind and joined the Underground. He was caught and shot in the last year of the war." Pierre's voice turned bitter. "I languished in Algiers for two years. Two *years.* I watched my friends give in to the hopelessness and the drink and the emptiness of life. But I fought it, my friend. I fought the only way I knew how. By hating. I hated the life. I hated the heat. I hated the foul things these losers did to their minds and bodies. I hated the politicians and the generals for their endless bickering. And I hated the Boche most of all."

"But you survived," Jake reminded him. "Don't forget that."

"Yes, it's true. But sometimes, Jake, when I look at you and see how you still care, I wonder if perhaps some part of me was destroyed by all that hating. My hatred is gone now. I lost it somewhere on the battlefield. It was burned up in the smoking ruins of another village whose name I don't recall. But nothing has come to take its place, Jake. Inside me now there is only emptiness."

Jake thought of his own struggles. "The chaplain told me to find the answers in prayer."

"Yes?" Pierre swung himself into a seated position. "And what do you think of that?"

"I don't know," Jake confessed. "But maybe I'll give it a try."

"But why, Jake? If you are not sure, how can you risk so much on the ramblings of a priest?"

"Because," Jake said, choosing his words carefully, "every time I look inside myself or let myself care, what I feel most is pain."

"Yes," Pierre murmured. "This pain I know very well. Too well."

Jake turned toward his unseen friend, an appeal in his voice. "I've got to try to find some way to be healed, Pierre. I've got to make this pain go away before I can start over."

"And you truly think this pain *can* be healed?" Pierre demanded.

"I've got to try," Jake repeated quietly.

Pierre slid back down, sighed, and said to the dark night, "Then perhaps I shall give this a try as well."

Chapter Nineteen

"*Y*OU HAVE HEARD from your colonel?" Konrad demanded when Jake arrived the next morning.

"Not a word," Jake replied, making no attempt to conceal his anxiety. He handed Konrad a steaming mug of coffee and sat down across the table from him. "The couriers have left for the border internment stations. I can't promise anything, but at least we are trying to have your partners released."

The German sipped, making his painful swallowing effort, then rasped, "But I have agreed to nothing."

Jake reached into his pocket and handed over a sheaf of folded papers. "Call it a sign of good will," he said. "Your documents, as promised."

With slow, deliberate motions, Konrad set down his cup and opened the papers. He looked at them for a long moment, then, without raising his head, said, "Very well, Captain. I agree."

Jake leaned back, releasing a sigh. "That's it, then."

The German pulled damaged facial muscles into the semblance of a smile. "No, Captain, that is where you are wrong. It is only the beginning."

* * *

When he left Jurgen Konrad's chambers, Jake walked outside for a breath of air. Konrad's news had shaken him to
the core. He stepped through the doors into brilliant winter
sunlight. It took him a moment to focus. When he did, he
found himself staring out over a field of green uniforms. All
eyes were upon him.

Sergeant Morrows mounted the stairs. "I guess word got
out, sir."

Jake surveyed the throng. "Is anybody shirking their
duty?"

"Not so far as I can tell," Pierre replied from below. "I've
checked with as many of the department chiefs as I can
find."

Jake raised his voice and said, "If anybody is out here
expecting to go home rich, you might as well return to your
barracks."

No one moved.

"You know how the army works," Jake continued in his
parade-ground voice. "Maybe your great-grandchildren
might get a penny on the dollar, but it's highly unlikely. If
the treasure really is there—and we don't have any guaran-
tee that it exists at all—the bigwigs will be quarreling over
it from now 'til doomsday."

The soldiers remained where they were. A voice from
somewhere in the crowd called back, "We know that, sir."

"You will all be searched thoroughly," Jake persisted.
"Don't think for a minute you'll be able to sneak something out."

They remained a solid wall of fatigue green. "All right,"
Jake relented. "Captain Servais and Sergeant Morrows will
act as liaison. Everybody is dismissed. Platoon leaders, report to the squad room in fifteen minutes. Anybody caught
shirking duty will be flailed alive—by me personally. Dismissed."

Jake walked back inside the headquarters building and
said to no one in particular, "Would somebody mind telling
me what's going on?"

"It's very simple," Sally replied, coming up beside him.
"They know a leader when they see one."

*   *   *

Jake unfolded the city map on the colonel's desk. "This is the best we've got?"

Sally nodded. "About a quarter of the streets don't exist anymore. Nothing's there but fields of scrap and waste. Survey has marked most of them."

"All right, then it will just have to do."

"Why couldn't it have been somewhere else?" Pierre muttered to himself.

"Because it isn't," Jake said, his finger tracing possible routes.

"And you're sure this isn't just a ruse?"

"Konrad insists he's giving us the scoop," Jake replied. "He says he even took a shipment in there himself just before the Allies arrived. One of the officers back on leave used him as a pair of trusted hands."

"What was it like?"

"Stolen Nazi loot from floor to ceiling, by the sound of it." Jake covered his own excitement with a scowl. "But you're right. They really picked the spot."

Morrows knocked on the open door. "The men are all assembled, sir."

"Right. Grab that map, Pierre. Anybody seen my hat?"

Sally walked over and handed it to him. "Here you are, sir."

"Thanks. Are you coming?"

"I wouldn't miss it for the world," Sally replied, her eyes bright, "sir."

Jake marched into the meeting hall and straight to the podium. The gathered squad and platoon leaders snapped to attention as he entered. "At ease," he said, taking strength from the fact that his voice remained steady.

He waited until Pierre, Sally, and Morrows were seated. Then he went on. "I've got good news and bad news. The good news is that it appears there is indeed a larger stash of treasure inside the city."

There was a moment's electric silence, then a raised hand. "Yes?"

"How large is large, sir?"

"I don't have the exact figures," Jake replied. "But from the sound of it, big enough to set off alarms from here to Madagascar."

A stir rippled through the group. "Settle down," Jake said. "You haven't heard the bad news yet. And believe me, it couldn't be worse. Captain Servais?"

With Sergeant Morrows' help, Pierre unfolded the large-scale map and held it up against the back wall. Jake walked over and pointed to an area, "The treasure is supposed to be located right here. Does anybody recognize the place?"

People half-rose from their seats as they strained and searched and finally started in alarm. "Sir, isn't that—?"

"That's right, gentlemen," Jake affirmed. "The treasure is right smack-dab underneath the stockade."

Chapter Twenty

"**N**OBODY MOVES WITHOUT an order from me, Sergeant Morrows," Jake said, climbing into the second jeep beside Pierre.

"But, sir—"

"I'll be back," Jake assured him.

"I will personally see to that," Pierre confirmed.

"But just six men, Captain, ain't that—"

"We can't tip them off, Sergeant." Jake stopped further conversation by rapping his knuckles on the side of the jeep. "Let's go."

When they arrived at the feeding station they found it in full swing, manned by the ten men Morrows considered most likely to keep a lid on their excitement. Still, despite the warnings, their arrival caused a major stir.

"Back to your positions, gentlemen," Jake ordered, his voice low. "We are being watched."

On the other side of the street a squad of MPs loitered around a couple of jeeps. They watched Jake's arrival through narrowed eyes, but made no move. Jake helped Sally down from the jeep and murmured, "Do you see Karl?"

"Not yet."

"I'll check around," Pierre said.

"Not alone," Jake reminded him, and turned with Sally toward the crèche.

Inside, all was normal and calm, or as calm as any room could be that held twenty-eight infants under the age of four. Sally was immediately engulfed in a press of little figures, their voices raised, their hands lifted to touch and be recognized and receive attention. Jake stood back and watched the transformation in her face, saw the love shining in her eyes, and felt himself a thousand miles from where he would like to be. When Pierre returned he walked over and asked, "Did you find Karl?"

"Outside. How do you want to handle this?"

"Not here." Jake pulled out pen and paper, scribbled a note, and handed it to Pierre. "Give him that."

When Pierre was gone, Jake turned back to the gathering of happy little girls. "Sally?"

"I think I'll stay awhile, Jake," she replied.

"I'll tell the kitchen detail to pick you up on their way out."

"All right." For a moment, a brief moment that seemed an eternity yet was over as soon as it began, she granted him the same look of love and tenderness she had bestowed upon the little girls. "Take care, Jake."

"I will," he replied, and because he could not say the other things tumbling through his mind, and did not want to risk seeing that look vanish from her eyes, he turned and left.

Jake walked across the vacant lot and pretended to inspect the kitchen. He accepted the smart salutes and brisk replies with an assumed calm. From the corner of his eyes he noted the MPs tracking his every step. When he deemed that the charade had continued long enough, he returned with his guard detail to the jeep.

"Where to?" Pierre asked.

"Head back toward HQ," Jake replied, determinedly keeping his gaze off the MPs. "Take it slow."

They were perhaps three blocks away from the center and rounding a corner when Karl and two of his companions popped up from behind the waist-high remains of a house. "Slower," Jake ordered, and then barked in German, "Move!"

The jeep continued rolling as the trio scrambled over the wall, covered the distance, and piled into the back. Jake signaled to the jeep behind them that all was well, checked swiftly for spying eyes, found none, and shouted, "Go!"

The kids sat bright-eyed and excited as they sped back out of town. Jake directed Pierre to turn down a dirt track not far from the HQ. When the second jeep had halted behind them, Jake turned to Karl and said in German, "We got the man."

"And the treasure, I hope," Karl said in his accustomed sharp tone. But the gleam in his eyes was strong. "The man is nothing without his hoard."

"That too," Jake agreed. "Or part of it, at least."

"And where is the rest?"

"That is what I want to speak to you about," Jake replied, reaching for the map. He folded it out to the appropriate section, pointed to the building with the circle drawn around it, and asked, "Do you know where this is?"

Clearly the boy had never been challenged in this way before. "I don't—"

"The stockade," Jake said.

"Where the white hats gather. Of course." Karl bent over the incomprehensible map. "They have taken the treasure there?"

"Not exactly," Jake replied. "The place used to be a bank. According to Herr Konrad, the bank's vault was in the cellar. What was not so well known was that they had also constructed a second cellar. Directly *underneath* the main vault."

Karl reacted with a hunter's eager tension. "A secret vault."

"Very secret," Jake agreed. "So secret not even the bank employees themselves knew of it."

"How was it reached?"

"Through a tunnel," Jake answered. "This much we know for sure. A tunnel at least forty paces long. With stairs leading to it."

"The man has seen this tunnel?"

"His name is Jurgen Konrad," Jake said. "And the answer is no, not exactly. Toward the end of the war, he was taken down there by his employer, who wished to get an inventory of some of his treasure and to make sure nothing had been stolen. He trusted Konrad enough to enlist his help, but before they began the journey, a hood was placed over Konrad's head. Though he couldn't see he could still hear, and he knows he was led through a narrow concrete tunnel before entering the vault itself."

"So how does he know that the vault is located there?"

"He says he heard them boasting," Jake replied. "Every time the officers would gather and drink too much, their talk would turn at one point or another to the cache beneath the bank."

The girl with Karl demanded, "And the treasure is still there?"

"Konrad's partners kept careful watch as long as they were free," Jake replied. "They hoped that someone would appear and lead them to the tunnel entrance. But not one of the senior officers returned from the last battles. Not one. Konrad believes they have all died or been arrested."

"So you want us to find this tunnel," Karl said.

"I want you to be extremely careful," Jake replied. "You will be walking through enemy territory."

"All life has its dangers, Captain. You should know that." Karl slipped from the jeep. "Do you have our money?"

Jake shook his head. "But I have some of Konrad's treasure in safekeeping for you. Do you want it now?"

"Later, yes. Not now, but later." The young man grinned for the first time Jake could remember. "We make a good team, yes, Captain?"

"A great team," Jake said, and meant it.

"There will be more rewards from this work?"

"Whether or not you succeed," Jake replied, "I will see that you are rewarded."

"We know where to find you," Karl said. He and his gang turned and raced off through the trees.

Chapter Twenty-one

$\mathcal{D}$USK WAS GATHERING when a muffled shout at the HQ's main gate brought Jake running.

Jake found Karl and three friends squatting in the guardhouse, far enough down to be invisible from the outside. Jake stood in the entrance and said to the nearby soldier, "Back up a pace, Corporal, so everybody can see you, and stand at attention. I want any unfriendly eyes to think I'm tearing off a piece of your hide."

"Yessir." The corporal gave a fair imitation of a soldier retreating before a storm of abuse.

"Did anybody else see them?"

"I didn't see them myself, sir. One minute I was looking down a lonesome road, and the next these four come piling in around me. Don't ask me how they got so close, 'cause I sure don't know."

Jake switched into German and said, "The soldier is impressed with your stealth."

"The shadows of this town are my friends," Karl replied. "You are being watched."

"Where?" Jake asked.

"Around the first corner going toward town there is a trail leading off into the woods."

"I know of it."

"They sit in their jeep and talk so anyone can hear," Karl said. "They do not sound happy. They care little for their work."

Jake said to the corporal, "We've got a surveillance team set up around the first bend."

"Doesn't surprise me in the least, sir."

"When we're finished here, go find Captain Servais. Tell him that one of our night patrols ought to take the first dirt track leading off the road into town. Anybody they find should be arrested on sight."

"Yessir. Consider it done."

To Karl he said, "You have found us an entry?"

"I have found many dark holes," Karl said wearily. "We are searching them all back as far as we can."

"With great care, I hope."

"The need to be quiet slows us down," Karl replied.

"Better at a slow pace than no pace at all," Jake said. "You have found no tunnel?"

"It is hard to say. Very hard. Every opening may be the correct one, especially if what you say is true—that there would be a door or barrier before the entrance."

"There must have been," Jake confirmed. "It was a closely guarded secret, so the tunnel would have been carefully sealed."

"Then I suppose that in front of each possible entry, we have to clean away the rubble as far back as we can," Karl said. Dust caked his clothes, his hands, his face, and frosted his hair. His trio of friends appeared more than content to sit and rest and let Karl make the effort to speak. "So many bombs fell in that area that shell holes are dug into shell holes. Sometimes we cannot see where the house stood, much less where there might have been a cellar. Or tunnel. All around the bank, there are piles of rubble higher than the remains of the bank itself."

"An impossible task," Jake said, momentarily defeated.

"A difficult one," Karl contradicted. "We have three possibilities. Good ones. Narrow stairs leading down to blocked passages. We are searching for ways through."

Jake decided it was time for a visit to the front-line troops. "Corporal, can you get some rations and water up here without anyone seeing?"

"No problem, sir."

"After that, find Sergeant Morrows. Have him fill five knapsacks with provisions."

"Five, sir?"

"Five. And three canteens per man." Jake turned to Karl and continued in German, "This man will bring you something to eat. Please wait here while I see someone."

"Any reason for a rest is welcome," Karl replied, and stretched out his legs.

When Jake told Pierre his plan, Servais was not enthusiastic. "You're not going up there to boost their morale," Pierre argued. "You're going because you think maybe you can find something they can't. Which is ludicrous."

Jake finished putting on his battle dress and pulled on well-worn boots. "The kids think they might have found the entrance. I need to check it out."

"You mean you want to be there for the kill."

"I need to see it for myself before calling out the troops."

"But to go out there alone is absurd," Servais continued anxiously.

"One man can probably slip through unseen," Jake replied. "Any more would just increase our chances of being detected."

"So what do I tell Sally?"

"Nothing," Jake said, with genuine alarm. "I should be in and out within a couple of hours."

"And if not?"

Jake opened the door and checked to make sure the coast was clear. "If I'm not back by midnight, you have my express permission to call in the cavalry."

His first thought upon seeing the dark set of stairs leading down into the gloom was, this is it. His second, upon reaching the bottom stair and being confronted by several tons of bombed-out rubble was, this is impossible.

But Karl was already scrambling through a miniature hole formed high in the dusty scree. Jake watched him disappear. He called to him, "Where is your gang?"

"Opening passages elsewhere," Karl replied. "There is an iron bar across the way here. We couldn't shift it. Watch your head."

Reluctantly Jake accepted the filthy dampened rag offered by one of Karl's companions. He tied it tightly across his nose and mouth and scrambled up and into the constricting blackness.

It wasn't easy, for the opening had been made by boys much smaller than he. As Jake inched forward, the light disappeared behind him. At times his shoulders jammed; it was only by sliding one arm down and lifting the other one up that he could make it through. The second time this happened, Jake was confronted by an iron bar slicing the tunnel neatly in half, and he almost gave up in defeat. Then he realized that going backward was impossible. He grasped the rod with panic strength, and wrenched himself up and around.

To his immense relief, the hole opened up on the other side, and Jake half-slid, half-dropped into an enclosure made from the remaining portion of a basement. Supporting himself on a fallen beam, Jake rose as far as the bowed ceiling would permit.

Karl turned and inspected him in the meager light from their single flashlight. "Where is your scarf?" he asked.

"I lost it in the tunnel," Jake admitted.

With a look that relegated him to the beginners' ranks, Karl came forward, tore off a segment of Jake's shirt and doused it in water from his canteen. He handed it over, saying, "If you don't keep this on you'll be coughing your lungs up in an hour."

Once Jake was fitted out again, Karl motioned him toward a narrow opening in the far corner. "We found this hidden behind a door."

Jake took the light and followed him. Entering the enclosure, his feet scrunched on a sheet of broken glass. The chamber was very narrow and lined on both sides by floor-to-ceiling cubbyholes. Jake looked around in confusion. He then spotted palm-size labels and corks amid the rubble, and understood.

"It's a wine cellar," he called back.

"A what?"

"Rich people sometimes have cellar rooms for wine," he replied. "The wine keeps best in coolness and dark."

Jake used the flashlight to search behind the shelves, finding nothing but solid concrete. The same was true for the back wall. He returned to the main room and announced, "Nothing there."

Karl had clearly seen many such dead ends that day. He contained his disappointment well. "The next one is not so difficult to reach."

"I'm glad to hear it," Jake said, and steeled himself for the return trip.

Once out, they took a moment to replenish themselves with deep breaths of the chilly night air. Then they were up and loping forward in a crouched run, passing within three dozen paces of the stockade's lighted back entrance.

Up ahead loomed a building whose four exterior walls were almost completely intact, though nothing but a waste heap stood within. Once they were safely inside the shadows, Karl said, "My friends will help you check this out. I will go on ahead to see if they are ready for us at the next one."

Jake glanced downward. A crater had been blown through the building's foundations. "You don't think it is here?"

"The same chance here as anywhere else," Karl replied wearily. "If there is a hidden switch to spring the wall back, we cannot find it."

"Why don't you call it off for the night," Jake suggested. "You can start again tomorrow."

"Because it is twice as difficult to move about in daylight," Karl replied. "We will rest at sunrise."

Jake watched him move off, then followed the three boys into the depths of what had once been a spacious basement. When he saw where they had led him, his heart began to race again. Set in the corner facing toward the stockade was a second set of narrower stairs descending yet farther still. They ended in a dust heap, as the basement overhead had shifted slightly and sent a crumbling load down to mask whatever had stood behind. Jake saw how the gang had painstakingly cleared away enough of the bricks and refuse to expose what appeared to be a door. But there was no handle, at least not that Jake could see. Nor were there any hinges.

As swiftly as the darkness and the need for stealth would allow, he searched the high reaches for a catch or switch that might swing the door open. He then joined the other three at the top of the stairs, searching through what remained of the central basement for something that might trigger the opening of the door.

Nothing.

Jake paused to wipe the sweat that had gathered despite the night's growing cold, and wished he could risk knocking on the door with something. He wanted to hear whether there was an echo beyond. He sighed as he realized it was impossible, and went back down the stairs to probe once more.

A scraping sound signaled what Jake thought was Karl returning. Jake mounted the stairs. It was time to tell Karl that unless one of the other entrances yielded something, he was coming back here tomorrow with a chisel.

But two steps from the top, a blow to his head sent him sprawling.

"Well, well, well," drawled an all-too-familiar voice. "Lookit what we caught."

"I told you I heard somebody messing around back here." Jake instantly recognized the voice as the MP called Jenkins. "I told you these weren't no rats, Sarge."

"So give yourself a gold star and shaddap," the sergeant rapped out. "Did you get them all?"

"All three," another voice replied.

"Bring them along," the sergeant ordered. "And keep a tight grip. Those kids are slippery as eels."

"Yessir."

"I think the captain's coming around," Jenkins reported.

"Not for long he ain't." A pair of boots scraped closer, and suddenly darkness descended on Jake with a thunderbolt of pain.

Chapter Twenty-two

*J*AKE AWOKE TO find himself suspended from the ceiling.

The rope tied to his wrists and flung over an overhead beam had been measured out carefully. His toes barely scraped the earth, but could not bear any of his weight. As he returned to full consciousness, he realized it was not just his head that was pounding. His arms burned from being stretched out of their sockets.

"Looks like the captain's about ready to join us again, sir."

"Give him another bucketful, Jenks," the sergeant ordered. "I want him all the way round for this."

A torrent of ice-cold water slapped Jake square in the face. He coughed, spluttered, and opened his eyes.

"There you are, Burnes," the sergeant sneered. " 'Scuse me for not saluting and all."

Jake licked his lips at the taste of water, then whispered, "I thought we were supposed to be on the same side."

"Yeah, I heard that too somewhere along the line. Guess all that went out the window when you started playing for the Germans."

"They were prisoners," Jake croaked. As his consciousness returned, fear gripped him. "They needed help."

"They were enemy, Burnes," the sergeant snarled. "Them and those kids you're always messing with."

The beast of fear filled the room, dominating Jake's universe. It was not like the fear of a coming battle. It was the terror of helplessness. Suddenly Jake's own life had been stripped from his control. There was no one to attack. There was no power to draw on for defense. The beast slithered its hands around Jake's entrails and squeezed with the awesome power of limitless dread.

Then the beast spoke with the sergeant's voice, "You can't imagine how much I've looked forward to this day, Burnes."

From the deepest reaches of his pounding heart came the silent cry, *help me*. Two words were all his mind could form.

"Now the first question is, what'd you do with the Kraut and his hoard? The second question is, what were you doing digging around here in the middle of the night?" The sergeant hefted his baton and gently pushed Jake in the chest, making him swing back and forth. "I'm gonna get the information outta you sooner or later. Just do me a favor and make it later, okay?"

Then it happened.

In a single wave that had no beginning and no end, Jake was enveloped in peace. Before and beyond his pain, Jake saw the room reduced to human proportions. The sergeant shriveled to an anger-filled puppet. The beast was vanquished. Jake knew that beyond the slightest doubt. Come what may, he was not alone.

The sergeant was watching closely, looking for the fear he expected his words to produce. When he did not find what he sought, he growled, "You don't think I'm bluffing, do you, Burnes?"

In a split second of piercing reality, Jake was granted a gift of sight beyond the coming pain. It was not a vision of the eyes, but rather of the heart.

"What, you think your little kids are gonna come running back, storm the place, and rescue you?" The sergeant sneered. "Think again, Burnes. We've got them all locked up." He gave a slow, measured nod. His eyes never ceased their probing search. "Yeah. Ain't much chance of your little buddies breaking out and coming to the rescue. Not this time. You're mine, Burnes. All mine."

Jake saw how the beast had come to feed upon his fear, and how the Invisible had now come to *give*. Giving was His very nature. Giving in creation, in love, in comfort, in peace. Even now. Even here. No matter what they might do to his body, Jake knew in that instant of overwhelming reality that the peace was his. Forever.

"Sarge," Jenkins called from the front hallway. "You gotta get out here."

"Later, Jenks."

"Now, Sarge. Right now!"

He flung the baton across the room and stormed out. Jake heard him snort, "You're next, Jenks."

"Just take a look out there, Sarge."

There was a long moment of silence, then, "Who—"

"The whole blasted city, by the looks of things, that's who." Jenkins was beginning to panic. "There must be a coupla thousand people, Sarge. More!"

"There's another group out back," another soldier called from farther away, his voice high with tension. "And more showing up all the time."

"They've all got candles," somebody else called. "Thousands of candles."

"Do we shoot?" called a frightened voice.

"Shoot? Are you crazy? Hold your fire, everybody!" Then out the window the sergeant shouted, "This is an unlawful gathering! You people disperse or else! Go home!"

"You are holding an innocent man in there," a woman's voice called back. Her English was precise, though she had a heavy German accent. "Release him and we will go home."

"I'm warning you," the sergeant bellowed. "Disperse or else!"

"We have had enough of such warnings," the woman called back. "Years and years of warnings and terror and screams in the night. Is that why you defeated the Nazis, so you could take their place?"

"Go home!" the sergeant shouted.

The quiet murmur grew in volume.

"What's going on?" the sergeant shouted.

"Are they gonna attack?" someone yelled back.

"Do we shoot?"

"Hold your fire!" the sergeant shrilled. "These are un-armed civilians!"

"Trucks, Sarge!" called a voice. "I hear trucks!"

Then Jake did too, and he moaned with relief.

A moment later the street outside was filled with the welcome sound of grinding motors. Then a blessedly familiar voice called out, "This is Captain Pierre Servais, liaison adjutant to the Badenburg garrison. I am acting on behalf of Colonel Beecham, commanding officer. You have Captain Jake Burnes in there. I am coming in to collect him."

"He's under arrest," the sergeant screamed back.

"I am coming in to collect him," Pierre repeated. "Along with fifty fully armed men. I suggest that you avoid a major incident and release him voluntarily."

There was a spell of heavy breathing in the other room, then, "Cut him down."

"Sarge—"

"Do it!"

The rope was released. Jake's legs crumpled under him and he slumped to the floor. He tried to catch his weight with his hands, and gasped at the shock. Then he cried out again as the blood started flowing back into his limbs.

Comforting arms were soon there to support him. "Take it easy, Jake." Servais and Sergeant Morrows lifted him in a double-arm sling. "Can you walk?"

"Maybe."

They made their stumbling way into the front room. A phalanx of men were still pouring in from the entrance and fanning out throughout the stockade.

"Hold it a minute," Jake ordered in a commanding yet weak voice. He nodded his head toward the MP sergeant and said to Morrows, "Let all but that man go."

"But, sir—"

Jake raised his voice as much as he could, and called out, "All who will leave peacefully are free to go, with the understanding that if any of you ever enter this city again you will be arrested on sight."

Morrows tried again. "Sir, I don't think—"

"Pass the message along," Jake cut in. "Take down the names of every man here. They're going to be shipped out by the next possible transport."

"Yessir."

"See they are loaded up and escorted out of town. Remind them there are a thousand witnesses outside ready to testify."

"More," Pierre offered.

Jake turned and looked at the sergeant for the first time since he had been cut down. He discovered that he felt no anger. "Morrows, place this man under arrest for Conduct Unbecoming."

"Try kidnapping and striking a superior officer," Pierre corrected. "Among other things."

The clarity of vision remained vivid, isolating Jake from the hatred in the sergeant's gaze. Jake saw a man shackled by his own rage, a mouthpiece for the beast. "I meant what I said," Jake replied. "All I want is a charge strong enough for him to receive a dishonorable discharge."

"Jake, listen to reason," Pierre insisted.

"What, you want my gratitude? You want me to grovel in the dirt and beg for mercy?" The sergeant snarled. "You're nothing, Burnes. And you never will be."

Jake was certain that all this man wanted, whether he knew it or not, was to provoke Jake into being like him. That was the purpose of the beast, to consume a person with rage and the desire for revenge. Then whatever happened, the outcome was sure. The beast would have conquered once more. Jake said quietly, "Morrows, I just gave you an order."

"Yessir. Consider it done, sir."

"Okay," Jake said. "Let's go."

As they moved for the door, Pierre asked quietly, "Are you sure you want to let them go like that?"

Jake struggled to put one foot in front of the other. "I'm sure."

He stepped through the entrance, and stopped once more.

Against the backdrop of a night untouched by city lights burned a sea of candles. Little flickerings of hope in an ocean of darkness. Jake's appearance was greeted by a rustling sigh, a sound as quiet and pleasant as the wind. He willed himself to stand erect, and proceeded down the stairs as best he could.

Frau Friedrichs, the woman whose son he had first taken into the clinic, was there to greet him. "I could not find your treasure," she said in her heavily accented English. "But there were other ways to help."

Jake nodded. "I cannot thank you enough."

She smiled, an effort which creased her face in unaccustomed lines. "So now we both share the same difficulty, how to repay what has no price."

He looked out at the surrounding faces and asked the woman, "How did you bring all these people together so fast?"

"I did not," she replied. "You did. You see, Captain, you have many friends."

Jake spotted Karl standing beside the closest jeep, and agreed, "Good friends."

"Come on, Jake," Pierre said. "We need to get you back to HQ."

As they passed Karl, Jake said, "I owe you much."

"A life, perhaps?" Karl asked, with a smile in his voice.

Jake nodded. "A life."

"It is good to settle debts," Karl said. "I shall report to you tomorrow, Captain."

"Not early," Jake said, and allowed himself to be bundled into the jeep.

Chapter Twenty-three

THE FIRST WORDS Jake heard upon awakening were, "I hope you are thoroughly ashamed of yourself, soldier."

Jake shifted his aching head, licked at a gummy mouth, and managed, "Water."

A hand far gentler than the voice slid in behind his neck and raised him up, while another brought the cup up to his mouth. Jake gulped greedily.

"Easy, soldier. There's no hurry."

He drank, sighed a deep sigh, and drank again. "Thank you."

The hand helped him to settle back, but did not pull away. Not yet. "Going into town all alone like that. I ought to shoot you myself."

"It had to be done," Jake whispered.

"So you say."

"I couldn't take an entire squad, looking for a tunnel that we weren't sure was even there." Jake cracked open one eye. "Is that coffee I smell?"

"I don't know if you deserve it," Sally replied, reaching for the thermos. She poured a cup and said, "Can you manage?"

"I think so." He pulled himself up, groaning at the thundering protest in his skull. Jake reached to the back of his head and felt a bandage. "What's this?"

"Six stitches," she replied. And with that the brave facade slipped away. "Oh, Jake," she whispered. "How could you?"

The sight of her quivering lip gave him the strength to push his feet to the floor. He reached over, grasped her arms, and drew her onto the bed beside him. He cradled her in his embrace, felt her trembling form, and closed his eyes to the sheer joy of nearness.

"When Pierre told me what you had done," she said, "I could have shot him, too."

"It's over, Sally," he whispered, kissing her hair.

"This time," she replied quietly.

He nodded. She was right. Now he said what he knew he had to say, what he had been thinking of on the drive into town the night before. "This is who I am, Sally. Risks are a part of my life."

The stark genuineness of his declaration brought her back far enough to look into his face. Jake went on. "I live on the edge. I guess I always will. I need you, Sally. I want you with me. But I can't change who I am just to allay your fears."

"Take it or leave it," she said bitterly.

"No," he replied, searching for words through the pounding in his head. "I will always take greater care if I know you are there waiting for me. Always. It gives me a reason to come home. The best reason a man could ever ask for."

She sighed and found her way back to his shoulder. "What on earth am I going to do with you?"

"Love me," he whispered, holding her close. "Please."

They sat like that for a time, until Sally forced herself apart once again. "They're all waiting for you."

"Who?"

"Pierre, Morrows, half the division that's not on duty, Harry Weaver, the kids, Buddy Fox—he's still here in the infirmary, by the way. Shall I go on?"

Jake dragged himself painfully to his feet. When Sally started to stand up to help him, he said, "No, I'm all right, thanks. Do you think you could find me a couple of aspirin?"

"Of course."

"Give me a few minutes to collect myself. Then I'll see Harry, okay?"

She nodded. "I'll think about what you've said, Jake."

He managed a smile. "A man can't ask for more than that."

When Dr. Weaver had finished poking and prodding and pronounced Jake as fit as any man could hope to be after what he had been through, Burnes walked down the hall and into Chaplain Fox's room. "What are you still doing in bed?"

"My ribs gave me more bother than Harry or I expected. He wanted to keep me still for another day. How are you, Jake?"

"Now that I no longer feel my head's about to come off in my hands, I'm all right."

"Pull up a chair and sit down. Sally told me what happened. You took an awful risk."

"Yeah, I guess I did." Jake eased himself down. "Something happened back there in the room when they had me tied up."

"It shows," Chaplain Fox replied.

"It does?"

"Sally noticed it too. She came down to talk with me while you were being examined. She says that when she looks at you now she notices something deeper." The chaplain gazed at him. "I agree. Do you want to tell me about it?"

Jake struggled for a moment. "I'm not sure I can," he said.

Chaplain Fox nodded. "Words can be so constricting sometimes. So incomplete. They are made for the things of this world. But sometimes our greatest revelations do not belong to this realm at all. We are given a taste of the beyond, where words do not exist."

"That's how it feels," Jake agreed. "Exactly."

"I'm glad for you, Jake," the chaplain said. "Very glad. But I want you to remember something. A life of faith is not based upon the moments of glory. Fireworks are splendid, but they soon fade. What is important is making steady, daily progress toward a life lived in Him, for Him. Do you understand?"

"I think so," Jake replied, thinking that maybe he really did. For the very first time.

"No man can keep up the walk alone through life. All of us need the impetus and the guiding light of faith in Jesus Christ to help us stay upon the Way." Chaplain Fox bestowed upon Jake his gentle smile. "Now go out there and face the world, and know that He will be there with you."

The morning sun was brilliantly clear, and strong enough to transform the icy winterland into a vista of dripping, dancing rivulets. Jake walked slowly, exchanged salutes with grinning soldiers, took in the day with the wonder of a newborn. When he came into view of the front gate, the corporal of the guard came rushing over to greet him. "Sure is good to see you up and about, sir."

"Thank you, Corporal." Jake waved toward where Karl and his friends stood waiting beyond the gate. "It's great to be here."

The corporal pointed in Karl's direction. "They've been hanging around all morning, sir. Sally—I mean Miss Anders, sir. She came out a while ago and said you were okay and got them something to eat."

"Thank you, Corporal." Jake limped over and asked Karl, "What have you found?"

"Nothing," Karl replied. "How are you feeling?"

"Sore," he admitted. "Nothing at all?"

"Now that we can move without worry," Karl said, "it is much easier. But no more fruitful. The best two chances we had were bombed shut. Permanently."

"The door at the bottom of the second basement stair-case?" Jake asked.

"That was one of the two," Karl confirmed. "The street was hit just down from there. Whatever was beyond the door is now no more."

"At least I don't have to go down there again," Jake said.

"What do we do now?"

Jake had already decided upon that. "Keep looking. I'll meet you there in an hour or so."

"And if we find nothing?"

"If at first you don't succeed," Jake said, turning back to the gate, "then it's time to call up the heavy artillery."

Chapter Twenty-four

JAKE'S WALK FROM the gatehouse to headquarters was interrupted numerous times by smiles and salutes and queries about his health. Everyone who had taken part in the raid on the stockade now felt they had a stake in his well-being.

The HQ central hall was filled to overflowing with staffers. Pierre, Sally, and Sergeant Morrows stood in front, taking charge of Jake's welcoming committee. Jake endured the attention as long as he could, but felt his patience ebb with his strength.

Finally he could stand it no more. "What is this, a holiday camp? We've got a garrison to run. Back to work!"

They responded with grins and a slow but steady withdrawal. Jake watched them go, then asked Sally, "Why is it when the colonel gives an order people jump, and when I do they grin?"

"If it had been the colonel talking under these same circumstances," Sally replied, "they would have reacted exactly the same way."

"For a moment there, I thought I was hearing the colonel," Pierre said.

"Me too," Morrows agreed, heading for the door. "Good to have you back, sir."

"Just a moment, Sergeant." Jake put a hand on his shoulder and drew him back. "Who's the best demolitions man on our silent squad?"

"The silent squad." Morrows' grin broadened. "I like that."

Jake shot him a narrow-eyed look.

Morrows straightened. "Oh, that'd be Parker, sir."

"Can he be cautious?"

"Pop a lid off a can of soup and not spill a drop, sir."

"Right. Have somebody round him up, tell him to get all he needs for a job. Then come back and join us in my office." He stopped, corrected himself, said, "I mean, the colonel's office."

"Right, sir. How large a job did you have in mind?"

"About the size of the stockade," Jake replied.

After the planning meeting was over, Jake rose from the desk. He was surprised when everyone else rose with him. "That's it, then," he said. "If we send for the trucks, it means we've struck gold. Everything goes into action then."

There were solemn nods and excited glances about the room. Jake thought to himself, time to fish or cut bait. The point of no return was about to be crossed. "Good luck, everyone. Dismissed."

As they filed out, Pierre approached him. "Are you sure you feel like going through with this today?"

"No," Jake admitted. "But we don't know if Connors is still looking, and if so, how much time we've got left."

"Or if he's found something already," Sally agreed, joining them by the desk. "If he has, or when he does, there will be no stopping him or General Slade."

Jake looked askance at her. "What happened to all your care and concern for my well-being?"

"You look pretty fit to me, soldier," she said.

Jake sighed in mock resignation. "Are you sure you know what to do?"

"If you say that one more time I will scream," she replied. "Five minutes after we get your signal, you'll have trucks and men flooding your area."

"They'll be ready and waiting for your word," Morrows agreed from his place by the door. "Good idea you had, sir, splitting up the contingents like that. Keeps them from moving unless there's a green light."

"Can't a man have a private conversation around here?" Jake snapped.

"Just going, sir," Morrows said, not moving. "I only wanted to say I wished I was heading out with the first group."

"I understand your concern, Sergeant," Jake replied. "But I need you here to muster the troops. Now move out." When Morrows had vanished, Jake said to Sally, "Don't forget the documents and supplies. And keep trying to find Colonel Beecham. If you do—"

"You go tend to your knitting, soldier," Sally retorted. "And let me tend to mine."

Jake nodded acceptance, then glanced at the lone figure still lingering in the doorway. Pierre rubbed his nose briskly and said, "Perhaps I should go make sure the lookouts along the roads into town are in place."

"Perhaps so," Jake agreed. When he and Sally were alone, Jake asked, "That's all the send-off you're going to give me?"

She looked long into his eyes and said quietly, "I'm a lot better at hellos than goodbyes, soldier. If you expect me to get used to your risk-taking, this is one little habit you're going to have to learn to live with."

"I hope you give me the chance," he replied.

"Come back to me," she replied, "and we'll see."

Jake arrived at the stockade sweaty and clammy; coming back to the place of his ordeal hit him harder than expected. As he was posting guards, a crowd of Germans gathered. They approached, asked of his health, showed him quiet respect. One old veteran from an ancient war even threw him a rusty salute. Jake responded with smiles and a few words, and found himself settling, centering, drawing from them the strength he needed.

By the time Karl appeared he was feeling ready. "Where have you been?"

"Checking up on one last possibility," the dusty, grime-streaked boy replied. "It's no good."

"Then round up your gang," Jake said, "and have them circulate among these people. None of my guards speak German. Tell them all we're going to be using dynamite, and that they should stand well clear."

Over the next quarter of an hour, Jake watched and waited as Parker and his two assistants wired the brig for demolition, and Karl's gang completed their passage through the throng. The crowd, however, did not disperse. As word circulated of what was about to happen, the gathering took on a carnival-like atmosphere. The crowd pointed and chattered and waved whenever Jake happened to look their way.

When Pierre joined him, Jake gestured toward the throng and asked, "Do you have any idea what this is all about?"

"You're the one who speaks their language," Pierre replied. "But I suspect they don't like Connors' men any more than you do."

"So?"

"Perhaps they think you are getting rid of the bad guys once and for all."

Jake mulled that over. "Don't contradict them."

"I wouldn't dream of it even if I could," Pierre assured him.

"And when you return to base, see if you can get word back to Connors that this is why we've blown up the building."

"That, my friend, is a grand idea. Consider it done."

Parker came hustling over. "Sorry it's taken so long, sir. See, the problem was, we've got this massive vault sitting right on top of where the second vault is supposed to be. So I had to figure out some way to blow a hole through to the bottom vault without shifting the support and sending the whole caboodle down."

"And you've done it?"

Parker grinned through the grit encrusting his face. "Sure hope so, sir."

"All right." Jake turned and surveyed the crowd of civilians. "Karl hasn't had much luck shifting them."

"They'll listen to you, Jake," Pierre said, pointing to the nearest jeep. "Stand up there where they can see you."

Jake did as he was told. Once he came into view, he raised his hands for silence and said in German, "I owe every one of you who was here last night a debt of thanks."

"Friendship is built upon mutual debts, Captain," called a stranger's voice.

"You are all friends," he agreed. "And I don't have so many friends that I can afford to lose any. So while we rid this city of a certain blight, I ask you please to disperse. And if you will not disperse, please go behind the next screen of buildings."

When the crowd had scattered, Jake turned around. "All right, Parker. Let's blow this sucker to the moon."

"It'll be a pleasure, sir," he said, and shouted, "Take cover!"

When the warning had reached the entire periphery, Parker attached the second wire to his trigger, checked the grounds once more for strays, ducked behind the jeep where Jake and Pierre were crouched, and pushed the plunger home.

The explosion rocked the site. Debris rained down for a full thirty seconds.

As Jake picked himself up, he said to Parker, "For your sake, I hope you didn't overdo things, soldier."

Parker answered with his customary grin. "So do I, sir."

"Let's take a look."

Lazy wafts of dust drifted in the unaccustomed warmth of a sunny, windless day. Jake carefully crept forward, up the front stairway, and to the other side of what remained of the entrance. A hole had been blasted neatly through the former floor of the front hall. It gaped black and gloomy at Jake's feet.

"I set the blasts for two holes, front and back," Parker said. "In case one didn't strike pay dirt."

"Let's see what you've uncovered," Jake said, his voice tight with excitement. "Somebody get me a rope and a light."

Pierre was at his elbow. "Don't you think someone else should go down first and check things out? Like me, for instance."

"Not a chance." Jake wheeled around, ordered, "Secure that line to the axle of a jeep."

"You've had a hard night," Pierre pointed out. "I, on the other hand, slept like a baby."

"Rank has its privileges," Jake replied. He accepted the rope and the light, and called out, "Stand back and give me room."

Jake scrambled down the steep ledge into the cellar vault, and dropped the line through the gaping hole blown in the floor. He slithered down hand over hand, ignoring the pounding in his head. Dust clung to his face and filled his nostrils. When he felt solid ground beneath his feet, he reached for the portable lamp and switched it on. In the instant that followed, his discomfort was utterly forgotten.

Jake had landed in the central hall of a chamber that stretched the entire length of the former bank. It was sectioned into concrete-walled compartments with stout mesh doors. Each portal bore a neatly printed placket stating a name and a series of numbers. Jake walked toward the nearest door and shone his light through the mesh. He trained the beam back and forth across the compartment and saw row after row of floor-to-ceiling shelves.

The shelves were filled with treasure.

Paintings were stacked like files against the back wall. Gold and silver baubles dripped and hung like ornamental spider webs from overcrowded ledges. There were so many objects so tightly packed together that Jake could not discern all that was there. The wealth of empires and the legacies of centuries were crammed in like innumerable trinkets at a costume jewelry emporium.

"Jake? Are you all right?"

Reluctantly Jake turned his eyes from the sight. He walked over to stand beneath the hole. He looked up and said to Pierre, "Go for the trucks."

Pierre hesitated. "You are certain?"

"This is it," Jake replied. "Hurry."

Chapter Twenty-five

*B*Y THE TIME Pierre returned with the convoy, Jake and his men had erected a series of tents; they extended in two unbroken lines from either hole to the front and back streets. Once the lines were set in place, men worked in utter secrecy, passing the treasure from hand to hand to waiting trucks. As soon as one truck was full, it moved forward to be enclosed by guards, and another empty one took its place.

Jake supervised one line of heaving, sweating men; Pierre the other. Morrows acted as a roving spotter, keeping an eye on everything, making sure that no one became greedy, watching out for anything unexpected. The trapped air within the enclosures was soon smelly and stifling, but the men did not slow down. Even when Jake ordered a halt or change of shift, they left their work with reluctance. The same air of electric urgency held them all.

Jake was on his second break, sipping a cup of soup prepared by the field kitchen, when Morrows caught his eye and motioned him over to the other side of the building.

Once Jake was out of sight of the others, Morrows said quietly, "Get a load of these, sir."

Jake stooped down. Five thick leather sacks the size of basketballs were gathered at Morrows' feet. "What have we got here?"

Morrows bent and loosened the thong holding the neck of one sack. He thrust one hand in, and came out with a fistful of gold and silver coins. "All five are just the same, sir."

Jake stared at the wealth for a split second, then came to what he would later recall as his first command decision. "Sergeant, these sacks do not exist."

"Sir?" Morrows asked, then snapped to with the light of understanding. "Right, sir. Figments of my imagination."

"Exactly. Stay here." Jake rose up, walked to the far corner.

He beckoned to Karl, who lay sprawled in exhaustion with several of his gang. Even after a full night and a morning of searching for passageways, they had insisted on helping with the loading. At that point, Jake could not have refused him anything.

When Karl joined Jake and Morrows out of sight of the others, Jake pointed to one sack. "This is yours if you like. Coins will be easier to use in these times than treasure," he said. "But it's your choice."

"It is much wealth," Karl said, reluctant to touch it.

"Hide it carefully," Jake ordered him. "If you like, when I return, we can talk about how you might divide it up. But the decision is yours. Yours and your gang's."

When Karl was gone, Jake hefted one sack and said to Morrows, "Those other three are for you and the men."

"Sir?"

"I can't spare you, Morrows," Jake continued. "So you'll have to find someone you can trust to stow this away." Jake's voice turned very stern. "When it comes time to divvy it up, I expect it to be done with complete fairness. Can I trust you with that responsibility?"

"Of course, sir," Morrows said, looking in wonder at the sacks.

Jake motioned to the sack in his hands and said, "This is for the people out there."

"They saved your life," Morrows said, nodding his understanding.

"No. I'm worried about the children. They need all the help they can get to survive this winter. And the next one."

"I understand, sir," Morrows said, but his voice was troubled.

"What's the matter," Jake demanded impatiently. The sack was proving to be very heavy. "Even split up among all the men, that is going to come to a hefty bonus. They may also receive a share of the reward someday. But I want them to have this now. It's all we can safely spare, Sergeant. These other items would do nothing but attract attention and put everyone at risk."

"Oh, it's not that, sir," Morrows replied. A shadow crossed his brow as he looked out beyond the barriers to the crowd watching with the patience of people with nowhere to go. Then he turned back to Jake and said, "I'll get Simpkins and Vance to handle this. And thank you, sir."

Jake nodded, then picked his way out of the building and on beyond the barriers. To his relief, he had no problem finding Frau Friedrichs. He walked up to her, trying to hide the strain of holding the sack, and said quietly, "Come with me, please."

Once they were well clear of prying eyes, Jake set the sack down, loosened the thong around its neck, and showed her what was inside. "You once told me your neighbors screamed at you because of your past," he told her. "If I entrust this to you, I want your solemn promise that it will be shared with all in need, without prejudice."

She gaped at the wealth. "This is Nazi gold? After all I have lived through, you wish to give me Nazi gold?"

Jake nodded. "Use it for the children and the people in most dire need."

She raised her head and searched his face for a long moment. "Someone should write a song to help us remember what you've done, Captain."

"I just want to help the children," Jake replied.

She bent over and retied the sack, lifted it to her shoulder, and said solemnly, "For the children. Upon my own son's life, I promise. For the children."

Chapter Twenty-six

A SOLDIER BANGED down the tailgate of the truck and flipped back the canvas cover. "We're nearly there, sir."

Jake rolled over, struggling to unzip his sleeping bag. "What time is it?"

"Almost nine, sir."

His mind showed its customary reluctance to shift into gear. "In the morning?"

"Yessir." A steaming mug was thrust under his nose. "Captain Servais said to give you this, and to tell you that there's a refill waiting just outside."

"Thanks, soldier." Jake raised himself up to a sitting position, accepted the mug, took a sip, blinked in the bright sunlight. As the world gradually came into focus, he gave thanks once again for the beautiful weather.

They had driven all night. The road had been full of potholes, rutted and bombed-out, poorly marked and icy. But at least there had been no more snow. Jake had forced himself to remain awake through the first three checkpoints, but when their documents and stories had gone unquestioned, he had given in to rising fatigue.

"If they ask," Jake had told Servais, "we are transporting a specially sealed shipment for General Clark in Frankfurt.

No one else may touch it. Any problems have to be referred to the general personally. Nobody else."

"I heard you discussing all this with Sally before she prepared the documents," Pierre reminded him. "I have also heard you give the same story at three different checkpoints. Now climb in back and get some sleep. You're dead on your feet."

Jake had awakened at the next checkpoint, heard all proceeding smoothly once more, then allowed himself to fully relax. No guard had chosen to question a convoy of this size carrying authentic documents and under the orders of General Clark himself.

Now it was morning. And they had arrived.

Jake crawled out of the truck and walked over to where Pierre stood surrounded by a group of drivers. Troops hung from the backs of their trucks or loitered alongside, heeding Jake's strict orders to keep the vehicles fully manned at all times. A kitchen detail made its slow way down the long line of trucks and jeeps, serving coffee and what passed for army oatmeal.

To his right stretched a seemingly endless high fence, beyond which rose the main Frankfurt base. It appeared less than half finished, with dirt tracks winding off across vast partially open fields to partially constructed buildings and hangars.

Jake greeted the drivers, nodding his thanks as Pierre refilled his mug. "Where is the main gate?"

"About a mile up ahead," Pierre replied. "How do you feel?"

"Stiff, but otherwise better. Much better." He drank the coffee, surveying the long line of vehicles pulled off the road behind him, and asked, "Is everybody ready?"

The drivers chorused a firm, "Yes, sir." Jake turned to Pierre and said, "You're in the front jeep with me."

"Everything is go, Jake," Pierre assured him. "Just as you planned."

Jake tossed the dregs of his coffee aside and handed back the cup. "Let's load up and do it."

*   *   *

The sergeant manning the main gates was clearly taken aback when a long line of vehicles pulled up and stopped right in front of the entrance, jamming it completely. Jake and Pierre jumped from the jeep while it was still moving; Pierre stood out in the road alongside the convoy while Jake rushed over to the astonished guardsman.

The guard saluted and said, "Sir, those trucks have got to be moved back—"

Jake handed over his fistful of documents. "Captain Jake Burnes with a special consignment for General Clark."

"Consignment of what, sir?"

"Call General Clark, Sergeant," Jake replied crisply. "Tell him that the consignment he *specifically* ordered to be delivered to him *personally*—and to *no one* else—is waiting for him at the front gates. Is that clear?"

"Yessir, I guess it is, sir." He cast a nervous glance toward the idling trucks, then started for the guardhouse phone.

"Just a minute, Sergeant. Aren't you forgetting something?"

"Sir?"

"Open the gate and let me get my trucks off this public road."

"Sir, I can't do that without—"

"I don't have time for your shilly-shallying," Jake snapped. "Those documents are all you need to get my trucks behind the safety of these gates." Jake wheeled around and shouted over the sound of the revving motors, "Do you see them?"

"Not yet," Pierre called back.

That put the guard on red alert. "See who, sir?"

"But there's some smoke in the distance," Pierre yelled with exaggerated concern. "Could be them now."

"Sergeant," Jake pressed. "I have an extremely valuable shipment that I have brought clear across this country in record time. See the date at the top of the first page?"

"Yessir. Dated yesterday." The sergeant went over and scanned the horizon again.

"I need to get these trucks inside and safe *now*."

The sergeant weakened. "I'll have to call out the guard until the general gives his okay, sir."

Jake released his pent-up breath. "That'll be fine, Sergeant. Call out anybody you like. Just open the gate, please. Now."

Reluctantly the sergeant turned to his man and said, "O.K., Charlie, raise the gate."

Jake joined his hands over his head and gave Pierre a pumping action, which Servais then repeated in plain sight of the convoy. At that, a cheer rose up and down the line. The sergeant's eyebrows went up yet another notch.

"I'll have to ask you to stay here, sir," the guard insisted.

"Of course," Jake replied. "Just remember, General Clark and no one else. He is here today, I hope."

"Yessir, I checked him in myself just under an hour ago."

Jake nodded, then yelled to Pierre as he passed, "Trucks alongside the wall, jeeps next, then the men!"

"Nobody goes near the goods," Pierre shouted back, and snapped off both a grin and a precise salute.

Fifteen minutes later, Jake was still standing there. "Still no word, Sergeant?"

"Sir, I've called every place I know and left word about you and your shipment for General Clark. Are you sure there's nobody else who—"

"This shipment is to go straight into the general's hands," Jake replied grimly. "And nobody else's."

Then a voice from behind him asked, "How about mine, son?"

Jake wheeled around, sputtered, "Colonel Beecham! What the—Where have you been, sir?"

"Hunting big game," the colonel replied, a glimmer of humor in his steely gaze. "Tell you about it later. Now then. Do you think maybe you could tell me what's got you in such an all-fired rush to see the general?"

Chapter Twenty-seven

STORING THE TREASURE and making an official handover took the better part of another day. By then the colonel had already left for Badenburg—called back, he said, to a desk which had been vacant far too long. Jake's men were then gathered and paraded so General Clark could thank them. Jake was mildly disappointed that the general had no personal word for him. Not the first word.

As they set off on the return to Badenburg, however, it struck him with full force that the reason for the general's silence was the coming interview with Colonel Beecham. Jake spent the journey cataloging the rules he had broken. It made a mighty impressive list.

Jake decided his homecoming was going to be rough. Very rough indeed.

The colonel insisted on hearing Jake's report in private and alone. Jake told Beecham the entire story, including what he had done with the coins, and then accepted all blame.

When Jake had finished, the colonel only asked, "What about this German ex-soldier? What's his name again?"

"Jurgen Konrad," Jake replied. "I had him released when we started off for Frankfurt. I figured he had suffered enough, sir."

"Sit down, Captain," Colonel Beecham ordered. When Jake had settled himself in his chair, the colonel went on. "You've stepped way out of line, mister."

"Yessir, I know that, sir," Jake replied, and readied himself for the worst.

"I am only going to say this once, Captain, so listen up. We are no longer at war."

"I'm not sure I understand, sir."

"We are no longer at war," the colonel repeated. "You can't get away with bending the same rules you might have bent a year ago." He inspected Jake to make sure the message had sunk home, then continued. "Still, I think I would have probably done exactly what you did."

That shocked him cold. "Sir?"

"Or I hope I would have, anyway." Beecham cocked his chair back and propped his feet on the corner of the desk. "Now I want you to consider something. The Occupying Forces need officers like you, son. There's work to be done here. Vital work. We're not just engaged in a police action. We are responsible for helping to rebuild an éntire nation."

"But, sir—"

Beecham held up his hand. "Just hear me out. Then you can say anything you like. There have been a lot of eyes on you recently. Most have liked what they've seen. A lot. These last few days were what you might call a final exam."

Jake could not help but gape. "You disappeared deliberately, sir?"

"More like we took advantage of the circumstances. The general's been busy forming the group he wants left in charge of reshaping this country. Had to make sure all the treasure hounds were rounded up and sent home. Looks like we've got them all." The colonel permitted himself a satisfied smile. "Wanted to see how you handled the pressure of command, son. You did well. Very well, in fact. The general agrees."

"He does? Sir?"

Beecham nodded. "I'm due for retirement in two months. So is Colonel Daniels up at Karlsruhe. Both of us are ready to go home. We've got families waiting, and we're not suited for what's coming next. I think you are, though, and Daniels' aide, Major Hobbs, agrees. Hobbs is scheduled to take the same ship we'll be leaving on, and feels you'd be a good man to place in charge of the new consolidated Karlsruhe command."

"Sir," Jake stammered. "I don't know what to say."

"We're pushing you for a battlefield promotion. Probably the last of its kind—in this war, anyway. Going to jump you a grade, put you right in as colonel, acting officer in charge, to be confirmed in ninety days. What do you say?"

Jake was left speechless.

"It's the chance of a lifetime, if you ask me. I'd urge you to jump on it with both feet." Beecham stood up. In a daze, Jake rose and accepted the colonel's hand. "You're a good man, Burnes, and a good officer to boot. One of the finest I've served with, and I've served with some dillies. Go think it over, and let me know what you decide."

Jake almost collided with Pierre as he left the colonel's office. Servais searched Jake's face. "It was bad, yes?"

Jake tried to collect himself. "I'm not sure."

"I don't see any blood. There are no guards. What happened?"

Jake pulled him into the hallway and told him the news.

Pierre said, "I don't understand."

"What's there to understand?"

"This is great news. Why do you look so glum?"

"I don't know whether I want to accept or not."

Pierre smiled broadly. "My friend, may all your life be filled with such troubles as this."

"This isn't a joke, Pierre."

"Wait. I too have news." Pierre drew himself up to full height. "You are now looking at the new commander of the French garrison at Badenburg."

"You?"

"Don't look so shocked. I think they have made an excellent choice." He patted Jake on the shoulder. "This of course would mean that I shall be close enough to offer advice whenever you are at a loss, Colonel."

Jake arrived back at the main camp to find Sally Anders pacing the length of his barracks. "I've been cooling my heels around here for over an hour, soldier. Are you going to accept?"

He gazed at her. "Aren't there any secrets around here?"

"Stow it, soldier. I asked you a direct question. I think I deserve a direct answer."

Jake sank down on the bed and replied, "I don't know."

She sat down beside him. "Would it help any if I told you I was accepting a posting to Berlin?"

Jake was both surprised and pleased. Then he thought for a minute, and pointed out, "Berlin is a long way from Karlsruhe."

"It's a lot closer than Ottawa," she replied. "Which was where I was headed until about three hours ago."

"You did that? For me?"

"I bet colonels in charge of bases can find lots of reasons to go hobnobbing with the senior brass in Berlin."

"Is that what you're going for? To hobnob with the officers?"

"Maybe. At least with one in particular. That is, if he'll let me. Hobnob, I mean."

"I can't see anybody turning you away, Sally," he replied seriously.

"I'm not interested in just any old officer body," she replied crisply. "One recently promoted colonel is the one I've got my eye on."

"Oh, really?"

She nodded. "If he'll have me."

"What if he wants you to give up the big city of Berlin for a little nowhere town like Karlsruhe?"

She took a deep breath. "Then I guess he's got his work cut out for him." She rose before he could reach for her, and said, "That's about all the risk-taking this girl can manage just now, especially with a desk piled high with transfer and promotion orders, and another soldier waiting to speak with you."

"Let him wait," he said. "Come and sit down."

"Later," she promised. She bent down and planted a solid kiss right where it belonged. Then she smiled, wiped the red smudge off his mouth, and said, "Can't have our newest colonel receiving his first official visitor wearing lipstick."

"Sally—"

"Don't, Jake. I'm shaky enough already." She bestowed upon him a trace of the tenderness he knew was there, and said in parting, "We'll have time for this later."

Jake was still staring at the door when Sergeant Morrows appeared, knocked, and asked, "Sir, could I speak with you for a moment?"

"Too much too fast," Jake muttered.

Morrows hesitated. "Sir?"

"Nothing, Sergeant," he replied. "Come on in."

"Thank you, sir."

Jake pointed to his footlocker. "I'm afraid this is the only seat I can offer you."

"Oh, no thank you, sir." Morrows remained standing, shifting his weight nervously from one foot to the other.

"What's on your mind?"

Morrows twiddled with his cap and said, "It's like this, sir. Me and the boys've been thinking."

"Always a dangerous sign."

"Yessir. Anyway, what we wanted to ask was, are you taking any share of the loot?"

Jake jerked to full-alert status. "What's that got to do with anything?"

"We'd just like to know, sir."

"I'll get a share of the reward, just like everybody else," Jake replied. "Someday. Maybe."

"That's not what I mean, sir."

"If you're talking about the coins, then the answer is no. That was intended for you men."

"That's sorta what we figured, sir. Me and the men, well . . . " Morrows hesitated.

"Go on, spit it out, man."

"We want to give it back, sir," Morrows said in a rush. "All of it."

Jake was completely dumbfounded. "Give it back?"

"The coins." The effort was costing Morrows dearly. "It's like this, sir. We got back pay coming outta our ears, at least compared to some. And with this new GI bill, we'll be getting a real leg up when we get home." He waved a hand to encompass the entire outside world. "But these folks, sir, what've they got going for them?"

"Nothing," Jake said quietly. "Absolutely nothing."

"That's what we mean." Morrows swiped at the perspiration beading his forehead. "They need it a lot worse than we do."

Jake shook his head at the enormity of what he was hearing. "I don't know what to say."

"The word's out that you might be sticking around, sir," Morrows went on. "We'd like you to keep it and use it wherever you think it'll do the most good."

Jake searched the sergeant's face. "You didn't pressure anyone to go along with this?"

"Nossir. It just sort of happened, I guess you could say. I can't explain it any better than that. But everybody agrees. All of us, sir."

"This will mean a lot to these people, Sergeant," Jake said solemnly. "It may make the difference between life and death for some. This is a very great and generous act."

Morrows shrugged and said, "We'll probably regret it like the dickens in the morning, sir."

"I doubt it," Jake replied. "I doubt it very much." He rose to his feet and offered the sergeant his hand. "For all those who will never know what you've done, accept my thanks, Sergeant. And pass it along to everyone else. Tell them . . ." Jake paused, then said simply, "I have never been prouder of anyone, at any time, than I am of all of you."

*   *   *

Toward dusk, Jake pulled out of the main gates and started down the road, only to find Karl walking up the road toward him. Jake stopped and turned off the jeep. "Where are your friends?"

"I wished to speak with you alone," Karl replied.

"Come aboard," Jake offered.

The boy took the seat beside him. "So it is done."

"Not entirely," Jake replied, thinking of the promotion he was about to accept.

"No," Karl agreed, misunderstanding him. Then he confessed, "I do not know what to do with our gold."

"It is a great deal of wealth," Jake agreed.

Karl slumped down even farther. "That all these riches could cause so many problems."

"There are banks with safety deposit boxes," Jake replied. "And there will be traders for the coins later when the markets are restored. And friends to offer help in the meantime."

"Banks and markets are for people with papers," Karl replied bitterly. "And friends go away to distant lands."

"Not this friend," Jake corrected him. "And papers can be arranged."

"What are you saying?"

"I happen to know for a fact," Jake answered, "that a certain commander of the Karlsruhe garrison is looking for a squad of young German men and women to help out around the base. Orderlies for the Officers' Mess, clerical help, assistants in the PX, that sort of thing."

"Commander?" Karl gaped. "You?"

"The job pays three square meals a day and provides a wealth of experience," Jake went on. "Along with a warm bunk and pocket money. This means you can leave your funds untouched until your feet and your nation are firmly established upon solid ground. The one condition is that all jobholders must go to school."

Karl made a face. "School."

"You will thank me in the end," Jake promised. "And I will see that you all receive papers."

"You will do this? For me?"

"A life is a great debt to owe somebody," Jake replied. "I recall someone telling me that once."

Karl's face split into a mighty grin. "We were a great team."

Jake corrected him, "We still are."

II
Gibraltar Passage

This book is dedicated to all our friends at Bethany House Publishers and the Bethany Fellowship. One of the great joys of this relationship is the opportunity it grants us to work with friends. Thank you for allowing us to be a part of your fellowship and mission.

Chapter One

MAJOR PIERRE SERVAIS, commander of the French garrison at Badenburg, wore a face that frowned from forehead to collar. At the sound of Jake's jeep, Pierre turned from his inspection of work on the refugee camp's sentry towers, walked over, and said, "First we worry because the ground is hard as iron. Now the thaw arrives and we find ourselves working in quicksand."

Lieutenant Colonel Jake Burnes, commander of the U.S. military base at Karlsruhe, watched the team of sweating soldiers struggle to steady a crosspiece while working in mud up to midthigh. "Maybe you ought to wait for the ground to dry out."

"I can't. The entire area has become treacherous. My sentries can no longer even stand, much less walk the perimeter. We must have these elevated positions." Pierre inspected his friend. "From your expression, I take it you could not convince her to stay."

"I didn't even see her," Jake replied. "She left Berlin the day before I arrived. General's orders."

"I am very sorry for you." Pierre reached over and patted his friend's shoulder. "She was posted back to America?"

"Six months," Jake said, her letter burning through his jacket pocket to sear his chest. "On the road almost the whole time. I can't even go see her because I don't know where she'll be. The whole business is classified. A great opportunity, she called it." He resisted the urge to pound the steering wheel. Again. "What does she call our relationship? A burden?"

"Sally must trust you very much," Pierre said solemnly.

"Or just not care one way or the other."

"That is not so, and you know it," Pierre countered. "What will you do?"

"I still have close to a month's leave. Almost wish I didn't now."

"Perhaps you would like to go home?"

"That's what the leave is supposed to be for. But there's not much for me to go home to, remember? My folks are both gone, and my brother didn't make it back from Normandy."

"I meant home with me," Pierre replied.

Jake showed a spark of interest. "To France?"

"That is where home was the last time I looked," Pierre said. "I have received another letter from my mother. She says that I have let the memories block my return for too long."

"You mean about your brother?" Pierre's twin had fought with the Resistance and had died in the war's final months.

"Among other things," Pierre said, his frown deepening. "Come. I need to check the other team's progress."

Jake sprang from his jeep and fell into step alongside his friend. He searched his memory and recalled references to a woman named Jasmyn who had betrayed Pierre during the war by taking up with a Nazi officer. Jake smiled grimly. He and Pierre made quite a pair.

Their way took them along the internment camp's outer fence. The open fields that had formerly bordered the Badenburg main base had been restructured as a holding center for paperless refugees.

Throughout the fierce winter of 1945–46, central Europe had remained awash in a human flood. Most refugees carried little or no identification, beyond perhaps the tattooed identity numbers of the concentration camp victims. Others were stragglers from farther east, uprooted by the invading of Stalinist forces and flung helter-skelter westward. Few families were intact. Husbands sought wives, wives children, children parents. Mornings in the camp were scarred by the wails rising from the Red Cross center when the daily reports confirmed that those being sought were no more.

Such camps were seas of humanity encircled by barbed wire. There was never enough room, or food or medicine, or news from the lands now suffering under Stalin's mighty fist. By midwinter, the number of homeless refugees in the American sector of the former Third Reich had risen to more than two million. The French sector had been similarly inundated.

The spring thaw had reduced the sentries' path to a muddy bog. Jake and Pierre stayed on the grassy verge and picked their way carefully as they skirted the camp. Jake resisted the urge to return the never-ending stares from behind the fence.

As they rounded the corner, a cry from somewhere inside the camp made Jake wince. No matter how often he heard the sound, he could not become hardened to the tragedy of another refugee's loss of hope. He steeled himself and continued onward until he realized that Pierre was no longer at his side.

Jake turned around to find his friend staring at the fence with a gaze of hollow agony.

Again there was the cry, and this time Jake heard it as a name. "Patrique!" Pierre recoiled as though taking a blow to the heart.

Jake spotted a girl struggling through the dense lines of bearded men and kerchiefed women waiting for food. The people were reluctant to let her through, both because of their obvious hunger and because a step in the wrong direction meant moving off the boardwalk and stepping into the mud. She ignored their complaints and curses, shoving and wriggling and fighting toward the fence. "Patrique!"

Pierre moved toward the fence, did not notice where he stepped, and sank to his knees in the bog.

The girl extricated herself from the final line, and promptly slipped and fell headlong into the mire. She scarcely seemed to notice. Even before the fall was complete, she was battling to right herself. Her feet spun for a hold in the slick mud. The front of her dress was encrusted. Dirt streaked her dark hair and painted one emaciated cheek. Finally she recovered her footing and flung herself at the fence. She thrust her face and one hand through the wire and screamed in a broken voice, "Patrique!"

A sentry called out a warning and started forward. Pierre barked out a command in French, but did not seem to have the strength to free himself from the bog. Jake walked over and offered a hand. "What's going on?"

Pierre accepted the help without really seeing. He mumbled something in French, his eyes fastened on the screaming girl.

"Try that in English, buddy," Jake told him.

Pierre swung around, seemed to have trouble remembering who Jake was. Then he said in a benumbed voice, "Patrique was my brother."

Chapter Two

*J*AKE SAT IN the corner of what once had been Colonel Beecham's office but now belonged to Pierre Servais. The former American base at Badenburg was presently a central French garrison, with Pierre as acting commandant. Pierre sat behind his desk, his hands shaking so hard he could scarcely bring the cup to his lips. Jake watched him listen to the girl's story, hoping that Pierre would begin to recover from the shock of having heard the young girl call out his dead brother's name. But if anything, Pierre was becoming continually more distraught. The young French major winced at the girl's voice. His own questions were hoarse and hesitant.

The girl was barely able to speak around her tears. It was hard to tell her age because she suffered from the refugees' most common ailment—desperate hunger. The skin of her face was like dry parchment, stretched tightly over bones of birdlike fragility. Her brown eyes watched a strange and dangerous world from dark-lined cavities. Yet her whole being burned with an intensity that belied her frailty. Jake imagined that given a chance to recover, she would emerge as a raven-haired beauty.

Seventeen, Jake decided, listening to her continue the halting discourse with Pierre. Maybe a year older. She spoke German with the lilting tone he had come to recognize as the result of speaking Yiddish at home. Neither her sadness nor the urgency of her words could obscure her voice's musical quality.

Her name was Lilliana Goss, she told them. She was half Jewish, half German. It was her mother who taught her Yiddish. Although she had been raised in a Christian home, her mother had insisted on keeping her Jewish heritage alive. Her father, a former university professor, had managed to bribe their way out of Germany when the Nazi sweeps intensified.

"My father was in contact with the Resistance across the border in France," she told Pierre. "That is what saved us. We were taken to Marseille, and from there to Morocco. We met Patrique, your brother, in Marrakesh. My father began working with him, processing the incoming refugees, arranging for false papers, keeping on the lookout for spies and turncoats.

"My father's health started to fail. I began helping out more and more with Patrique's operations. I became a local messenger for the group and helped to forge documents. I had nothing else to do with my time, and I enjoyed the feeling of being useful. One night, a few months before Morocco was liberated—"

"When exactly," Pierre grated.

She thought a moment. "The first week in April," she replied with confidence. "I remember because my birthday had been only a few days before."

The news visibly shook Pierre. "Go on."

"I was working alone in our offices, they were hidden under the eaves of the Red Cross building, when Patrique rushed in. He startled me, because he had been called away in March. Nobody knew where he was. There had been all sorts of rumors floating around about how he had been captured or killed, but I had refused to believe them."

Pierre was taking the story very hard. The longer Lilliana continued, the more he seemed to shrink inside himself. Jake watched him, recalled the day news had come of his own brother's death on the Normandy beaches, and ached for his friend.

"Patrique was furious to find me there. I did not understand his anger, because I had feared the worst and was overjoyed to see him alive. He said that a messenger was to have met him that night but had not arrived at the meeting point. Patrique had waited three hours, then risked going to the offices, where he found me. Since I knew nothing about a messenger, Patrique was forced to assume that the French conspirators had captured him."

Pierre roused himself enough to rasp out, "You mean the Nazis."

Lilliana responded with an adamant shake of her dark locks. "He said the French. I asked the same thing. He *insisted* it was the French, which made him extremely distressed. But he refused to explain. He said the less I knew the better. Then he asked me if I would take on a dangerous assignment. He hated to use me, but there was no one else, and he had to leave that very night. He knew the forces were hard on his trail. I adored your brother and would have done anything for him. He asked me to take a message to his friends in Marseille. He said a boat was waiting for his messenger in the Tangiers harbor. I was to go there, take the boat, deliver the message, and return immediately."

Again Pierre stirred himself enough to ask, "What was the message?"

"Beware the traitor," the girl replied, "I have the proof you need."

"Which traitor?" Pierre demanded.

"Patrique did not say," Lilliana replied. "Only that it was no longer safe for him in Morocco. That he was going to try to make it to Gibraltar. And that they should not believe overmuch in rumors of his death."

Two days after finding Lilliana, Jake and Pierre boarded the train for Marseille. Lilliana had been examined by the local Red Cross doctors and proclaimed unfit for travel—acute malnourishment and a persistent low-grade fever. Be-

sides which there was still no word from her family. Three
inquiries had been sent to Morocco, with no reply. Pierre's
last action before departing had been to place yet another
request through official channels.

The train was crammed to overflowing. Every compartment was full. People jammed the aisles outside, sitting on
their luggage, standing, crushed together like sardines. Yet
there was no pushing, no shoving, no arguments over
places. With their officers' passes, Pierre and Jake were assured seats. Twice they rose and tried to give their places to
ladies. Both times they were refused—not only by the
women themselves but by all the people surrounding them.
When the people saw that Jake did not understand their
words, they motioned him down with hand signals. Sit, sit.
Officers deserved a place.

Of Pierre they asked as much as politeness allowed.
Where were the gentlemen coming from? And where,
might one ask, were they headed? Ah, Marseille. A beautiful city. To see the family. How nice. And the first time
since the end of the war? Oh, how exciting it must be for
you, sir. And for your friend, this will be his first time in
France? Welcome, welcome. Smiles and bows were presented in Jake's direction. May your stay in France be a
glorious one. That was the word they used, Pierre assured
him. A *glorious* stay. This from people who wore their hunger as evidently as the frayed elbows and carefully darned
tears in their clothes. They wished him a glorious stay in
their beloved land.

Once they were settled in their seats, Jake asked Pierre in
a low voice, "Why did you keep asking Lilliana to repeat
parts of her story, you know, about when Patrique came
back to Morocco unexpectedly?"

"Because, my friend," Pierre replied, "this entire episode
took place a month after my brother was supposed to have
died."

Jake turned back toward the train window and mulled
this over. The others in their compartment showed polite
disinterest, granting them as much privacy as their
crowded surroundings would allow.

Lilliana's story had not ended there. She had done as Patrique had requested, traveled to Marseille, and hurried to the designated address. But the building had been destroyed in the war, and she had no other way of contacting Pierre's friends. In desperation she had walked the streets until a roving German patrol spotted her and arrested her for being out after curfew. She soon found herself on a train with other detainees, heading north.

Once inside Germany, the train had been halted and left to languish on a siding for three days. Finally the soldiers in charge had forced those still alive to continue onward by foot. They had walked for a very long time—Lilliana was not sure exactly how long, the days had melted together. She had ended up in a workers' camp and endured the grueling weeks of autumn and winter working in an unheated bomb factory. Then with the spring had come the Allied liberators, and after that she had been passed from one camp to another, awaiting papers and word of her family.

"I am tempted to travel directly to Gibraltar," Pierre broke in, "but I know I must first go to my family in Marseille."

"I thought you said they were in—" Jake searched his memory, but could not recall the name. "Some other town."

"Montpelier," Pierre supplied. "My family originally came from Marseille, and we spent much time there when I was growing up. During the war my parents moved back there because survival was easier when surrounded by family. Now my uncle, my mother's brother, is one of the President's team in Marseille. Not one of the cabinet, mind you. One of the local staff. He is in charge of food distribution for that area of Provence. My father works with him. Marseille is where the Americans offload all supplies."

As soon as he had recovered from Lilliana's story, Pierre had applied for and been granted long-overdue leave to visit his family. The brigadier general responsible for Jake's region had then personally authorized his own travel to France—not because of Pierre, but because he knew of Jake's lack of family and his distress over Sally.

The train that took them through the Alsace countryside was from a bygone era. Plumes of smoke and cinders flew by their closed window. Jake gave thanks for a chilly day. If it had been warmer and the windows open, they would both have arrived blackened by the chuffing locomotive.

"Gibraltar," Pierre murmured. "Why would he choose to go there, of all places? Why not home?"

"It seems to me that if your brother really had survived," Jake cautioned, "he would have gotten in touch with somebody long before now."

"Do not rob me of hope, my friend," Pierre said, his eyes still on the countryside. "Already it hangs from the slenderest of threads. Do not swing the knife."

"I just—"

"Don't," Pierre repeated, turning away from the window. "Let me sit for now, this moment, this day, and believe that there might indeed be a chance that Patrique is still alive. My mind too is full of all the arguments, but my heart does not wish to hear them. Not now. Not yet."

Jake nodded his understanding. "So tell me more about your brother."

Pierre was silent a long moment, then began. "Marseille is a funny place. For the first three years of the war, it was occupied by the Italians. Between the mentality of the Italians and that of the Marseille people, life there was what we call 'soft.' People got on with the business of living. There was laughter. There was smuggling. That is what my brother did. He smuggled bodies."

"Warm ones, I hope."

Pierre smiled. "My brother operated the Marseille end of an underground system that smuggled out people wanted by the Nazis. About half were Jews. The others were mostly German intelligentsia, people who publicly opposed Hitler's madness—professionals, priests, teachers, writers. He was very successful, my brother. At least, as long as the Italians were there."

"After that?"

"After that, well, after that came the Nazis. And life became very hard."

"And your brother?"

"Patrique stayed for as long as he could. Then one night the Nazis came for him, and we all thought he had been taken. But somehow he had managed to escape at the very last moment. He went to Morocco and operated there for a while."

Jake inspected his friend's somber face. "He was killed there?"

"So we were told," Pierre sighed. "Where exactly I have not been able to determine. Everything after his departure from Marseille remains a mystery."

Jake said quietly, "You miss him."

"There is a bond between twins that only another twin can understand," Pierre said. "It is for me like an invisible connection from the womb. More than sympathy. We *share* in the emotions and the experiences of one another. Across distances, across time. We are different, yet the same."

Jake listened and heard the way his friend spoke. We *are* these things, Pierre was saying. Not were. Not in the past. Still today. Jake heard, and understood, and dared hope for his friend as he had not been able to hope for his own family.

"I am the cautious one. Reserved. Deliberate. I am the one who made the good army officer," Pierre continued. "Patrique is bold. More than that. He is reckless. I was the reins that held Patrique in place. I think he understood this better than I. Through Patrique I felt the emotions I never allowed myself, and through me Patrique knew a balance between caution and abandon."

The emotions that etched themselves on Pierre's features were too naked for Jake to feel comfortable watching. He turned his attention to the window, listening carefully, but granting his friend the only privacy he could offer.

"Patrique was younger than me," Pierre continued, pitching his voice softly. With the noise of the locomotive and the train's rattles and squeaks, only Jake could hear him. "He was younger only by two minutes in time, but always I was the older brother. I went through life feeling that I watched over him. I was responsible for him. I was the rock. Patrique was the wind."

The train did not go fast. Nothing seemed to move fast in this land. The entire country appeared to be gradually recovering from shock, stumbling a bit as it found its footing.

Their journey was one of stark contrasts. Some towns and villages were left virtually untouched by the war, at least as far as Jake could see. Others were pitifully scarred. All wore the same run-down look as the people.

"When Patrique was fifteen," Pierre told Jake, "he got a job working at the local hippodrome, the racetrack. He became an excellent rider. In his free time, he began hunting the wild white stallions of the Camargue. I can still remember him flying across the great salt flats, both hands busy with his lasso, guiding his horse with his knees. The weekends he went hunting, my mother used to spend at the local *église*, praying that her son would come home in one piece.

"Patrique sought out the Resistance within days of the German invasion," Pierre went on. "He proposed that they use the hippodrome as a gathering point for the fleeing refugees. In his first letter to me, he bragged that already they had ten times as many Jews as horses in the stables. It gave him great pride to help these people."

Pierre was silent for a time, then said to himself, "I think I have always seen my brother as the hero I never was."

"That's crazy and you know it," Jake protested. "Where did you get those medals on your chest, a bazaar?"

The journey from Karlsruhe to Strasbourg to Lyons to Marseille took twenty-eight hours. For the majority of the trip, Pierre remained immersed in his thoughts and his memories. Jake did not complain. His own ruminations were more than enough company. At times he would emerge, look about, return the smiles of the people whose eye he caught. But soon enough the blanket of sorrowful thoughts tucked itself up tight around his chest and he retreated into missing Sally.

Six months. The time stretched out before him in endless emptiness. It did not matter how much he argued with himself. It did not matter that she had been ordered to go. It did not matter that her work was important. Jake found it impossible to see beyond the painful fact that she was not there beside him.

Near Avignon the train chuffed around a high rock ledge just as the sun cleared the horizon. Gray-faced rocks drank in the morning light and were transformed into shades of soft coral. The train's brakes squealed on a sharp decline, the whistle blew a greeting to the new day, and they were swallowed by the ancient town.

From Avignon the train followed the Rhone River's winding path, never leaving its side for more than a few minutes. The air was scented with olive trees and pines and awakening spring. The sensation of entering a new world grew ever stronger. Behind them northern Europe still struggled to cast off winter's cloak. Here in the Provence, spring had long since been welcomed home with open arms.

The faces surrounding Jake seemed to lose some of their deeper lines. Eyes shadowed by years of strain and worry and war took on a glint of newfound humor as breakfast provisions were brought out. The woman next to Jake unfolded a checkered bundle to reveal a round loaf of bread, home-whipped butter, and a honeycomb in waxed paper. Shyly she offered him a portion. The entire compartment watched as he bit and chewed, then shared a smile as he moaned his pleasure.

Jake offered his handful to Pierre. "You want some?"

"What?" Startled by the words, he turned from his endless perusal of the window. "Oh, no thank you."

"It's great."

The woman next to Jake spoke up, urging Pierre to take a portion. He dredged up a smile and shook his head. Pierre remained the only one of their compartment untouched by the new day.

He felt Jake's eyes on him and turned a sorrowful gaze toward his friend. "I was thinking of Jasmyn."

Once more Jake recalled late-night talks. "She's the woman who betrayed you by taking up with a Nazi officer, right?"

His friend nodded and confessed, "The closer we come to Marseille, the harder it is to keep the memory of her behind me. You remember how I said that there could never be another woman for me?"

"I remember," Jake said quietly.

Pierre sighed his way back to the window. "All she did, all that was, and still I yearn for her."

"Would it help to talk?"

"Thank you, my friend," Pierre replied to the unseen day outside the train. "But more words about Jasmyn would be lances to my spirit."

Outside Arles, a new conductor made his way down the crowded train. He was an ancient survivor of the First War, the chest of his heavy blue conductor's uniform sporting three rows of ribbons. When they handed over their official passes, the old man drew himself to attention and threw them a rusty salute.

For the first time that morning, Pierre showed a spark of life. He asked the old man a question and received an overloud reply. Pierre smiled, only his eyes holding the stain of unspoken memories. He motioned toward Jake and spoke at length. All eyes in the compartment turned his way. Pierre pointed to the ribbons on Jake's own chest and gave a name to several of them. His words were greeted with appreciative oohs and aahs.

Jake objected with, "You mind telling me—"

But Pierre cut him off with further words in French. He grew fervent, his voice rising to reach more of the passengers who now crowded into the compartment's open door. The woman seated next to him had eyes as wide as saucers. Jake felt his face grow hot.

The ancient conductor handed back Jake's papers and snapped off a second salute. Jake accepted the papers and brushed one hand across the front of his close-cropped hair. The conductor spun around, shut the compartment door behind him, and talked excitedly with the people jamming the corridor who immediately crowded around him. From the looks cast through the smudged glass partition, Jake assumed the old man was recounting Pierre's story.

Jake leaned forward and muttered, "What was that all about?"

"I was simply telling them a little of who you are," Pierre replied.

Jake shot a glance toward the growing number of faces pressed against the glass. "You don't say."

"Believe me, I was defusing trouble before it could take hold," Pierre replied. "Not everyone you meet in Marseille greets Americans as friends."

"Why is that?"

"There was a terrible bombing here in 1944," Pierre answered. "The city's worst destruction from the entire war."

"By the Americans?"

Pierre nodded. "The Allies decided the city was important enough to be bombed, since Marseille was a German submarine harbor. They wanted to destroy three points— the central train station, a storage center, and the submarine base. The Americans came with their great bombers called Superfortresses. But not one bomb found its target. Not one. Bombs fell all over the city. The worst destruction was in the Quartier Saint Charles, not far from the station. Over three thousand people were killed that night, all within two hours. It was tragic. The city's highest death toll in all the years of war."

Jake sat back in his seat. "I'm really sorry, Pierre."

His friend replied with another smile that did not reach his eyes. "In some ways, the city of Marseille is but a very large village. By tomorrow it will be known all through the markets that a great American hero has come to visit their beloved town. And that he will stay in the home of their own Resistance hero, the famous Patrique Servais."

Marseille was a bustling, thriving city. It was also a city wed firmly to the sea. The Bay of Marseille bit out a mighty chunk, as vast as a great inland lake. Hills rose on the north and east, giving the impression from seaside that the entire town looked out upon water. The deep blue Mediterranean waters caught the sun's rays and brushed the tired land with hope of a new tomorrow.

As the train wound its way toward the station, Pierre pointed out a great medieval castle, rising from the city's southern tip. It was the Fortress of Saint John, he said, from which Crusade ships journeyed into the unknown dangers of the Ottoman Empire.

The train platform was jammed solid. When Pierre stepped into view, a great cry of joy arose from the throng. He was immediately swept into a huge crowd of laughing, crying, singing, shouting people. Jake stood on the train's top step and watched as a diminutive woman in black stepped forward. The crowd quieted and drew back a step as she reached up one age-scarred hand to stroke the side of Pierre's face. When Pierre reached down and enveloped the woman, a second great cheer arose. He reached out behind the woman and made room in the embrace for a bespecta-cled man who held his sparse frame rigidly erect. Tears streamed from every face in view.

A champagne cork popped, then another, and suddenly every hand was holding a mug, a cup, a glass. Pierre turned to find Jake still standing at the crowd's periphery and shouted for silence. He waved Jake over and said in English, "Come join me, my friend."

A space was made through which Jake walked. Pierre raised his voice and spoke briefly in French, ending with the words, "Colonel Jake Burnes." A murmur of greeting rose in reply.

"These are friends and family," Pierre explained. "Many have traveled from Montpelier to welcome me home."

Pierre's mother reached over and gripped Jake's arm with surprising strength. She spoke rapidly, her voice trembling slightly, her eyes shining despite the tears.

"My mother tells me to apologize for her lack of En-glish," Pierre translated. For this moment at least, the shadows were gone from his eyes. "I am to tell you that she has read from my letters about your parents' accident and the loss of your brother in the war, and that she grieves for you. She says that she would consider it an honor if you would consider our family to be your own."

A pewter mug full of champagne was thrust into Jake's hand. A great salute rose as Pierre raised his own cup and toasted the crowd and his parents. Then he turned to Jake and said, "Welcome home, my friend."

Chapter Three

*J*AKE AWOKE TO the sound of church bells clanging
directly beside his head.

He groped his way upright, rubbed his eyes, and realized
that the bells were ringing through his open window. He
stumbled across the room, but just as his hand gripped the
ledge the clanging stopped. The air ached with the sudden
stillness.

Thoroughly awake, Jake took in his surroundings. The
Servais family did not live in the city of Marseille itself, but
in Le Rouet, a small farming village near both the city and
the sea. The village church stood to Jake's right, bordering
the cobblestone plaza. To his left rose houses so old they
appeared to have grown naturally from the earth. Beyond
the village stretched vast fields of verdant green.

Jake leaned on the windowsill and watched the gentle
colors strengthen into full-fledged day. Great wild birch
and umbrella pines acted as natural windbreaks for the ancient houses. Hoopoes and robins and nightingales and
song thrushes sang the glory of Pierre's homecoming.

Through his window Jake saw a fox shepherd her three
cubs across the field. Herons stood in white calmness about
the edge of a distant lake. Flamingos fed with the foolish
intricacy of ballet dancers. Ducks mocked all Jake's wor-

ries. Beyond the fields and lake stretched the wetlands, silver-white with salt.

His attention was drawn downward at the sound of a closing door. He watched as Pierre's father and mother, dressed in suit and dress of basic black, exited the house and walked arm in arm toward the chapel.

Pierre swung the bedroom door open. "Ah, you're awake. Good."

"It'd be easier to sleep through D-day than that racket."

"Yes, my father says he has never found it so easy to be on time for morning Mass." Although the joy of yesterday's homecoming had dimmed, Pierre's sardonic smile appeared to be firmly in place. "I spent much of last night going over places we need to check. Shall we get started?"

"Give me two minutes to throw on some clothes," Jake replied, "and I'm with you."

First stop was the port of Marseille. The harbor seemed to be flourishing. Fishing vessels of every size and make bustled in smoky confusion between the great gray hulks of the American battleships. With the Sixth Fleet using Marseille as a major center for offloading supplies, the streets were full of American uniforms.

Tankers and cargo vessels lay at anchor or vied for space at the crowded docks. The surrounding streets were jammed with every imaginable form of transport, from donkey carts to military trucks to human-powered pushcarts. People shouted and cursed and fought their way through the crawling traffic. The air stank from rotting fish and seaweed, from the refuse of a thousand broken food crates, from the fumes of the overheated trucks.

Pierre did a slow circle, took a deep breath, and smiled with vast pleasure. "Ah, my friend, it is so good to be home!"

Alleys opening off the main thoroughfares widened into markets selling everything from fish to fashionable clothes, from seaweed fertilizer to silverware. Time after time Pierre and Jake's progress was stopped by stall holders who dropped their wares, shoved aside impatient customers, and rushed to greet Pierre with cries of welcome. Large women swathed in layers of frayed sweaters and stained with fish scales enveloped Pierre in their fleshy arms, tears of joy streaming down their broad faces. Old fishermen overturned packing crates and scattered ice and nets in their haste to rush over and pound his back.

Each time Pierre extricated himself from their blows, he pointed toward Jake and spoke an introduction. They turned and doffed battered berets, their hands curled into stone-hard rigidity by decades of fighting nets and fish. Leathery seams creased until dark eyes almost disappeared, and smiles revealed a few remaining smoke-stained teeth. Then Jake was pulled into the back-slapping circle, where his total lack of French in no way slowed down the questions thrown his way. Jake replied with shrugs and smiles, while Pierre tried to keep up with a dozen people demanding answers at once.

Whenever the name of Patrique was brought up, the crowd quieted. A moment of reflecting upon the ground, the sky, the harbor's scummy waters, and then quietly Pierre would ask his question. Eyes widened, the group tightened, voices tensed. Jake watched faces, since he could not understand the talk, and repeatedly saw a struggle pass over their weather-beaten features. They drank in Pierre's news with breathless unease. They wanted to believe, tried to believe. But in the end they turned away with sorrowful shakes of their heads. Patrique, to their minds, was no more.

"They don't know anything," Jake said with certainty when they stopped for a breather at a harbor cafe. The air was redolent with the pungent odor of French cigarettes and cheap wine. Jake followed Pierre's example and hunched down over his coffee. That appeared to be the universal signal for privacy, and no one approached them unless one or the other straightened up.

"I think you are right," Pierre said. "No one has heard anything to suggest Patrique is alive."

"You don't seem surprised."

"No," he agreed. "If Patrique had made it this far, the family would have heard. Of this I am sure."

"Then why are you doing this?"

"Planting seeds," Pierre replied. "All I need is for one to grow and bear fruit. The fishermen and the smugglers and these local traders often work together, you see. There is the chance that someone stopped somewhere to pick up an illegal shipment and heard something which he discounted."

"Up to now," Jake added.

"Exactly. So he hears that Pierre is back and is spreading word that Patrique might be alive. Of course, most people will say it is a futile hope, but who knows what might turn up?"

"They all seem to think a lot of you."

"Patrique and I both worked as boys on fishing boats," Pierre said. "We had an uncle who was a fisherman, and he used to tell us stories of foreign ports and mysteries of the sea. My father is a very wise man. He knew that if he was to forbid our going to sea, we would both have run away. So instead he urged us to spend our summers working for my uncle. Although we learned to love the sea, we also learned that the hard life of a fisherman was not for us."

Pierre sipped his coffee, then continued. "When the Resistance was starting here, Patrique used his old connections to organize those smugglers and fishermen who wished to help. When I was home on leave, I worked with him."

"Patrique led the local Resistance?"

"There was no single leader. Cells, or units, were formed. Patrique worked with a number of these units."

Jake decided he could ask what had been on his mind since his arrival. "Will you tell your parents what you've learned?"

"My father only," Pierre replied, his face somber. "I told him last night. He agrees we must say nothing of this to my mother."

"That's probably wise."

"Losing Patrique almost killed her. We cannot speak with her until we know for certain, and then only with the greatest caution." He dug in his pocket, tossed a coin on the counter, and rose to his feet. "Come, let us go plant some more seeds."

They exited the cafe, crossed the main port road, passed through a tiny arched portal, and descended a dozen grime-encrusted stairs into a miniature market square. Another shout greeted their entry. Jake held back and watched Pierre being swept up by another joyful crowd.

A gentle tug on his sleeve caught Jake's attention. He turned, the smile in place, expecting to find some ancient fisherman wanting to pump the hand of Pierre's friend.

Instead, he confronted a slender figure covered from head to toe in a great gray cape. The hood was slid so far forward that the face was totally lost in shadow. A honey-coated woman's voice said in English, "Step back away from where he can see us."

"What?" Jake took a reluctant step as the figure backed between two stalls toward the ancient stone wall. When he hesitated to move farther, the figure raised one fine hand and beckoned impatiently.

"Who—"

His words were cut off as the hood was folded back to reveal one of the most beautiful faces he had ever seen.

Great eyes of darkest jade captured him and held him fast. High cheekbones slanted above a finely carved jawline, the sharp features balanced by full red lips. Rich, dark hair was gathered over one shoulder and held by a silver clasp inscribed in a writing that Jake could not fathom.

The eyes. They held him with a sorrowful calmness that stilled his ability to question.

"You are Pierre's friend," she said, her voice as soft and rich as her gaze.

Jake could only nod.

"I am Jasmyn." Her gaze flickered behind him. Slender hands rose to sweep the hood back forward, and the beautiful face was lost once more to the shadows. "We haven't much time. Pierre turns this way. Tonight or tomorrow he

will take you to a restaurant called Le Relais des Pêcheurs.
There is a cafe next door. I will await you."

"Jake!" Pierre's voice called from amidst the throng.

The hand reached out and grasped his arm with a power
that seemed to scald through his uniform. "Do not tell him
I have seen you. But come. Please come."

"Jake! Come on over here!"

"I have heard of your search for Patrique," said the hidden woman. "You *must* come. I have news."

Then she swept around and vanished, her absence a vac-
uum in the bustling market.

Chapter Four

"**I**T'S COLD TONIGHT," Jake said as they bicycled back into town that evening. Although there were a few cars around, including one used by Pierre's father, petrol was almost impossible to find. Bicycles remained the most popular and dependable means of transport.

"This is the home of the mistrals, the winter winds," Pierre replied, pedaling alongside him. "They funnel down through the Alpine foothills and strike Marseille with brutal force. On nights like this, we say that winter has returned to remind us of what was and what will be again."

Just as Jasmyn had predicted, Pierre had invited him to eat at a restaurant near the harbor, one run by an old friend. But Jake found it difficult to concentrate on the coming meal and their conversation on the way. He found it even harder to keep quiet about Jasmyn's presence in the city. "From the sound of things, you must like this restaurant a lot."

"Marseille is the most ancient town in France," Pierre replied in his roundabout manner. "The Romans used it as the port for all the upper Mediterranean. From the old harbor, when I was growing up, there was a major thoroughfare that split the town into two sections. The one nearest to the old fortress was called Le Panier, the Basket. It was the oldest part of town. Very, very ancient. And very crowded. A lot of bars, prostitutes, fishermen, tiny market areas, very small shops." Pierre waved and smiled a reply to the greeting of an old gentleman seated beside a roadside cafe. "Le Panier was always full of life. The restaurant we are going to tonight is on its border. Whenever I think of Marseille, I think of that area. It was where my brother operated from."

Jake's breath pushed out wispy clouds as they crested a ridge and the harbor came into view. A greatcoat that had once belonged to Pierre's brother flapped around his legs as he pedaled. "Why is that?"

"A person who knew the area could remain hidden in the maze of alleys and stairs and passages for a lifetime. It was possible to go from the central train station to the water, a distance of perhaps two kilometers, and never walk upon any road or path that could be found on a map."

"Incredible."

"Yes, exactly that. The entire history of that area was incredible. It was built during the time of the Crusaders, upon ways that had existed since Charlemagne. The second time I visited during the war, my brother took me down what I thought was a blind alley. But there in the back were carved these small stone steps that would go unnoticed unless you knew what you were looking for. Then up above, on top of the wall, a narrow path intersected three small gardens and joined a bridge which from below looked to be merely two overlapping roofs."

"Sounds like an amazing place."

"It was, yes. And there was such a great mixture of people in that area. Many small-time gangsters, who ran the gambling and the prostitutes. Many shop owners, whose families had been there, probably working the same tiny shop, for hundreds and hundreds of years. And fishermen, extremely conservative families who kept to themselves. Somehow my brother managed to make friends with all those people, and all of them helped him with his smuggling work."

As they approached the water's edge, the evening crowd thickened to the point that the road became impassable even for bicycles. They dismounted and walked.

"So what happened?"

"When the Germans came in, they demolished the entire area. It was impossible to control, so one day they simply went in and leveled it." Pierre swept his hand out. "One day home to several thousand families, the next rubble."

"What happened to the people?"

"Ah, that is another mystery." Pierre stopped and shook the hands of a young couple, exchanged greetings with three others, then rejoined Jake and continued. "According to what we learned later, the Germans planned to round everyone up, interrogate them to find out who was involved in illegal activities—which of course meant almost everyone—then ship them off to the camps. But instead, almost no one was there! The entire area had been cleared out overnight, right under the noses of the Nazi guards. Poof!"

"An informer," Jake guessed.

"Yes, that is what I think as well. But who would have had access to such information? And who could have gotten that information back to so many families so fast?"

Pierre smiled fondly at the ancient facades lining the harbor. "So many mysteries," he murmured. "That is the nature of Marseille, my friend. It is close enough to the Arab world to have learned to treasure its secrets."

Their entry into the restaurant was greeted with a roar of approval. Chairs were shoved aside and napkins flung onto tables as waiters and patrons together rushed forward to hail Pierre Servais. Jake allowed himself to be swept up in the hubbub. His coat was slid from his shoulders, a chair was jammed up behind him, and friendly hands forced him down. A glass was slapped into his hand. A bottle appeared. But just as the room quieted for a toast, a rotund little man in a chef's apron and hat pushed his way through the crowd to stand before their table. His cheeks were the color of ripe apples, and below his nub of a nose sprouted a curling waxed moustache. He sprang to attention, which shoved his belly out at a ridiculous angle, and snapped off a parade-ground salute. "A votre service, mon Capitaine!"

"Major," corrected a voice from the crowd.

"Jake, allow me to present Sergeant Roncard," Pierre told him. "Formerly the greatest scrounger in the Fighting Free French."

"True, true," the rotund little man agreed merrily in English.

"In the middle of the Algerian desert," Pierre went on, "the illustrious sergeant fed his troop so well we actually gained weight."

"I took my duties most seriously, mon Capitaine," Roncard replied, still at attention.

"When my men began wondering if we would ever be permitted to fight, and I was growing weary of fighting for the attention of deaf officers, the grand sergeant told me to invite the general for a dinner. After finishing off the only wine within a hundred kilometers—"

"Two hundred," the little man murmured.

"—not to mention dining on desert grouse and wild onions—"

"Ah, you remember," Roncard said, and stuck out his pigeon's chest even farther.

"—the general was made to see reason, and we were sent into action with the Americans. Not, I must add, without a struggle, for the general wanted to keep the sergeant for himself. The sergeant, being made of hero material, insisted on his right as a French soldier to fight alongside his brothers." Pierre grinned. "After that, our brigade saw more of the general than any other. Not to mention being the first to receive scarce supplies."

"You do me great honor, mon Capitaine."

"None but what you deserve." Pierre rose to his feet and raised his glass. "A toast."

"To a free France," Roncard shouted.

"Vive la France!" cried the room with one great voice.

Jake raised his glass with the others and silently blessed the fate that had brought him here.

*   *   *

A steaming bowl of bouillabaisse was followed by partridge stuffed with mushrooms and cooked in fresh spices, cream, and white wine. Every few minutes Roncard popped back through the kitchen doors to make sure that everything was satisfactory and to apologize for the paltry meal. *Dégoulas,* he moaned, dragging the word out like a chant. How was he to run a first-class restaurant when everything had to be purchased either with coupons or on the black market? When Jake assured the little chef that the meal was the best he had eaten in ages, Roncard puffed up like a pink balloon.

When they had finished, chairs from other tables were drawn closer, and the air soon thickened with the scents of Gauloisie cigarettes and syrupy coffee. Pierre switched to French and began telling his story once more.

Jake stood. "Think maybe I'll get a breath of air."

"Don't stray where there are no lights," Pierre warned. "Marseille is still Marseille."

Then Roncard was at his elbow, leading him toward the door. When they were away from the group of locals, he said quietly, "You are a good friend, Colonel Burnes."

"I try to be."

"Go," he said softly. "She awaits."

That stopped him. "You know about Jasmyn?"

"All know," Roncard said simply. "All know, all approve, all hope against hope."

"I don't understand," Jake replied. "All know about what?"

The little man opened the door and permitted in a breath of fresh night air. "A good friend," he repeated and ushered Jake into the darkness.

The cafe was as crowded as the restaurant, but the atmosphere was more subdued. Jake pushed open the glass portal and squinted to see through the smoke. There in the center was a table made noticeable by its isolation. A woman sat alone, her back to the door, her long dark hair gathered and brought over one slender shoulder. Hers was the only table occupied by one person. The card playing and smoky companionship swirled around her, yet left her untouched.

Jasmyn looked up at Jake's approach. When he stopped before her table, she said quietly, "Thank you for coming, Colonel Burnes."

"I don't even know what I'm doing here."

"Sit down. Please." Her voice was as softly sad as her gaze. As Jake slid into a seat, the barkeeper came around the counter and stopped before their table. His eyes flickered over Jake, then turned to Jasmyn. She asked, "What will you have?"

"Coffee, I guess."

"Café, s'il vous plait," she said. The bartender gave her a respectful bow and returned to behind the counter.

Jake felt eyes turning his way. He glanced around, saw people at every nearby table watching him speculatively. "What is this all about?"

Jasmyn seemed uncertain as to how to proceed. She fiddled with her spoon, asked, "They say you are a hero."

"I was in the war. I survived. That's true for a lot of people."

"They say your brother died on the beaches at Normandy."

The sudden piercing ache hardened his voice. "It's not my brother we're here to talk about."

A warning appeared in the eyes of those patrons close enough to have heard the change in his voice. Jake held their gaze and had a sudden realization that it was not mere curiosity he saw, nor hostility toward a stranger.

"It means a great deal to these people that you have suffered a loss here in our land."

Jake nodded. He was beginning to understand. They were not isolating them because she was not welcome. They were doing it out of respect. He looked around the tables and saw how faces throughout the room turned their way, then looked away. Checking on her. Watching him carefully. They were *protecting* her. They were protecting *her*.

He asked, "The folks here are friends of yours?"

"I was born and raised in the area of Marseille called Le Panier. You have heard of it?"

"The Basket, sure, Pierre told me how the Germans tore it down."

"Walk one block and you can see the destruction for yourself. Many of these people you see here were scattered to the wind. Now that the war is over, they shall come back and rebuild. This cafe and the restaurant next door are gathering places."

Her face was a remarkable mixture of fragility and strength. Every feature was drawn as with a chisel, clear and distinct. Yet there was a delicacy to her, as though the sorrow in her voice and her eyes could overwhelm her at any moment.

"My father was a fisherman. His family had lived in Le Panier since the Middle Ages. My mother was Moroccan. From a desert tribe. She was sent to Tangiers to study, a great rarity in her day, but she was a beauty even at a young age and the apple of her father's eye. She yearned to know the world beyond the desert, and her father could not refuse her anything."

Jake nodded as the barkeeper set a tiny cup down in front of him, then demanded, "Why are you telling me this?"

"They met when my father began traveling to Morocco on smuggling runs after the First War," she went on, ignoring his question. "After they married, she returned with him to a little fisherman's cottage by the Bay of Marseille and filled it with books and songs and light and laughter. We learned the English language together, my mother and I. She loved learning for learning's sake. They both died in the first year of this war, when an epidemic swept through the city and there were no medicines." Jasmyn raised her gaze from her own cup. "So we share a sorrow, you and I."

Jake could not believe he was hearing this. "Pierre has been telling the whole city about my folks?"

"No," she replied quietly. "Only his mother."

"You still see his mother?"

"Every week," she replied, her gaze steady. "Sometimes every day."

"This is crazy," Jake muttered. "You ought to be talking with Pierre, not me."

"You know that is not possible," she said, pain blooming in her eyes like dark flowers. "Tell me, Colonel Burnes—"

"Jake."

"Jake, then. How is Pierre?"

His answer was halted by the veil that drew back from her face to reveal a naked, aching hunger. He forced himself to reply, "He misses you."

"Yes? You are sure?"

"It's hard for him to even mention your name." Jake wondered whether it was right for him to be saying this, yet something drew him on. Perhaps just the desperation with which she drank in his words, or perhaps something more. "He says he will never be able to love again."

A single tear escaped the jade-green eye and trickled unnoticed down her cheek. "Another thing which we hold in common," she said, her voice a throaty whisper.

Jake felt seared by the pain he saw and the pain he had seen in his own friend's face. "Why did you do it? Why did you betray him?"

"Betray," she repeated as another tear escaped. "Have you ever faced an impossible choice, Jake?"

"I'm not sure—"

"Have you ever seen the only way to save what is most precious to you is by destroying all that you hold dear?"

"No," Jake said, for some reason shaken to his very core by the fragile power of Jasmyn's words.

"Pray that it never comes, Colonel Jake Burnes. Pray that you are never seared by the flames of impossible choices." Jasmyn rose to her feet by pushing upon the table with both hands. Then she leaned over and spoke intently. "There are others who have been asking about Patrique. Evil men with evil intent. They were among the smugglers. But if you speak with them, take great care."

Jake started to his feet, but was stilled by the motion of one slender hand. He asked, "When was this?"

"Two months ago, and then again the week before last. I know nothing more, except that one man bears a scar from forehead to chin and another is called Jacques. And also that you must watch your back if you search among the smugglers."

She looked down at him a long moment, with a gaze that was tormenting to behold. "Take care of my Pierre," she said quietly, then turned away.

Jake watched her slow passage through the cafe. As she passed each table, many people rose from their seats and gave little half bows in her direction. She walked with head held high, acknowledging none of it. A trio of men at the bar turned and lifted glasses in her direction, murmuring a salute that Jake could not understand. The barkeeper hustled out from his station, wiped hands on his apron, and opened the door with a bow. Jasmyn raised the hood up and over her beautiful face, gently touched the barkeeper's hand, then stepped into the night.

Chapter Five

*J*AKE WAS ALREADY downstairs and seated at the kitchen table when Madame Servais appeared on her way to morning Mass. She smiled and wished him *bonjour*, then placed her hands together and raised them to the side of her face—did he sleep well?

Jake seesawed a hand. Not so well.

Bright, birdlike eyes peered closely, then the old lady spoke the single word, "Jasmyn?"

Reluctantly Jake nodded yes. He remained troubled by their encounter.

"Ah, oui. Jasmyn." She sighed the words, then happened to notice the little volume that Jake half hid with his hands. She peered around his fingers, showed widening eyes, and asked, "La Bible?"

Jake lifted his hands. Although he had discovered no answers to the many questions scurrying about his head, he still found comfort in his morning routine.

They both started at the sound of another tread descending the stairs. Madame Servais motioned with one finger to her lips, shook her head, then pointed to her heart. Jake understood. He should not mention Jasmyn to Pierre's father because of his bad heart.

The look in her dark eyes deepened and she said the single word, "Pierre." Then she shook her head once more and again pointed to her heart.

Jake sighed agreement as Madame Servais turned to her husband. So many secrets entrusted to him. So many questions without answers.

He exchanged greetings with the old man, then accepted the look of approval when his wife pointed out the small New Testament Jake had been reading. Madame Servais turned back to Jake and motioned an invitation for him to join them for Mass. Jake thought it over and decided to accept. Perhaps the answers would come to him in church.

He was surprised by the number of people entering the church for early Mass. Almost every seat was taken. Jake followed Pierre's parents up to what was undoubtedly their customary pew. People slid over to make room for him, then offered little seated bows of welcome.

The church was built of ancient dressed stone. Small alcoves held narrow stained-glass windows, statues, paintings, and row upon row of candles. The people were of every age and description, from local farmers to stern-faced dignitaries in shiny dark suits. Jake followed their lead, standing and sitting and kneeling, understanding nothing, content to listen as the refrains echoed about his head.

He tried to pray, but the confusion only seemed to grow as he sat isolated by his lack of comprehension. Sally, his own future, his friend's distress, Patrique, Jasmyn, Lilliana's rumors—he did not even know where to begin. He began with a simple prayer for guidance and felt as though the words bounced about his own internal inadequacy. So he stopped praying and sat in silence.

It was not until he was leaving the church that Jake noticed a change. He stepped from the ancient dimness with its cloying scent of incense to be greeted by the sun cresting the buildings across the square. A brilliant ray of light shot over the rooftops and almost blinded him. In that instant came a sense of illumination, of answer. He could not explain why, not even how he could be so sure that here was a message intended for him. But he knew. He was being guided. There was a purpose to it all.

Jake walked back home, slowing his pace to match those of Pierre's parents, and knew peace. He was not alone.

"You say someone approached you last night?"

"Just after I left the restaurant," Jake agreed.

"You're sure you've told me everything they said?"

"I'm sure. It wasn't much."

"Enough," Pierre replied, pedaling alongside Jake on the now-familiar road into Marseille. "It appears, my friend, that one of our little seeds has sprouted."

"You know where to go?"

"The smugglers are a clannish lot," Pierre replied. "They stick to their own cafes, their own streets."

"I had the impression that just about everybody here is on the fiddle."

"There is a difference between a fisherman who smuggled a load of weapons for the Resistance and another who lives from nothing else. Many people barter on the black market, selling chickens they have failed to register or butter from a cow hidden far from home. Such things are a way of life for us now. But with the smugglers it is different. War or no war, shortages or not, they would do nothing else."

"You know them?"

"Not well. I know where to look because my uncle knew them. All fishermen do. And Patrique used them from time to time for smuggling people."

Many of the people they passed were pitifully thin, especially the children. Young people sprouted from old clothes that fit their bodies only because they had not grown out as well as up. The men wore dark suits and hats or berets, the women simple print dresses and coats. All their clothes bore multiple repairs; all were burnished by age and wear.

And yet the people of this town remained erect. Proud. Confident. Determined. Jake wondered if he would have noticed it as strongly had he not just arrived from a defeated nation. Here, unlike Germany, there was no air of pervading dejection. Here there was hope.

They stopped as they crested the final ridge and the sparkling blue of the Mediterranean stretched out before them. Pierre asked, "What did he look like?"

"Who?"

"The man who spoke to you in the night."

"It was a woman," Jake said, wiping his brow as the sun rose higher in a cloudless sky. The previous night's chill had proved as fleeting as a bad dream.

"You're sure?"

"The street was very dark," Jake hedged, wishing he could just speak the truth and get it over with. "But I'm pretty sure. Small, slender, a hood over the face."

Pierre mulled that one over, then decided, "I want to go back there first and ask around. Perhaps someone else saw something more."

Jake shrugged as though it was the least of his concerns. If somebody talked, he would be happy. He hated this subterfuge. "You're the boss."

Pierre grasped his handlebars and pushed off. When Jake was alongside and coasting downhill, Pierre said, "Still I wonder why the woman came to you, and not me."

"Maybe she was afraid," Jake said.

Pierre picked up speed and called out over his shoulder, "Why would any woman be afraid of me?"

As they entered the crowded market area, Jake felt himself lifted and carried along by the general sense of contagious excitement. The air was charged with rediscovery. Still, there were ruins and want and decay and loss. Yet the people seemed to draw hope from this very hopelessness. They were seized by a wild spirit of reconstruction. They were free of the fascists' grip. The blindfold was off. What they saw was painful, yes, but at least they *saw*.

Jake balanced his bicycle outside the cafe and waited by the side wall while Pierre popped into numerous doorways and asked his questions. The cafe's barkeeper came out to clean the two rusted roadside tables and set chairs in place. He ignored Jake completely.

Jake turned his face to the sun. The roofs of the surrounding buildings were steep-pitched and clay-tiled. The
walls were mostly of dressed stone. The roads were dusty
clay or crumbling asphalt or bricks smoothed to glassy
roundness by decades of hard use. Even in the middle of the
city, the air was sweet with awakening springtime. The sky
was an open, aching blue. Jake could not get enough of the
air, the sky, the scent of sea.

Eventually Pierre returned, his face creased with
thought. "All right. We leave our bikes here and go on by
foot."

"No luck?"

Pierre hesitated. "I have the feeling . . ."

"What?"

Pierre struggled with words that made no sense even to
him. "I have the feeling that they are all waiting."

"Who?"

"My friends. The homecoming celebration is over, or so
it seems today, and now they are waiting. All of them.
Everyone I knew and some I didn't. Watching me and waiting."

"Waiting for what?"

"This is what confuses me most," Pierre replied. "It is as
though they think I already know."

"You realize," Jake pointed out, "that what you're saying
makes no sense at all."

"They are waiting," Pierre insisted. "I felt it at home this
morning as well, but did not think of it at the time. They
give me only half a greeting. Half a welcome. The other
half they hold in reserve."

Jake thought of the way Jasmyn had been bowed from the
cafe the night before and said nothing.

Pierre started forward. "Come. Let us see if the smugglers can make more sense than my friends."

Their way paralleled the harbor. Two streets farther
along, the cramped orderliness gave way to ruin. The
dwellings had been flattened as with a giant's hand. Streets
were buried under a field of rubble. A few chimneys rose in
mournful monument to what once was. In the distance, a

pair of buildings stood isolated and naked, the only surviving structures in the vast acreage of desolation.

Grimly Pierre surveyed the specter, then said simply, "Le Panier."

Something tugged at Jake, a thought that remained only half-formed. "And you say nobody was hurt when the Nazis did this?"

"A mystery, yes?" Pierre turned and started down the lane bordering the destruction. "I must ask my friends how that came to pass."

The lane meandered along the brink of devastation. The buildings lining its right side looked out over a vast field of dusty stone and sorrow. Pierre stopped in front of a glass door and said, "I wish we were armed."

Jake glanced at the utterly silent glass-fronted shop. Overhead were the vestiges of a name painted long ago, now so covered in dust and time that it was illegible. "We're going in there?"

"We must." Pierre reached for the door. "Full alert, my friend. Watch both our backs."

They entered a narrow cafe, and were enveloped in gloom.

The pair of cramped windows flanking the door were so coated in grime that little light could enter, and the cafe had no other illumination. The patrons stood cloaked in shadows. Jake felt unseen eyes fasten upon him as he stepped through the doorway.

Pierre moved up to the bar and gave a quiet salutation. The barkeeper responded with stony silence. As Jake's eyes adjusted to the poor light, he saw a man slip through a back passage and disappear from sight. His mind shouted a warning.

Pierre seemed utterly unaware of the silent hostility that gripped the room. He leaned against the bar, calmly pointed to a bottle behind the barkeeper's head, and spoke with casual politeness. Jake sidled over to a spot next to the window, from which he could watch the whole room.

The barkeeper lifted down a bottle and poured out a measure. His eyes did not leave Pierre's face. Pierre lifted the glass and offered the blank-faced man a toast. Then he took a sip, set down the glass, and spoke a name.

The silence was taut as a scream.

Pierre took another sip. His hands were as steady as his gaze.

"So, the famous captain finally comes to see his brother's old mate," boomed a guttural voice from down the passage, "and brings an American officer to keep him company."

"Major," Pierre corrected, his eyes still on the barkeeper.

"Captain, major, what is a little more gold braid between friends?" A great mountain of a man appeared in the hallway. He was not simply tall. He was huge in every way. A vast frame was covered in so many layers of fat that he had to turn sideways in order to pass through the doorway. "It is not often that an officer of the law dare enter these portals. Not even one who has a great American hero to guard the exit."

"Colonel Jake Burnes," Pierre murmured, remaining where he was. "May I introduce Abdul Hassad, smuggler king."

"Yes, one who needs no ribbons to gain the fear and respect of his fellow man." The man lumbered across the room to stand alongside Pierre. "By Mohammed's beard, if you did not wear the uniform, I would swear I stood before your brother."

"The same brother who brings me here," Pierre replied.

A slight thrill of movement coursed through the room. Jake watched the room and wished for a gun, a platoon, and another pair of eyes. The huge man's gaze narrowed slightly. "You have news?"

"Rumors only," Pierre replied. "But enough to want to know what you know."

"What I know," Abdul Hassad rumbled. Despite the room's closeness, he wore a voluminous navy duffle coat over shapeless trousers and boots so large that one would have held both of Jake's feet with room to spare. "As you say, rumors only."

"I hear that you know something more," Pierre said.

"You hear?" The deep chuckle carried no mirth. "Then whoever speaks of my affairs has seen his last sunrise."

"Tell me what you know," Pierre said, his voice stony cold.

Dark eyes flickered in the barkeeper's direction, then returned to Pierre. "What I know is yours, Major Servais. For a price."

With subtle ease the barkeeper flicked the towel off his shoulder and began polishing the bar. His other hand drifted down below the counter. Instantly Jake vaulted over the bar and locked one arm about the barkeeper's neck while he seized the unseen hand in an iron grip. The man struggled, but his strength was no match for Jake's. Tables and chairs crashed as men about the room leapt to their feet. Jake squeezed until the man yelped in pain, then wrenched the man's hand out and up, revealing a revolver which was now pointed directly at Abdul Hassad's massive chest.

The huge man barked out a command, and the room froze. Dark eyes held Jake with a baleful glare, and watched as Jake forced the gun out of the barkeeper's grasp and into his own.

Pierre had not moved. He took another sip from his glass and repeated, "Tell me what you know."

His eyes still flickering from Jake to the gun and back again, the smuggler replied, "Others have been asking questions."

Pierre nodded as though expecting nothing else and said calmly, "Jacques and the scarred man."

Dark eyes blazed with fury. "Tell me who has spoken," Abdul Hassad snarled. "By the Prophet's beard, he will dine upon his own tongue."

"Where were they from?" Pierre demanded. "Morocco?"

Abdul Hassad ground his teeth in silence. The barkeeper tried to struggle, and Jake screwed up his arm lock until the man squealed in pain. The greasy little barkeeper smelled of old sweat and cheap tobacco and new fear. Jake raised the gun until it was focused directly into Abdul Hassad's glowering eyes.

"Marrakesh," the huge man conceded.

Pierre nodded at the news. "Did they speak of a traitor?"

A snarl from across the room was cut off by a roared command from Abdul Hassad. "Get out while your legs can still carry you," he growled at Pierre.

"What about Gibraltar?" Pierre pressed.

"I have said all that is to be said," the huge man muttered.

Pierre glanced toward Jake and motioned his head toward the door. Dragging the barkeeper along with him, Jake circled the bar, the gun never leaving Abdul Hassad's face. Pierre opened the door, waited for Jake to exit, then said to the huge man, "You have been most helpful."

The barkeeper struggled harder when Jake started down the sidewalk without releasing him. Jake tightened the choke hold and picked up the pace. The barkeeper wrapped both hands around Jake's arm and shuffled along on legs that could scarcely hold him up. His two-day stubble burned Jake's forearm like sandpaper.

Pierre stuck his face up close to the man's and snarled words in French. Then to Jake he said, "Keep walking toward the harbor."

"No problem," Jake said. "Take the gun, will you? I'll be able to move faster."

Pierre accepted the gun from Jake's grasp and snarled something more to the whimpering barkeeper. Jake asked, "Are they behind us?"

Pierre glanced back. "No. It is not their way. They will wait until dark and try to strike us in the back."

"Sounds noble." Jake shook the man hard as fingers tried to pry his arm loose. "Then why are we bothering with this guy?"

"I want to get him out of sight. Down here."

They turned down a narrow, filth-strewn alley that emptied directly into the bay. When the water came into view, the barkeeper wailed and struggled anew.

"Wait," Pierre said. When they stopped he stuck his face within inches of the barkeeper's and roared. The man whimpered a reply. Another angry command. The bar-keeper spewed a fear-filled response.

Pierre took a step back, his face filled with cold loathing. "Let him go."

The man dropped to all fours, coughed and rubbed his neck, then struggled to his feet. With one vengeful glance back at Jake, he turned and fled down the alley.

"What did you learn?"

"The hunters were indeed here," Pierre replied, his eyes upon the now-empty alley. "They have traveled on to Gibraltar."

Chapter Six

*J*AKE RETURNED TO Mass the next morning, trying hard not to hope for a repeat of the previous day's revelation. Still, when he remained untouched by the liturgy, he could not help but feel disappointment.

After the service, Pierre's mother motioned for him to remain behind while her husband exited the church. A familiar figure rose from one of the side alcoves and approached. Despite his surprise, Jake noticed the respectful greetings and formal half bows with which many people greeted Jasmyn. Madame Servais smiled sadly at the dark beauty, patted Jake's arm, and joined her husband outside the church.

Jake followed Jasmyn back to the side alcove. When they were seated and alone, she asked him quietly, "Do you believe in God, Colonel Burnes?"

"That's a strange question to hear in this place," he replied. "And the name is Jake."

"I come here to see Pierre's mother," she said, "and to know a moment's peace. That is such a hard thing to find in my life that I dare not doubt or question or search too deeply."

As gentle as the beat of dove's wings, as powerful as the rain, Jake felt a gift of words descend into his mind and heart. In the instant of receiving, he knew that by sharing the words he could make the Invisible real. "Perhaps if you dared to search and question, the peace would not be so fleeting."

"I see you have answered my question," she said softly.

But the giving was not yet complete. "True peace carries with it the gifts of healing and of forgiveness. Not for an instant, but for a lifetime."

She was silent for a time, then asked, "And what if the forgiveness I seek is not from God? What if I pray to be forgiven by one who can never do so?"

Jake waited, but further words did not come. Instead, his heart filled with a silent compassion. For her, for Pierre, for a world awakening from the tragedy of war. He tried to make the feeling live for her as well by giving words of his own. "Then I will pray for you both."

"I wonder if Pierre understands," she said softly, "just how special a friend you truly are."

To that Jake had no reply.

They sat in shared stillness for a moment until she asked, "I have heard of your conflict with the smugglers yesterday."

"How?"

She waved it aside. "I will speak to friends. Pierre's family will be guarded against attack. Can you tell him that?"

"I don't see how," Jake replied. "Not without telling him about you and—"

She interrupted him with, "What will you do now?"

Jake sighed acceptance of her refusal. "We have heard from the smugglers that the hunters have traveled on to Gibraltar. Pierre wants to leave tonight on the train for Madrid, and travel on from there as swiftly as we can."

She thought for a moment, then decided. "I shall take a compartment well away from yours."

"How?" Jake looked down on her. "From the sound of things, unless you have a military pass, seats on the international trains are booked solid for months."

She rose to her feet. "I have very few contacts in Gibraltar, but perhaps another pair of eyes and ears will be of help. And if your way leads from there to Morocco, I will be able to do more for Pierre."

"You still love him," Jake said quietly.

"Love?" Sorrow filled every pore of her being. "Last night I dreamed of holding his hand once again. I knew contentment for the first time in years. As I sat there, I looked down at the hands in my lap, and I could not tell which fingers were my own."

"Pierre," Jake said, then stopped. He was going to say, Pierre is a lucky guy, but caught himself just in time.

"Pierre," she sighed, and reached out one hand to steady herself upon the back of the pew. "Pierre was more than a part of me. He was all of me."

"Then why—"

"If I hear of something, I will search you out," she said, and raised the hood to veil herself once again. "The shadows have become my friends, Colonel Burnes. There is a chance that I can find what remains hidden to you."

Chapter Seven

*B*EYOND THE CERBÈRE border station, the track changed gauge. All passengers alighted and carried their bags through customs before boarding the Spanish train. The French customs' search was perfunctory. The Spaniards' inspection was anything but. Fascist soldiers in gleaming black leather and funny feathered caps watched over the scowling customs officers. Above them all hung a brooding portrait of General Francisco Franco, undisputed leader of fascist Spain.

The mountainous terrain was far more arid on the Spanish side of the Pyrenees. Beyond Barcelona they entered the vast plains of the Spanish heartland, which baked under a sun already eager for another summer.

At Madrid, before boarding the Gibraltar-bound train, Pierre and Jake scoured the area for food. Like many of the Spanish towns through which their train had passed, Madrid was a patchwork of normalcy and war-torn destruction. For several blocks they saw little indication that the country had recently suffered through a horrific civil war. Then scars emerged, destruction so severe Jake doubted if the country could ever recover.

The streets near the city's central station were so jammed with people it was almost possible for Jake to lift his feet and be carried along. Police and black-belted military were everywhere. The atmosphere was tensely unsettling, yet without any clear indication that anything was wrong. The entire region held a sense of forced gaiety, like the laughter heard at a wake.

There was little automobile traffic. Jake saw a number of army transports, a few ancient cars hung together with rust and baling wire, the occasional overloaded truck, sporadic tired and wheezy buses. But in truth the streets belonged to the pedestrians and the bicyclists and the soldiers.

There was little food to be had until Jake entered an apparently empty store and pulled out American dollars. Then everything was laid out before him—flagons of wine, a huge pie-shaped hunk of cheese, smoked beef, dried tomatoes, the season's first fruits, bread still warm from the oven. What the shopkeeper himself did not have, he scurried out and obtained from his neighbors. Pierre and Jake filled two sacks, in case provisions were scarce in Gibraltar, and hurried back.

As they entered the station, Pierre confessed, "I thought I would be leaving a great burden behind in Marseille, but I find I carry it with me still."

Jake swerved around a porter struggling to maneuver a bulky wheeled wagon through the crowds. "Why's that?"

"I have been so afraid," Pierre said.

The words sounded so alien, coming as they did from Pierre's mouth, that Jake had no idea what to say except, "You?"

"All the while that we were in Marseille. Strange, yes?" Pierre's smile meant nothing. "Every time we went into town, I was filled with terror at the thought that this street, this cafe, this turning, would reveal her."

"Jasmyn," Jake said, hating the subterfuge more than ever. It was there on his tongue to say that she was here, on the train, to push Pierre to go and find her, speak with her, make peace with her. But he could not. Something held him back. Amid the clamor of the Madrid station came a calm understanding that they themselves would have to choose their own time, their own way.

"So often I imagined seeing her," Pierre went on, his eyes pained by the vision of what only he could see. "My mind would become filled with the sight of her, and I would be so terrified I could scarcely go forward. There she would be, walking toward me, looking as only she could look. And the thought alone would be enough to almost shatter my world. Break it into a million pieces that would never fit together ever again."

"You should have sought her out," Jake said quietly.

"You think so?" Pierre turned sorrowful eyes toward him.

"You can't go through the rest of your life like this."

To his surprise, Pierre did not object. Instead, he set down his sack like an old man releasing a too-heavy burden. Slowly he straightened and said, "There was a voice in my heart which said the same. But my mind would scream, what if I did and it destroyed me?"

"It's a risk you need to take," Jake said, wondering at the strength that let him say such things with such confidence.

"You speak as though it is still a possibility," Pierre said. "Do you think I should give up this search for my brother? Return to Marseille and seek her out? Is that what you are saying?"

There in a silent thunderbolt of power came the answer. Unbidden, unexpected, yet in his heart to be spoken, given, shared with one in need. "You don't need to see her to forgive her," Jake replied.

The words seemed to strip Pierre bare. "Forgive," he said.

"It's the only way you will ever leave the burden behind," Jake said, knowing it was the truth, yet wondering still.

"You know what she did," Pierre protested.

"I know," Jake said.

"Then how can you speak of such a thing?"

"Because I want to see you healed," Jake said. "If you punish her, you punish yourself." As suddenly as the power had arrived, it departed, leaving him embarrassed for having spoken at all. He hefted his sack and walked away. "Let's get on board."

Once the train was under way, he left Pierre in their compartment and maneuvered down the jammed hall to the back of the railcar. A narrow door opened onto a gangway connecting to the next car. The passage was metal floored and open to the wind and the heat and the train's rattling roar. Jake stood with two other young men and swayed in rhythm with the train. It was far too noisy for conversation. The engine's smoke blew past in great swirling puffs, except on the slower curves, when it forced its way into the gangway and made breathing difficult. The two other men soon had enough and returned to the train's more protected interior.

Jake stared out over the brilliantly lit Spanish landscape and felt ashamed for having spoken with such authority. Now that it was over, he wondered how he could ever have felt so sure of anything. Especially faith. Even more, how faith could be applied to someone else's problems. First Jasmyn at the church, and now Pierre. Spouting off answers as though he knew everything, even though he had more questions than answers about his own life. Jake stared at the earth rushing by just below his feet and shook his head. It did not make any sense at all.

Words chanted through his brain in time to the train's rhythmic rattle. Sally is gone. Sally is gone. Jake rubbed his face, tried to squeeze silence in through his temples. How could he give advice about relationships when his own love life was in shambles? Sally is gone. Sally is gone. Sally is gone.

Chapter Eight

*A*T THE FRONTIER between Spain and Gibraltar, Jake was jerked upright by the sight of an officer in American naval whites passing their compartment. The man was clearly as surprised as Jake to see a fellow American, for he was already out of sight before the facts clicked into place. He backpedaled, inspected Jake with widening eyes, then pushed open the compartment door. "Afternoon, Colonel."

Jake was on his feet. "Commander. Care to join us?"

"Don't mind if I do. Seats are as scarce as hen's teeth on this train." He cast a glance at Jake's medals, then said, "Don't believe I've seen you around here before."

"Official leave. First time in these parts. Like to introduce Major Pierre Servais, commander of the French garrison at Badenburg."

"Major." He nodded toward Pierre, then offered Jake his hand. "Harry Teaves. Adjunct to the supply depot on Gibraltar."

"Jake Burnes. I run the Karlsruhe base."

Commander Teaves seated himself, asked, "So what brings you fellows to Gibraltar?"

Jake cast a glance Pierre's way. The Frenchman's mobile features furrowed momentarily before he gave Jake a single nod. Jake turned back to Teaves. "It's a long story, Commander. Might take awhile."

"We've got half an hour before we arrive. If the train's on time, which it hasn't been since sometime last century."

Jake recounted their search, beginning with Lilliana's disclosure. Harry Teaves proved to have two of the most expressive eyebrows Jake had ever come across. By the time Jake finished his explanation, the eyebrows had crawled up so high they were almost touching his hairline.

"That's some tale," Commander Teaves said, looking from one to the other. "So you think maybe there are a couple of thugs hunting your brother in Gibraltar?"

"We do not even know if my brother is alive," Pierre replied. "But the barkeeper in Marseille did say they were coming here."

"Got any description?"

"Again, we're not sure, but they might be the same people I was warned against," Jake replied.

"By the woman who just happens to find you in the middle of the night, did I get that one straight?" Teaves shook his head. "Lemme tell you. If you two weren't about the soberest looking officers I'd ever met, with a string of ribbons suggesting you're on the up and up, I'd say it was time to pop you in the loony bin."

"I realize the chances are long," Pierre said. "But I must at least try to check this out."

The commander nodded as he mulled it over, then said to Jake, "Mind if I ask what's in it for you, Colonel?"

"Pierre is a good friend," Jake said, then after a struggle he went on. "I lost my own brother at Normandy. If it was Jeff we were talking about here, I'd travel to hell and back on the breath of a chance."

"Not me," Teaves replied conversationally. "My brother sat out the war in a cushy office, pushing papers for the war effort. We never got along."

"You saw action?" Pierre asked.

"Little bit. Here and there. Joined up in '41. Got to see some too-hot Pacific islands I don't ever want to visit, not ever again." He inspected Pierre. "You?"

"North Africa. Then the push through Belgium."

"Heard it was nip and tuck there for a while."

"As you say," Pierre replied, "I have no desire to retrace my steps."

"What about you, Colonel?"

"The name's Jake. I spent more time than I wanted walking Italian back roads."

"Between the three of us, we've got just about the whole world covered," Teaves said. "Sounds like a pretty good reason to offer my help. That and the fact that you've told me the biggest whopper I've heard since getting assigned to shore duty."

"It's the truth," Pierre declared. "All of it."

"It better be," Teaves said, his tone easy. "One thing I discovered while dodging incoming shells was life's too short to go goose hunting unless there's a goose to be caught."

Even in its tatty post-war state, Gibraltar was a monument to British imperialism. The official buildings were strong and sturdy as the cliffs towering overhead. Porticoes were supported by great pillars atop flights of steps fifty feet wide. Sweeping parade grounds of immaculate green were bordered by flowers and flagpoles. The air was a strange mixture of Spanish spice and British formality. Uniforms were everywhere.

Teaves led them to the main British depot. Beyond endless rows of squat warehouses stretched the combined might of the Allied navy. The war-gray battleships were too numerous to count. Flags fluttered in the strong sea breeze. Klaxons sounded their whoop-whoop in a continual shout of comings and goings. Tugs worked frantically to maneuver the great warships to and from anchor.

He left them at the main gates and returned a quarter hour later to announce, "Admiral Bingham of the Royal Navy wants to check you out."

As they followed him down the rank of weary buildings, Jake asked, "How do we handle it?"

"Straight as an arrow. Bingham is rumored to keep a set of bone-handled skinning knives for people who waste his time. I've been careful not to find out if it's true."

They were ushered into a room dominated by a crusty old warrior with a manner as clipped as his moustache. "Teaves reports you are here on unofficial business."

"Strictly, sir," Jake agreed, remaining at rigid attention.

"May I be so bold as to see your papers?"

Together he and Pierre handed over their leave and travel documents. The admiral inspected them carefully before announcing, "They appear to be in order." He raised his eyes. "Very well. I'm listening."

Jake went through their story much more concisely with the admiral. When he was through, Bingham inspected them thoughtfully for a moment, then declared, "I am in full agreement with Commander Teaves. Yours is an admirable quest. Nasty business, this destruction of families. How can I help?"

Jake was caught flat-footed. "To be honest, sir, I don't have any idea. This was the last thing we expected."

"Well, if something arises, don't hesitate to contact me through Teaves here." He looked at the commander. "I assume you were going to assign them berths."

"With your permission, sir."

"See to it." He turned back to Jake. "The governor is giving a little do this evening. Seven sharp. Did you bring a dress kit?"

"Yessir."

"Bound to be a bit rumpled after your travels. I'll have my aide stop by and give your kit a good pressing and polishing."

"That won't—" Jake was stopped by the commander's discreet cough. He immediately changed tack. "That's most kind, sir. Thank you."

"Right. Until seven then."

When they were back outside, Jake and Pierre released a joint sigh. "I didn't realize what a chance you were taking," Jake said, "bringing us in like that."

"We are in your debt," Pierre agreed.

"Now that's what I like to hear," Teaves said cheerfully. "Nothing like a little gratitude to set the day straight. Let's see you to your quarters, then I'll have to get to work. As you can see, Bingham keeps this place running like a top."

"The whole of Gibraltar is a fortress town," Teaves told them. "Its population has lived under the shadow of attack for over a thousand years."

A gentle spring dusk painted Main Street with swatches of gay pastels. The thoroughfare was crowded with people taking their traditional evening stroll. Jake spotted uniforms from half a dozen different nations.

Commander Teaves kept up a running commentary as they walked toward the Governor's House. Above their heads, the Rock was a timeless gray bastion that dominated the peninsula. Its peak remained enshrouded in a faint veil made multicolored by the setting sun. The high ridge stretched out like the bleached backbone of some great prehistoric beast.

"Gibraltar was one of the two ancient pillars of Hercules," Harry Teaves explained, "and has been fought over since the dawn of history. Whoever controls Gibraltar controls entry into the Mediterranean. Modern Gibraltan history began with its Moorish capture in the eighth century. Since then it has belonged to the Spanish, the Portuguese, and now the British for the past two hundred years."

At the great iron gates flanking the Governor's House, Teaves stopped before two honor guards in burnished helmets and presented their names. "Don't know if you'll find anything of use here," he said, "but contacts like these can never hurt."

"We are truly grateful," Pierre replied solemnly and followed Teaves through the semitropical garden surrounding the palace.

"I'll have to leave you to your own devices for a while," Teaves said as they mounted the great steps. "This is my chance to bend the ear of the ones in power. Come find me if there's anything you need. I'll join you as soon as I can."

The British High Commissioner's residence was a former Franciscan convent. Its formal gardens overlooked a cream-colored palace of Spanish-Moorish design.

Jake and Pierre repeated their names to the majordomo, heard themselves announced as they entered the reception line, and allowed themselves to be passed down from hand to hand. Then they were released into the crowd.

The great reception hall was lit by chandeliers holding hundreds of flickering gas flames. The light was caught and reflected by the medals and gold braid and shining dress scabbards worn by many of the officers, as well as by the king's ransom of jewelry worn by many of the women. Yet no amount of refined dress could mask the fact that most of the people here looked exhausted.

Jake moved from group to group, smiling and bowing and shaking hands. Inwardly he reflected that almost everyone looked as though they had been old all their lives.

"Colonel Burnes," a voice said from beside him, and instinctively Jake stiffened. "Good of you to join us."

"Nice of you to invite us, Admiral Bingham," Jake replied.

"Not at all, not at all." Bingham walked up and said, "Perhaps you would allow me to introduce you to an old friend."

A husky voice behind Jake said, "What an utterly dastardly thing to say about a lady."

Admiral Bingham looked behind Jake and smiled, a feat Jake would not have thought possible. "Now, Millicent, you know exactly what I meant."

"That does not excuse your ill manners." A diminutive woman of extremely advanced years tottered into view and looked up at Jake. "Why is it, sir, that you Yanks insist on growing your men so overly tall?"

"Colonel Burnes, allow me to present Lady Millicent Haskins, the grande dame of Gibraltar society."

"Nonsense. I am simply an old busybody who does not have the good sense to lie down and give up the ghost, as most people around here wish I would."

"None of that." Admiral Bingham's bark was softened by his second smile of the evening. "We would all be positively lost without you."

"Very well, you are forgiven." She patted the admiral's arm. "Now, run along and let me wring this picture-perfect officer of all his gossip."

Admiral Bingham bowed and spun on his heel. Millicent Haskins then guided Jake toward an empty sofa by the side wall. "I do hope you will permit me to sit down, Colonel. One of the greatest afflictions of old age is the inability to remain comfortable upon my feet for more than a few moments at a time."

"I feel that way already," Jake replied, "and you must have a good ten years on me."

Age-spotted cheeks dimpled with a smile. "Why, how gallant." She eased herself down. "Ah, that is much better. Now then, Colonel. Tell me about this quest of yours."

"It is my friend's really." Swiftly Jake recounted his tale. Then he allowed himself to be taken back through the story in far greater detail.

When he finished to his companion's satisfaction, she was silent a moment, then said, "I am not sure how much I can help you, Colonel. You see, I have only returned here to my homeland three months ago."

"You've been away?"

"We have all been away. In 1940, the entire civilian population of Gibraltar, some thirteen thousand people, was evacuated. The main reason was defense. The Rock was the key to passage into the Mediterranean, you see, and way had to be made for the incoming soldiers.

"First we went to French Morocco, but we were there scarcely a month before France fell. We were then shipped to England. It was only this past winter that we were permitted to return." She looked out over the swirling, sparkling crowd and smiled at the memory. "When the ship neared the strait and we first caught sight of the Rock, the feeling was indescribable. It was a dream come true. I had been so afraid that I would not live to see the day."

"From what I have seen of the place," Jake said, "your home is beautiful."

"Yes, it is. We are dominated by the sea and the mountain and the military. Either you love such an atmosphere or you leave."

"You certainly look at home here." Jake drifted into polite conversation. No matter how charming Lady Haskins might be, she did not appear to be the kind of person with connections to the local underworld.

Shrewd eyes showed awareness of his wandering attention. "Have you wondered, Colonel, why a member of the French Underground would seek to flee to territory firmly in British hands?"

Jake looked back down at the tiny woman and reflected that perhaps Admiral Bingham had been right in bringing them together after all. "No, I hadn't."

"I find that most intriguing." She thought a moment, then said, "Traitor. You are sure he used that word?"

"It's what the girl reported to us. She was absolutely positive about the message."

"Then hard as it may be for your French friend to accept," Millicent Haskins said, turning her bright gaze back toward Jake, "I think it would be wise to consider that the traitor is one of his own countrymen."

"There is much truth in what the old woman has said to you," Pierre said as they made their way back to naval quarters.

"Yeah, Millie Haskins is some lady," Commander Teaves said. "She's got the vision of an eagle. Sees right to the heart of an issue."

"You know her well?" Jake asked.

"Everyone knows Millie. She makes it a point of making everybody's business her own. Sort of considers all who live here as part of her extended family. The locals call her the Matron of Gibraltar."

"I have been troubled by Patrique's travel to Gibraltar without knowing why," Pierre went on. "Now I can see no other reason for it but this one."

Teaves skirted around a pair of quarreling curs. "Any idea who this traitor fellow might be?"

"None." Pierre hesitated, then said, "Perhaps it is because I do not wish to think too deeply."

"May be your only way of finding out who was behind your brother's disappearance," Teaves pointed out.

Jake was beginning to realize that the commander's easygoing voice was a velvet glove cloaking a steel-keen mind. "That makes very good sense."

"Just conjecture, but maybe the way to find your brother, or at least find out what happened to him, is to hunt down the hunters."

"If it was indeed a traitor," Pierre said to the night, "it would have to be someone who has something to hide *now*."

"I get you," Jake said. "Not something from the war. Nobody is going to chase across the Mediterranean to settle a wartime grudge. Not now."

"Somebody with something to hide," Teaves said. "Something big."

"Or somebody in a big position," Pierre mused.

"A turncoat," Jake suggested. "Played both sides of the fence during the war, and now he wants his secrets to stay good and buried."

From the far side of the road came the faintest of sounds, a gentle snicker of well-oiled metal upon metal. Yet for Jake the almost inaudible noise shouted loud across the years. Without an instant's thought his wartime reflexes had him down and flying with outstretched arms for his friends' legs. *"Down!"*

The wall that was now over their heads erupted with dust from a barrage of bullets. Before the machine gun's roar was silenced, Jake was rolling and crawling for the gutter.

The shadows from across the street emitted a faint curse, then the gunner aimed his weapon lower and traversed a second time. Jake pressed himself to the smelly, slippery stone of the shallow ditch and wished for a weapon of his own.

A shout from farther down the street. A scream from a window above their heads. The sound of running feet. The machine gun made a third swipe at the street fronting the gutter and at the wall above their heads. Dust and rock chips flew in every direction. Then silence.

As the footsteps and yelling approached, Jake risked raising his head. The smell of cordite hung heavy in the air. "Are you all right?"

Pierre rolled over and heaved himself up. "Fine. Commander?"

"All in order," Teaves said, emerging into view. "Other than a little shaken."

"And angry," Pierre added. "I have a distinct dislike for people who shoot in my direction."

Shutters overhead flew back, and a shotgun-bearing moustachioed man scowled down at them. "What's going on here?"

"I wish I knew," Teaves said to the street in general. "Did you see where they went?"

Jake pointed down the alley across from them just as the group of a dozen or so men, some in uniform, came racing up. "I think they were back in there." The men, jabbering in Spanish, turned and chased down the dark alley.

"You gentlemen all right?" demanded the man over their heads.

"Shaken," Jake said.

"And dirty," Teaves said, picking a bit of filth off the front of his dress whites. He glanced Jake's way. "Do you realize you're bleeding?"

Jake swiped at his face, and only when he saw the blood on his hand did he feel the sting. "Must have been hit by a flying rock."

Pierre inspected the cut, decided, "A flesh wound." He stepped back. "That is the second time you've saved my life since all this started."

"You don't say?" Teaves said, joining them. "When was the first?"

"A barkeeper pulled a pistol on me," Pierre replied, his eyes still on Jake. "My friend moved as fast then as now."

The crowd returned, dejected and angry. They exchanged shouted words with the man overhead, who glowered over his shotgun barrels, clearly wishing he could find somebody to shoot. He said to the trio, "They have found shells, nothing more."

"Let me have some," Teaves said. "Bingham will want to see them."

"You have to tell the admiral?" Jake said.

"He'll hear about it all by himself," Teaves replied. "News like this spreads by osmosis."

Someone in the crowd chattered to the man overhead, who translated, "Do you know who it was?"

"Brigands," Teaves replied, his eyes warning Jake.

"We saw nothing," Jake agreed.

The police arrived, took statements. The alley was searched a second time. Nothing. Weary, dirty, and bruised, the three men were finally permitted to return to base.

On their way back, Jake asked Teaves, "Why didn't you want me to say anything to them?"

"Just a hunch," the commander replied. "Thought it might be easier to track those guys if they don't know how much we know."

"The commander is correct." The light of a flickering street gas lamp showed Pierre's expressive face cast in a fierce scowl. "It is time, as you say, to hunt the hunters."

Chapter Nine

"*T*HIS WILL NOT DO, mister," Admiral Bingham barked. His anger was fierce enough to blister the air. "I will not permit officers under my command to be shot at!"

"Aye, aye, sir," Harry Teaves replied, his voice as laconic as ever.

Jake, Pierrc, and Teaves stood in the center of Bingham's office, while the admiral stalked the floor in front of them, arms lockcd behind his back. "You say you did not catch sight of the men?"

"We don't even know if it was more than one," Jake replied. "Sir."

"Have a seat, gentlemen." The trio slipped into three high-back chairs. "The bullets tell us nothing, I'm afraid. German make, but they fit any number of weapons. There's a glut of those on the black market just now. Remnants of war and all that."

Bingham stopped before Jake. "That was fast thinking on your part, Colonel."

"More like an automatic reaction, sir."

"Indeed. Your reactions served you well. You saw active duty, I take it."

"Mostly in Italy. But I am stationed in Germany now."

291

"Yes, so Commander Teaves informed me. Karlsruhe, do I have that right?"

"Yessir."

"I shall inform your superiors of this, Colonel." He resumed his pacing, forming the letter in his mind as he spoke. "They should know that your performance has saved the life of an American officer assigned to my depot."

"Ah—" Jake was stopped before he could start by another of Harry Teaves' throat-clearing exercises. "Thank you, sir."

"Don't mention it." Bingham turned to Pierre. "Would you happen to have a picture of your brother, Major?"

"Yessir. One I borrowed from my parents."

"Let me have it, please."

Pierre unbuttoned his side pocket and drew out a jagged-edged print. The admiral inspected it and gave a start. "I say. Identical twins."

"Yessir."

"Most remarkable. Has it occurred to you, Major, that the assailants might not have been after you at all?"

Pierre opened his mouth, shut it, tried a second time. "Now that you mention it—"

"Indeed." Bingham thrust the photograph at Teaves. "Assign a squad to show this around. They are to take their time, Commander. Stress in the strongest possible terms that they are to visit every bar, every hotel, every boarding-house, every back-room dive. Ask both after this man, and anyone else who might have been inquiring after him. I want no stone left unturned."

Teaves accepted the picture. "Aye, aye, sir."

"Shoot at one of my officers, will they?" Bingham fumed his way around his desk and back into his seat. "I'll have their guts for garters. All right, gentlemen. Dismissed."

As they left the garrison headquarters, a midshipman approached them. "Commander Teaves?"

"That's me."

"Message for you, sir."

Teaves unfolded the paper, read the few lines, and announced, "We've been summoned, gentlemen. It appears that Millie Haskins has need of our presence. And when that lady speaks, you better answer on the bounce."

The old woman lived in a stout colonial residence, one clearly built with solid confidence that the family would remain there for centuries to come. The house was almost buried under its ballast of bougainvillea. Great clusters of the rich purple flowers grew in such profusion that Jake was on the front stairs before he realized he was entering a deep porch and not the house proper. He spotted a pair of rainbow-tinted hummingbirds feeding delicately from the blossoms, then stooped and stepped into the perfumed shade.

Millicent Haskins sat enthroned on a high-back brocade chair. "Good morning, Commander. Hello, Colonel. So kind of you gentlemen to stop by. I hope I did not pull you away from anything important."

"Not at all, ma'am." Commander Teaves took her hand and bowed stiffly from the waist, but did not quite bring it to his lips. Millicent Haskins accepted the gesture as her due. Afraid that he might do something wrong, Jake simply accepted her hand and said, "I didn't have an opportunity to introduce my friend last night. This is Major Pierre Servais."

"Welcome to my humble abode, Major."

"Enchanté." Pierre bowed over her hand with the polish of a courtier. Millie flashed her eyes in reply, giving Jake the impression that she must have been a beauty in her day.

"Do sit down, gentlemen. Hodgewell, I'm sure the officers would like a glass of fresh lemonade."

"Very good, madam," replied a desiccated butler in formal black.

"And ask Lavinia to join us for a moment."

"Please don't trouble yourself on our account," Harry Teaves said.

"Nonsense. That is the pleasure of having servants. It permits one to go to great bother without rising." She glanced at the bandage on Jake's forehead. "I see you have been injured since our last encounter, Colonel."

"Nothing serious," Jake replied. "We had a little run-in last night."

"So I heard. From the sounds of things, you are all lucky to be alive."

"Luck had nothing to do with it," Teaves replied. "Jake here has the reaction of a leopard."

"You must tell me all about it." She looked over their heads. "Ah, Lavinia, excellent. Gentlemen, may I introduce the finest cook on the peninsula."

They stood and turned and found themselves facing an inscrutable woman of advancing years. Her hands were plump and strong and so chapped they looked bruised. Her steel-gray hair was pulled back into a tight bun. Her face was as chapped and puffy as her hands. Her eyes were hidden within deep folds, offering only brief glimmers of a shrewd gaze.

"Lavinia has a relative who operates a small restaurant for the locals up near the Rock. Upstairs he has rooms which he rents. He has had a pair of men staying with him now for over three weeks. Tell them what he said to you, please, dear."

"Bad men," Lavinia said, her English heavily accented. "One man has scar." She traced a line down the side of her face from forehead to neck.

Jake and Pierre exchanged glances. "Did they mention a name?"

"No name. But men speak French, little English. No Spanish. Not from here."

Pierre asked, "Why do you say they are bad?"

"Not speak with others. Have much money. Carry knives, maybe guns. Cousin not sure, no saw, smelled grease."

"Oil," Jake corrected quietly, suddenly chilled by the memory of that snickering sound. "Gun oil."

"Yes, so. Cousin know smell. He is hunter."

"You mentioned, did you not," Millicent Haskins pointed out to Jake, "that one of the men you are pursuing has a scar?"

"It's what we were told," Jake said. "We haven't seen either of them."

"Still," Millicent Haskins said, "perhaps it would be something worth investigating. Lavinia would be happy to take you to the establishment, wouldn't you, dear?"

"This is great stuff, Millie," Commander Teaves said, rising to his feet. "If you don't mind, we'll give you a rain check on the drinks."

"I'm sure Hodgewell will recover from the disappointment. Only do stop by and let me know what develops, won't you?"

Despite her age and size, Lavinia set a pace that had the men scrambling to keep up. As they left Main Street for smaller byways, Jake asked, "Should we stop off for reinforcements?"

"Time for that later," Commander Teaves replied. "Let's check this out for ourselves, make sure there's something to the rumor."

"No rumor," Lavinia huffed, and picked up the pace even further. She wore a flat, black reed hat held in place with a pair of enormous pins. Black lacquered cherries trembled with each substantial step. She gripped an enormous shiny black purse with both hands, holding it defiantly before her body like a battering ram. "No rumor. Is truth."

Teaves lowered his voice and finished, "Bingham is not the kind of man you want to bother with too many false alarms."

Their way took them ever farther from the prosperous central districts. They passed through a market square fronting two older residential areas. The buildings were seedy and sagging, with rusting ironwork and facades shedding paint. Yet the brisk sea air and bright sunlight graced the entire area with a cheerful, picturesque charm.

People used the most remarkable contraptions as vehicles. Bicycles had grown homemade side trolleys and rear

carts. Reinforced baby strollers served as all-purpose carriers. Horse-drawn hay wagons did duty as city buses.

There were smiles. Hunger, yes. Hardship, certainly.
Pain was etched deep into some of the faces. Yet everywhere there were smiles. Jake found himself searching
them out, hungering for the sense of being around people
who dared to be happy.

Their way took them directly beneath the Rock. The
gray behemoth dominated the horizon, rising from rich,
verdant growth at its base to stand exposed and proud,
splitting the sky, defying the elements as it had through
the ages. There at the base, ancient homes bordering the
untamed parkland bore evidence of a grander age.

The road took a final sharp turning, from which they
could see lines of newer military warehouses flanking what
appeared to be a great hole carved into the mountainside.

Lavinia halted just beyond the turning and pointed to
one of the old houses. "There. Go there."

Harry Teaves grunted at the sight of a mass of men milling about the dusty front yard. "What is that, our welcoming committee?"

"Don't know. Cousin and friends maybe. You go. I have
work." With that Lavinia settled her hat more firmly into
place, wheeled about, and stumped off.

"Some of them have clubs," Pierre said doubtfully.

"Maybe there's been some mistake," Jake suggested.

Teaves took a tentative step backward. "Why don't we
just—"

But someone in the group spotted them, and with a great
shout a number of men peeled off and hustled over. "Too
late," Jake said.

A crowd of angry, shouting men raced up and surrounded
them. All were hard-faced working people, grizzled and un-
shaven, with sleeves rolled up to reveal arms knotted from
lifetimes of hard work. Most waved clubs overhead. The
weapons were long and polished and black and dangerous.
The three officers eased into a tight cluster, standing back-
to-back, and waited.

A broad little bantam of a man pushed his way through and shouted the crowd to silence. He then turned to the trio, his chest puffed out with importance. "You friends of Señora Haskeens?"

"That depends," Jake replied.

"Yes, yes," Teaves countered energetically. "Bosom buddies. Known her for ages."

"Good. You seek two men, yes?"

"That's right."

The little man spun around. "You come."

Encircled by the group of muttering men, Jake and the others were ushered back to the ancient sagging house. More men massed upon the broad veranda, filled the doorway, spilled up the sweeping interior stairs. Through vast windows, Jake could see that the ground floor was a single open room. Tables and chairs had been plucked aside and heaped in various corners.

The little bantam wore a great fuzz of curling reddish-gray hair that shook about as he cocked his head and announced, "I am Fernando. This my restaurant. Upstairs have rooms. Two men, they stay three, maybe four weeks. You understand?"

"Loud and clear," Teaves replied, giving another glance at the mass of clubs and the angry, eager fists clutching them. "Whatever you say."

The little man shouted and gestured. A canvas sack was passed from hand to hand and deposited at their feet. The sack was covered with dirt and leaves.

"My son find this under my house," Fernando said, his neck growing as red as his hair. He stooped down, released the leather catch. Flinging open the sack, he revealed three machine guns, extra clips, two revolvers, boxes of ammunition, and several sticks of dynamite.

"Bingo," Jake said.

"*My* son find under *my* house," the little man cried, almost dancing with rage.

Teaves had a battle-hard glint in his eyes as he said to Pierre, "Before we turn this over to the authorities, I would imagine you might have a couple of questions you'd like to ask."

"One or two," Pierre growled, his eyes still on the sack.

"Yes, yes," Fernando agreed. "First questions, then police."

"A man after my own heart," Teaves said. "I take it the prey are upstairs."

The little man bobbed affirmative. "Trapped in room. My friends and I, we have plan. You come?"

"No lynching allowed," Teaves warned.

Fernando frowned. *"Qué?"*

"We want to deliver these men to the police intact," Teaves explained. "Not in separate little bits and pieces."

"Yes, yes, understand," the little man said impatiently. "You come?"

They exchanged glances. Jake asked, "What choice do we have?"

"As long as I get my answers," Pierre grated, "I will go to the ends of the earth."

"Not so far," Fernando said, his grin exposing discolored teeth. "Okay, we begin."

A narrow way opened for them through the men thronging the stairs and the second-floor hallway. At the hall's far end a door stood open. Passing through it, they saw more armed men lining the room. Seated on the floor in the center were two very disgruntled men in T-shirts and skivvies. Both men had their wrists and ankles firmly tied.

"Catch while asleep," Fernando announced proudly.

Both men had the leathery complexion of those hardened by long marches under desert skies. Blue eyes attested to non-Arab blood. The younger of the pair bore a knife scar that traced its way from temple to collarbone, just missing the left eye. It gave his fierce expression an even more sinister cast.

The elder was nursing his hands close to his chest. He looked up at the sound of Fernando's words, glanced at the trio filling the doorway, spotted Pierre, and emitted an involuntary gasp.

"It's them," Pierre cried exultantly. "They recognize me."

"Find more guns under beds," Fernando said, pointing to yet another pair of revolvers. "One man try to shoot, but my brother, he move very fast."

A burly man standing over the pair hefted his club and gave them a proud gap-toothed smile.

"Bet that hurt," Jake said conversationally, then turned to Pierre. "You realize these guys are not going to be very helpful."

"With time they will," Pierre replied grimly.

"No time, no time," Fernando said impatiently. "Police must be called, yes? We learn what we need now."

"Just exactly what do you have in mind?" Teaves asked.

"You see." He motioned at the men and spoke a torrent of Spanish. Immediately the room was filled with a hungry roar.

The pair of prisoners showed wide-eyed alarm as arms hefted them aloft and carried them from the room. The noise was picked up by the men crowding the hall and the stairs and the veranda as the procession made its way down and out of the house. The prisoners struggled, but were held fast by more hands than there was flesh to hold.

As Jake was carried along by the fierce horde, he said to Pierre, "I hope they leave enough for you to ask questions to."

From Pierre's other side, Teaves shouted back, "You think you can stop them, be my guest."

The throng made its way around the house and entered the vast, overgrown stretch bordering the Rock. Their own shouts were soon joined by barking cries emitted from the surrounding growth. Jake shot wide questioning eyes to Teaves, who shouted, "Barbary apes. They live here."

For some reason, the chattering screeches raised the crowd's excitement to a fever pitch. The prisoners were hefted up higher, and those arms that could not reach the men lifted a forest of black clubs. A few men slowed and lit fire-blackened lanterns.

A jink in the path revealed a mammoth opening at the base of the Rock. As the men started in, Teaves said, "There are over thirty miles of tunnels carved into the Rock. Hospitals, kitchens, barracks, weapons stores, you name it. There's place here for keeping an army of four thousand men."

The short tunnel emptied into a vast cave. The roof was so high that in the glint of feeble lanterns it was lost to shadows. Stalactites broader than a man hung down in grand natural splendor. The ground was a soft sandy shale, littered with refuse and animal droppings. The odor was fierce.

The men crowded about a pair of metal frames. Jake stepped closer and saw they were white hospital beds, minus their mattresses. The prisoners struggled frantically, but powerful hands held them fast as their ropes were untied. The prisoners were then laced spread-eagled to the bed frames. Each rope was tested carefully a dozen times; then Fernando straightened and motioned. Gradually the hubbub settled into silence. He gestured toward the trio. "You speak now."

Teaves stepped forward. "Do you two understand English?"

There was no reply.

He made a broad gesture, taking in the tightly packed horde of armed and scowling men. "I don't know exactly what they've got in store for you, but I think we can all assume it's not going to be pleasant. So why don't you do us all a favor, answer this man's questions, and we'll ship you off to a nice, safe, comfortable cell."

The scar-faced man spit in Teaves' direction. Pierre stepped forward and barked a command down at the prisoners in French. They glowered and remained silent. Again he tried, and received the same response as Teaves.

Fernando stepped forward, as puffed-up as an actor on the stage. "Is enough, yes? You wait, we get answers."

"That's very kind of you," Teaves said, showing a moment's squeamishness. "But to be honest, perhaps this is a matter for the police."

"No, no, no police," Fernando said impatiently, pushing the officers back. "Not now. Later, but not now. Now we get you answers." He grinned fiercely. "And payment for room, yes?"

"I'm not sure I want to watch this," Jake said quietly.

"You go stand there," the little man said, directing them to where many of the others were already headed. "Now."

Reluctantly they allowed themselves to be led into the shadows. As their eyes adjusted, they saw that the other men were climbing up a series of narrow steps and crowding into broad alcoves carved from the walls of the cave. Room was made for them at the front of one alcove. They stood on the edge and looked out to where the two men lay tied. The last man to retreat from the cave floor was Fernando. He took a sack from his brother, then stooped and slid several objects under each bed. Then he ran over and joined the others in the alcoves.

The cave grew quieter still, until the only noise was the squeaking frames as the prisoners tried to free themselves.

Faintly at first, and then more clearly, Jake heard a series of loud, barking cries. Yes, he was certain now. The cries were growing closer, close enough to echo about the vast cave.

The prisoners stopped their struggles for a moment, their faces turned toward the opening through which they had been carried.

Suddenly Fernando's brother came racing into the cave, screaming at the top of his lungs, his eyes almost popping from his skull. In his panic he lost his footing and sprawled face first into the sand. But before he was completely down, his legs were already churning him back upright. Spitting sand and howling with fright, he raced past the beds and out of sight.

Then the first apes appeared.

They loped forward on arms longer than a man's. Their great reddish-blond manes flowed back and forth as they raced into the caves. Their barking cries filled the air as more and more emerged through the tunnel.

The prisoners emitted their first sounds since capture, shouting with fear and struggling madly against the frames.

Their voices rose several octaves as the first apes loped over to stand above them and grin with long, fiercely yellow teeth.

One of the apes grabbed the arm of the younger man. Jake flinched at the sight and saw Pierre blanch as the prisoner screamed with terror. Jake started down, not sure what he could do by himself, but knowing he could not stand and watch this happen. Half a dozen hands grasped and held him. He turned and stopped his struggling. The men surrounding him were grinning. *Grinning.*

The apes circled the pair of beds, barking their great cries and rummaging about, using the frames as jumping platforms. The two prisoners, although hidden from view, were shouting at the top of their voices.

A chuckle rose from several of the men near Jake.

One ape clambered up onto the head-frame, bent his head far over, and barked down at the prisoner. The prisoner replied with a howl of his own. The chuckles took on strength. Pierre looked a question in Jake's direction. He could only shrug in reply.

Someone jabbed Jake in the back. He turned, saw a man gesture with his chin. Go ahead. He caught Pierre with an elbow, said, "Try your questions now."

Pierre shouted something across the floor in French. A pair of panicked voices screamed back their reply. Pierre turned and nodded.

Immediately several men jumped down, sacks in hand. They called out, raising the sacks as they came into view of the cave floor. Standing well back so that the prisoners could not see, they began scattering objects around one side. Jake craned, made out oranges and apples and bananas. The apes immediately lost interest in the beds and came loping over. The men stood their ground as several of the apes plucked up fruit and then leapt into the men's arms.

Suddenly Fernando was beside them. "Gibraltar apes tame," he explained. "My brother chief keeper. He feed them here. Others help." He grinned proudly. "Was good idea, yes?"

"Outstanding," Teaves said, his voice as shaky as Jake's knees.

"Go," Fernando said. "Ask questions. Men talk now for sure."

Chapter Ten

ADMIRAL BINGHAM GLOWERED at each man in turn. "I must say that I disapprove strongly of your methods, gentlemen. I condemn them in the sternest possible terms."

"They weren't ours," Pierre replied for them all. "Sir."

"We sort of got swept up in it all," Jake agreed.

"Officers under my command are expected to behave in a gentlemanly fashion at all times," the admiral bristled. "Am I getting through to you?"

"Loud and clear, Admiral."

"Aye, aye, sir."

"Then we won't say anything more about it. Where are the prisoners now, Teaves?"

"In the brig, sir."

"Well separated, I hope."

"Yessir. Saw to it myself."

"Their injuries seen to?"

"They were delivered undamaged, sir. That is, except for chafed wrists and ankles and one pair of rapped knuckles."

The admiral nodded once. "Very well. Tell me what you have learned."

Pierre took a breath. "They assume I am Patrique."

"They do not know your brother has a twin?"

"I did not ask."

"I see." The admiral mulled it over. "Interesting."

"A price has been put on my brother's head. Fifty thousand francs."

Bingham's forehead creased until his eyebrows almost joined. "The price was set in French currency, you say."

"That may not mean anything about where the traitor is from, sir," Teaves offered. "The contract was set in Morocco."

"French-controlled territory. Quite. Very well, proceed."

"They only had two leads," Pierre went on, "Marseille and Gibraltar. They found nothing in Marseille, but it seems they expected that from the instructions they were given. Their orders were to first check Marseille and then to come to Gibraltar and wait."

Steel-gray eyes bore down hard on Pierre. "When were these orders issued?"

"Just over two months ago."

"And that was after your brother was supposed to have died, I take it."

"Yessir. By many months."

"Fascinating." Admiral Bingham leaned back in his chair. "It appears, then, that your search is not entirely in vain."

"My feelings," Pierre replied, "exactly."

"So what do you intend as your next step, Major?"

"The orders were issued by one Ibn Rashid in Marrakesh," Pierre answered. "Does that name mean anything to you?"

The admiral thought it over, decided, "Nothing at all. Teaves?"

"I came up blank as well, sir."

"Colonel Burnes and I have discussed it. We think we should try to find passage to Tangiers, go immediately to Marrakesh, and try to find this Ibn Rashid."

"Take the struggle to the enemy's lair," Bingham said. "A risky business."

"I see no other way."

"No, perhaps not." He turned to Teaves. "What do you think, Commander?"

"Me, sir? I didn't realize I was paid to think."

"Only when so ordered," Bingham replied.

"Well, it seems to me they could use all the help we could give. Passage on one of the regular weekly transports, to begin with. I believe one departs tomorrow."

"See to it."

"Aye, aye, sir. And perhaps you could write your contact in Tangiers. The harbor commander."

"Quite so. Admiral Peltier. Draft a letter. No, belay that. Send an urgent communication, mark it highest priority, requesting that every possible assistance be granted to Major Pierre Servais and Colonel Jake Burnes."

"Aye, sir."

"Supply them with revolvers and ammunition. I will sign the authorization. Can't have them traveling to the back of beyond unarmed. Then issue these gentlemen travel documents and copies of the communiqués. Duplicates in French. To whom it may concern, from the commandant of Gibraltar garrison, you know the proper form."

"Consider it done, sir."

"Thank you, Admiral," Pierre replied quietly.

"Very much," Jake added.

"Don't mention it. Least we can do here. I'll also be sending a note to your commanding officers." A gaze as domineering as a pair of gun barrels swiveled in Jake's direction. "That wouldn't be General Clark in your case, would it, Colonel?"

"Yessir. But it's not necessary—"

"Know him well," Bingham said, overriding his protest. "I'll give him a call. I intend to do the same with your commander, Major. Let them both know personally how impressed I am with your performance here."

A glint of humor returned. "This matter of the apes, however, should perhaps best be held strictly between us, wouldn't you agree?"

*　　*　　*

The air was as fresh and clear as the sea. Gentle rollers lifted the aging steamer and sent it splashing eagerly on toward a new and unseen shore. Jake stood at the bow, the salt-laden breeze cleansing him of wrong and doubts and regrets. He looked to his right, where the sun descended in a cascading symphony of colors, and thought of Sally. Here, he discovered, such thoughts were possible without pain. Here the sea and the adventures ahead granted him sufficient distance to look at the past few months as though examining the life of another man.

Whatever happened, he realized, it had been her decision. He had done as much as he could to make his feelings known. He hoped that they could be reunited. He prayed for it. He yearned for her look, her voice, her touch. But here and now there was a peace in his heart. He had given it his best. The rest was up to God and Sally. For the moment, for this glorious moment of limitless horizons, he was able to let go and turn the future over to more capable hands.

He sensed more than saw Pierre move up beside him and grasp the rail as the ship descended easily into the next deep-blue trough. "The skipper says we should be able to spot land just before nightfall."

Jake allowed his thoughts to return earthward, to matters at hand. "You still planning on heading straight to Marrakesh?"

"It seems best. Then the element of surprise may still be with us."

Jake was about to speak further when in the corner of his eye he spotted another figure move hesitantly toward the railing. One cloaked from head to foot in gray folds. Slender and graceful. Jake watched as one delicate hand reached and grasped the rail to his other side.

As smoothly as he could, Jake allowed the next roller to push him back a staggered step. When he returned to the bow rail, it was to Pierre's other side, so that he no longer stood between them. He sidled up close to his friend so that with the next gentle roll Pierre took a step away. Closer toward the cowled figure, whom Pierre had not yet spotted.

Jake held his breath.

An endless moment later, one hesitant hand rose and clutched the hood. Another breathless wait, and the hood was drawn up and away. A breeze caught Jasmyn's dark hair, and flung it up and out like a dark mane. She stood revealed, exposed, trembling.

Pierre raised his eyes from the waters below, cast a half glance toward the figure to his right, and jerked around with a cry of genuine pain.

Jasmyn turned slowly toward him. She stood tall and regal, her eyes wide and defenseless. The wind tossed her hair high enough for the setting sun to shine through and burnish it like a lustrous copper crown.

Jake turned and silently left the bow. As he reached the shelter of the side deck, he thought to himself that there stood the bravest woman he had ever known.

Chapter Eleven

*T*HE TRAIN RATTLED so hard that conversation was impossible. The windows had rusted partway open, which meant both the night's chill and the locomotive's smoke billowed through continually. But this was not all bad, as it kept the compartment's stench from overpowering them.

Goats and lambs bleated and roamed the aisles. The five Arabs crammed into the wooden benches alongside Jake and Pierre passed around a hookah stem, while the tall brass pipe stood at their feet, bubbling merrily and sending up great pungent clouds. Every now and then the Arabs huddled together, shouted fierce arguments, then subsided into sullen, smoky silence. The overhead railings were packed with rolled carpets and bulky sacks and chickens that fluttered futilely, their legs fastened to nearby bundles. Pierre ignored it all, his face turned stonily toward the dark window.

Jasmyn was nowhere to be seen.

Jake had waited almost two hours by the boat's starboard railing until his friend had reappeared. Pierre had remained silent ever since, his face clamped down tight. Jake had let him be as the ship pulled into the Tangiers harbor. When the gangplank had been laid in place, the first officers up the walk had called in French for Major Servais. Pierre had roused himself to exchange salutes and to be ushered from the boat.

Jake had struggled to keep up. As he had pushed his way through the throng eager to descend the gangway, Jasmyn had appeared at his elbow. He had shouted over the clamor, "Last I heard, we were planning to head directly for Marrakesh."

She had nodded as though expecting nothing less. "Find Father Mikus. You will be safe there."

Before he could ask more, he had been pushed forward and away from her. The last he had seen of Jasmyn, she had been staring after Pierre, her jade-green eyes soft and aching with unanswered yearning.

Once into the waiting car, Pierre had adamantly refused what Jake assumed was an invitation to return to headquarters. Their guide had finally responded with a Gallic shrug and driven them to the train station. With the aid of two other officers, places had been found for them on the night train south, a feat that to Jake had appeared next to impossible. The entire station had been flooded with humanity and animals, all shouting and struggling for space on the already packed train. The officer had seen Pierre off with another salute and a stream of words that Pierre had accepted with a single nod. Since then, he had not spoken once.

Three hours into their journey, the train pulled onto a siding and stopped. Jake poked his head through the window and saw nothing but stars and desert and a single wood-lined water tower. A team of shouting Arabs struggled to draw a great hose down and over the locomotive's boiler.

Jake drew his head back in to find Pierre staring at him. "You knew, didn't you."

"Yes," Jake said, determined not to flinch, not to lie to his friend.

"And yet you said nothing."

"Jasmyn asked me not to, as did your mother."

The pain-edged gaze drew even tighter. "My mother?"

"She sees Jasmyn every week," Jake said, glad despite Pierre's agony to have this in the open.

The facts somehow did not mesh in Pierre's mind. "My mother?"

"There is something we don't know about Jasmyn," Jake said. He struggled to describe the reaction Jasmyn had received from the cafe patrons and the churchgoers.

Pierre listened with growing confusion. "You must have imagined it."

"Almost every man she passed bowed toward her, Pierre. I was watching. This was not something they did to other women. They treated her with special respect." Jake leaned forward. "You remember telling me about Le Panier? How everyone escaped unharmed before the Nazis destroyed the district?"

Pierre's eyes widened. "You think Jasmyn warned them?"

"Think about it. There's something we're not seeing here. Even you told me that after the welcome was over, people seemed to be watching you and waiting for some reaction."

Pierre shook his head slowly, struggling hard with what his mind could scarcely take in. "She told you this?"

"She's told me nothing. Nothing except that she loves you."

Bitter, time-hardened anger leapt into the Frenchman's features. "She chose a strange way to show this love."

It came to him then. There in the tumult of an ancient Moroccan train, in the middle of a dark and empty desert, Jake felt himself filled with the same comforting wisdom as before.

This time he struggled a moment, afraid to give in. He found himself able to push it away. Yet as he did so, he caught a fleeting glimpse of an aching sorrow, of a chance lost, of a gift refused. So he stopped, and listened to the silent voice, and found the message waiting. Along with the strength to speak. "Did you ask her how it was?"

Pierre waved the air between them, a gesture so weak he could barely raise his hand. "Words."

Words. They rang in his heart with such gentle power that Jake felt his entire being vibrated. He did not need to raise his voice to command, "Tell me what she said, Pierre."

His friend did not have the strength to refuse. Pierre replied in a hoarse whisper, "She claims she was not his mistress."

"I believe her," Jake said firmly. "And I think you should too."

Pierre remained trapped within the shocking anguish of that unexpected encounter. "She claims to have led this Nazi officer on. He sought to impress her with his power by boasting of his knowledge and his position. He seemed to care less for her as a woman than as a prize to be shown about. She allowed him to parade her about the city as his woman, but she says she never . . ." Pierre hung his head, unable to go on.

"It is the truth, Pierre."

Slowly, gradually, as though raised by unseen hands, Pierre's head rose back up to reveal a gaze torn to heart level by doubt and confusion and pain. "How can you say this?"

"I say it because it is the truth," he replied. "I have seen how she loves you."

Pierre shivered under the weight of those words. "But I heard—"

"Listen to your heart," Jake urged quietly. "It will confirm what I am saying. I *know* this, Pierre."

He waited until his friend was focused upon him before saying as forcefully as he could, "Jasmyn loves you too much to lie."

The desert night lay unbroken across the city when the train pulled into Marrakesh. Feeble lanterns glimmered from some hands, and a few flickering headlamps bumped their way down deeply rutted roads. Otherwise the brightest lights were the ones glittering overhead.

The only taxi outside the station was a vintage Model-T flatbed truck. Piles of carpets lined the back, where passen-

gers could sit or sprawl as they chose. Jake and Pierre flung
their cases on board while the driver fluttered officiously,
proud of his Western patrons. Pierre started off in French,
and Jake caught the word *hotel*.

"No hotel," Jake said, pushing himself onto the truck.
The carpets were kept soft and well preserved by the dry
desert air.

"Where do you expect us to sleep?" Pierre demanded.
"Under a date palm?"

"No hotel," Jake repeated, glad to see a spark of the old
Pierre surfacing. "What if the Tangiers authorities have
passed on information to the wrong people?"

Pierre nodded at the sense of this. "What did you have in
mind?"

"I was told to find somebody called Father Mikus."

The taxi driver started to full alert. "Le Pere Mikus.
L'homme de Dieu. Oui, oui, je le connais."

Pierre's eyes remained fastened upon Jake. "Jasmyn?"

He shrugged. "Who else?"

"Tell me what she said."

"Only that we would be safe there."

Pierre stared at him a moment longer, then nodded. "We
go."

The ride was brief yet exhilarating. Jake saw little of
what they passed—shadows upon shadows, starlight etch-
ing strange silver forms which he assumed were houses and
mosques. The truck bounced and squeaked down empty
streets, grinding gears and sending up great oily plumes
with the dust. But the chilly air was spiced with the fragrances of the unknown, and every dark corner held the
promise of untold mystery. Jake clung to one side post and
raised himself to his knees, so that his face was above the
cab and exposed to the fresh night breeze. He took great
drafts of the cold, dry air and felt that he had never been so
alive.

The ancient car chugged to a halt outside a crumbling
clay-brick home. The aged structure was set into one corner of a square turned silver and weightless in the moon-

light. "Mikus, Mikus ici," the driver cried, climbing from the cab.

As Jake was clambering down, an irascible voice called out in heavily accented English, "Who dares to disturb the night?"

"Friends," Jake called back.

"I'll be the one to decide that." A burly figure in a full cassock stumped through the gates. He raised his lantern high enough to reveal a heavy-jowled face with bristling eyebrows. As the visitors came into view, gray eyes popped wide open and his free hand reached up to clutch at his chest. "Patrique!"

"No, monsieur," Pierre said. "I am his brother."

The priest squinted and stepped close. He gave Pierre's face a careful inspection in the lantern light. "Incredible," he murmured. "For a moment I thought—"

"Were it only so," Pierre said solemnly.

The priest stepped back and motioned brusquely. "Pay the man and come inside. Quickly now. The night is full of prying eyes."

The priest heard them out in impatient silence. When Pierre faltered, which happened several times, Jake picked up the pace, filled in the gaps, watched his friend with worried eyes. Finally Mikus waved his hand for silence. "Enough, enough. Two people telling the same tale is worse than no tale at all. You are tired, yes? You need a bed, a bath, food? Very well. All else will wait for the dawn. Come along."

The walls were of hard-baked brick, roughly plastered about great half timbers. Threadbare carpets covered the uneven floor. The only light was the priest's flickering lantern, which he held before him as he stumped up two flights of stairs. He flung back a creaking door and motioned them into the low-ceilinged space under the eaves. "Mattresses and blankets there in the corner. The pitcher holds water. Use it with care. Water must be brought from the well at the far end of the square." He motioned for Jake to follow him. "You can come for the food and save me another trip."

As Jake followed the priest back down the stairs, he said, "It is very kind of you to help us."

"I am not the least bit kind," Father Mikus snapped back. "I am disagreeable, and I am impatient. The great Lord above no doubt finds me difficult. But Patrique was a friend, and there are few of those about in this evil time."

The kitchen was a crude brick annex fastened to one wall of the cluttered house. Everything in it was battered and used long beyond its natural life. The grizzled man moved about, setting bread and cheese and olives and dates upon a simple wooden platter. "This water is twice boiled. Drink nothing else."

"Again, thank you," Jake said, taking up the tray.

"Wait." Steel-gray eyes fastened upon him. "What is the matter with your friend?"

"He is troubled," Jake said simply.

"His brother?"

"Not only."

The priest nodded as though satisfied. "It is a troubled world. I myself am from Austria, the land that spawned the evil called Hitler. I stood and watched my beloved land prostrate itself before the monster, and I did the only thing I could: I condemned all who chose to follow him. I barely escaped with my life. Patrique brought me here, arranged for me to take over this work for the local Red Cross. Do you understand what I am saying? Your friend's brother saved my life and then gave me a reason to continue living."

"I understand," Jake said quietly.

"Whatever you need," Father Mikus said. "Whatever I can do. Now go and see to the needs of your friend."

It was not a peaceful night. Jake lay awake in the dark and listened to Pierre toss and turn and heave deep sighs. Finally he asked, "You want to talk about it?"

The silence lasted so long that Jake took it for the answer. But then Pierre said, "I feel as though my mind and my heart are being torn in two."

Jake searched the dark before his eyes, waiting for the sense of being guided toward a response. He sat up, feeling as though something was coming, something greater than either of them, greater than the problem, greater than the very night.

"One side of me yearns to hold her," Pierre moaned. "I feel the need in my very bones. And yet I cannot."

A silent herald called to Jake's heart. All he said was, "You're trapped."

"It is an impossible life. Everywhere I turn I am faced with the daggers of an enigma for which there is no answer. No matter what I do, I am pierced to my very soul." Pierre beat the mattress with a feeble fist. "I cannot go on. This much I know. I cannot live with this. I cannot. I lie in the darkness and know a thousand deaths."

A flame ignited in Jake's heart. A power so vast it filled his being with strength that could not be denied. The instant of its coming lasted less than the span of a heartbeat, yet in that immeasurable moment he saw his own life linked to Infinity. The flame was a gift, one somehow granted through his meager faith and his love for a friend, given so that it might be shared.

"There is an answer," Jake said softly, and in the moment of speaking felt the light of his heart illuminate every shadow.

Pierre responded with a groan of defeat. "Impossible."

"Listen to me, Pierre. The answer is yours for the asking. I *know* this. All you have to do is turn and ask."

The mattress next to his grew still. "What are you saying?"

"You are lost because you insist on going through this alone. But God has an answer for you. There is someone there, waiting for you to open your heart and your mind to Him. I feel this with every fragment of my being, Pierre. He knows your distress and wants to offer you peace. Healing. He waits to offer you *hope*."

The stillness lengthened, then, "You truly believe this?"

"With all my heart."

There was a shifting in the darkness. Then the broken voice of his friend asked, "What must I do?"

"Pray," Jake said. "Ask for His help and guidance. Confess to your own failings. Turn to the Son and ask Him into your life."

A time passed, measured in waiting breaths, before Jake heard shaky murmurs in French. A love so strong it could not be contained filled his heart. A love meant not for him, but for his friend. Jake sat and added his own silent words to those of his friend and felt the freedom of hope fill the night.

Chapter Twelve

THE NEXT MORNING Jake clattered down the stairs to find Father Mikus seated at the rough-hewn table. He sipped from a glass of tea and asked, "How is your friend?"

"Still asleep."

"A good sign. Sit, sit. Do you take tea?"

"If it's not too much trouble."

"All life is trouble in troubled times." The priest rose to his feet, moved to the coal-fired stove, grasped a singed towel, set the blackened pot in place. "You come from Gibraltar, did I understand that much?"

"Yesterday. Then the night train from Tangiers."

"And you found no sign of Patrique?"

"Nothing except the hunters."

"Then I fear the worst." He inspected a glass, decided it was clean enough, dumped in a fingerful of shredded leaves, and added water. "Bread and dates and goat's cheese are all I have to offer."

"That sounds fine. Thank you."

"Patrique told me he was headed for Gibraltar." He sipped noisily. "There he would find safety, he said."

Jake blew upon his glass. "Safety from what?"

"He would not tell me. He said the less I knew the safer I would remain. Two nights after he vanished the third time—"

"The *third* time?" Pierre appeared in the doorway.

"That is what I said." The priest waved Pierre toward the only other chair. "I suppose you'll be wanting tea as well."

"He can have mine," Jake offered.

"Nonsense. The air is dry, and so the body is fooled, but this desert chill can seep into a man's bones." Mikus hovered over the stove and filled a third glass. He returned to the table, set it in front of Pierre and said, "Twice before, Patrique disappeared, and each time there were rumors of his death. Each time he was brought back by something that troubled him greatly. The third time was to see if word had arrived back from Marseille. He had sent a messenger, he told me, a young girl—"

"Lilliana," Jake offered.

The priest gaped. "You know of her?"

"That is why we came. We told you last night."

"Last night you spoke gibberish. Lilliana is alive?"

"She is in a camp in Badenburg. I have a letter for her parents. She has suffered from a fever but is recovering and soon should be well enough to travel."

But Father Mikus was already on his feet. "Up, up, leave your breakfast. We must hurry."

Pierre protested, "But we have questions—"

"Questions we shall have until the day we die," the priest snapped. "A good family has suffered the agony of the damned. I shall not force them to wait a moment longer for this news."

"I'll go," Jake said, patting his friend on the shoulder as he rose. "You take it easy until we return."

"Just one question," Pierre demanded. "How did Patrique know of this danger?"

"The second and third times he returned and spoke of it, I have no idea. The first time, he knew the same way he learned to escape from Marseille when he did." The priest impatiently reached from the door. "From Jasmyn. Is she not your woman? Do you not hear these things from her?"

The news shook Pierre to his deepest foundations. "Jasmyn?"

Father Mikus loomed large and crooked in the doorway. He turned back to Pierre. "What is this I hear? You do not honor the woman who has twice saved your brother?" Then he gave his head a curt shake. "No, no, that too can wait. This news cannot. Do you have the letter? Good. Then we go."

The priest set a hasty pace across the dusty square. Although the sun had not yet risen high enough to crest the surrounding buildings, already the night's chill was fading. All the buildings Jake could see were alike—low and brick and daubed with yellow clay and roofed with dry thatch. Walls ran around many of them. Portals were arched in the form of the Orient. The doors themselves were thick and studded with iron.

In the square's far corner, beyond the well, stood a squat building with a pole set over its door; from the pole hung a Red Cross flag. As they approached, a gang of young children came squealing into view and danced a joyful racket around Father Mikus. He ignored them completely, and they paid his scowl no mind whatsoever. All of them were barefoot, all wore the simple cloth shift of the desert Arab, all laughed and danced and tried to work eager fingers into the priest's pockets.

"Wait here," he said gruffly to Jake, and disappeared into the building. The children knew better than to enter with him. They stood around, eyed Jake with shy curiosity, peered through the open door. A moment later Mikus appeared and announced, "Too early. He is still at home. Come."

The children ran and chattered about them as the priest hurried down narrow ways. After several twists and turns Jake was completely and utterly lost. Suddenly their passage opened into a main thoroughfare that ran parallel to a tall city wall. Already the street was busy with vendors and merchants and herdsmen and donkeys piled high with wares.

A hundred meters farther, Mikus bounded up crumbling steps to enter a derelict abode. The filthy entrance hall opened into a broad central courtyard lined with rusting balconies and laundry. Its center boasted a well, a carefully tended patch of green, and three date palms.

Mikus reached the far corner of the courtyard and climbed the wooden staircase in great bounds. He reached the top floor, walked to the first entrance, and pounded on it with his fist.

A moment later a bespectacled man, burdened by the sorrows that lined his face, opened the door. In German he said, "Ah, Mikus. Good. You are just in time for tea."

"I bring news," the grizzled priest replied abruptly, also in German. "May God be praised, your daughter is alive."

A shriek rose from the apartment's depths, and the bespectacled man staggered against the doorpost. Before he could bring himself to speak, a woman appeared, an older image of Lilliana, dark and sharp-featured and beautiful in a tired and world-worn way. She clutched at the priest's frock with desperate fingers. "My baby? Lilliana? Alive?"

Father Mikus motioned toward Jake. "Calm yourself. He has just come from her."

The priest looked surprised when Jake stepped forward and added in German, "Lilliana is alive and well. I spoke with her eight days ago. She has had a fever and is still too weak to travel, but she is recovering."

The woman broke down and wept so hard her legs gave way beneath her. Together the priest and her husband helped her inside the apartment. Jake stood awkwardly in the doorway, fumbled with his cap, and watched as Lilliana's father held and soothed the old woman, ignoring the tears that streamed down his own face.

When a semblance of calm was restored, the husband motioned for Jake to enter and asked quietly, "What can you tell us?"

"Lilliana was arrested in Marseille," Jake replied. "But only for not having papers. She was shipped to a Nazi prison camp and put to work in an armament factory. She stayed there until the Allies liberated her. She recognized my friend Pierre, mistaking him for his brother Patrique."

"The brother of Patrique is here?"

"At my house," Mikus replied. "He has word that Patrique is still alive."

"Perhaps," Jake amended.

"That such a man would send my baby off like that," the woman moaned. "May he roast in hell."

The husband became rigid. "What do you say!"

"That such a man would risk his own life time and time again to save ours," the priest said gravely, "as well as the lives of countless others, may the dear Lord reward him well."

Jake unbuttoned his jacket pocket and extracted Lilliana's letter. "I have brought this from your daughter."

Instantly the woman leapt up, tore the letter from his grasp, ripped it open, scanned the page, and crushed it to her breast. She rocked back and forth, sobbing, "Alive, alive."

Gently the husband reached for the letter, read it, and looked up at a room he did not see. "I must go for her."

"It would be tough but probably not impossible to arrange for you to travel," Jake said. "I can write a couple of letters that might help, but my influence is barely above zero here, and you'd have to expect long delays on the way. Transport is extremely crowded."

"Pay attention, Peter," Father Mikus urged. "Listen to the colonel. This is important."

The bespectacled man struggled to focus. "What do you suggest?"

"We have arranged for her to be issued papers—ID card, travel permits, assistance requests, official passage, the works. All we need is for you to write the Red Cross in Badenburg and confirm where you are. We can even arrange for an escort, with time—an older woman or another family traveling in this direction."

"My wife and I will speak of this," Lilliana's father said in a trembling voice. "We are in your debt for all time."

"Could I ask, did Patrique mention anything to you about a traitor?" Jake asked.

"Not to me," the husband replied. "Three weeks after Lilliana disappeared, Patrique came to us and told us he had news that had to be delivered in person. He said that she had gone to Marseille as his messenger, and had not returned. He feared the worst. My wife," he paused, then went on more quietly, "my wife was hysterical. Lilliana is our only child. She came late in life, after we thought children were denied to us." He looked down at the letter. "All this time I have tried to hope, but it has been hard. So very hard."

Father Mikus patted the man's shoulder. "We will leave you. I shall return later. Arrangements must be made." He stood and motioned Jake from the apartment.

Once they were outside, Mikus said, "They are too distressed to say it, so I shall do it for them. Thank you."

"You are welcome."

"Come." As they made their way back downstairs, Mikus said, "Your German is good, very good."

"Thanks. I was studying it when the war broke out." Jake followed him through the courtyard and back out into the dusty street. There the children gathered, waiting for them.

He watched the priest walk over to a vendor, buy a fistful of sweets for a single copper, and begin distributing them to all the little hands. Somehow he seemed to know when one had already received a sweet, for several times he slapped away an eager palm and directed the candy into another mouth. When all the sweets were gone, he waved impatiently and spoke harsh words in Arabic. The children laughed as though it were part of the game and continued to dance along behind him.

Jake drew up alongside him and asked, "Do you know the name Ibn Rashid?"

"Do not speak those words in public," Mikus snapped. He picked up the pace. "Why do you ask?"

"The assassins we captured in Gibraltar were sent by him."

"Then this is both good and bad news." They turned into narrow passages just as the sun cleared the city wall. Suddenly their entire world became one of brilliant light and impenetrable shadow. "Good because the man whose name you spoke is no fool and would not spend money chasing after one already dead. Bad because he is a jackal, a hyena, a robber of graves, and will do his best to ensure that Patrique's life is as brief as possible."

As they entered the square, Jake found the courage to venture, "May I ask you something?"

"You may ask anything you like. Whether or not I answer is an entirely different matter."

"From time to time people have been coming to me for advice. About spiritual matters. I try to help them. I pray," Jake said, and faltered.

Father Mikus stopped and turned to him. "You are a believer?"

"I try to be. But when I try to help people, I feel . . ." He searched for the word.

"You feel human," the priest said. "You feel trapped within all that is not perfect within yourself. You feel empty."

"That's it," Jake said, glad he had spoken.

"Good," Father Mikus said, turning back around. "Only when we are faced with our own emptiness can we open ourselves fully to be filled by the Spirit." He started forward. "Come, let us get out of this heat."

Jake hustled to keep up with him. "But I feel like there has to be somebody else who would be better—"

"Look around yourself," Father Mikus snapped. "Do you see crowds of perfect people? Do you see a world filled with the Savior's love? Do you find a thousand people calling out to be used by our Lord? No. You find nothing of the sort. You find bitterness and pain and wounded spirits. You find unanswered needs crying out to uncaring hearts."

He stopped once more and fixed his impatient gaze on Jake. "Accept that the Father is calling you, Colonel. Accept that in your imperfections grow the seeds of His divine love. Be content to know that no matter how flawed you may be, no matter how great your failings, the Lord sees in you the *possibility* of perfection. Why? Because you have opened yourself up to be used by Him, the One in whom perfection is complete."

Chapter Thirteen

WHEN THEY RETURNED to the priest's house, Jake found that Pierre had returned upstairs. Jake sat on the crumbling stoop and watched the day's growing heat gradually beat all life from the dusty square. There was little to be seen beyond a series of tumbledown French colonial structures, a few tired donkeys, and a handful of dusty Arabs intent about their business. Yet he could not get enough of the scene. He sat and watched the day take hold, and decided that he would go exploring on his own if Pierre did not rise soon.

Jake stiffened at the sight of two figures in Western garb crossing the square toward him. As they drew closer, he recognized Lilliana's parents. The mother was carrying a steaming cauldron, her hands protected by layers of padding. Jake hurried over and asked in German, "Can I help you with that?"

"I am sure the good father has shown you as little concern over food as he shows for himself," she replied, ignoring his offer. "So I have brought you some real sustenance."

Father Mikus appeared in the doorway. "You can scarcely afford to share the little you have, Edna."

"Nonsense. This is a time for celebration. Move aside, Father, and see to plates and spoons for these hungry men."

As Edna bustled into the house, her husband stopped in front of Jake and solemnly extended his hand. "I failed even to introduce myself properly. Please forgive my bad manners. I am Peter Goss."

"Nice to meet you. Jake Burnes."

"The honor is mine, I assure you." The handshake was firm, belying the man's frail image. "You cannot imagine what joy you have brought into our lives."

"My husband speaks for both of us." Edna Goss appeared in the doorway, nervously wiping her hands over and over with her cloth. "I wish to apologize for my words about Patrique."

"They were understandable, given the circumstances."

"They were unforgivable," she replied sternly, her hands still busy with their cloth. "Almost as unforgivable as my thoughts."

"Edna," her husband murmured.

"I have raged against Patrique ever since my daughter's disappearance. But in my heart I have always known that the girl probably thrust herself upon him and demanded that he send her."

"Lilliana positively adored the man," Peter Goss added. "She would have done anything for him. Anything."

Pierre appeared behind Frau Goss and asked, "These are the parents of Lilliana?"

The sounds of English words turned both their heads. Peter Goss was the first to see, and gasped at the sight. Frau Goss cried aloud. "You!"

"Allow me to introduce Patrique's brother," Jake said, "Major Pierre Servais."

"I would never have believed it," Peter Goss murmured. "Even seeing it with my own eyes, I still am having difficulty."

Edna Goss had staggered back to be steadied by her husband. "Patrique told us he had a twin, but never would I have imagined the resemblance."

"Forgive me," Pierre said, his German halting. "Do you perhaps speak English or French?"

"Our English is much better," Peter Goss replied for both of them and released his wife to offer one unsteady hand. "It is an honor to meet you, Major."

"Please, call me Pierre." Despite the extra sleep, distress was clearly taking its toll. His skin was drawn taut over his features, and his eyes bore the weight of exhaustion. He bowed toward the mother and said, "You have a most remarkable and brave daughter, madame."

"Thank you," Edna Goss said, finding her voice. "The colonel tells me she was ill."

"Jake," he corrected.

"That is so," Pierre replied. His tone was formal, his bearing rigid, as though holding himself erect by strength of will alone. "But when we left she was recovering nicely. Hopefully by now her strength will be restored."

"You look as though you have been ill yourself," Frau Goss said.

Pierre did not bother to deny it. "In spirit," he replied, his eyes seeking Jake. "Thankfully I have friends who minister to me in my hour of need."

"Enough of this chatter," the priest said crossly, poking his grizzled head out of the doorway. "There is food, and it is hot, and I am hungry. The talk will keep, the food will not. Come and sit."

The Moroccan lamb stew, called tangeen, was delicious. It was cooked in a clay pot, with quarter moons of potatoes set in a rich sauce of meat and pungent spices. Jake took three heaping portions and stopped only when his belly positively refused to accept another bite. "That was wonderful, Frau Goss."

"Indeed, indeed," Father Mikus agreed, his eyes turned owlish from an overstuffing of rich foods. "Your cooking is a blessing, Edna."

"It is the least I could do," she replied, her nervous hands again busy with the cloth in her lap. "After what I said—"

"Enough," the priest said, but without his customary rancor. He switched into German and said, "The good colonel has demonstrated the best kind of forgiveness by forgetting what you have said."

"It is true," Jake agreed.

"If you find Patrique," she said hesitantly, her eyes on her ever-active fingers, "tell him," and here her voice became as downcast as her gaze. "Tell him I forgive him and ask his forgiveness in turn."

"You have it," Jake replied. "If he is half the man I know his brother to be, I am sure he has long since done what you ask."

"Excuse me," Pierre said in English, rising from the listlessness that had held him throughout the meal. "You are speaking of my brother?"

"Only that he is a fine man," Frau Goss replied in her heavily accented English. "Would you tell him that for me, please? That I said he is a good and fine man."

"After you left us this morning," Peter Goss said, picking up for his wife, "I had a thought. There was a very dear friend of Patrique's, the son of friends, people who escaped with us."

"Erich Reich. Of course. I should have thought of that myself," Father Mikus agreed. "He was Patrique's confidant. Erich was not actually connected to the Resistance. He worked in his father's shop. Only Patrique, Peter, and I knew of his true role. We decided it was better that way. You see, many of our funds came from his father's shop."

"He was killed toward the end of the war," Peter Goss said sadly. "Such a waste. There were several uprisings as the Nazis were pulling out of Marrakesh. It appears that Erich was caught in one by accident and shot. Frau Reich died two months later, they say of an illness, but we know it was from grief."

"We understand from Lilliana," Jake said, "that Patrique had come to the office that night because he was supposed to be meeting a messenger. He sent your daughter because no one else was there."

"And because she insisted," Frau Goss said to her lap and shook her head. "I know, I know. I can hear her now. Ach, Lilliana, Lilliana, what you have done."

Peter Goss reached over and patted his wife's hand. Then he said, "Perhaps it would be worthwhile for us to go and speak with Herr Reich, Erich's father."

"I am not sure that would be a good idea," Father Mikus said worriedly. "Anyone who sees Pierre will immediately think it is his brother. And the Kasbah is Ibn Rashid's domain."

"Even more reason to go now." Pierre was immediately on his feet. "We shall take the battle to the lion's lair."

"But without the two of you," Jake said to Peter Goss. "It may be unsafe for you to be seen with Pierre, in case he is mistaken for Patrique by the wrong people."

"It is a good point. I will lead you there myself." Father Mikus raised his hand to still Peter Goss's protest. "You have a daughter to think of now."

Frau Goss asked, "And yourself?"

"I am an old man who has nothing to lose but his troubles." He turned to Pierre. "You should wear something other than your uniforms. The Kasbah has defied control for centuries. It is full of great hatred for all foreign armies."

The city's walls were high and entered through great domed portals. Squadrons of Foreign Legion soldiers stood sullen guard. Through the entry poured a vast rainbow of humanity. They paid the desert dragoons no heed whatsoever.

The Arabs surrounding them wore a variety of robes and headdresses to mark their tribes—multicolored robes with knitted caps for the mountain Berbers; long, embroidered white robes for the city nobility; sky blue for desert Moors. The women sailed by in isolated majesty, some covered from head to foot, others holding a symbolic scarf entwined with two fingers, their beauty as striking as their fierce pride. Seldom would a man risk a glance, no matter how covered or uncovered she might be; to do so invited the vengeance of a jealous guard or tribesman, never far away.

The favorite city transport seemed to be either by foot or by donkey. Arab traders sat with shoulders bowed low, their turbans unwound to veil their face in cooler shadows, their side bags bulging with the day's wares.

"This is the central square," Father Mikus said as he led them through the jostling throngs. "The locals know it as the Place of Heads. Before the French arrived, all public executions took place here. Then the heads were set on stakes as a warning to all who passed."

Jake felt the thrill of stepping into the unknown. "This place is beyond anything I've ever seen before."

"The Moors and Berbers, the first settlers of Marrakesh, were ancient peoples, old as the human race," Father Mikus went on. "Their heritage was mixed and rich with legend. In the twelfth century, these tribes became swept up in the Arabs' tide of conquest. They heard the stories of Mohammed, the prophet of Allah. They were granted the choice of either submitting to Arab rule and accepting Islam, or knowing swift death."

The great Khutubian mosque dominated the Marrakesh cityscape. It was visible from everywhere inside the ancient walled city. Not even the great wall was permitted to rise as high. They passed by a crowd of Arabs washing their hands and faces and feet at a communal trough as part of the ritual required before entering the mosque.

"The conquerors mingled with the local tribes and left behind civilizations which were both Arab and African," Father Mikus went on. "Though their religion became Islam, it was an Islam decorated with countless centuries of legend and superstition and African desert ways."

Water sellers cried their raven calls, their backs bowed by heavy copper urns. They wore broad, fringed hats to keep off flies that gathered at the scent of water.

"Marrakesh means 'the red city.' Under the Moorish empire, Marrakesh became the foremost city of Africa, the link between the conquered territories of Spain and those in the lands south of the great Sahara. The city and the countryside has changed little from its foundations in the twelfth century until the end of this war. But now Winston Churchill comes here to convalesce, and airplanes have begun linking Marrakesh to such far-flung places as London and New York. The modern world is crowding in. Whispers of change are being heard, at least within the city walls. In the rest of Morocco, time remains frozen as it has been for seven hundred years."

At a second set of older, derelict gates, Father Mikus stopped. "From here on you must take great care. It is doubtful that Ibn Rashid would strike in the light of day, but one can never tell with the likes of him. This is the entrance to the Kasbah, and within these walls the traders are a law unto themselves."

Chaos ruled beyond the ancient portal. The ways grew ever narrower, ever more crowded with camels and donkeys and traders and Arab patrons. Every two or three paces opened a new stall, each staffed by two or more people, all shouting the worth of their wares. They passed down great open halls of copper, of carpets, of spices piled into multicolored mountains. The smells were rich and redolent and as heavy as the heat.

Moorish wood turners fashioned everything from table legs to statues. They spun the wood at a blinding speed, using a one-handed instrument that looked like a clumsy bow. With their free hand they held the cutting instrument, which was set in place through the toes of one foot. Father Mikus told Jake and Pierre that the quality of this work had won fame throughout the world.

The wool market was a separate entity within the Kasbah. Long before the Europeans discovered modern colors, the priest explained, the Moors were exporting their brilliantly dyed wools, fashioned at the wells of Marrakesh. Here the brightly colored strands were looped on poles and hung overhead. Great rainbows of reds and blues and violets and sunburst oranges festooned the passages and transformed the crumbling market buildings. The winding Kasbah paths became tunnels with shadows of gloriously rich hues.

Beyond the wool market, the way became quieter and less crowded. Beggars abounded, their pleas a plaintive chant as constant as the dust. "The gold market," Father Mikus explained. "The beggars become far worse when one departs. Thus it is that few come here unless they intend to buy, and then only with the company of guards."

"Patrique!" The cry was so piercing it shocked the entire venue to stillness. A chubby, gray-haired man wearing a remarkable mixture of Arab djellabah and dark suit coat and vest came bustling up. "Am I dreaming? Can this truly be?"

"Swiftly, inside, all of us," Father Mikus urged, herding them all back down the path and into an open-faced shop lined with wooden-and-glass display boxes. The boxes contained a king's ransom in gold—necklaces, bangles, nose rings, book covers, stamped blocks.

"I regret, monsieur," Pierre replied once they were inside, "that I must disappoint you."

"Herr Reich, this is Major Pierre Servais," Father Mikus said as gently as his rough demeanor allowed. "Patrique's brother. And Colonel Jake Burnes."

The man deflated at the news. "Of course, of course. It would be too much to hope." He fumbled about for chairs and set them in the shop's cramped little center. "Sit, sit, please, you are my guests."

Pierre seated himself, asked, "Then you have heard nothing from my brother?"

"Nothing since, since . . ." Herr Reich allowed the sentence to dissolve into empty space. His words and motions appeared slightly out of focus, as though his hold on reality hung by a slender thread. He blinked and looked about, forcing himself to remember who they were. "You will take tea?"

"Tea we can have anywhere," Father Mikus said, leaning forward. "How are you, old friend?"

"I go through the motions," he replied faintly. "Buy and sell, pretend that it all matters. But there is little left for me now."

"Lilliana is alive," the priest told him. "These men brought word with them."

"Oh, that is good news," Herr Reich said, brightening momentarily. "The Goss family will be delighted."

"You know they have spoken of immigrating to America," Mikus went on. "Perhaps you should think of joining them."

The plump little man hesitated, then shook his head. "My wife and son are buried here. How could I leave them behind?"

"A new life," the priest murmured.

For a moment Herr Reich appeared not to have heard. Then he looked at Pierre and demanded, "You think that your brother might still be alive?"

"A rumor, nothing more," Pierre said, every word an effort. "But we must be sure."

"Yes, of course you must. Patrique was like a second son. He brought me and my family out. He helped me set up this little business. My Erich thought the world of him. I was a jeweler in Frankfurt before the Nazis destroyed our world. I was condemned for the crime of having a Jewish grandmother."

Herr Reich stared at Pierre as he rambled, but clearly was seeing another man. "Patrique was a friend. He was a *mensch*. If you find him, tell him I wait and hope for his return. Tell him all I have is his."

"I will do so," Pierre replied quietly.

When Pierre seemed unable to press the matter home, Jake said, "It appears that a man called Ibn Rashid believes Patrique is alive."

Herr Reich jerked as though struck by an electric current. "You know this for a fact?"

"He sent two assassins first to Marseille and then to Gibraltar hunting for Patrique."

The jeweler became increasingly agitated. "Then there is hope. Real hope. Ibn Rashid is not one to chase after shadows."

"Can you think why he might want Patrique dead?" Jake pressed.

"No, but whatever it is, rest assured that the reason is big. Very big. Ibn Rashid is a power here in the Marrakesh Kasbah. Not even the Nazis were able to dislodge him. They found it better to use him, which strengthened his

power even more than before. They say his tentacles reach
all the way to Paris."

"Paris," Jake glanced at Pierre, but his friend sat mute
and blind to all but his thoughts. He said, "We heard from
Lilliana that Patrique had evidence of a traitor."

"Of this I know nothing," Herr Reich said definitely.
"But if the traitor was high enough to grant Ibn Rashid
protection in the present transition, and if Patrique knew
enough to topple the traitor from power, that would certainly be reason for the thief to send his minions hunting."

Jake felt that something was coming within grasp, something that would help unravel the puzzle. "Our trail goes
cold here. We heard Patrique was headed for Gibraltar, but
it looks like he never arrived. If he had started for Gibraltar
and then found his way blocked, could you think of anywhere else he might have gone?"

Herr Reich pondered long and hard, then announced,
"Telouet."

"Where is that?"

"A fortress kingdom high in the Atlas mountains. It is
older even than Marrakesh, older than the first Moorish
Empire. The sultan there holds life-and-death power over
the entire central Riff plains. And all highland trade routes
traverse the Riff valley, which means tribute must be paid
to Sultan Musad al Rasuli. The kingdom's power had
waned early in the century, once the Barbary pirates were
cleared away and the seas around Tangiers had been made
safe for traders. But when the Nazi chokehold became too
tight, some of us began shipping in supplies along the ancient Atlas passes."

"Supplies and people both," Mikus added.

"Indeed," the gold merchant affirmed. "Erich and Patrique often spoke of using Telouet as an emergency escape
route." Herr Reich shook his head. "I was against it. I have
worked with Sultan Musad al Rasuli enough to know him
as a man who stays trustworthy only so long as there is
more gold to be had."

Jake turned to his friend, but Pierre remained locked within himself. Jake touched Pierre's shoulder and urged, "Did you hear this?"

Pierre roused himself with visible effort. "It appears that we must go and check out this, this . . ."

"Telouet," Jake supplied impatiently.

"Difficult," Herr Reich said doubtfully.

"Dangerous," Mikus added.

"We must," Pierre said. "Can you help?"

"There is a Berber supply caravan leaving at dawn to cross the mountains," Reich said. "I know because they are delivering what I hope will be my final request for supplies. The French are still not in full control of the harbors, and shipment of anything except emergency goods remains sporadic, so I must transport overland. But the tribute I must pay, as well as the payments to the tribal chieftains who bring in my goods—" He shook his head. "Together it is almost as much as the goods themselves. I hope this will be the last time. As I do with every shipment."

"Will they take us with them?" Jake pressed.

"If there is a reason." Herr Reich pondered a moment, then brightened. "What do you know about automobiles?"

"Excellent," Father Mikus muttered. "A splendid idea."

"You mean, as in repairing?" Jake shrugged. "As much as the next guy, I guess." He looked at Pierre, willing his friend to hold the world in focus. "What about you?"

"Some. Before the war I enjoyed tinkering about."

"The sultan has a fleet of Rolls Royces," said Herr Reich. "Four, to be exact. None of them run."

"You're kidding."

"It is a story that has been told in the lowlands for years," Father Mikus replied, "as an example of the sort of man who rules the Riff highlands. Once his stables held only horses. Then in the thirties he took delivery of four Rolls Royce automobiles. Thirty men lost their lives widening the highland trails to deliver them, and still they were unable to drive across the steepest slopes—they were pulled by teams of horses and slaves."

"Slavery's been outlawed," Jake pointed out.

Reich cast him a sardonic glance, then continued. "Gasoline had to be brought by donkey over the mountains. As long as the cars ran, the sultan could only drive up and down the Riff plains; beyond that the roads were not extended. But when war broke out, the sultan's mechanic ran away to join up, and now the cars no longer run. I know this for a fact because the Berbers are taking back spare parts, and they joke about it because there is no one to replace them or even to say whether they are the correct pieces."

Jake turned to Pierre and demanded, "So what do we do?"

"Do?" Pierre rose slowly to his feet. "As Herr Reich has said, we go through the motions. We continue the search."

"The Berber tribesmen will leave with the sun," Herr Reich offered, rising with them. "I will arrange for them to come by Father Mikus' house to fetch you and will pay for your passage. I shall call it a further token of my esteem for the great sultan."

"Thank you," Pierre managed.

"It is I who offers thanks," Herr Reich replied. "Even this talk has done my spirit a world of good. And if ever you find Patrique, remember my words to him. All I have is his."

Chapter Fourteen

PIERRE RETREATED BACK into himself and re-
fused even to speak with the others for the remainder of the
day. That evening he retired to his mattress immediately
after dinner and did not respond when Jake spoke his name.

Jake was awakened before dawn by faint sounds echoing
outside the priest's hovel. "Pierre?"

"Yes?"

"I hear horses," he said, fumbling in the dark for his
clothes. "Hurry."

As Jake dressed and threw his belongings into his satchel,
Father Mikus appeared in the doorway bearing an oil lamp.
"Ah, you're awake. Good. A rider has appeared with your
horses. You are expected at the main gates at dawn." He set
down the lantern and turned away. "I will see to your
breakfast."

Jake asked Pierre, "Can you ride a horse?"

"As well as I can repair an engine. I would sometimes
ride the salt plains with Patrique. And you?"

"I learned in the Poconos. They're mountains back
home." Jake grinned as he buckled his bag. "It seems like
another lifetime."

"Everything that came before the war is from a different
life," Pierre replied.

"How do you feel?"

"Bruised, battered, and horribly confused," Pierre said, not looking Jake's way.

"Don't you think—"

Pierre raised his hand. "I think too much. Night after night I rack my brains. Day after day I search my mind. All it has done is to lead me in hopeless circles."

He snapped the satchel's catches and straightened. "So I try to do as you say. At night I talk to the stars and in the day I plead with the dust. I try to listen to the infinite. I struggle to see the invisible. And all it has left me is more empty than I have ever been in my life. Empty and lost and without hope." Pierre turned and left the room.

Jake sat by his mattress, waiting for guidance. He heard nothing, felt nothing save an aching worry for his friend. Then he sighed his way to his feet, grasped his satchel, and followed Pierre downstairs.

The Beshaw Berbers spoke only Arabic and their local dialect, so Jake and Pierre journeyed in silence once Father Mikus saw them off at the gate. Jake did not mind, nor was he troubled by the dark-eyed stares sent his way. He was among an unknown folk, journeying into lands where legends were born. Not even Pierre's morose silence could still the humming excitement that coursed through Jake's veins.

Farewells with Father Mikus had been awkward. Pierre barely roused from his reverie long enough to offer thanks. Jake had taken it upon himself to pull the priest aside and ask, "Can you tell me anything about what's up ahead?"

Father Mikus thought a moment, then replied, "Morocco became a protectorate of France in 1912, but this has had little effect outside the major cities." He stretched out one hand toward where the mountains rose, pink and glorious in the distance. "In the lands beyond the hills, time is measured by centuries and not by days. The French will come and go and be granted little more than a sentence in the tales of tribal life."

Mikus called to where the tribesmen waited patiently. They responded with a few words. "You should arrive late tomorrow," he told Jake. "They will take you straight into the mountains. You must cross the Tizian-Tischka Pass, then enter the highland plains. This will take you to Telouet."

"You know the way?"

"I have been there. Twice. But one could spend a thousand lifetimes in those hills and not know them."

Jake felt the rising thrill of adventure. "If Jasmyn shows up—"

"Jasmyn?" the priest cried. "She is here?"

"She may be," Jake hedged. "She was with us, sort of, as far as Tangiers."

"Sort of?"

Jake glanced toward Pierre. "There are problems."

"Ah." The priest's jowls shook as he gave a jerky nod. "Now all is made clear. But how will I know her? I have never seen the woman before."

"If it's her, you'll know," Jake said definitely. "Tell her where we've gone, and why."

"Very well." The priest offered a gnarled hand. "Go with God, Colonel Burnes."

"Thanks. I appreciate your help. And advice. We both do."

"Find Patrique. Tell him his friends await his return." He gave Pierre a searching look. "And see to the needs of your friend."

The mountain tribesmen rode gleaming steeds which handled the rocky terrain with sure-footed strength. Their stout saddles rose high in front and back. Saddle blankets bore the markings of the Beshaw tribe, three stripes interwoven with the mark of Allah.

The hard-faced men all wore white voluminous trousers and high boots as supple as the ammunition belts that crossed their chests. Their turbans were of dark blue, and matching robes hung about their necks—there to be wrapped about in strong winds and morning chills or flung aside in heat.

Their rifles were ancient to Jake's eyes, a museum of armaments from other eras. Most were single-fire weapons with stocks layered in filigreed silver and barrels as long as a man was tall. But the men carried them with the ease of those long accustomed to bearing arms, and gave little notice to their great weight.

They followed the path of a wandering stream out of town and up toward the mountains. Wild scrub fought for place with the towering palms. The air was sweet with the scent of endless spices and blooming flowers.

Morocco was indeed a land of contrasts. Wherever there was water and arable land, life bloomed in profusion. Where water was absent, rock and shale and sand dominated, and the land was dry and dead as old bones. The distance between these two contrasting lands was often less than a hundred meters.

The mountains garnered rainfall from clouds grown full in the tropical south, so even the dry reaches of their early journey held many oases, with calm waters surrounded by palms and Berbers and camel herds. Water dictated where life could flourish. The villages they passed bordered either oases or rivers. The houses were made of the region's red clay.

By midday the first rise was behind them, and Jake's legs and seat were rubbed raw. His lower back burned from the unaccustomed motion. But he strove to keep his discomfort from his face, and concentrated upon the wonders about them.

After they had crested the first rise, the road became rougher, the air dryer. The lowland's bright, leafy greenness gave way to scrub and stubborn fir trees stunted by trying to grow in meager soil.

The path was little more than a flattened trail up the rocky scree. The horses, mountain born and bred, found footing with the ease of mountain goats. The higher they climbed, the colder it became.

They camped for the night just below the snow line. While the tribesmen made camp and prepared their meal, Jake eased bruised muscles and looked out over a sunset-lit vista of gold and russet hues. The great plains of western Morocco stretched all the way to the sea, while to either side of him rose the jagged Atlas peaks in all their glory. The view added spice to an otherwise unappealing meal of dried lamb strips and corn gruel, and made Pierre's morose silence much more bearable.

As the camp settled for the night, Jake lay beneath his saddle blanket, watched the stars circle just out of reach, and thought of his silent friend lying there beside him. The wind spoke to him then, and the clarity of the night sky helped him see and understand.

Pierre had spent the years of war conditioning himself to revile Jasmyn. All that bitterness, all that raging fury had carried him through the dregs of war-torn Europe and kept him alive when many other good men had passed over. Now Pierre's world, bitter as it might be, was being torn asunder. And his best friend responded by saying that help could come only from a God in whom Pierre did not believe. Jake lay still and felt the cold pinch at his face, and did the only thing he could think of to help his friend. He prayed.

Frost whitened their blankets when the travelers awoke the next morning. With a minimum of discussion, camp was broken, horses packed and mounted. The trip resumed.

The pass was recognizable as such only because the ridge they crossed was three thousand feet and more below the surrounding peaks. But there was no path over the saddle of ice and snow, and the wind howled with fierce fury as the men dismounted and walked the horses up and over the steep ridge. Twice during their passage, heavily laden packhorses broke through the permanent ice coating and sank to their chests in the deep snow. Each time the entire tribe jumped into action, shouting and heaving with all their might, struggling to free the animals before they disappeared completely into the ancient snows.

On the pass's other side, going was faster but equally dangerous. A misstep meant a slide down icebound slopes with nothing to stop the plummet for a thousand feet. By the time the snows began to give out, Jake's legs were trembling from the strain and the fear.

When they were safely beyond the snow line, the horses were hobbled and fitted with feed bags. Tea was brewed and served with chunks of sticky-sweet cakes made from layer after layer of paper-thin pastry, filled with crushed nuts and lathered with honey. Jake felt his tired body soak in the energy from the provisions, and again he found himself able to look at the surrounding vista with interest.

The road to Telouet descended before them into a wide, flat highland plain. Most of the valley floor was dry and void of life. The road was the same hard-packed scrabble as had borne the feet of Roman legions two thousand years earlier. Through the highland valley's heart flowed a river, which from Jake's lofty perspective appeared as a silver ribbon lined on both banks by broad stretches of green. Along the river's path rose a city as yellow as the barren earth that stretched out beyond the water's reach.

Although in the dry highlands air the city seemed close enough to touch, still it took them three long hours to work their way down the steep-sided hill to the point where the path broadened into the ceremonial road of packed shale. As soon as the horses touched the road, the tribesmen raised their rifles and fired a volley into the air. Jake guessed the time-honored custom had two purposes. First, it announced their approach loudly and long in advance. Second, for the single-fire weapons of old, the volley cleared the guns' chambers.

The city hid behind the tall, sturdy walls of a medieval fortress. Only the great dome of a palace and the tower of a mosque were high enough to be seen as they approached. The portals of the keep were fifty feet tall, curved and peaked at their summit, and fashioned from thick oaken planks studded with iron crossbars. A score of turbaned men with scimitars and well-oiled rifles guarded the approach.

When the Berbers were within hailing distance, the chief separated himself, trotted forward, slid from his horse, and greeted the captain of the guard with a bow. Three fingers of his right hand touched heart and lips and forehead. The guard captain responded in kind. They spoke for a long time while Jake tried to match the tribesmen's silent patience. Pierre seemed oblivious to his surroundings.

Jake stiffened as attention of the entire guard party swung toward them. The captain examined him with an impenetrable gaze, then turned and barked an order. His subordinate scurried away. There followed a long and careful scrutiny of the cargo. Each packhorse in turn had its leather covering slung aside. Some carried delicacies— small eggs of pastel blue, salted fish wrapped in seaweed, fine fruit, fresh spices. But most carried metal components clearly meant for machinery. Jake looked at one horse bearing a pair of mufflers and three tires, and understood why the animal had broken through the packed ice.

A pair of guards came hustling through the portals, trying to keep up with a diminutive official. Jake sucked in his cheeks to hide a smile. He knew that kind of man. General staffer, his sort was called in the army, a man who loved giving orders and fled at the first sign of a fight. This particular one was extremely proud of his ill-fitting Western suit and tie and Brylcreamed hair. His manner was officious and bossy and superior.

Experience had taught Jake that the best way to deal with such a man was by meeting him head on. As the official bustled toward him, Jake slid from his saddle, came to bristling attention, and snapped off a parade-ground salute. "Jake Burnes, formerly of the United States Army, at your service, sir!"

The action generated the desired response. The little man ground to a halt, faltered, then drew himself up and sniffed, "Is true, you are mechanic for Rolls Royce motor vehicles?"

"Yessir!" In the corner of his eye Jake caught Pierre swiveling and giving him a questioning gaze. He willed his friend to remain silent. "My assistant and I, we have positively years of experience with motor cars of all shapes and sizes, sir!"

The power of Jake's voice drove the official back a step. "I am Hareesh Yohari. Official assistant to great Sultan Musad al Rasuli, ruler of all Riff." He had to cock his head back to a ridiculous angle in order to sniff down at Jake. "Sultan orders you to fix motor vehicles. How long it take?"

"Hard to tell until we check them over, Lord Hareesh, sir!"

Being accorded a title consistent with his over-inflated ego helped puff out the official's chest and ease his concern over admitting strangers into the palace keep. Hareesh cocked his head back even farther so as to inspect Pierre, who eyed the scene from the safety of his horse. "You, why you not standing and giving proper greetings to sultan's official assistant?"

"My assistant has been ill, and the trip has tired him out, sir!" Jake answered for him.

"Better not illness to slow down repair of motor vehicles," Hareesh warned. "Sultan not patient man."

"Oh no, sir! We'll be starting on repairs this very day, sir!"

The official sniffed and turned away in dismissal. He snapped out orders, and the guards waved the company through. The tribesmen watched Jake snap off a second salute, then heave himself back into the saddle. Once they were through the massive portals, several turned toward Jake, gave him ridiculous parodies of salutes, shouted nonsense in Arabic, then howled their mirth. Jake shared a smile. Officials were the same the whole world over.

He walked his horse alongside Pierre's and tried hard not to gape. The city was as ancient as time and mysterious as the desert mountains that enclosed it. Crowds of people stopped and pointed up at them; clearly few had seen a white man before. Jake smiled and touched his forehead in greeting and received gap-toothed grins in return.

The streets teemed with raucous Arab life. Berbers fresh from the empty reaches strode with confidence down the packed market ways. Their eyes held the far-seeing gaze of those used to desert distances. Princes with eunuchs in cautious attendance stepped casually from stall to stall, the gold and jewels woven into their robes glittering in the harsh sunlight. Snake charmers and water sellers and musicians and acrobats and storytellers vied for attention in the crowded ways.

Doors to the imposing structures they passed were all tall and domed, meant to be opened fully only for riders mounted upon proud Arabian steeds. Set in their middle were smaller doors for foot traffic. And in the center of these were hand-sized openings with stout iron grillwork, through which guards scowled fiercely at all who sought entry.

The tribesman nearest Jake noted his excited gaze, smiled with pride at the stranger's interest in the man's homeland, and pointed up ahead. Jake heard strange calls and cries, and craned in his saddle. Their way opened into a tightly packed square, and suddenly he was riding through an outdoor aviary. Birds of every size and description stood upon wooden crooks or fluttered inside hand-woven reed cages. Their plumage was a blurred riot of color. Their calls and shrill songs echoed back from the surrounding walls in never-ending symphony. Jake laughed his delight and was rewarded with a clap on the shoulder from the closest tribesman.

They were stopped a second time at the portals to the inner keep, and held until the little official appeared. When Jake slid from the saddle, the tribesmen were ready and kept straight faces only by tugging fiercely on their beards. The official puffed out his chest and motioned for Jake to move up beside him. Jake handed his reins to a tribesman and stepped to the head of the procession. They walked past scowling guards and entered the palace grounds.

The road changed instantly from dusty stone to polished, close-fitting brick. They circled a third wall, over which peeked the heads of tall date palms.

"The sultan will personally wish to ask when Rolls
Royce motor vehicles ready," Hareesh warned. "Best you
know when he ask."

"Tomorrow, sir!" Jake said, keeping to a quick-step
march and ignoring the suppressed chuckles behind him.
"We'll know by tomorrow, definitely!"

Hareesh sniffed his acceptance, passed under a tall portico, and entered a cobblestone yard lined by servants'
quarters and fronting a long line of stables. A large well
dominated the center of the yard. "Rolls Royce motor vehicles in four left stalls. You to make most careful inspec-
tions, yes?"

"We inspect, sir!"

The official bristled at the sound of mirth behind him,
wheeled about, and was met with stony expressions. He
turned back and cocked his head suspiciously, but Jake responded only with the blank stare of one long trained in
dealing with officers who led from the rear. Another sniff,
then, "You sleep with cars. I order food."

"Very good, sir!" Jake snapped off his salute, then went
back to his steed, untied his satchel, accepted the handshake and salutations of the tribesmen, and motioned for
Pierre to join him. Together they crossed the yard, the
tribesmen calling farewells behind them.

The stable doors at first refused to give. Jake had to borrow a guard's rifle and bang long and hard on the rusty
hinges before they were able to swing the heavy door wide.
Clearly no one had entered these stables in years.

They set down their satchels in one corner and together
drew back the dust cover from the first vehicle. The sight
was enough even to raise Pierre from his stupor.

The great gleaming hood appeared to go on for miles. A
pair of burnished headlights as big as soup tureens flanked
the massive chrome grillwork, which was crowned by the
silver angel with swept-back wings. Huge fenders curved
over the front tires swept down and flattened to become
chrome-plated running boards. The driver's compartment
had a roll-back leather roof that was cracked along the
seams, as was the seat. Yet the damage was nowhere near

what could have been expected. The dry desert air had held deterioration to a minimum.

Jake opened the carriage-type door to the back compartment. The musty air was redolent of saddle leather and luxury. Elegant seats faced a bar of crystal and chrome and walnut burl. A swivel writing desk contained a silver-plated inkwell, leather writing postern, and two gold pens in tortoiseshell holders.

Jake looked back to where his friend was unfastening the engine cowling. "All the comforts of home."

"Come take a look at this."

The engine was a straight-eight and appeared to be about fifty yards long. It looked as clean as it had when rolling off the assembly line fifteen years earlier. Jake declared, "You could eat your dinner off this thing."

"Nothing looks wrong with this," Pierre agreed. "Nothing at all."

Jake looked at his friend. "You ready to rejoin the land of the living?"

Pierre kept his eyes on the motor. "We need to talk."

"Anytime," Jake said quietly. "I've been waiting—"

"Ah, gentlemens already at work, is most excellent." Hareesh bounded into the stable. "Is everything you require?"

"We could use some tools, sir!" Jake said, coming to rigid attention. He found extraordinary pleasure in seeing Pierre snap to alongside him.

"Tools are many, on wall in next stable. And equipments. We have much equipments." He motioned imperiously to a guard, who turned and barked a command. A line of servants began parading in, depositing the tribesmen's cargo on the car's other side. "Is good, yes?"

"We should have enough for the job, yessir," Jake said, eyeing the heap, wondering if any of the pieces would actually fit a Rolls.

Pierre heaved a silent sigh when one of the porters dumped a pair of batteries at their feet. Hareesh squinted up at him and demanded, "Assistant is fainting now?"

"He'll be fine, sir, just give him a couple of days."

"No have days. Day. One. Tomorrow sultan will ask how long to repair motor vehicles. You will tell, yes?"

"We'll do our best, sir."

"No best. You do. Sultan want Rolls Royce motor vehicles for to drive, not keep in stables." Hareesh spun on his heel and departed, flinging over his shoulder, "Servant bring food. Sick man eat much, feel better, work hard."

When the livery was again empty, Jake ducked inside the driver's cab, inspected the controls, and announced, "This car has been driven a grand total of three hundred and thirty-seven miles."

"My guess is that all it needs is an oil change, new tires, and a charged battery," Pierre said, his head deep inside the cowling.

"Can't make this look too easy," Jake warned.

"Go see what kind of tools they have," Pierre said, "and don't try to teach a Marseille boy how to work a scam."

Chapter Fifteen

*A*T DUSK THE city sang its throbbing beat. The air cooled, the dust settled, the sun descended. During their meal Jake tried to urge Pierre into talking, but his friend would say no more than that he was not yet ready to find the words. Afterward Pierre curled himself into blankets on the backseat of one Rolls, and Jake set off alone to enjoy the dying day's cooler hours.

The guards by the inner keep's portals eyed him with stony silence as he walked by, but did not attempt to stop him. Jake could feel their eyes remain on him up to the next corner. Beyond the turning, however, he was able to give himself to the sheer joy of exploration.

The city's narrow ways and cobblestone squares were a distillation of the entire desert nation. Members of virtually every tribe wandered its dusty courses. Porters streamed by under the watchful eyes of guards armed with great long rifles and viciously curved scimitars. Traders hawked everything from beads to camels. Painted ladies wore veils which fell away in indiscreet folds. A bearded giant, carrying a full-grown sheep across his shoulders, passed him. A native child drove a herd of goats down the lane, then paused to gaze up in astonishment at Jake's blue eyes.

Desert folk shielded themselves against the growing evening chill with hooded djellabah of soft goat's wool. No man's head was uncovered. Turbans of white or checkered cloth, peaked hats, knitted caps—all denoted tribe and region as clearly as did robes and speech.

Women of the orthodox tribes were dressed in either all white or all black, their faces covered by embroidered shawls with rectangular slits for vision. No part of their bodies was permitted to be exposed, not even their hands, which were kept hidden within the flowing folds. Other women walked with no head covering at all save for sheer silk kerchiefs. Cascading gold bracelets on their ankles and wrists marked a cheerful tune with each step.

Jake climbed the outer ramparts of the city walls just in time to see the sun's final rays transform distant snow-capped peaks to bastions of molten gold. Guards standing duty along the wall glowered in his direction, but made no move. Clearly word had spread of the strangers who were there as guests of the sultan.

A cannon boomed from somewhere down the ramparts. As the echo rumbled like thunder through the valley, Jake watched the city's great outer doors draw shut. They rolled on ancient stone wheels, each pushed by six men, while another six heaved on a rope as thick as a man's thigh. As the doors rumbled closed, the muezzin's call rose from the mosque's minaret.

Jake looked out over a desert landscape gradually disappearing into a sea of blackness. Tiny orange fires shone from tribal campsites like mirrors of the stars appearing overhead. He watched the night gather strength, wished that Sally were there to share it all, and wondered at the strange new vistas opening up inside him.

He had long since learned to live with the responsibility of leadership. Before, he had always known that the answers had come from *him*—from his experience, his intelligence, his ability to see a situation and know the correct answer.

Now was different. Now the answers were not his own. They were from beyond. He *knew* this, knew he was being used as a conduit. It was not a comforting knowledge.

Jake found himself forced to accept his own weaknesses and lack of wisdom. And alongside this were the questions of who was using him, and how he could be sure he was hearing correctly.

The answer was there waiting for him, carried upon a wind which gathered force as the evening's chill took hold. Just as he stood strong and stable upon two legs, so his spiritual foundation needed to be based upon the dual pillars of prayer and daily study of the Scriptures.

In a sudden sweep of understanding, Jake saw beyond his own dilemma to the *opportunity*. By accepting the challenge, he was also being invited to grow. By seeing to the needs of others as well as to his own needs he was given great opportunities to deepen, to have more in order to give more.

A confirming grace of silence descended upon him, as powerful and far-reaching as the star-flecked heavens. Jake climbed back down from the ramparts, carrying the silence with him. This he understood as well. There would often be a need to rest in stillness, to listen without responding, to *wait*. To be sure that the answer was not his own. To give the questions over in prayer and study of the holy pages. To have the strength to remain quiet until the answer was given.

He returned to the stables and found Pierre seated beside a battered gas cooker, his eyes dark and downcast. Pierre raised his cup. "They brought the makings for tea. Apparently it is our only heat. Would you like a cup?"

"Sure." Jake squatted down beside the stove. "Beautiful night."

Pierre poured the steaming brew into a mug, added sugar from a small leather sack, and handed it over without meeting Jake's eyes. "You have been a good friend."

"I haven't done anything."

"You have done more than others with a world of words." Pierre raised his gaze. "You have given me the space to think."

Jake sipped the steamy liquid. "Want to tell me about it?"

Pierre's gaze dropped back to the flickering flame. "I feel . . . hollow."

The silence was captivating. Jake found himself hearing it almost as clearly as the words of his friend.

Pierre drew the blanket closer about his shoulders. "There have been moments. I am not sure if I can describe them."

"Try," Jake urged quietly.

"I have spent much time talking to what I am not sure is even there. That is how desperate I have become." Pierre hesitated, and lowered his head farther until his features were lost to shadows. "I am ashamed to tell you."

"No need," Jake said, his voice soft, trying hard to be there without disturbing the peace, the strength of silence.

"There have been moments when the unspoken words of my mind and heart have become alive." Pierre stopped, as though expecting Jake to laugh. When there was no sound, he went on. "I have felt almost as though there was something unseen there, not just listening, but guiding me as well."

Jake took another sip, his eyes steady upon his friend.

"Moments have passed when I am lost to all but the feeling of not being alone. Then the moment goes, and I am left with a greater torrent of doubts and worries than ever before."

Pierre heaved a sigh. "More and more the only peace I can find is in searching my heart's empty spaces with these unspoken words, begging for what I cannot even name to return with this gift of peace. Yet I do not hear the answer I seek. I do not hear what I should do about Jasmyn. Still, this moment of peace is the only answer that makes sense to my fevered mind."

Jake unbuttoned his shirt pocket and drew out his New Testament. "Here."

Pierre raised his head, hesitated, then accepted the book.
"We'll have to share it," Jake said. "It's the only one I
have."

"You think I should read this?"

"It's time," he replied. "Begin with Matthew, the first
book. If you like, we can talk about what you read."

Pierre fumbled, opened the cover, lowered the volume
until its pages were illuminated by the flame. Jake watched
him for a moment, his heart filled to bursting. He reached
over, set his hand on his friend's shoulder, and offered up a
brief prayer of his own. Then he stood and walked to the
neighboring stall.

Jake awoke to the sound of a cannon's thundering boom.
As he swung his feet down from the rich leather seat, a
muezzin's cry rose in the chill dawn air. He flung on his
clothes, washed in the outdoor trough, checked and saw
that Pierre was still asleep, and decided to take his breakfast in the city's market.

He walked through gradually awakening streets, savoring
the sights and sounds and smells. Old men greeted the new
day seated along sun-dappled walls, hoarding the meager
warmth of old bones by wrapping themselves in goat's-hair
blankets and sipping loudly from steaming vases of tea.

Jake stood at a tea stall, eating cold unleavened bread and
sweet honeyed dates spiced by the flavor of a new world.
He was so wrapped up in the moment that when the voice
spoke he very nearly cleared both feet from the ground.

"Jake," the voice behind him said.

He spun so fast he spilled the hot liquid over his fingers,
shouted his pain, and dropped the vaselike glass. The stall
holder cried his outrage when the glass shattered. Immediately Jasmyn spoke soothing words and reached in her belt-
purse for coppers. The man subsided under her voice and
her beauty, relenting so far as to offer Jake yet another
glass.

Gingerly he accepted the tea and demanded of her, "How
did you get here?"

"My mother's tribe is from east of these hills," she replied, her proud stature and her quietly spoken English garnering stares from all who passed. "When I was twelve we returned, my mother and I. She was not able to have other children, and she wanted her heritage to live in me. I spent half a year traveling the dry reaches, as long as my mother would remain apart from my father, who was too wedded to the sea ever to travel inland. So it was not hard for me to arrange transport with a hill tribe related to my own."

Jasmyn wore sweeping robes of black, lined with royal blue and a long head scarf of the same rich azure. She accepted her own cup of tea, sipped cautiously, and asked, "How is he?"

"Better," Jake said. "I really think he is better."

Great jade eyes opened to reveal depths of such painful yearning that they twisted his heart. Her voice trembled as much as the hand that held her tea. "Do you think there is a chance for us?"

"I hope so," he said with a fervor that surprised even himself. "But I don't know."

Jasmyn was silent for a time, and when she spoke again her control had returned. "You are in danger, but how much I cannot say."

"How do you know?"

"The Marrakesh jeweler, Herr Reich, was approached by the minions of Ibn Rashid after your departure. Herr Reich found them very willing to accept that he had made a mistake, and that the man with whom he had spoken was not Patrique. Too willing. So he made inquiries. Herr Reich is a well-connected man. It did not take him long to hear that Ibn Rashid had already received word that Patrique was being held for ransom by Sultan Musad al Rasuli."

Jake almost spilled his tea a second time. "He's here?"

"Somewhere," Jasmyn replied quietly, her eyes discreetly focused on the ground at her feet. "I have a relative in the sultan's service. I have sent word that I must speak with him."

"I don't understand," Jake muttered. "The sultan's assistant was the one who saw us into the city."

"He saw Pierre?"

"He was as close to him as I am to you." Worriedly Jake shook his head. "He's bound to know who's in the prison."

"This I do not understand. But still I believe the information to be true. According to Herr Reich's sources, Ibn Rashid has been arguing for over a month about the bounty demanded by the sultan. He would not do this unless he had solid evidence that Patrique was here. And alive."

She thought a moment. "Pierre must stay hidden as much as he possibly can. There is too much risk of him being recognized."

"That shouldn't be difficult. The official already thinks he's sick."

Concern swept over her features. "Pierre is ill?"

"Only for you," Jake said quietly. "He feels torn in two."

"But you said he was better."

"I hope he is."

"Tell him," she hesitated, and her eyes opened once more to reveal those endless green depths. "Tell him that my heart is his. My heart, my love, my reason for living."

Jake nodded. "How will I find you?"

"Come here again at midafternoon." Slender fingers rose to adjust the folds of her scarf. She then turned and vanished into the swirling throngs.

Jake stood for a long moment, sipping lukewarm tea and marveling at the strength contained in that fragile-seeming woman.

"She said that?"

"Those exact words," Jake confirmed. "She loves you with all her heart. All you have to do is look into her face to see that's the truth."

"And Patrique may be here. So much to think on." Pierre dropped his head into his hands. "I wish I knew—"

"Ah, gentlemens, excellent." Hareesh Yohari appeared in the stable doorway. He stared disdainfully down at Pierre. "Assistant is still with illness?"

"The altitude," Jake said, drawing himself erect. "But he's still working hard, sir."

The little official sniffed. "You come to sultan alone. Better for assistant to stay and work. Now. You have answers to question?"

"Hope so, sir."

"Yes, hope, for you and assistant, I so hope." He motioned. "You come."

Great bronze doors five times the height of a man opened into the inner residence. Geometric mosaics tiled the walls and floors. The air was rich with the fragrance of scented water spouting from a dozen fountains. Hundreds of birds sang from gilded cages. Flowers and palms grew in rich abundance. Servants scuttled in silence along the arched colonnades.

Another set of doors, these of intricately carved sandalwood, were pushed open by a pair of dark-skinned southerners. The official straightened to his full diminutive height and motioned Jake to walk behind him. They passed through stout pillars supporting a domed portico decorated with ivory mosaics. Sharp-eyed courtiers gathered about fountains of sparkling silver and grew silent and furtive at his passage. Stern warriors stood at attention, gleaming scimitars at the ready. Peacocks squawked a raucous greeting from tall cages.

A third pair of doors opened before them, these inlaid with intricate patterns of silver and ivory and semiprecious stones. Jake stepped inside, looked up, and gasped. The high dome was layered in sheets of gold.

The official murmured a salutation and bowed low. Jake decided a salute suited him better. When the sultan motioned them forward, Jake proceeded at a stiff-armed march. He approached across a sea of bright carpets, stopped before the dais, and saluted a second time.

The sultan wore an elaborately embroidered cloak of gold and black, sealed at the neck with a ruby the size of a hen's egg. His trousers and curled cloth slippers were sewn with shimmering gold thread. His be-ringed fingers grasped a staff of gold topped with an emerald half the size of Jake's fist. But nothing could disguise the flabby folds of the man's indolent body, nor the cruel glint of his hooded dark eyes.

The staff dipped in Jake's direction and the sultan spoke languidly. His official translated, "Great sultan asks, why you not bow like other mens."

"In my country," Jake replied, still at rigid attention, "the greatest sign of respect a soldier can give to a superior officer is the salute."

"Superior, yes, is good answer." The official turned and replied with a torrent of words and florid hand gestures. As the sultan listened, he gave a tiny flickering motion with one finger. Instantly a servant appeared at his side, stoked the bowl of a silver hookah, set a smoldering coal on the top, then with an elaborate bow handed the sultan the pipe. The sultan sprawled upon his dais, settled within gold-embroidered velvet cushions, and drew hard until the pipe gurgled and threw up great clouds of pungent smoke. Finally satisfied that it was drawing well, he spoke again.

"Great sultan ask, when are cars ready."

"The first should be up and running in two days," Jake replied. "Three at the most."

The official risked a warning glance. "Is best not to be wrong."

"My assistant and I are working around the clock," Jake replied solemnly. "Can't have the great sultan kept waiting."

"No, yes, is true." Hesitantly the official turned back and replied.

The sultan, his face wreathed in smoke, watched Jake. Again Musad al Rasuli spoke. Hareesh translated, "And the other Rolls Royce motor vehicles?"

"A couple of weeks. Probably not more than that."

"Great sultan say, he wait a year, more, and you fix Rolls Royce motor vehicles in days, maybe he keep you here, give you job in stable. Permanent retainer."

"Tell the great sultan it would be an honor to serve him," Jake replied solemnly, keeping his thoughts to himself about being made a slave. Years of dealing with superior officers had taught him that a direct refusal was the worst possible reply to an order.

"Great sultan say, what you expect for these workings."

"The great sultan strikes me as a fair and generous man," Jake replied straight-faced. "Why don't we let him decide what the work is worth."

The official tossed him another uncertain glance, then replied. The sultan contemplatively drew upon his hookah, then motioned his dismissal. Jake threw another exaggerated salute, spun about, and marched back alongside the little official. Only when the great doors had closed behind them did he permit himself a quiet little smile.

Every sense was on full alert as together they went to the rendezvous with Jasmyn that afternoon. His mind shouted danger, but Jake could not refuse Pierre's insistence that he come along. Despite the heat, Pierre wore the black knit cap many older Arabs used against the night chill. With his shoulders hunched, walking half a pace behind and beside Jake, he remained as much hidden as possible.

Jasmyn's calm demeanor dissolved when she spotted Pierre. She rushed up and shepherded them into a refuse-littered alcove between the stalls. "Why do you come?"

"To see you," Pierre replied.

"Oh, oh, oh," she said, reaching for him, pulling back, her face a tormented mask of fear and hope. "How I have dreamed of hearing those words."

"I have thought and I have thought and I have thought," Pierre said, speaking to the stones at his feet. "I speak now so that my friend can hear this as well. Without him I would be lost in the darkness still. I do not know what the answer is, but I know that my life without you is no life at all."

Tears streamed unheeded down her face as she reached with trembling fingers and took one of Pierre's hands in both of hers. Jake blocked them from the view of passersby as much as he could and felt his own heart sing. Jasmyn stroked Pierre's hand and whispered, "Pierre, oh, Pierre."

"Perhaps," Pierre said, his voice unsteady, "perhaps you can help me to find the answers."

"There is nothing I would rather do," she whispered. "For now, for tomorrow, for all the tomorrows to come."

Jake felt eyes searching his back, probing the shadows where a fair-skinned stranger held the hands of a weeping woman dressed in the garb of the desert tribes. "I think we'd all have a better chance of seeing another tomorrow if we continued this somewhere else."

Pierre nodded. "You will come with us?"

"I cannot," she said, and released one hand long enough to wipe her face. "I would never be permitted entry into the palace grounds. And I have news."

Pierre stiffened. "Patrique?"

She nodded. "He is here."

"But how did the official not recognize me?"

The tears started anew. "I have word that he is not as he once was."

The glint in his eyes turned fierce. "What have they done to him?"

"Pierre," she whispered. "You are hurting me."

Immediately he slackened his clenched fist. "Tell me."

"He is held in the palace dungeon. I have a map." She reluctantly released his hand to extract a slip of paper from the folds of her robe. "There is a barred window high up in his cell wall. It opens onto the yard just beyond the stable courtyard."

"We will find it," Jake said, an idea taking form in his mind.

"You must hurry," she said. "Ibn Rashid's men are said to be here now, striking the final bargain."

"Tonight," Pierre hissed. "My brother will greet the next dawn as a free man."

"But how can you escape?" Her tone became increasingly frantic. "They would shoot you on sight. I could not bear—"

Jake interrupted her with, "Would your people offer us shelter?"

She showed confusion. "How—"

He leaned down. "Would they?"

Jasmyn forced her mind to work. "Some of my mother's tribe are camped at the valley's far eastern end. This I heard from the kinsman who works in the sultan's palace. If I left now, I could be there before nightfall. If I ask for help, they are bound by custom to grant it."

"Better and better," Jake said. "We should be at the road's far eastern end just after dawn tomorrow."

"How is that possible?" She turned to Pierre and begged, "Do not get yourself hurt. If you were to die, I would as well."

He reached for both her hands, held them a moment, then asked Jake, "You have a plan?"

"The bare bones is all."

"Go to your people," Pierre told her. "Tell them we come. Ask them for shelter."

She looked long into his face, drinking in what had so long been denied her. Then she leaned forward and kissed him once, twice, a third time, before releasing him and pulling up her scarf. "Promise me you will come."

"With the dawn," Pierre said, his eyes kindled with a new light. "Now go."

Chapter Sixteen

"*T*HEY FIRE A cannon to open and close the main gates?"

Jake stared at his friend. "You really have been out of it, haven't you."

"I don't understand. How can we be sure exactly when it fires?"

"We can't. But the mountains throw the sound back and forth for a while."

"How long?"

"Long enough. That is, if we're ready."

Pierre was silent.

"What do you think?"

He rose to his feet. "I think I need to hear this cannon for myself."

As they walked the crowded ways, Jake told him, "That was a great thing you did, speaking to Jasmyn like that."

"I confess to you and you alone that it would have been impossible without your help, my friend."

"Without God's help, you mean."

"Perhaps," Pierre said, climbing the rampart's ladder behind Jake. "Still, I find it easier to credit you than the Invisible."

They stood in silence and watched the evening descend. When the cannon boomed on cue, Jake counted off the rumbling thunder. "I give it ten, maybe twelve seconds. More than enough time."

"For what?" Pierre demanded.

As night draped the highlands in a blanket of darkness and the immense doors rumbled shut beneath them, Jake outlined his idea. He finished just as the muezzin's wail began to fade. Pierre remained silent for a time, mulling it over in his mind before declaring, "It is a good plan."

"You think it'll work?"

"We can only hope." He clapped his friend on the shoulder and turned for the ladder. "Come. It is time to see if the directions are correct and my brother truly languishes in an Arab's dungeon."

Night cloaked their movements as they walked past the stables and entered a narrow connecting passageway. Eighty meters farther on, the passage opened into a second yard, this one for farm animals. Cows, chickens, ducks, geese, goats, and even a few sheep filled the muddy area with their noise and their smell.

Together the two scouted the surrounding walls and saw, to their immense relief, that the map was correct—no windows faced them from the upper palace walls. They stood and listened to the cacophony and searched the walls of the inner keep.

Jake's guess appeared to be correct—guards were concentrated along the outer keep and within the palace itself. The inner wall was unguarded except for the sentinels at the gate.

They could see only one opening into the palace foundations, a low window just beyond the trough. The air rising through the thick iron bars was so foul that Jake had trouble approaching. Pierre fell to his knees, clenched the bars, and hissed into the fetid darkness, "Patrique!"

From the pit came a stirring, clinking shuffle. At the sound of chains dragging across stone, the cords of Pierre's neck and arms stretched taut, as though he sought to tear the bars from the wall. He hissed a second time, "Patrique!"

"C'est qui?" came the fearful reply.

"Pierre."

A long pause, then the tremulous murmur, "Mon frère?"

Jake examined the crossbars and knew a qualm of doubt. They were not bolted to the wall, but imbedded deep into the stone. "Ask him if he's chained to the wall."

Pierre did so. The reply wafted upward with the stench. "Oui."

"Three ropes," Jake muttered.

"What?"

"Give him the scoop," Jake replied. "Hurry."

Pierre spoke at length while Jake nervously watched the shadows. Seconds stretched like hours until Pierre sighed, released his hold, and stood. "We go."

When dinner was brought, they sent the servant to summon Hareesh Yohari. The official bustled in more than an hour later, clearly miffed at being disturbed. "What this is, hey? You tell servant go bringing sultan's personal administrator, better having good reason."

Jake straightened, wiping his hands on an oily rag. Pierre kept his burning rage hidden beneath the engine cowling. "This one's almost ready," Jake replied, unable to drag up the pretense of respect. The sound of Patrique's fearful voice rising from the foul darkness hovered still in his mind.

"Yes?" The official was too pleased to note Jake's casual manner. "Is two days early for Rolls Royce motor vehicle to running."

Jake nodded. "We need to take it out for a trial spin tomorrow morning."

Hareesh's brow furrowed. "What this is, trial spin?"

"We need to take the car, the motor vehicle, out to make sure it's running right. You wouldn't want it to break down with the sultan driving, would you?"

The diminutive official showed real horror. "By the Prophet's sword, no, no, is great danger. Heads watching sunset from spike on wall."

"Right. So before the city wakes up and the streets become crowded, just after the cannon fires and the doors open, we'll drive the car out a ways and check it all out. Then we'll bring it back, give it a good polish, and send for you."

Hareesh bobbed his head like a feeding waterbird. "Yes, yes, is smart thinkings. You going for trial before sultan waking."

"Gotcha. You better tell the guards so they don't wonder what we're doing."

"Yes, am telling all peoples tonight."

Jake played it casual, asked the inevitable, "You want to come along?"

Hareesh pretended to give it serious consideration before replying, "No, is not necessary. I drive with sultan." He smiled in utter superiority. "Where are mens to going with car? Valley closed, no roads out, yes?"

"Exactly," Jake agreed, and heaved a great internal sigh as the little official spun on his heel and paraded off.

Pierre chose that moment to extract his grease-smeared face and demand, "Why did you have to ask him that?"

"The only way I could be sure he wouldn't pop up unexpectedly," Jake replied. "The car ready?"

"This car has been perfectly ready," Pierre replied, "for fifteen years."

"Then let's fire the sucker up."

With a new battery and tires and oil and filters, not to mention a careful adjustment by two semiskilled mechanics, the Rolls fired on the first try. Jake swung the cowling closed, fastened the great leather straps, and stepped back. From a dozen paces the sound was barely audible.

He walked over to where Pierre sat behind the wheel. "Who drives tomorrow?"

"You," he replied immediately. "I will be far too nervous."

When their preparations were completed, neither man showed any interest in sleep. They hunkered down by the cooking stove, sipped cups of steaming tea, and silently mused upon what lay ahead.

Finally Pierre raised dark eyes over the rim of his cup and asked, "Do you think it would be a good thing for us to pray?"

"I think it would be a very good thing," Jake said, setting down his cup, realizing he had been half-hoping Pierre would ask. "A very good thing indeed."

Chapter Seventeen

WHILE IT WAS still pitch black, they drove the Rolls through the narrow passage separating their stable from the animal yard. The engine purred with silent grace as Jake eased it forward with scarcely an inch to spare on either side. The yard was quiet save for the bleating of an amiable goat and a single rooster anticipating the dawn. Jake backed the big car up close to the dungeon window, then went back to help Pierre with the ropes.

While his friend lowered the pair of ropes down into the stinking darkness, Jake ran the thickest strand they had found in the stable yards back and forth among the crossed iron bars, then tied both ends to either side of the Rolls' bumper. After carefully testing the knots, he helped Pierre measure out and prepare his own lines. "You better hope your brother understood to tie the longer one to his waist and the shorter one to the wall. Otherwise we're going to stretch him to the limit."

"He understood," Pierre said, frantically tugging on the lines.

"You're sure there's enough play in those lines so they go taut in turn?" Jake cautioned. "The bars have to give first, then the chain is pulled from the wall, then he's raised up to safety. Otherwise—"

371

"Enough, enough," Pierre hissed, pointing to the lightening sky. "Get into position, Jake. It is almost time."

His heart in his throat, Jake climbed into the quietly idling automobile and waited. Minutes stretched out endlessly, granting him ample time to worry through all the possible things that might go wrong. The sky continued to brighten until he finally decided that the cannon had misfired, that the gates were long since open, that they couldn't hear the muezzin's cry from this end of the palace, that soon a guard was going to appear and point a great blunderbuss down on their heads and—

The cannon's boom caught him totally by surprise. Jake's hand slipped off the gear lever in a sweaty jerk. He fumbled, meshed into first, eased the clutch, and started forward. As the rope connected to the bars pulled taut, he turned back, saw Pierre check the other two and give him a pumping action with one fist. He gunned the engine and willed the bars to give.

Nothing.

The motor roared, the tires spun, Pierre was pelted by a storm of dust and gravel and barnyard filth. His anger mounting, Jake eased off, reversed back, slapped it back into first gear, and tried again. The bars refused to give.

Jake felt something snap in his head. Casting caution to the wind, he slammed the car into reverse, swiveled in his seat, stomped on the accelerator, and roared with the bellowing engine.

He struck the wall with a crashing thud.

Pierre inspected the wall, shouted, "Again!"

A second time he drove forward, raced back, and slammed into the palace.

"Again!"

Jake shouted his frustration and did as he was told.

"Good! Now *pull*!"

Jake rammed the car forward, and the entire section of the wall came away with him.

A second smaller tug signaled that the chain was free from the wall. Jake slowed, turned in the seat, and drove forward while watching back as Pierre fell to his knees by the gaping hole and began guiding the third rope up and out. A shout and Jake stopped and flung open his door. He skidded to a stop at the sight of a herdsman staring wide-eyed at them from the doorway of his stable-yard hovel. Jake opened his jacket to reveal the pistol stuck into his belt, then motioned with his head. The man understood perfectly and vanished back into his hut.

Jake raced back and found Pierre struggling to help a scarecrow of a man clamber up and over the ledge. He was little more than skin and bones and matted beard, clothed in stinking rags. Pierre was almost weeping with rage. "Look at what they have done to my brother."

"He's alive," Jake said tersely. "You want to keep it that way, get him in the car."

Together they bundled Patrique into the back compartment and hid him on the floorboards under a heap of blankets. Jake used his knife to slice the ropes free from the bumper, then returned to where Pierre was tucking blankets around his brother and demanded, "Do you speak English?"

The man was trembling too hard to reply with more than a nod.

"There's a sack of food and water there by your head," Jake went on. "Hold off until we're outside the gates."

Pierre hissed as he shifted the chain still bound to Patrique's leg and revealed great weeping sores circling the ankle.

Jake had opened his mouth to urge Pierre into the front seat when a cry rose from deep in the palace's bowels. They jerked up as further shouts rose from the dungeon, then slammed the passenger door and scrambled into the car. Stiff with alarm, Jake found first gear and slammed the accelerator home.

The Rolls scattered a vast assortment of squawking birds and raced into the narrow passage. Sparks flew from each side in turn as they ricocheted from one stone wall to the other. They exited the passage, roared through the first stable yard, slid into second gear, and passed through the portals of the inner keep at almost thirty miles an hour.

An invading army could scarcely have caused more alarm than the Rolls. Early morning traders, owlish with sleep, cleared their stalls in single bounding leaps at the sight of the great silver eyes roaring down on them. The central passage descended in a series of long sloping steps. Jake managed to clear all four tires a dozen times or more before the great outer doors careened into view. The guards had clearly been forewarned about their intended test drive, for as the car hurtled over the final square and through the portico, they lifted weapons high and shouted their approval. Jake slammed the car into third, took the curve by the river in a dusty four-wheel spin, and roared away.

The road leading east was rough and cobblestoned and blindingly bright from the sun's rising glare. Jake was literally on top of the first goat before he saw the herd, and carried two of the animals a good thirty yards before he managed to shake them loose. He then remembered that the car probably had a horn, and hit every surface on the dash before discovering the switch by his right hand. He then drove by horn and feel, his eyes squinted up against the blazing orb. The horn was a splendid three-tone affair, blaring out its royal aaah-oooh-gah in time to their jouncing progress.

To Jake's relief, the road took a gentle turning, and a high central peak blocked the sun. Jake managed a swift glance at his companion. Pierre sat wide-eyed and rigid as the car frame. Jake shouted, "You all right?"

"How fast are we going?"

Jake checked the controls, replied, "A little over seventy."

"You will never speak to me about my driving again," Pierre shouted back. "Is that clear?"

Jake grinned and swerved to avoid a shepherd glued to the center of the road with terror. His sheep had shown more sense and were scattered to the wind. The mountains were drawing closer, shielding them from the dawn's glare. They passed through two villages in turn, the villagers frozen to the ground. Jake had sufficiently recovered by then to bestow a few regal waves as they breezed bumpily through.

They were almost upon the mountains before Pierre pointed and shouted, "The cliff at eleven o'clock!"

Jake craned and spotted the blue-robed Arab waving and pointing them toward a crevice opening at his feet. Without slowing, Jake wheeled the big car off the rapidly deteriorating road. The engine roared in mighty fury as the tires spun through softer sand before catching hold and hurtling forward. Careening wildly from side to side, Jake scrambled through the yielding drift, willing the car onward. The steep rock side rose up around them, and they hit harder ground. Jake eased up on the accelerator as they hurtled ever deeper into the rock-walled crevass.

They continued on this winding course for almost ten miles before the walls closed in so tightly they threatened to jam the car to a halt. Another sharp turning, and suddenly the walls opened to reveal a great open space where tall date palms sheltered an open well. At the car's unexpected appearance, camels reared, sheep scattered, goats bleated, and Arabs came streaming toward them.

Jake was too caught up in the adrenaline rush to just sit there. He slammed back the roof, stepped up on the seat, raised two fists high over his head, and shouted up at the heavens above, *"Yee-ha!"*

"My cousin says your greeting is worthy of a great warrior," Jasmyn said, hastening forward, her eyes fastened upon Pierre. At her side strode a tall Arab of proud bearing and evident strength. "My cousin, Omar Al-Masoud, leader of the Al-Masoud tribe, bids you welcome."

Jake grinned down at the pair. "Tell your cousin we're mighty grateful for his hospitality, and ask him if he's in the market for a slightly used Rolls Royce. We'd like him to accept it as a little token of appreciation and all that."

Dark eyes gleamed brightly at the translation. He stared up at Jake for a long moment, then nodded once. Jake felt a thrill of having gotten something very important very right. "My cousin asks if this is the sultan's car."

"It was."

"Then he accepts your gift and asks if you can drive it into the cave there behind you."

"No problem." Jake watched Pierre step from the car and walk stiffly over to Jasmyn. She stared up at him, searching his face for a long time. The Arab observed the scene with an unreadable gaze. Pierre nodded once, then said quietly, "At times I wondered if perhaps my memories had painted you to be more beautiful than you were. No one could be so lovely, I told myself. But I see that I was wrong to wonder."

Jasmyn lifted one hand to touch his face, then stopped herself. Her voice was shaky as she said, "I have told my people that you are my fiancé. It does the tribe honor to have me return with you before, before . . ."

"Before our marriage," Pierre said quietly.

She gasped a single quick sob, but with great determination drew herself up. "They will help us go where we wish."

"A doctor," Jake said, motioning to the back compartment. "Patrique is in pretty bad shape."

Jasmyn turned and spoke to her cousin, who called over a pair of women. Pierre tore himself away from Jasmyn to help them bring Patrique out. "There is a healer two villages away," Jasmyn translated. "We will go there."

"Jasmyn," Patrique murmured. "Is it truly you?"

She walked over and touched the gaunt man's trembling hand. "You are safe now, my friend."

"Again you have saved me," he said hoarsely. "How can I ever repay you?"

Pierre started. "Again?"

"There is no debt, and thus nothing to repay," Jasmyn replied.

"Because of her I escaped from Marseille just ahead of the Nazi raid," Patrique said. "How can you not know of this?"

"Because I am a fool," Pierre replied, gazing at her.

A call hallooed from above and beyond the rocky confines. A guard above their heads called back and away from them. A distant call drifted back upon the wind. The entire

camp seemed to hold its breath and listen. "Horses," Jasmyn said. "Many horses. Coming this way."

Omar shouted instructions. Jake saw a group gather up
branches and began brushing away the car's tracks. "Please,
Jake," Jasmyn urged, "you are to drive the car into the cave
now. We must hurry. The sultan's men are after us."

Chapter Eighteen

IT WAS THREE days before Omar felt safe enough to bring them into a village. They walked twenty miles or more each day, passing through narrow defiles which opened suddenly into boulder-strewn pastures. Always their destination at day's end was pasture and water. Seldom was there warning before the rocky gorges spilled them into the great open spaces. Their path wound through chasms and passes and bone-dry valleys, jinking back and forth so repeatedly that Jake could never have found his way out alone. Somewhere up ahead, Omar told him through Jasmyn, the jagged Atlas foothills joined the Sahara. There in the first desert reaches waited the remainder of his tribe. That was their destination. For now, they took a course uncharted by any save those trained by their fathers, and they by their fathers before them. Such, proclaimed Omar, was the desert way.

They met other people only once in that three-day stretch, another desert tribe sending wool and hand-woven carpets toward Telouet. Jake crouched in the shadows of the great central tent, dressed in the same desert robes as all the other men, and watched as solemn greetings were exchanged.

Patrique rode hunched on a camel, recovering slowly, sleeping much and eating with the hunger of one who could never be sated. Pierre and Jasmyn tended to him constantly, but in truth Jake felt they saw little save each other. He did not mind. A whole new world opened up before him, one of silence and heat and sun and wind. Omar saw that Jake's fascination was genuine and accepted him into the fold. Their lack of a common tongue was no great barrier. Speech was not so important here in the reaches where silence reigned.

On the third day, Omar entered the quiet stucco village with Jake and Jasmyn. Pierre had elected to remain behind with Patrique. Jake wore the royal blue of the desert tribes, belted and robed and turbaned. The clothes still carried a hint of alienness with them, but they no longer hung as strangely as they had the first day. Jake was swiftly learning to appreciate them and the life they stood for.

The village was composed of two dozen meager huts, more camels than people, and more goats than both. A single wire strung limply from pole to pole connected the village with the outside world.

They followed the wire to the village's main store, a fly-infested pair of rooms stocking everything from saddles to salt. Barefoot children in filthy miniature robes scampered in the dust outside the doorway. Jake walked in after Omar, waited while the formal greetings were exchanged, and watched the storekeeper enter into a paroxysm of refusal when Omar made his request. Not content to simply shake his head, the storekeeper rose to his feet and twisted his entire body back and forth. Although Jake could not understand a word, the message was clear. Under no circumstances would he allow a stranger to send a telegraph on his set. No matter that the storekeeper could only send and receive in Arabic. The message must be translated and sent by him, the one and only official telegraph operator in the valley.

Jake then reached into his belt pouch and displayed his dwindling wad of dollars. The storekeeper deflated like a punctured balloon. His entire demeanor changed. He pushed open the stall door, shoved papers and forms and sheets off the cluttered desk and onto the floor, dusted off his chair, and held it as Jake sat down.

Through Jasmyn Jake made his request. No, the storekeeper replied, there was no problem in making a connection to Gibraltar. Of course, he had never done it, but yes, it was possible through the operator in Tangiers. They had communicated several times, and he knew the operator to be a good man. Yes, of course, for the desert sahib he could make the connection. It would be an honor. One moment, please.

They waited out the interim in the shadowed coolness of the village's only teahouse, which in truth was simply the front room of the shopkeeper's own three-room shanty. As they sat and sipped the sugary tea, Jasmyn said, "We have been ignoring you these past few days."

"You have every reason to," Jake replied. "I'm not much competition for true love."

Dark green eyes raised to gaze at him. "I am in your debt," she said gravely. "You have restored to me my reason for living."

"Not me," Jake countered. "It was all God's work."

"Yes, I have heard the same from Pierre," she said, "and this is as great a miracle as the fact that he is here with me." She watched Jake for a long moment, then asked, "Could you perhaps teach me how to find God so that I may thank Him?"

"There is nothing on earth," Jake replied sincerely, "that would give me greater joy."

The moment became almost an hour before the storekeeper, now swelled with importance, announced that his Tangiers connection, whose name by the way was Mohammed, had succeeded in making the link to the central Gibraltar operator, who happened to be at the naval base. Oh, that was exactly the person with whom the sahib wished to speak? Then indeed Allah must be smiling on their proceedings. Please, please, the sahib must now sit and communicate with the Gibraltar operator.

Jake approached the telegraph key with trepidation. He had no hope of arriving back on time, and his commanding officer was a firebrand for discipline. Jake knew there was a very good chance that General Clark would tear his story apart, especially with him not there to defend it. But he had too much respect for the general to offer anything but the truth. He hoped fervently that Bingham would weigh in on his behalf and confirm at least the beginning of their journey.

He unfolded the paper bearing the message he had composed the night before, bent over the key, and began. It took almost forty-five minutes to transcribe the message, partly because it was long and partly because his Morse code was so rusty. When he finished, Jake sighed his way to his feet, unbent his back, and said, "I guess we might as well go."

The storekeeper accepted the dollars with unbridled greed. He salaamed repeatedly and shook each of their hands half a dozen times before finally permitting them to depart.

They were almost at the outskirts of the village before the cry rose up behind them. "Sahib, sahib!"

The storekeeper raced up, fought for breath, and jabbered away while plucking at Jake's sleeve. "He has received a reply from Gibraltar," Jasmyn told Jake. "He cannot understand it, and says you must come back now."

Jake raced back to the store, slid into the seat, and keyed in the repeat sign. The reply came back immediately:

BINGHAM HERE STOP HAVE BEEN IN FREQUENT TOUCH WITH CLARK STOP NUMEROUS DEVELOPMENTS THIS SIDE STOP REQUEST CONFIRMATION THAT BROTHER OF MAJOR SERVAIS ALIVE AND WELL STOP

Jake pushed aside all wonderment and keyed back:

PATRIQUE ALIVE AND RECOVERING FROM ORDEAL STOP IS HERE WITH US STOP

ASSUME FROM YOUR MESSAGE THAT TRAVEL
BACK TO TANGIERS OR RABAT IMPOSSIBLE STOP

AFFIRMATIVE STOP WE ARE HUNTED BOTH BY
IBN RASHID AND THE SULTAN'S MEN STOP

A longer pause, then:

URGENT YOU AND MAJOR SERVAIS ESCORT HIS
BROTHER TO PORT OF MELILLA STOP WILL HAVE
BOAT RENDEZVOUS WITH YOU THERE STOP EX-
TREME CAUTION REQUIRED STOP REQUEST ETA
STOP

Jake turned to Jasmyn and asked, "Ask Omar if he can
take us to Melilla."

Her eyes widened, as did his at the translation. "You seek
to cross the Hamada and the Jebel Sahara? Those reaches
are called the Great Burn. They are most dangerous."

"Does he know if it is possible?"

Omar drew himself up to full height. Through Jasmyn he
replied, "I hold the desert wisdom of twenty generations.
No one but I could see you across the Hamada hill country
and the eastern Sahara. No one."

Jake recognized a negotiating ploy when he heard one.
"Hang on a sec." He keyed out:

HAVE POSSIBLE GUIDE AND COVER BUT EXPEN-
SIVE STOP

BOAT WILL CARRY ADEQUATE SUM AND AU-
THORITY FOR PAYMENT STOP REQUEST ETA
STOP

"We will pay you well," Jake replied to Omar. When that
was translated he asked Jasmyn, "Would you come with
us?"

"Pierre will be traveling with you?"

"I think so. And Patrique."

"Then I will go." Definite. Unequivocal. Determined.
"Ask him how long it would take, please."
The translated reply came back, "Two weeks if the wind and Allah are with us. If not," Omar shrugged his reply.

UNDER A MONTH STOP

TOO LONG STOP YOU ARE HEREBY COM-MANDED TO MAKE FOR MELILLA WITH ALL POS-SIBLE HASTE STOP WILL CLEAR WITH YOUR SU-PERIORS THIS SIDE STOP CONFIRM BROTHER OF MAJOR SERVAIS HAS PROOF OF TRAITOR STOP

AFFIRMATIVE STOP BUT HE IS ILL AND MAY SLOW US DOWN STOP

MAKE HASTE BUT WITH PRUDENCE STOP HOW RECEIVED STOP

LOUD AND CLEAR STOP

GODSPEED

III
Sahara Crosswind

*This book is dedicated to
Samen Mina
A man wise in the ways
of both desert and city
A friend who hears the music
of the heavens*

Chapter One

SULTAN MUSAD AL RASULI'S dungeon passage was foul with odors and centuries of agony. The jailer led the little group down the stairs, wheezing through lungs tainted by years of breathing the imprisoned air.

Behind him puffed the sultan's assistant, Hareesh Yohari, trying futilely to mask his nervousness by adopting an even more officious manner than usual. He cast a furtive eye back at the two Tuareg. The desert warriors followed close at his heels. Tall and hawk-nosed and cruel of gaze, they had been sent across the mountains from Marrakesh by Ibn Rashid, the undisputed master of Marrakesh's old city. Their orders were to make a final payment to the sultan, witness the demise of the prisoner called Patrique Servais, and return with the unfortunate's head.

At the passage's end the jailer stopped by a stout iron door. He rammed back the great iron bolt, shoved the door upon its complaining hinges, and motioned the other men through.

Hareesh Yohari stopped by the portal and announced, "The honored guests are to follow the sultan's jailer. I shall await you here."

"The sultan ordered you to be his official witness," hissed one of the men.

"Is not necessary, not in the least," Hareesh Yohari replied, drawing himself up to his full diminutive height. "The jailer will make a perfectly good witness to all that transpires."

The second man, darker and taller and far crueler looking than his minion, leaned down until his great beak of a nose was within an inch of Yohari's face. His voice was as quiet and dry and deadly as a desert wind. "The sultan said *you*."

Hareesh Yohari swallowed with great difficulty. "Of course, if the honored guests wish for me to accompany them, who am I to refuse?"

Beyond the door stretched a great chamber, its alcoves and arched roof hidden in shadows cast by the smoky torches. The chamber was filled with hanging cages and vats and instruments of torture. This slowed down their progress considerably, as the two Tuareg showed great interest in all the implements, and the jailer responded to their queries with professional pride. Hareesh Yohari hovered just beyond the trio, almost dancing in his nervous desire to get the task over with and be gone from this foul and fetid pit.

Scarcely had they made their way through half the chamber before a great noise boomed, and the solid rock floor beneath their feet shuddered. The jailer started and dropped the red-hot branding iron he had been demonstrating. With a sizzle, it made contact with his sandaled foot. While he shouted and leapt about, the others searched and craned to discover the source of the noise.

A second noise, louder than the first, drowned the jailer's anguished cries. The Tuareg drew their daggers, the only weapons permitted them in the sultan's palace, and bounded toward the far wall, from beyond which the noise had come. They pulled futilely at the second great door. Then with an oath the taller of the pair raced back, plucked up the wailing jailer by his leather apron, and dragged him over. Hareesh Yohari scuttled fearfully along behind them.

As the jailer moaned and jangled his keys, a third booming explosion shook the chamber, this one followed by a great crashing and rending. Shouts resounded through the palace overhead.

The Tuareg buffeted the jailer with a pair of great blows before he managed to fit in the proper key and unlock the door. Together the Tuareg lifted the man and carried him down to where a final door stood between them and the sound of chains being plucked from stone and dragged across the floor. The jailer's hands were trembling so hard it took several further blows about his head before the proper key was found. The door was flung back, and with a great cry the Tuareg bounded in.

The chamber was empty. A ragged-edged hole gaped high overhead where before had been only a narrow, barred slit.

The taller Tuareg lifted the jailer with one mighty hand, placed his curved dagger across the man's neck, and hissed, "This was the cell of the one called Patrique, the one sought by Ibn Rashid?"

The jailer managed a terror-stricken nod. "I know nothing, masters, please, I—"

"Listen," hissed the other Tuareg.

In the sudden silence they heard voices speaking foreign words, then a roaring noise, followed by scraping, rending sounds. "A motor car," said the Tuareg.

"It can't be!" shouted a wide-eyed Hareesh Yohari.

"And ferengi are driving," the other said.

"Impossible!" Terror drove Yohari's voice up a full two octaves.

The taller Tuareg tossed the jailer aside and raced through the cell door. "To the ramparts, swiftly! We must signal to close the outer gates."

"Yes, of course, of course," the diminutive official agreed, but for some reason appeared in no hurry to follow them. "You must hurry, of course. And I must alert the guard. And the sultan, of course—he must know all."

But as the Tuareg raced through the outer dungeon, Yohari stopped, turned, and scampered to a small, hidden side door. He pushed the secret handle, slipped through, and quietly closed the door behind him.

Chapter Two

*I*T WAS THE desert way.

Lieutenant Colonel Jake Burnes had heard that phrase so often from his tribal hosts that it had begun to echo in his mind.

For a week and a day he had walked through reaches so empty they had ached with their burden of void. And yet it was in this arid emptiness that his heart had begun to fill with appreciation for the men and women and children who allowed him to travel in their midst.

The Al-Masoud tribe were a people who defined who they were not by what they owned, not by their houses or jobs or ambitions, but by tradition. Theirs was an extended family of some eighty souls, bound to one another and to the past by centuries of tribal lore.

The desert way.

The phrase wafted through his thoughts as he stood on a rise above the camp, watching a heated discussion between the tribal elders and their leader, Omar. Even at this distance, their voices floated clearly through the desert air. Jake had by then begun to recognize Omar's style of leadership. Every major decision was first given over to open debate. But once the judgment was set, any further argument was met with savage fury. That, too, was the desert way, and for the moment it seemed more real than all that lay behind him and all that lay before.

So much seemed so distant here in this parched land of sand and scrub and stone. The States, which had birthed him and raised him and then sent him off to fight against Hitler's forces. Europe, where he had fought a war and fallen in love and forged the friendship with Pierre Servais that had brought him to this vast desert. Even the mountain fastness of Telouet, not so many days behind them, where he and Pierre had breached a sultan's dungeon and narrowly escaped with the prisoner and their lives. And faraway Gibraltar, the source of their telegraphed orders to cross the desert at all possible speed with their recovered comrade and his important secrets.

All these places and events haunted his memory and directed his plans. Yet somehow they seemed infinitely removed from his present reality.

A strange dark cloud hung low on the horizon, hiding the sinking sun and staining the landscape the color of dried blood. Down in the camp, Jake saw a brown arm extend from a sweeping robe to point toward the cloud, then another gesture toward the pristine blue sky that still arched overhead. More voices. More discussion. Nods of concern and knowledge and understanding. The desert way.

Now he saw Jasmyn Coltrane detach herself from a cluster of women and walk over to where he stood.

Jasmyn. He had first heard that name as part of a bitter tale of treachery—the mysterious half-French, half-Moroccan woman who was said to have betrayed his friend Pierre for a Nazi officer. Then he had learned that her true story was one of love and loyalty and sacrifice.

It had been Jasmyn who helped them find Pierre's twin brother Patrique in the sultan's palace, who had arranged with her tribal kinsman to help them escape. And it was for her sake that Omar had taken them in and offered to guide them from the mountains outside Telouet to the Mediterranean port city of Melilla.

"There is a storm," Jasmyn told him, dark green eyes showing worry under her blue headkerchief. "A khamsin, it is called. A desert wind."

"So I see."

"It is tracking parallel to our course, but Omar thinks the night currents will turn it toward us. This is a risk we must prepare ourselves to meet, especially with the new lambs."

Jake had been up much of the night before, along with many of the others, watching the miracle of birth. Six lambs had appeared in the space of twelve hours. Within minutes of taking their first shuddering breath, the tiny animals had risen upon trembling legs and made for the udder. Their approach was greeted by a deep chuckling sound from their mothers. Little tails fluttered with the thrill of eating. Jake had stood with the others in the cramped paddock, watching and pointing and laughing with unbounded hilarity at their antics. And feeling lonelier than he had felt since beginning his desert journey.

Jasmyn touched his arm. "Jake?"

He looked down at her and confessed, "I was thinking of Sally."

"You miss her." It was not a question.

"Very much." It was a ridiculously inadequate answer. "It seems like everywhere I turn, I discover something new I wish I could share with her. Like the lambs."

"From everything you have said, I feel I know this woman Sally." Jasmyn inspected his face. "I have started a letter to her. I would very much like her to know how grateful I am for all you have done. If you give me an address, I shall be mailing it as soon as we pass a village with a postal system."

"I don't even know where she is myself," he replied sadly. "I have to send my letters in care of the U.S. Embassy in Paris. She's traveling around with some high-powered Allied generals. They forward mail by diplomatic pouch. But thank you."

"Poor Jake," she said, and reached over to touch his sleeve. "So much you have done for Pierre and me, and for

Patrique. And now, when you need us most, we are so caught up in ourselves we scarcely speak to you."

"I really don't mind all that much," he said truthfully. In the distance, a whirling beacon of dust rose from the cloud's mass, lifting higher and higher, a fragile tower turned ruby red by the sun's final rays. "You and Pierre have years of catching up to do, not to mention an invalid to watch over. Besides, there's a lot to take in here."

"You like the desert," she observed.

"It's a world I never imagined existed," he said, "not in my wildest dreams."

"All the tribe are speaking of you," Jasmyn told him. "How a stranger has come and drinks in their world with his eyes. How he seeks to learn everything he can, do all he can, be as much a part of the tribe as he can."

She rose to her feet. "Come, Jake. We must break camp and walk by moonlight for the cliffs."

The children were whimpering with fatigue when they arrived at the first great outcropping four hours later. By then the tribe had been walking with few stops for a day and much of a night. Omar pushed them as hard as he could, barking his worry at everyone, rushing back and forth, trying to ensure that neither animal nor tribesman was lost in the headlong rush for safety.

Suddenly one of the outriders hallooed from atop his camel and pointed skyward with his great, silver-clad rifle. Jake looked up with the others and watched open-mouthed as a coiling tendril of shadow drifted overhead. One moment all was clarity and a sea of silver stars. The next, a silent menace blotted out half the universe.

Omar's shouted instructions required no translation. Jake raced with the others toward the cliffs, which jutted out into the sand like giant sharp-edged buttresses. As they approached, Jake realized that the cliff face was pocketed with shallow, bowl-shaped caves. Eons of wind and sand had hollowed the sandstone into a series of natural chambers.

While the children formed a natural paddock for the bleating animals, Jake and all the other adults raced to raise three goat's-hair tents abutting a trio of neighboring caves. It was hard working by torchlight, men and women snapping in frantic haste and shouting words he could not understand. But by then he had grown accustomed to the task, pulling the heavy ropes taut and hammering down the ironwood stakes as long as his thigh. So he ignored the others as best he could and simply went about his chores, feeling the fitful breeze blow gritty breaths against his face and hands.

A great cry arose from several voices at once, and the entire tribe held its breath. In the distance Jake heard a sound that raised the hairs on the nape of his neck, a basso moaning that died away, then mounted to a force that left the ropes under his hand trembling in fearful anticipation.

At that the tribe doubled its already frenetic haste. Jake joined with the other men to mount a fourth tent, this one as a simple protective flap over a cave farther down the cliffside. The camels had both forelegs and back legs hobbled, then were tied in a long string to a series of stakes hammered deep into the earth just inside this protective awning.

The other three tents were joined side by side, fronting onto a trio of caves set close together in the cliff. The sheep and goats bleated in panic as they were herded into the left-hand tent, the one fronting the largest cave. By the time the double flaps were dropped and tied securely into place, the wind was growling about them.

Jake allowed himself to be herded into the middle tent, which was crowded with milling bodies. Normally they had twice the number of tents, and none used by animals, but there had been neither time nor nearby caves to set up more. Jake helped where he could as the others sorted themselves into family groupings. Lamps were lit and hung from supporting ropes. Carpets were unrolled to form a comfortably padded floor. A shallow hole was dug at the tent's center, rocks found and set in a circle, coals laid, a cooking fire started, a tea canister set in place.

Everyone paused to listen as the first great blast descended upon them, buffeting the tents with sandy fists. All eyes and ears searched the unseen spaces to either side, then gradually relaxed when it was decided that all the tents were holding well.

Within an hour the camp had settled into family groupings. Jake found himself a corner at the back of the cave, eased down on a pile of carpets woven in desert colors, and gave in to exhaustion.

The tribe slept a day and a night and into the next day, taking in sleep and storing it as they did water at the wells. Trips outside were battles against the wind and sand, and nobody went far, or for very long. Jake spent many hours dozing in solitude.

Once a waking routine was resumed, Jake visited occasionally in the third tent with Pierre and Jasmyn. But Pierre's twin brother Patrique, still weak and sick from his stay in the brutal Telouet dungeon, required much of their attention, and what was left they preferred to lavish upon each other. Their tent contained the old and infirm, the families with the very young or the very sick, as well as the unmarried women, and in quiet desert ways Jake was urged not to linger.

Jake found himself making numerous trips with Omar to check on the animals. The tribe's children spent most of their waking time there, filling the odoriferous tent with their delighted laughter. The newborn lambs were little bundles of black and white fluff. The animals frisked about, bleating their high-pitched cries, jumping and spinning in midair. Jake watched the children as much as he did the animals, marveling at how contented they were with the simplest of entertainments. They rarely cried or fought or whined, despite a life that was harsh by any measure. And here they were, cooped up in a tent with over a hundred milling animals, not a toy or a book between them, utterly content.

Jake found himself thinking that he, too, could be content in this sand-bounded desert world if only Sally were here with him. But the pain of missing her, which had

dulled to an inner ache during the course of rescuing Patrique, now throbbed into anguish during the long hours of
waiting.

When he dozed, he could see her clearly. Sally tall and
lithe, cool and confident behind her desk in Badenburg.
Sally strong and tender, kneeling to comfort one of the im-
poverished orphans the war had left scattered in its wake.
Sally beautiful in the candlelight, her auburn hair gleaming. Sally sad but determined, telling him about her orders.
Telling him goodbye.

And then he would wake to the reality of sand and wind
and children and animals and Sally would be gone once
more.

It was around noon of the third day that disaster struck.

By then, Jake had almost grown accustomed to the
wind's continual growl. He was caked from head to foot
with grit, and his hair felt like a used paintbrush that had
been left to dry in the sun. But he watched the others and
saw how they ignored what they could not alter, and he
resolved to try and do the same. By the third day, the dry
crunchy feeling of his skin seemed almost as natural as the
thundering gusts that shook their tent from time to time.

The change came without warning. Jake sat cross-legged
in what had come to be his corner, trying to concentrate as
two men laid out a complicated game of rocks and shells on
a board design drawn in the sand. He nodded as though he
understood as they pointed at each rock or shell in turn,
then gave lengthy explanations. Clearly they had decided
that his lack of Arabic could be overcome by shouting, because their explanations were as gentle as artillery bar-
rages. Jake found the game totally incomprehensible, but
since they were tugging at his sleeve with one hand and
fondling their daggers with the other, he tried to pay attention. He felt like his mask of wide-eyed interest had become glued in place.

Suddenly the wind's pitch rose to a horrendous shriek.
The flickering lamps shook as the tent's guide ropes threatened to give. A terrific blast fought its way through the

double flaps over the portal, blew out all the lamps, lifted up a great fistful of coals from the central fire, and flung them haphazardly about the room.

The tent went berserk.

Screams and shrieks competed against the wind's overpowering noise. The cramped space was instantly filled with jumping, whirling bodies, tumbling onto one another, tripping and falling onto yet more coals. Jake struggled out from under one writhing body, only to see the robe of a man next to him shoot up in flames. He tackled the man, tore up a carpet, and flung it together with his own body over the flames. Only when the fire was out and he raised to his knees did he realize the man he had saved was Omar.

Before the tribal chieftain could speak, another blast of wind split the night. In its midst came another sound, an explosive ripping followed by animal screams. Omar's eyes opened wide in the dim light and he shouted words Jake did not need to understand. The animals' tent had collapsed.

Somehow he managed to struggle across the mass of teeming bodies behind Omar and push himself through the tent's portals. Immediately the wind grappled with him, searching with harsh gritty fingers to pluck him up and hurl him against the cliffside. There was neither night nor day nor left nor right, only the golden-brown swirling mass that flung itself at him with such force that it threatened to rip the skin from his face.

Out of nowhere appeared a great looming shadow, one dusty brown shade darker than the storm itself. The shadow passed, to be followed immediately by another, and yet a third. When the fourth shadow appeared, Jake did not hesitate or think. He reached and found himself grasping at the sand-sodden hairs of a camel's neck. Somehow a string of camels had broken free of both their hobbles and their stakes.

The pelt ran through his fingers until he came to the thick harness guide rope. He grabbed hold and allowed himself to be flung from a standing start to a pace so fast that his feet scarcely touched the ground. With his free hand he reached blindly and felt a second rope trailing down from the camel's hump, the leader used to lash down the loads. Without thinking of the risk, he took two further great strides and flung himself up onto the camel's back.

The panicked beast was too busy running blind to bother with him. Jake struggled and managed to raise himself up and into the lumpy fold between the beast's double humps. He struggled against the jouncing gait that slammed him up and down and threatened to dislodge him with every step. Working his feet through the ropes running around and under the camel, he pulled his cape down far over his face and hung on for dear life.

Chapter Three

ALTHOUGH HE DID not ever really sleep, still Jake had a sense of awakening to the hush and the heat.

The wind and the camel's bruising gait had buffeted him to an aching numbness. Jake had been unable to unmask his face or hold his eyes open against the storm's blistering force. He had ridden scrunched over, his face pressed close to the camel's hide so that his hood was kept in place, blind to all but his growing pain. The jouncing, panic-stricken race to nowhere had bruised him from head to toe. Jake had hung on with the grim determination of one who knew his only hope of safety lay in not being tossed off. The enforced blindness and the relentless wind and the jolting ride had gradually melded together, until time had lost all meaning and Jake had been swallowed by a welcome nothingness.

Then he opened his eyes to a brilliant desert sun.

After three days of howling storm, the stillness was frighteningly alien. Jake struggled upright, wiped his eyelids with an inner sleeve, blinked, squinted, and laughed a hoarse croak.

The seven camels all wore remnants of their hobbles around their ankles. They were linked by halters, and dragged the uprooted staves as they cropped at meager desert shrub. The scene was so calm and normal it was funny, despite the fact that the cliffs were a distant smudge line on the horizon.

The camel upon which Jake sat was the only one with two humps. All the others had the more common single hump. Jake inspected them, doubted if he would have been able to keep his hold upon one of those.

He ran his hand tentatively down his camel's neck, fearful that at any moment the animal would recognize him for the novice he was and attack him with those great yellow teeth it was using on the shrub. But the camel paid him no mind. Jake snagged the rope attached to one of the staves, pulled it toward him, and grasped the wood. He leaned back as far as he could and tapped behind the camel's rear leg while trying to copy the "tch-tch" sound he had heard from the drovers.

Obediently the camel lowered itself in the slow rocking motion of a boat on high seas. When it was fully down on its knees, he croaked another laugh. Jake Burnes, camel driver.

With the motions of an old man, Jake half clambered, half slid down onto the ground. Keeping a very firm hold on the guide rope, he struggled up from his knees. Every muscle, every bone, every joint groaned in protest. His first few steps were little shuffling motions. His throat was too dry to permit much sound, so he had to make do with little ahs of agony.

Had the camels decided to desert him then, there would have been nothing he could do about it. But they remained motionless, save for the constant scrunch-scrunching of those grinding jaws on the dry scrub.

Jake shuffled up to the next camel, touched the back of its leg, tch-tched a second time, and marveled as the great beast obediently buckled down to its knees. Now that the storm was over and they had run through their panic, they seemed almost to welcome a semblance of their normal routine. He moved to a third camel and was met with the same dutiful response.

With the line now anchored by three settled camels, Jake began reshaping the line. First he untied the remaining staves so that they could not tangle about the camels' legs. Then he unleashed one halter at a time, leading the camels back and retying them so that the double-humped camel was placed in front.

After moving the three still-standing animals, he approached the center kneeling beast. Touching the stave to its side as he had seen the herders do, he gave a sharp "hup, hup," then jumped back as the neck swiveled around and the animal let out a deep, yellow-toothed groan. His heart in his mouth, Jake stepped forward, touched the side a second time, and hupped as loud as his dry throat could manage. The camel groaned another loud protest, but this time it lurched upright. Jake led it around and tied it in line, then did the same with the second kneeling animal. By then all six standing beasts were groaning in unison and stamping their pie-shaped flat hooves on the dusty earth.

Even though the lead camel still knelt in patient watchfulness, Jake had to use both hands to lift his leg up and over the animal's broad back. He too groaned as aching muscles fitted themselves back into the uncomfortable position. He tapped his camel's side, hupped a sharp command, then hung on and groaned again as the camel rose, its pitching motions reeling him back and forth.

But then he was up, high off the desert surface, with seven great animals groaning and stamping and waiting his command. He tapped his camel's side, hupped as loud as he could, and watched as the animal lumbered forward. He felt the line tug taut and begin moving behind him. Jake pulled his dry, cracked lips into a grin and raised the stave over his head with the sheer joy of getting it right.

By the time the sun began its rapid descent from late afternoon into night, the thrill had long since faded. Jake's entire body was one great thirsty ache. He had stopped trying to peer through the dimming light at the cliffs. Despite hour after hour of jouncing pain, they did not appear to have come any closer. Jake kept his head down, piloting his string of animals by their lengthening shadows.

Even with his eyes focused downward, they were almost through the patch of meager green before Jake's mind lifted

from its fog of fatigue and thirst. He pulled on the bridle
rope with what strength he had left and managed a single
tched croak from a throat almost swollen shut. Thankfully,
the camels appeared as ready to stop as Jake. At his tap the
lead camel swung down in a motion so abrupt that Jake
almost tumbled over. Once down, he found himself without the strength to lift his leg free. Jake gripped the camel's
hide with both hands and slithered groaning to the cool
desert floor.

Only the fear of the string pulling free and leaving him
lost and alone in the desert vastness kept him from giving
in to his fatigue. Jake scrambled to his feet, found himself
unable to straighten up. Gripping the stave and hobbling
forward like an old man, he walked to each camel in turn
and touched them behind the knees. Three welcomed the
invitation to kneel, three growled and snapped in his direction with their great yellow teeth. Jake was too tired to
jump away. He responded with a raised stave and a hoarse
growl of his own. The camels grumbled and turned away.
Jake was more than willing to call it a draw and leave them
standing.

The sandy earth revealed nothing large or solid enough
with which to pound in the staves. Jake was not sure it
mattered, as he doubted he had strength left to drive them
home. In desperation he noosed a second line around the
lead camel's neck, then tied both ropes to his ankles. In the
last light of a dying day, Jake checked the knots, then
groaned his way down to the sandy earth and gave in to his
exhaustion.

It would go down as the worst night in living memory.

In what seemed like only seconds after he had closed his
eyes, Jake was jerked awake by the lead camel lumbering to
its feet, grumbling its great guttural roar, then swinging
about and trotting away. Dragging Jake along as though he
was not even there. The rest of the string following as
though a midnight stroll was the most natural thing on
earth. Jake scrambled upright only to be tossed back with a
thud. He gripped one of the ankle ropes, shouted hoarsely

for the camel to stop, endured having his backside scraped across plants and rocks and sand and twigs, growing angrier by the second.

As abruptly as it had started, the camel stopped, dropped its great head, and began cropping on a bit of wild scrub. Jake scrambled upright, his chest heaving. He raised the stave, decided crowning an animal five times his size was not in his own best interests, dropped it, looked around, and wondered what was so doggone special about that particular scrub. The other camels were contentedly cropping away, paying him no mind whatsoever. Jake gave a single dry chuckle of defeat, lowered himself back to the desert floor.

And realized he was freezing.

With the sun's descent the temperature had plummeted. The flickers of night breeze drifted through his clothes like iced daggers. Jake drew his legs up, wrapped his arms around himself, and wished for fire. And thick desert tea. And blankets. And day.

The night was endless. Every time he drifted off he was jerked awake by the camel moving to another shrub. Jake slipped further and further into a dull half-awake state, suspended in a freezing netherworld of sand and fitful dreams and fatigue and aches.

When dawn finally arrived, Jake peered at the lightening horizon through grit-encrusted eyelids, scarcely able to accept that the night had finally come to an end. He used both hands to push himself to his feet, then shuffled over and tapped the lead camel behind its knee. The camel was as displeased with the night as Jake, for it rounded on him with a roar of complaint. Jake stood unmoving and watched the great teeth open in his face, too far beyond caring to be afraid. Clearly the camel realized this, for it retreated, grumbled, and sank obediently to its knees. The camel then endured a full ten minutes of Jake slithering and sliding and groaning until he managed to right himself on its back.

Hours into the day, the heat and his thirst and the unrelenting jouncing ride began to play tricks with his mind.

Jake had an image of himself standing at attention before General Clarke's desk, pointing at a map and trying to explain just exactly where he was. Which was impossible, because the entire stretch of area through which he passed was blank. Across the empty yellow expanse was printed, "Demarcation Uncertain, Reliable Data Unavailable."

Next to the map stood a glass of sparkling ice water. Jake could not take his eyes off the glass, with the cold condensation rolling down the sides in tantalizing slow motion. Every once in a while the general would raise the glass and sip. But he never offered any to Jake, even though he could see Jake's mouth and throat were so dry he could not even swallow. Jake knew if he could just pinpoint his location, the General would reward him with a sip. But he could not find any way of telling where he was on that blank map. And the heat beating down on his head made it harder and harder to think.

The sun had passed overhead and was drawing a second set of afternoon shadows when the cliffs finally rose high above them. Jake bounced up and down, each step agony, and prayed with all the might his exhausted mind had left that he would not be forced to spend another night out in the open. Each breath rasped noisily through a throat almost closed by dust and dryness. His eyes were squinted down to sandy slits against the reflected glare. His legs and back burned as if branded. His arms were too tired to hold upright. His fingers were coiled loosely to the guide ropes. It was all he could do to keep from sliding from the beast's back and plunging in defeat to the desert floor.

A distant rifleshot crackled like lightning across the empty reaches. Jake jerked upright, then reached forward to pat the camel's neck as it snorted and faltered. Not another panic. Not now. He did not have the strength left to hold on. He searched the distance and saw five figures moving through the wavering heat lines, seeming almost to float toward him.

Another rifle crackled. This time the camel remained steady under Jake's hand. An instant of clarity granted Jake the chance to see that the figures were in fact sitting astride galloping camels and headed his way, rifles held up high over their heads. Another few moments, and he could hear their shouting and excited laughter. A sudden flood of relief washed through him. Tiredly he waved his own stave overhead.

He was safe.

Chapter Four

T HE TRIBE REWARDED his return with great shouts of joy. Jake was pulled from the camel by a dozen eager hands, his back pummeled so hard his legs gave way. A bladder of water was thrust into his hands. After five days of resting in the distended animal skin, the water smelled foul and tasted brackish. Jake squirted a flood of warm liquid into his parched mouth, and thought he was feasting on nectar.

They ignored his protests and herded him up into one of the dark tents fashioned upon a larger camel's back, where the infirm and elderly normally rode. Omar came to see that he was settled in well and explained through Jasmyn that they must make all haste for the next oasis, as the waterskins were almost dry and the animals were growing too parched. Another day of walking in the heat would doom the weaker beasts. Omar knew exactly where they were, he said; the oasis was a five-hour march due north. They could follow the cliffs and the stars and would arrive near dawn.

The tribal chieftain then looked up at Jake's resting-place and said, "The tribe is most grateful for your acts of courage. For myself, I will hold my thanks until later."

Jake dozed much of the journey. The ocean beast rocked as gently as a ship riding over great rollers, and Jake's berth was made soft by layers of carpet. Overhead, the tent's cloth sides flapped with each swaying step, like sails set to snare the stars and power them through the dark reaches. The desert floor was transformed by moonlight into a frozen silver sea. The loudest sound he heard as he drifted in and out of sleep was the bleating of the animals.

The sky had not yet gathered enough light to banish the stars when they arrived at the oasis. Long before the camp came into view, however, the sheep and camels smelled the water. Their cries and increasing pace awoke Jake from his deepest slumber of the night. He pushed aside the tent flaps to breathe the crisp night air and watch as silhouettes of palms appeared on the horizon.

The sun was well over the horizon by the time the animals had drunk their fill and the paddocks and tents had been erected. Once the chores were finished and most of the tribe vanished into the shade for much-needed sleep, Jake reveled in a long bath. The oasis lake was shallow and sandy-bottomed and lukewarm. Yet the waters were clearly replenished by an underground spring, because now and then he would pass through unseen ribbons so cold they raised gooseflesh. Jake swam the few strokes from one bank to the other, feeling his parched skin drink in the liquid. He floated for a long time, his only company the ravens that populated the oasis.

Eventually he stepped from the water, let the sun dry him off, dressed, and walked over to where the two tribesmen watching the animals were having great difficulty keeping their eyes open. With sign language Jake showed how he had slept on the camel and then offered to take their watch so they could sleep. The astonished tribesmen bolted for their tents before Jake could change his mind.

That evening, Jake sat with his back resting against a date palm and watched as night descended. The easy day had done much to restore both his body and his spirits. He looked out beyond the scrub and palms to the great golden emptiness, a land ruled by heat and dust and hardship. It made their tiny island of green and water a jewel of incredible value, something to be treasured, a place of restoration and peace.

The tribe was preparing for a feast. Gradually all the tribe approached to sit or sprawl in a great circle. In the center, an entire sheep turned upon a great spit. One of the women prepared semolina in the time-honored manner, drying the ingredients in wooden bowls, mixing them by hand and stirring, stirring constantly. Her arms flashed a blurring motion, her tribal tattoos of vines and fishes denoting one who had been married into the Al-Masoud from some place closer to the sea.

The sea. Jake leaned back comfortably, tried to take his mind from the fragrances that crowded the night, and wondered what it would be like to see the sea again.

Jake observed the gathering tribe. He had come to see the desert folk as a closed lot, suspicious of all outsiders, even those who were granted entry by custom. Hospitality was offered only within the tight barriers of formality. The more he came to know the world in which they lived, the less he found himself minding their ways. The desert was a harsh teacher, yet he found himself valuing the few lessons he had already learned.

Tonight, though, there was a difference. Tribesmen stopped to offer him faint greetings before dropping to their places. Some even granted small smiles. Jake found himself treasuring them, knowing they were neither common nor lightly given.

Pierre and Jasmyn pushed their way into the circle, supporting Patrique between them. Like Jake, the French officer wore the tribal clothing of voluminous white desert trousers, embroidered white-on-white shirt, and light blue cloak. Jasmyn wore the royal blue djellabah of the desert women with elegant ease. With Pierre's dark, expressive features and her exotic, black-haired beauty, they made a striking couple. Their good looks accented the fragile condition of Patrique, whose sunken eyes and hollow cheeks made him a shadowy copy of his twin. It was hard to think

of this emaciated, dozing man as the former bold member
of the French Resistance in Marseille.

They eased Patrique down on a cushion, then took up
places to either side. "The tribe is calling you a hero," Jasmyn said, settling down beside Jake.

"If I had taken the time to think," Jake replied, "I would
have never grabbed for that camel. Not in a thousand
years."

"I have often thought that is what separates the coward
from the hero," Pierre mused. "Just one split second of
hesitation."

To change the subject, Jake looked over to offer greetings
to Patrique, only to discover that Pierre's brother had already fallen asleep. Not a good sign. Jake asked quietly,
"How is he doing?"

"The stop forced on us by the storm has not been altogether a bad thing," Pierre replied worriedly. "He is not
improving as I would hope. His ankles and his feet are hurting him."

"And he has a fever," Jasmyn said softly. "I suspected it
before, but today I am sure."

Jake examined Patrique more closely, saw a pallor that
not even the fire's ruddy glow could erase, and felt the chill
of one who had seen war wounds fester and turn gangre-
nous. "This is not good news."

"I fear he will not make the trip without better medical
treatment than Jasmyn and I can give him," Pierre agreed.

Jake mulled this over as the meal was served and eaten.
At Jasmyn's urging, Patrique woke up and ate, but as soon
as his meager appetite was sated, he forced himself to his
feet. Jasmyn was instantly there beside him, even before
Pierre could rise. Patrique motioned for Pierre to remain
seated, bid Jake a quiet good-night, and with Jasmyn's help
stumbled back toward his tent. Pierre watched him go, an
enormous frown creasing his expressive face.

Eventually, Jake admitted defeat to the challenge of eating an entire sheep by himself and set his platter aside. He
eased himself back, belly groaning, and smiled his thanks
when a glass of tea was passed his way. He then turned to

Pierre and said quietly, "It may be a good idea if you wrote down everything he knows about this traitor in the French government. Make sure the evidence is clear enough to stand without him there to back it up."

Pierre looked over and replied fiercely, "My brother will survive."

"Just in case our ways split up," Jake soothed.

Pierre examined his friend. "You have a plan?"

Jake nodded. "Just the bare bones is all."

"I find that reassuring," Pierre said, subsiding. "Myself, I have been far too worried to come up with anything."

Jasmyn returned to the fireside and eased herself down. "He is resting as well as can be expected."

"Tell me again about this guy in the French government," Jake said, "the one Patrique thinks is a traitor."

"He does not just think," Jasmyn murmured. "He knows. You have not sat with him, listened to him speak for hours about this man. Even his fever dreams are filled with the urgency of his mission to expose this traitor and bring him to justice."

"Monsieur le Ministre Jacques Clairmont looks like a snail without his shell. He made a name for himself as a politician, even when he was in uniform," Pierre said bitterly. "Adjunct to de Gaulle's military staff, rich, from one of France's oldest families."

"From the tone of your voice," Jake observed, "I get the impression you don't much care for the gent."

"There were rumors," Pierre replied. "Even an officer in the field heard such things. Of orders that made little sense to those who had to carry them out. Of decisions taken that cost too many men's lives."

"I know the feeling," Jake said. "Only too well."

"He stayed on in North Africa long after the remainder of the staff followed the European campaign northward. There were sound reasons for this—needing to hold someone there, especially when ground forces in Algiers were cut to the bone and all possible resources flung at the enemy in Europe."

"Which would have given him the perfect opportunity to line his pockets," Jake said.

"Patrique says he is both greedy and ruthless," Jasmyn confirmed. "A man who would do anything to increase his wealth and power. Anything."

"What is he doing now?"

"Deputy Minister of the Interior," Pierre replied, the growl in his voice drawing attention from all sides. "And adjunct to the President's cabinet. Perfect for a man such as this. Responsible for all transport, all distribution of supplies, all economic contact with the colonies."

"Powerful," Jake said.

"Dangerous," Pierre agreed. "He will do anything to protect his position."

"But is his position," Jake demanded, "great enough to warrant the American and the British taking such an interest in our getting back safely with Patrique's information?"

"Of this I had not thought," Pierre admitted.

"It's been on my mind," Jake said, "ever since we received that telegram from Admiral Bingham. If the army taught me anything, it's that the brass wouldn't go to all this trouble just for the sake of two officers. No matter how much we might think our own skins are worth." He shook his head. "I'd give you thousand-to-one odds there's more to this than we think."

Discussion halted about the campsite as Omar stood and signaled for silence. He spoke at length, gesturing from time to time in Jake's direction. Jasmyn's gaze turned with the others toward him. "I did not know you saved Omar's life."

"That's blowing things a little out of proportion," Jake protested, but already her attention was turned back to the tribe's leader.

"What is he saying," Pierre demanded.

"That Jake threw himself on Omar and put out the fire burning Omar's robes with his own body." She looked round-eyed at him. "Is this true?"

Jake shrugged. "I tripped over the carpet I was holding."

Omar continued speaking.

Jasmyn went on, "Omar says that afterward as he stood blinded and deafened and helpless in the storm, a string of the tribe's best camels thundered past. One moment you were there beside him and the next you had disappeared. It was only when he realized you had risked your life to save the tribe's wealth that he himself was forced into action. He managed to hold the remaining staves in place while other tribesmen erected shelter around the cave." Her gaze rested solemnly upon Jake, as did those of the others gathered about the fire. "To have saved the animals in the midst of such a storm is the stuff of tribal lore."

Omar motioned to a man standing beyond the fire. The tribesman stepped forth and deposited two cloth-wrapped bundles at the chieftain's feet. Omar then turned his attention toward Pierre.

This time it took a long moment before Jasmyn was able to speak. "He says that all the tribe have witnessed the love with which you accept a daughter of the desert and the wind and the wild reaches," she said, her gaze fastened upon Pierre. "No one could see this love and remain untouched. He says that you have done the tribe, and their daughter, great honor. This too should be rewarded."

Omar picked up the first bundle and passed it to Pierre. He unwrapped the oil-stained cloth to reveal a gleaming rifle. Pierre hefted the weapon and breathed, "A mitraillette."

"It is not fitting for a man to walk these reaches armed only with a revolver," Jasmyn continued, translating Omar's solemn words. "All who are accepted by the tribe have a responsibility to guard and protect."

Jake asked, "You know the gun?"

"Ah," Pierre sighed, checking the action, stroking the stock. "This weapon and I are old friends. Look, no safety. Instead, a trigger that folds up and out of the way. Ingenious, no?"

"Fascinating," Jake said, smiling in spite of himself.

"No single-shot mechanism, and wild as a frightened recruit beyond fifty paces. But it has the muzzle velocity of a lightning bolt, and a steady touch can hold the bullets to one at a time." Pierre hefted the weapon toward Omar and said, "Tell him that I am honored to carry such a weapon on behalf of the tribe."

But Omar did not wait for the translation. Instead, he reached down and hefted the second bundle. He held it a long moment and said through Jasmyn, "These were the weapons of my father, a great leader of the Al-Masoud tribe."

A murmur rose from the tribe as he walked around the fire to set the bundle at Jake's feet. Jasmyn interpreted, "My father would be pleased to see you so armed."

With numb fingers Jake undid the leather thongs, rolled out the covering, and felt the whole world focus down upon this instant. A dagger as long as his forearm rested in a leather sheaf dressed in silver, its haft formed by woven silver wire.

"These are on loan only," Jasmyn said. "They are part of the tribe's heritage and wealth. Still, this is an honor, Jake. A very great honor. I have never heard of an outsider being granted such a boon."

Omar squatted down in front of Jake, showed him how to lace his cloth belt around the sheath and then knot it through the silver loop before tying it about his waist. The dagger rested snug against his belly, angled so that it would not get in the way when he sat or ran, rising so that the haft pressed against the muscle over his lower rib.

Not waiting for Jake to respond, he stood and strode back to his position at the head of the fire. Jake forced his hand to reach out and take the rifle. It molded to his hand as though it had been made for him and him alone.

Pierre demanded, "What is it?"

"A Springfield .30-.03. One of the finest guns ever made." Jake worked the bolt, so smooth it almost slid on its own. The stock was layered with filigreed silver that shone in the firelight. "I've read about them. Never held one before."

He raised his eyes to meet Omar's gaze. "Tell him thanks. I don't have the words just now, so please say it for me."

When Jasmyn had translated, Omar said something with mock severity, which brought a chuckle from around the fire. Jasmyn explained, "Now that you are one of us, Omar says you should begin standing watch. Pierre has his brother to look after, but you have already shown your first concern lies with the animals."

"I'd like that," Jake replied.

"He was only joking."

"But I want to," Jake protested. "Tell him."

The announcement silenced the camp. Omar examined him, then shook his head. "Standing watch once in a while is disruptive," Jasmyn translated. "The routine must be maintained with discipline."

"Fine with me," Jake said, meeting the chieftain's gaze.

"Watchkeepers hold their position every third night," Jasmyn translated. "Punishment for any who sleep through duty is fierce."

"I want the dawn watch," Jake replied.

That brought yet another murmur from all who watched and listened. "That is usually the duty assigned to the youngest," Jasmyn said.

Jake could not have explained it, but for him the desert sunrises were very special. A quiet time, when the world belonged to him and to God. There often came a moment so precious and so fragile that even to speak of it might shatter the experience. So he simply replied, "Seeing as how I'm the newest man on duty here, I'd say that fits me down to the ground."

"It means a day two hours longer than all the rest of us," Omar warned. "There will be no time for rest between end of watch and breaking camp."

"Even so," Jake replied, "that is what I want."

Across the fire from where he sat, a suspicious old goat of an elder, the man who had remained most hostile to their being taken in by the tribe, rewarded Jake with a single curt nod.

Jasmyn told him, "You are fast building friends here, Jake Burnes."

Omar spoke at length, directing his words to Jasmyn. When he finished, there was another chorus of quiet approval from the gathering. Jasmyn said, "Omar has requested that I spend a part of every day translating, so that he may speak with you. He sees that your interest in the tribe and our land is genuine and wishes to reward you by teaching you of the desert way."

Jake searched for something to convey his thanks. "Tell him his gift has a value beyond measure."

Strong black eyes held him from across the fire. Jasmyn translated his response, "As does friendship between brave men."

Jake scrambled up the hard scrabble rise that separated oasis and camp from the cliffs. He had been awakened for his watch by a guard who had planned to step up quietly and then feign alarm. Jake's wartime reactions had served him well, and before the man could approach he had already rolled free of his cover, weapon in hand. The man had grunted approval and walked away, assured the camp would be safe in Jake's care.

Jake had stopped by the campfire to bolster himself with a glass of tea. After simmering on a rock close to the coals all night, the beverage had the consistency of liquid cement. The tannin was so strong the first few swallows sent shudders down Jake's frame and threatened to remove the first layer of skin from his tongue. But it succeeded in kick-starting his reluctant heart and guaranteeing that his eyes would not sink shut.

He chose his position well, far enough below the peak that he would not be silhouetted against the night, yet high enough to capture all the camp with one glance. He settled himself down on the flat escarpment, set his gun within easy reach, and began a slow, steady sweep of the entire area. A savvy old sergeant with whom he had served in Italy had taught him that good infiltrators were hard to catch moving, because they knew to keep their movements small. Night creepers, the sergeant had called them. The best way to catch one was to commit the vista to memory, and then if a boulder or shrub or hillock suddenly appeared from nowhere, to go and inspect. Cautiously.

Jake was not by nature an early riser. Under most circumstances, he listed dawn patrols just a notch or so above getting caught by crossfire. But twice already he had awakened in time to step beyond the camp and become captivated by the unfolding desert dawn. The memory was bright enough for him to seek out the experience yet again and even to look forward to its being part of every third day. Strong enough to stay with him for the rest of his life.

He released the cloth button sealing his vest pocket and took out his small New Testament. The moonlight was strong enough for him to read the tiny script with ease. The silence was so powerful the words rang through his heart like thunder.

Every minute or so he raised his head and scanned carefully. The oasis was a sharp-edged shadow staining the silvery, moonlit plain. Animals shuffled and bleated quietly, their every sound carrying clearly across the distance.

Jake raised his Bible once more, then took another glance upward. He searched the vast river of stars, savored the brilliant clarity of the almost-full moon, breathed in the air's bracing chill, listened to the wind's gentle whisper, and counted the night as his friend. The desert world was vast and endless and alien. He felt enthralled by the vista, captivated by the night on display.

Jake sighed and wished once more for Sally, aching to share the moment with her. As Jake watched the first glimmers of dawn take hold he wondered if this almost constant yearning was a sign of true love.

Light came swiftly in the desert as though dawn were too fragile a gift to last for long. Yet no matter how fleeting, still there was a moment. A single ephemeral instant when all the world held its breath, when all creation lay open and poised and fresh and new. The light grew full and yet remained gentle. The camp was utterly still, the great reaches achingly open and exposed. He and he alone was there to know this moment, the only man awake in all the world.

Then the instant of breathless perfection was shattered. The sun rushed over the horizon and blazed with fierce pride upon its harsh desert kingdom. Jake shaded his eyes against the sudden onslaught and saw the first stirrings of life within the camp. He sighed, knowing the moment was gone, yet reluctant to release himself from the thrall of what he had just seen and felt.

He started to reach for his weapon, then stopped. As cautiously as possible, he swiveled about, an inch at a time. Yes. There it was. Some flicker of motion had alerted him, and now he could see clearly. On the cliff behind and overhead and to his right a head was raised, clearly silhouetted against the new dawn sky. And there beside the head a dark line protruded over the edge, far too straight and true to be anything but a gun barrel.

Jake sat in utter stillness, wondering if the intruder realized he had been spotted. Eventually the gun barrel was drawn back, and the head disappeared. Only then did he risk a full breath, rise to his feet, and scramble back down the hillock to the camp.

Chapter Five

OMAR LISTENED TO Jake's report with the focused alertness of a hunting falcon. When Jasmyn finished translating, Omar called for the three elders to join him and the story was told yet again. Jake watched them digest the news in silence and then waited for the eldest to speak first. Jasmyn translated the old man's question as "How long a gun?"

"Hard to say how much of the barrel I saw, but I'd guess it was man-sized. And he had a ribbon or tassel or something dangling off the end."

Tension crackled through the group. Omar demanded, "He wore a large blue turban?"

"The color I couldn't tell," Jake replied. "But the headdress was broad and flat, yes."

It was enough for the senior elder. "Tuareg," he declared.

"Tuareg are desert warriors," Jasmyn explained to Jake. "Mercenaries."

Omar spoke harshly, and Jasmyn translated, "They were once a tribe like ourselves. Now they are jackals and vultures. No longer do they hold animals nor wells nor pride of their own. They are a scourge, killing the weakest men and beasts when they can. They take anyone's silver and accept any task. Nothing is too low for the Tuareg."

"It's us they're after," Jake said, and knew a sinking sense of defeat. He said the words so they would not come from Omar and the elders. "Maybe we should take off on our own. No need to put your tribe at risk."

But his offer was met with vehement refusal. "No desert hyena will stop us from our task," Omar replied for them all. "We know now to move with caution."

"You think they'll attack?"

Omar shook his head decisively. "It is not their way. Even if they were certain of your presence, the Tuareg would not attack the Al-Masoud. We are too strong. No, they would harry us like the vultures they are. But for now they are armed only with suspicion and greed. First they will seek to learn if we harbor their prey."

"So what do we do?"

"Prepare," Omar replied, and strode back into camp.

The mountains that paralleled their course were barren and bleak, shaped by wind and heat so fierce that Jake often heard rocks splitting open at midday. They cracked with lightning force, frightening the animals and causing the men to raise weapons and search the empty peaks. But not for long. Experience had taught them that few bothered to stalk the occasional traveler here so far from water. Greater dangers lay closer to the wells.

Jake walked alongside Omar and Jasmyn, trying to match the chieftain's long strides, falling into the rhythm of Omar's speech and Jasmyn's translation. "Ours is the tribe of Al-Masoud," he said through Jasmyn. His voice took on a timeless timber, chanting words spoken by countless generations, teaching Jake as he himself had been taught. "We are known as the desert foxes, for those of us who wish can travel great distances at great speed and be seen only by those to whom we grant vision."

He stretched out his hand. "Ask anyone in the desert. They will speak of us with respect. No one has ever said a bad word of our tribe. We follow the command of hospitality. We give of our best. This is the way of honorable men."

Today the move was short, less than twenty miles. It was part of a yearly cycle that took Omar and his tribe across eight hundred miles of desert and mountain and sand and rock and scrub. The search for pasture never ended in this, their arid homeland. They walked and rode with all their belongings strapped to their camels' backs, and earned the right to stand with pride by the simple act of surviving.

"We follow the customs," Omar went on, his voice rising and falling in practiced cadence. "We respect our tribe and our elders. We love our children and our animals. It is enough. Dawns begin with prayers and the lighting of fires and the milking of animals. Milk and fresh curds are our lifeline. Our animals feed us and clothe us and grant us the products which we can trade in the cities. We show our gratitude by treating them well. Normally we do not trek every day. This we do for you. Normally, when the milk bowls are not filled at dawn, it is our animals' way of telling us that the grazing is poor and it is time to find new pastures."

Omar's commanding presence made him appear much taller than he truly was. Although he stood an inch below six feet, Jake often had the impression of looking up to him, especially when he was speaking. His features seemed carved from the rough red sandstone of the surrounding cliffs, his body lean and hard and sparse. His bearing was erect, his dark gaze farseeing and direct, his voice solemn and sonorous. Omar was every inch a leader.

They tracked a narrow flatland that was bordered on one side by the sandstone Atlas foothills and on the other by the sand mountains of the Western Sahara. To either side the dry and looming shapes were as mysterious and beckoning as death.

"The sheep need water every three or four days," Omar went on. "The camels can last up to two weeks, but that is not healthy for them."

Jake nodded and heard not just the words but the message. Here the options were simple and stark, either water and life or thirst and death. It was a leader's responsibility to know every well, every seasonal creek, every sinkhole within a range of eight hundred miles. And in a world where sand mountains were carved and shifted overnight this was the task of a lifetime.

A young man walked two paces behind them, proudly leading Omar's camel with its high-backed, embroidered leather saddle. This duty was passed to each adolescent of the tribe, boy and girl alike, granting them an opportunity to walk with their leader and learn from seeing him in action.

"This has been a good year," Omar continued through Jasmyn. "The sheep and camels have been fruitful. There has been grazing, there has been water. Only two wells were dry, and one choked with the poison of salt. A good year. And your coming shall hopefully make it better."

"We will hold to our pledge of payment," Jake promised.

"It is good to speak with one who honors his debts," Omar replied when Jasmyn had finished translating. "But life teaches us to count the silver pieces only when they ride in the purse at our belts."

Jake nodded but didn't answer. He could feel himself storing up lessons with every breath, as he had little chance now to ponder them deeply. This life was too new and too hard to allow much contemplation. The land through which they passed was one vast anvil, the sun and the heat dual hammers that pounded constantly upon his body and his spirit and focused his energies toward survival. But still he knew, on some deep visceral level, that much was being taken in and stored for an easier time, when he could sit and reflect and understand.

If the heat and the trekking bothered Omar, he did not show it. With natural motions he swung his body in time to his strides, constantly checking in all directions, inspecting the outriders, the shepherds, the animals, the children, the women, the way ahead. Jake asked, "Where do we stop tonight?"

"Ras-Ghadhan," Omar replied. "A village of shadows, some of them our own."

In translating Omar's words, Jasmyn's voice took on a slight tremor. Jake glanced down. "Is something the matter?"

"My mother told me once of this place," she replied. "I had nightmares for many weeks."

"While my father's father was still chief and my father was still young," Omar intoned, his voice a chant as constant as the wind, "the droughts came and the animals died. We trekked from oasis to well to lake to oasis and found no water. Wells that had known water from the dawn of my tribe's history, a dozen generations and more, gave us nothing but mud and dust and despair. So we went to the village of Ras-Ghadhan. There was water and work and a moneylender who owed my tribe enough silver to feed us until the waters reappeared.

"Aiya," Omar sighed a painful breath. "The stories we gained from that city. The scars. Those are stories we shall ever wish to forget, stories we shall carry untold to our grave."

"His father's father," Jake mused. "It must have been, what, sixty years ago, and he talks like it happened yesterday."

"Every village and every tribe has a storyteller," Jasmyn explained. "Their job it is to make the past live again for yet another generation, to remind them of the great, the glorious, the sorrow, the traditions, the heritage. For these people, the past is not a half-forgotten legend. The past is as real and as vital as the present. It gives definition to both their lives and their tomorrows."

"The Tuareg are a people who were once like us," Omar continued, and Jake's head jerked upward at the name before Jasmyn had a chance to translate. "The drought came and they went to the city of Raggah, five days north from here. They, too, were scarred. Like us, they had the city's stories branded upon their hearts. But the Tuareg were not strong. It is only at a time like this, when the world strips away all that was, that a man comes to know his secret strength. The Tuareg had no well of strength to draw upon, so in the end they sold their souls to the city. Now they wander the streets. They slave at tasks meant for no man. They stoop in the market and argue for hours over a penny. Their lives are filled with words and money and city smells. The Tuareg, who were once like us, are no more a people of honor. They have been devoured by the city. They are shadows."

Omar raised his head and said to the empty desert sky, "The Tuareg are no more. Behold the danger of looking to the city when the drought comes. The Tuareg are no more."

Chapter Six

*T*HE VILLAGE OUTSKIRTS were marked by the roadway becoming imprisoned. Walls of clay-daubed stone grew and enclosed them. After his time in the desert, Jake felt as though he were suddenly gasping for air.

Clearly Omar shared his unease. Through Jasmyn he said, "I for one will know comfort only when my back is toward this place."

"Then why are we stopping here?"

"Because it lies directly in our path," Omar replied. "If it was indeed Tuareg you saw upon the cliff, they will most likely seek to inspect us here, as this is a village to their liking. To avoid it would draw undue suspicion our way. And if they do appear, we will know with certainty that unwelcome eyes are turned our way."

The walled path narrowed further until two camels could scarcely walk astride. Through a sudden gap in the wall, Jake caught a final glimpse of the desert; as far as he could see in every direction was nothing but flatness and sand and sun and heat. Then the village swallowed them.

The hamlet was tiny by Western standards, smaller even than the grounds of a large Western estate. His hood drawn down far enough to shield his blue eyes from sight, Jake followed the others down the dusty way, past two small squares where women drew water from stone wells. He had the sudden impression that these walls had been built to protect the village's most precious possession—water.

The caravansary was a dismal affair, a litter-strewn walled plaza utterly barren save for a well and two bedraggled date palms. Their only way in or out was by a narrow passage leading back through the heart of the village. Jake watched Omar bow and salaam to the village elders who hurried over, and knew he would sleep with one eye open that night.

Taking water from another tribe's well meant more than an hour of negotiation. All that while, beasts and children bellowed from thirst, pressing Omar to make a hasty bargain. But he was a man of strength and patience and did not turn away until he was satisfied with the deal.

Jake helped raise the water by harnessing camels to long ropes and drawing up skin after skin, which was then tipped into metal cisterns. As always, the animals drank first, then the people. When it came his turn, Jake bent over the cistern to wash his face, and was startled to find a German air-cross staring back up at him; the cistern had been fashioned from the wing of a downed fighter plane. He carried that thought with him as he helped erect the animal paddocks. Here in the desert, nothing was wasted. Nothing.

Omar walked over holding a bloodstained bandage. Through Jasmyn he explained, "Wear this about your forehead, and if we are approached you must draw the edge down over one eye, and keep the other in the bandage's shadow."

Gingerly Jake accepted the cloth and inspected the red stain. "Who wore this last?"

Omar granted him a small smile. "Even the sheep make sacrifices to keep you safe."

His chores finished, Jake joined the other men by the smaller cooking fire. Omar himself saw to the little teakettle and the leather bag of sugar, pouring out thimblefuls of black, highly sweetened tea, making sure each man had his glass before serving himself.

Traditions like this ruled the tribe's daily existence, offering a framework for living in this harsh and desolate land. This time before the evening meal was always a moment of peace and satisfaction. The tribe had been brought safely through another trek, there was food, there was water, there was safety. Now was the time for talk.

The day was dissected. The animals would be discussed one by one. It was the one time of day when the men spoke with ease, without guarding each word as they did their animals. Jake stood with the others, listening to words he did not understand, watching the tribe's life unfold and fill even this bleak little square.

The women were beautiful, their features as clearly defined as the desert shadows. Their skin was the color of honey, their eyes dark and fathomless. They wore the traditional black headkerchief, but most kept their faces open to the wind and the sun in the Berber fashion.

The first tent poles were struck with an invocation to Allah the merciful, the compassionate, to shield them in this their home for one night. Curved hoops were set in the earth, then great sand-colored sheets were slung up and over and tied in place. A woman sang a haunting melody as she unfurled the great tent's sheet. Her voice rose and fell in a cadence timed like a camel's steps, her words as lilting as a desert wind at dawn.

While the meal was prepared, the children lined up before one of the aged grandmothers. The children's heads were shaved once a week. The grandmother used a flat razor blade, kept in a special pouch. She entertained them with a story as her hand scraped, scraped, scraped away at their dark locks. If the children began howling when the razor was brought out, their cries were the signal that it was time to barter for another blade.

Jake made hand signals requesting two full glasses of tea, then carried them over to where Pierre sat with Patrique. They were stationed at the opening of the tent farthest from the narrow entranceway. With his dark eyes and his features worn by days in the desert, Pierre could easily have passed for a member of the tribe.

Jake worked to keep a smile from his face as he squatted down and offered the two glasses. "Nice to see you looking so fit, Patrique."

One hand emerged from dark folds to accept the glass. "I am hot and I am uncomfortable. It is not proper to make jokes at one so trapped."

"Sorry. You've got to admit, though, the outfit does have a lot going for it."

Before entering the village, Patrique had reluctantly accepted Omar's orders and donned the garb of an elderly woman—black djellabah draped from head to fingertips to toes. The hunters would be searching for one with scars on ankles and wrists. The only person safe from such inspection would be a woman. It would also be easier to hide Patrique's evident weakness behind the dark head-scarf.

Jake pointed to the pen and paper in Pierre's lap. "I didn't mean you had to do it all the time."

"I insisted," Patrique said. "It is good insurance, in case—"

"Stop," Pierre ordered sharply.

Patrique drew back the head-scarf and sipped from his glass, his hand trembling slightly. "Pierre tells me you have a plan."

"Maybe." Jake settled on the ground in front of them and began talking. The three of them were soon so intent on the discussion that they did not notice Jasmyn's approach. But when Jake finished, she was the first to speak. "It is a good plan, Jake. I think it will work."

"I don't like it," Pierre declared.

"Which would you prefer, my brother?" Patrique asked, his eyes glittering with feverish intensity. "Either we accept the fact that some action must be taken, or I shall be laid to rest here in this land."

"Do not speak like that," Pierre said. "I forbid it."

"Forbid all you wish," Patrique replied. "But it will not change the fact that I cannot continue much farther."

"He is right, my beloved," Jasmyn agreed.

"Listen to your woman," Patrique urged, the effort of seeking to convince his brother bringing a clammy sweat to his forehead. "Twice already she has saved my life. Three times, if you count her part in the nightmare of Telouet. She knows, Pierre. I cannot go much farther."

"But to split up," Pierre protested, weakening.

"Someone must carry on," Patrique said. "This news must be passed on to those who can stop the madness. Think, my brother, I beg you. We owe this to all who have fought and died to make France free once again. We cannot stand aside and allow her to become imprisoned by other dark forces."

Jake sat and watched as the internal struggle was mirrored on Pierre's mobile features. But before he could speak, the normal rhythm of the tribe faltered. There was nothing marked, nothing to which Jake could point and say, here, this is what I noticed. Yet the time in the desert had sharpened his awareness, and he knew without understanding exactly why that danger had entered into their midst.

The others noticed it too. Patrique dropped the dark head-scarf over his features. Pierre rose smoothly to his feet, the mitraillette suddenly appearing in his hand. Jake paused long enough to veil his gaze with the bloody bandage, then stood and turned toward the entranceway, his hand on the knife at his waist.

There were three of them. The central figure was sleek and self-assured and wore fine robes woven with threads of silver. The other two were obviously men of the desert, but the difference between them and the Al-Masoud could not have been greater. In place of strength and quiet pride, their faces held only cynical cruelty.

Jasmyn slipped up close behind him and Pierre and whispered, "The central one is a trader."

Pierre whispered back, "The others?"

Jasmyn replied with the single word, "Tuareg."

Omar approached and salaamed formal greetings. The trader bowed low, his left hand sweeping up the folds of his robe while the right touched heart and lips and forehead. The Tuareg stood and glared and said nothing. Taking no notice of the pair, Omar led the trader over and motioned for him to be seated on a carpet rolled out ceremoniously by the central fire. The Tuareg followed with an insolent swagger, their dark eyes sweeping the camp.

When the trader had settled, Omar remained standing, and for the first time he looked directly at the taller of the Tuareg. There was no change to his features, but the challenge was clear. Omar extended a hand, half in invitation, half as an order, for the Tuareg to take seats by the trader. Clearly this was not what the Tuareg wished.

As the pair locked eyes and wills, Jake looked from one to the other and glimpsed the two paths taken by these men and the tribes they represented. Upon Omar's features were stamped the strength and power and determined focus of one who lived by honor and traditions. The Tuareg's features were little different from Omar's, with the same hawk nose and fierce dark desert eyes, yet the Tuareg's face was shaped by unbridled cruelty.

The tension mounted until the entire square was held in the grip of the silent standoff. Then the Tuareg snorted his derision, and settled down upon the carpet. Only when the second man had also seated himself did Omar take his place by the trader and motion for tea to be brought.

The trader spoke with rolling tones and florid gestures. Jake did not need to understand the words to know this was one who lied with the ease that others draw breath. As he watched the discussion proceed with formal precision, Jake could feel the danger heighten his perceptions.

He looked from Omar to the trader to the Tuareg and back again. Here, he sensed, was an important truth. Something essential about the desert life was displayed here before him. This was why the tribe clung so determinedly to their traditions and their lore. The desert's harshness was always there, ever ready to steal away the moral fiber that bound them together. As Jake stood and watched and listened to words he could not understand, he knew a pride for Omar and these people, an affection so strong that the flame burned his chest.

Omar turned and gestured to one of the men standing behind him. A moment passed before several of the tribe stepped forward and unrolled richly colored carpets. Jake had watched the old women weaving these, working as they traveled upon the camels' backs and sitting by the fireside in the evenings, chattering and laughing among themselves, their hands never ceasing their nimble dance. In the sunset's burnished glow, the carpets' rich red and orange hues shone as though lit by a fire of their own.

The trader glanced casually down at the offered rugs and then swiftly turned away, continuing with his elaborate talk. Others stepped forward and set upon the carpets more of the tribe's handiwork—hair and hides of desert goats fashioned into waterskins and tent coverings, and lamb's wool spun into soft blankets and vests for the cold desert nights. Again the trader paid them scant mind, seemingly lost in his conversation.

With formal correctness, Omar hefted a belted vest, the stitches worked with brilliant thread and patterned after the flowing Arabic script. He ran his hand over the rich wool and spoke in a voice that did not require volume to demand a response. Reluctantly the trader cut off his flow of words and accepted the vest. He picked at the wool, frowned with theatrical concern, then spoke a few words.

With a speed that surprised them all, Omar was on his feet, lifting the trader by one arm and gesturing for the wares to be taken back and stored away. The trader yelped in protest, clearly having been prepared for hours of bargaining. But Omar was having none of it. Polite yet determined, he signaled that the discussion was at an end.

Recognizing that this was not a ploy, and seeing the wares vanish from view, the trader yelped a second time. Omar replied by silently waiting and watching as the two Tuareg rose to their feet. The trader plucked at his sleeve, smiling nervously, reaching out into the gathering night toward where the wares had vanished.

Suddenly the Tuareg were less interested in the argument than they were in examining the camp's periphery. Jake felt their gazes rake across him, pass on, then return for a second inspection. He forced himself to stand still and unflinching. But only when the gaze moved onward was he able to draw breath again.

The taller mercenary stepped away from the fire as though wishing to enter deeper into the camp. Instantly a phalanx of tribesmen were there to bar his way. The Tuareg snarled a curse. The trader moved forward and spoke with eyes closed to cunning slits, his eyes now on the animals paddocked at the square's far end. Caught in a quandary, Omar hesitated only a moment before waving for the tribesmen to let them pass.

A passage opened, barely wide enough to permit one visitor to pass at a time. The trader stepped forward, a nervous giggle escaping under the pressure of the tribesmen's stares. The Tuareg swaggered after him, hands on knives, their eyes sweeping back and forth through the camp as they walked.

At the paddock, the trader went through an elaborate charade of inspecting several animals before speaking a question. Omar responded with a single snort of humor and jerked his head upward in the desert signal of negation.

The trader spoke again, his voice rising. Omar replied by steering the man about and directing him toward the square's entranceway. The tribesmen closed in about them, forcing the Tuareg to follow. Seeing that his protests were to no avail, the trader gathered himself, flung his robes up and about his left arm, gave Omar a single cold nod, and stomped off.

Only when they had left the square did Jasmyn venture to speak. "Omar refused to deal with him."

"I understood that much," Jake said, and discovered that his voice was as shaky as his legs from the aftershock of passing danger.

"Omar accused him of offering prices meant for those who had returned from unsuccessful trading at Raggah. But since we are headed there, we shall simply wait and trade in the souq ourselves."

"Raggah," Jake said. "Isn't that the city where the Tuareg live?"

Before she could reply, Omar walked over and spoke. Jasmyn translated, "Danger has passed for the night."

"That trader was a piece of work," Jake said.

"Indeed, a man so oily he could escape the tightest shackles," Omar agreed. "He also talks too much. In the desert way, we say that here is one who scolds the trees. When the trees do not answer, he scolds the stars. But we say there remains hope, so long as he scolds only the made things, rather than the Maker. Before, I thought there was hope for this one. Now that I see him in the company of vultures, I am no longer certain. It is doubtful that we shall trade with him again."

Jake asked, "Is it true we are headed for Raggah?"

"It is the natural destination of all on our course," Omar explained. "To the west are mountains without passes. To the east, desert without water. All who go north must stop at the oasis of Raggah."

"Will we be safe?"

"The danger will be no greater there than elsewhere. There is a small French garrison, or there was the last time I passed. The war drained it to a symbolic force of three or four, but still the French soldiers held the Tuareg from doing their worst."

Jake glanced Pierre's way and said, "Better and better."

Pierre stepped forward and said, "Ask him if there is any chance that we might find medicines in this village."

"Doubtful," Omar replied. "The nearest healer is in Raggah. But I am going now to the village tea house to sit and listen and see what I can learn. I shall see if the merchants have anything. This is for your brother?"

"He is growing worse," Pierre said, concern creasing his features.

"This is not good. The way to Melilla is long yet. And the healer of Raggah will not be one to trust overmuch."

Pierre turned to gaze thoughtfully at Jake, then reached some internal decision and gave a single nod. "Please tell Omar we are sorry to have brought peril upon him and his people."

"The Al-Masoud are men of honor," Omar replied. "We would not pass a cur into the clutches of the Tuareg."

"Even so," Pierre went on, "we are indebted to you and your people. Our duty shall continue long after the money has been paid."

Omar gravely accepted the translation, inspected Pierre for a long moment, then said, "It is good to know that one such as yourself is to wed one of our own. Long after you have departed, we shall remember that our daughter's husband is a man close to our hearts."

Chapter Seven

JAKE AWOKE THE next morning to the comfortable sound of coffee being pounded in the tribe's brass mortar. The young girl timed her strokes to the song she sang, a warbling melody that pealed like bells in the still air.

Breakfast was the same as every morning—treacly thick coffee, dates, unleavened bread, milk curds, and honey. Jake took his portion over to the side wall, drew out his Bible, and read as he ate. The sounds of the camp awakening were a reassuring chorus, familiar enough now not to draw his attention. The children laughed and scampered in scarce moments of playtime before the chores of breaking camp were begun; camels bellowed and complained as they were made to kneel and the saddle blankets were set in place; a group of men knelt toward Mecca and murmured their morning prayers; several of the older women sat and spun silky goat's hair with blinding speed, their mouths open and gossiping and laughing in the morning sun.

The village *kunta*, a nomadic spiritual leader, arrived and passed from person to person. He made talismans, said the special healing prayers, taught a few new verses from the Koran, and offered the traditional blessings for good grazing and much water. His final blessing was the special one, offered for a safe and healthy passage through the desert reaches. Each person in turn held out their right hand, which was first touched by the kunta's cane, then spat upon. The nomads then wiped the spit over their faces and down the front of their robes.

Omar gave the call to break camp. Jake rose, tucked away his Bible, and joined the others. Again he had the sense of gathering lessons, storing up information and knowledge and newfound wisdom but being unable to digest what he was learning. Even so, he felt a sense of rightness to it all, a knowing on some deeper level that this need to sit and reflect would be granted him at the proper time.

When they had left the village and its confines well behind, Omar sent word for Jake and Jasmyn to join him. As the two of them walked toward the head of the caravan, Jasmyn said, "Pierre agrees with your plan."

Jake nodded, too full of sudden doubt to be very pleased. "How is Patrique?"

"There were no medicines in the village. Did you see him try to mount the camel?"

"Yes." It had taken three tries and the aid of both Pierre and Jasmyn to get him into the saddle-tent.

"Pierre walks with him now, writing whenever he has strength to speak." Jasmyn shook her head. "I hope your plan works, Jake."

"So do I."

"Even Pierre feels it is our only hope to save him now."

As they approached, Omar said to Jake, "Several mornings now I have seen you separate yourself and read from a book you carry."

"It is a Bible, the holy Book," Jake said, answering the implied question.

"It is good for man to be bound by the custom of his religion," Omar said.

"It is more than that," Jake said, seeking a way to explain that would invite and not offend. "This is the story of Christ, the Son of God. His is a story of salvation for all who choose to believe. And His lessons are those of love."

Omar walked ahead in silence for a time, then said through Jasmyn, "Yesterday I sought to teach you of our ways. Today I would ask a question of you, a man of the world who speaks with wisdom of his own and who does honor to our desert ways."

"I would be honored to help," Jake said, "if I can."

"I have heard of this Christian god," Omar said. "There is a school now in Colomb-Bechar, five days' march from Raggah. It is run by families who claim to serve this god of yours."

"We call them missionaries," Jake offered.

"I have two of the tribe's children, a boy and a girl, who beg to go and learn. Day and night they are after me. Even when they do not speak, still I can hear their little hearts crying through their eyes." He looked at Jake. "Sending a child to school means losing a herder. I must also pay for a family to keep them. While they are gone, their own mother's heart remains empty. A young boy's bed goes cold with his absence. A father misses the songs that his lovely daughter sang to the waking day."

"They might return and enrich the tribe with what they have learned," Jake ventured.

"Yes? You think this school will make them better people? That their lives will be better? Yes? Then tell me. What will they know, my children, that has enough value to wrench them from the heart of my tribe?"

"They will know languages. History. Math."

"Already they know their father's tongue. They learn the history of their father's father and their fathers before them. They can count their sheep and their goats. What more will they know?"

"They will know the world."

"No!" Omar pounced upon Jake's words. "They will know *your* world, not mine. They will know *your* knowledge. And then whose child will they be, yours or mine?"

"Everything you say is true," Jake agreed, marveling anew at the man who strode along beside him. "There is a risk that they will choose not to return. But what right do you have to refuse them their heart's desire?"

Omar subsided. "You speak a truth that has echoed through my nights since learning of this school. This is a question for which I have yet to find the answer. Tell me, man of the world who honors our desert ways. What would you do if you were faced with such a dilemma?"

"Pray," Jake said simply. "Pray and wait for guidance."

They walked for a time in companionable silence until Omar said, "I want my children to know the value of wisdom, but I also want them to know the wealth of the desert. I want them to have the city and the wider world to call upon when there is drought, but I want them to return to the desert in the rainy season. Is that so much to ask?"

"No," Jake replied, liking him immensely.

"Our world has changed," Omar declared through Jasmyn. "For many past seasons we stood upon our desert hills and watched the thunder of war from distant lands coming ever closer. No matter how far into the desert we went, still guns split the heavens and called to all the world that a new time was upon us. It does not matter what I like or what I wish. The seasons change, and only a fool refuses to accept what is."

He drew himself up to his full height. "But I am still leader of the tribe. And as leader it is my duty to see that the desert's wealth and wisdom is not lost. We shall change, yes. But we shall take with us what is ours. What others do not see, do not know, and cannot understand. What makes us who we are."

"It is a worthy aim," Jake said, and meant it with all his heart.

"I am a man of the desert," Omar said. "The desert is all I know."

"But you know that well."

"I know the wind," Omar went on. "I know the great emptiness that is as close to death as a living man can ever know. I know the feel of rock and the smell of water. I know the dry mountains. I know the dusty graves of ancient rivers. I know . . ."

"You know," Jake murmured, thinking of all he had learned.

"*Aiwa*. I know. And yet this, this is a new thing. A thing of wars and machines and cities. This new thing I do not know. And I do not know what is to be done. Not for today, not for tomorrow, not for all the days yet to be granted my people."

"Perhaps," Jake ventured, "perhaps you could find this answer also in prayer."

"Yes? You think this Christian god might turn to help a man of the desert?"

"He has promised to be there for all who seek Him," Jake replied. "All men, all nations, all times. A God who seeks only to give peace and love and salvation. To all."

That day they entered the area known as Zagora. Most of the desert through which they had passed was rock and shale and hard and flat, bordered by mountains and great, billowing desert hills. But Zagora was a region of sand. Oceans of drifting, golden sand. Gradually the Atlas foothills turned and moved away, leaving them enclosed by endless sand. Ever-changing, always the same. Hills and valleys and great, ghostly shapes that lasted only until the next great wind.

It was hard going for all but the camels, whose great wide hooves splayed out flat and kept them from sinking down. For the others, each foot dragged, every step sucked from the blistering sand. By midday, even the nimble-footed goats were complaining.

They walked nine hours with only two short breaks, yet managed only six miles. Jake knew this only because Omar told him. Distance meant little in this barren world. For a while that afternoon, as they struggled onward, Jake had wondered if perhaps Omar had led them astray. Each crested sand dune revealed nothing in any direction but more sand, more undulating hills, more heat. There was no track whatsoever, no road signs, no directional markers, nothing with which to determine either progress or bearing.

But then, as the sun began its grudging descent, a paint-daubed thorn tree came into view. All the tribe offered loud cries of relief and pride that Omar the desert chieftain had led them correctly yet again.

Around the thorn tree spread scattered desert scrub on which the animals could feed. It was the first vegetation they had seen all day. Jake helped form the paddocks with shreds of wood bleached white as old bones, then gathered with the others for the customary evening tea. There was no firewood; by tradition the bits of wood kept at the site were to be used only as paddocks. Their tea and the evening meal would be cooked over portable stoves, a necessity that everyone loathed because it left everything tasting and smelling of kerosene.

Sunset that evening was transformed by clouds gathering on the horizon, an event so rare that all work was stopped. As the orb slipped behind the cloud, a silent symphony of colors lit up the sky, and drew appreciative murmurs from them all. Jake watched the others as much as the sky itself and wondered at a people who could stop and share in the beauty of something that for himself had so often gone unnoticed.

When the spectacle finally dimmed, Jake asked through Jasmyn, "Does it ever rain here?"

"Oh yes," Omar replied. "I remember it well. It turned the plain we were walking into a river and swept away several of the animals. Then the next day the entire desert bloomed. I will never forget that vision. Good and bad together."

"When was that?"

The entire group entered into a spirited discussion. Jake waited and watched, wondering if perhaps he had broken some desert etiquette. The argument continued on until night veiled the camp and the tribe was called for the evening meal. Jake followed Jasmyn toward the cooking fire and, when they were apart from the others, asked, "Did I say something wrong?"

She looked at him with genuine surprise. "What could be wrong in asking an honest question?"

"Never mind. Come on, I want to speak with you and Pierre."

Together they walked over to where Pierre sat brooding over the sleeping form of his brother. He lifted his head at

Jake's approach and declared, "We no longer have any choice, my friend."

Jake squatted down beside him. "He's worse?"

Pierre nodded, his face deeply furrowed. "I am greatly troubled. We must get him to a facility that can offer proper medical care."

"Do not trouble yourself so, mon frere," said a weak voice. All eyes turned toward Patrique. He smiled faintly and went on, "Pierre always did the worrying for both of us."

Jake asked, "How do you feel?"

"That I have more than enough strength for the task at hand," Patrique replied. "It is a good plan."

"I think so too," Jasmyn agreed.

"For myself, I am too worried to think," Pierre said. "So I must trust in the judgment of you three. Though I confess it tears at my heart to do so."

Jasmyn reached over and took his hand, her gaze as soft as her touch. "It is only for a short while, my beloved. We have been separated before, and for much longer, and much farther apart in spirit. This shall pass in the blink of an eye."

"Even that is far too long," Pierre replied.

Jake cleared his throat, the night filled by the love that spilled out from them. "You two need a couple of nights off. I'll stand watch with our friend Patrique here until we arrive in Raggah."

"They were right in what they have told me," Patrique said. "You are indeed a good friend."

Pierre looked torn. "You are sure—"

"Thank you, Jake," Jasmyn said, rising to her feet and drawing Pierre up with her.

But before they could depart, Omar walked over with two of the elders. He spoke briefly to Jasmyn, who turned and said to Jake, "Twenty-four years."

"What?"

"You asked when it had last rained. It was twenty-four years ago. They are sure."

Jake struggled to his feet. "They've spent all this time trying to figure out when it rained?"

"Smile and nod your gratitude," Jasmyn said quietly. When Jake had done so, she went on, "You are an honored guest. You asked a question, and they wished to answer you honestly. It was not a simple matter. You see, Jake, there are no calendars here, no birthdays beyond the one marking a child as an adult. Time is measured by events. They had to tie the rainfall to the events of that period, measuring back by other events. This camel had foaled, that person was born, another died, counting back over the seasons until the date was arrived at. Twenty-four years ago it rained."

"Please thank them," Jake said feebly. His mind rang with the impact of foreignness. The desert way.

Jasmyn turned and bowed and spoke solemnly. The men responded with beams of real pride. Omar patted Jake on the shoulder, turned, and walked away.

Chapter Eight

*A*LTHOUGH PATRIQUE HAD a restful night, Jake found himself sleeping with one eye and ear open. So it was that he was up and ready before the guard came within ten paces. He slipped on his boots, grabbed his rifle, stood, and bent over to check on the sick man one last time. Then he heard the whispered words, "Take me with you."

He jerked. "I thought you were asleep."

"I sleep far too much. It comes and goes like the wind. You're going out on watch, yes? I want to come with you."

"I'm not sure—"

"Please, my friend. Let me share your sunrise."

Jake helped him rise and dress, then with one hand holding his rifle and the other steadying Patrique, they made their way out of camp. Awkwardly they climbed a nearby rise. When Jake had settled Patrique near the peak, he descended to the camp and returned with two glasses and the pot of watch tea. They sat and sipped in silence for a time until Patrique spoke. "I have seen you walk out while the camp was still sleeping and seen you return after the sunrise. Your face changes while you are away."

Jake hid his embarrassment behind noisy sips of his tea that cooled the liquid as he swallowed. "You've been watching me?"

"Not intentionally. But I often find it hardest to sleep around dawn." Patrique paused to sip from his own glass. "Pierre has told me of your faith. I hear in his voice how it has given him strength. But I *see* it most clearly in your face, when you return from watching the sunrise."

Patrique lifted his gaze toward the star-flecked heavens. "There were times of great despair in that dungeon, Jake. I felt as though the darkness would crush my very soul. That day, when I heard a voice call out my name, I thought at first it was death come for me. I thought the tragedy of my imprisonment had given me the power to hear what should always remain hidden."

Jake sipped quietly and shivered from more than just the night's lingering chill.

"But the voice came from above," Patrique went on. "From the only place where light entered into my dark hole. And then I knew. I was hearing an angel. An angel with the voice of my brother. Even after I knew it was real, and my nightmare might indeed come to an end, still I knew that the angels had been at work. I knew that it would take the power of heaven to pierce the darkness that enslaved me with chains upon my heart as well as my limbs. So I was not surprised when Pierre began speaking of this new power in his life. I had already seen it at work, you see. I had already sensed this power at work."

He turned to look at Jake. "So tell me, friend of my brother. What is carried upon the sunrise that leaves you with the power shining from your face?"

"I couldn't put it into words," Jake replied, ashamed by his inadequacy.

"Then show me," Patrique quietly implored. "Please."

Jake nodded once, closed his eyes in a moment's prayer, then turned his face toward the awakening east. Patrique followed his example, sitting in utter silence there beside him, his eyes searching in the gradually strengthening light for that which remained unseen.

Little by little the silence drew into their souls, stilling their mind, opening them to the quietest of sounds. Breaths of dawn wind puffed about them, whispering gentle secrets.

Sand shifted and cascaded, an animal bleated, a loose fold on one of the tents flapped open and closed. The light strengthened, and with it the sense of sharing more than that which was seen with the eyes. The veil of night lifted enough to reveal an ocean of softly undulating sand waves stretching into the horizon. All was still and silent and timeless.

Jake reached into his pocket for his Bible, found his place, and read the next verse from John's gospel, "Verily, verily, I say unto you, Whosoever committeth sin is the slave of sin. And the slave abideth not in the house for ever: but the Son abideth ever. If the Son therefore shall make you free, ye shall be free indeed."

He stopped, lifted his gaze, and heard Patrique murmur to the horizon, "Free."

Jake reached over, clasped Patrique's shoulder, bowed his head, and spoke the words resounding through his silent mind and heart.

Chapter Nine

*T*WO DAYS LATER they arrived at the oasis of Raggah, a broad lake sheltered by a veritable forest of palms.
When he crested the final rise and the lake came into view,
Jake stopped and gaped with the others, mesmerized by the
sight. In the space of three weeks, he had forgotten how
beautiful so much water could be.

Swaths of green stretched down two neighboring gullies,
marking the track of streams that broke through the rock
and delivered their precious load overland. Amidst the
trees and brush raced a wealth of wildlife—ostriches, hye-
nas, gazelles, monkeys. Butterflies by the millions scoured
the lake's surface, feeding upon the water flowers and the
blooming reeds that lined one bank. After days in the barren sand, Jake had difficulty taking in this sudden wealth of
life.

Across the lake from them rose a city as yellow as the
barren earth that surrounded it. The Atlas Mountains rose
majestic and ocher in the background. This was the first
real town Jake had seen in what felt like a lifetime. Jake
was not sure he liked it. He was amazed by how his perspective had changed. When he had first left the city for the
desert, he had felt he was leaving all civilization behind.
Now, as he left the desert for the city, he felt as though the

joys of living were soon to be lost, the beauty of life re-caged, and his world filled with meaningless clamor.

Omar and Jasmyn climbed the rise to stand behind him. "Raggah is a place of great glory," Omar said, looking out over the city. "And like all such places, a home to much tragedy. It was here that the lords of the western deserts ruled the trade routes of the northern and western Saharas. Gold, ivory, myrrh, frankincense, salt, slaves—all traders paid tribute to the rulers of Raggah."

He pointed out over the cloudless distance. "From that citadel they held life-and-death power over the local tribes. The chieftains were all-powerful, ruthless, and often cruel. When the great drought drove the Tuareg into this city, Raggah and the chieftains devoured their souls. Now the French have restricted their evil, but only to a point. Their cruelty is not ended, only held in check, like a vicious dog on the Frenchmen's chain. Be careful here."

"Don't worry."

Still Omar stood and gazed out over the city. "To my people I give the wisdom of the desert and the wealth of my camels. People in towns such as these live for money. That is not our way. That is the hunger that never ends, the thirst that is never quenched no matter how deeply they draw from the well. No, money is for those who have chosen to live as the blind."

Jake stood and looked out over the city and felt the words settle to the very depths of his soul.

"We hold the wealth of blood," Omar said quietly. "By this we mean the good name of our tribe. It means we treat our animals well, we pass on the tribe's wisdom and lore to our children, we show the desert hospitality to all. It is a wealth that lasts and does not blind one to the power of the day."

He turned and faced Jake square on. "I have thought long on your words of our walk together. I have decided that our two who beg to learn will go to the Christian school. They will study the knowledge of which you have spoken. They will return and teach our people the meaning of this Christian love and Christian peace."

"You do me a great honor," Jake said, humbled by the man's gift of trust. "I will hope and pray that your decision brings new and eternal wealth to your tribe."

"This also do I hope. Come," Omar said. "Let us descend and make camp."

Travel-weary caravans from a dozen different locations took rest along the lake's shoreline. As they walked the long path skirting the oasis, Omar intoned each name in turn. "They are of the Al Moyda'at. And those the M'Barek, a good people and our friends for many generations. And on the other side, the Mahmoudi. They are not to be trusted. Beyond them the Tebbeh from the reaches far to the south, here to trade their gold for salt and wares."

Each camp was carefully guarded, showing fierce hostility to most who passed or looked their way. At one camp a man strode forth, bowed and spoke and gestured for the chieftain to join him. Jake walked on with the rest of the tribe, drawing the desert hood down farther to shield his eyes, and watched as Omar respectfully declined the invitation.

They kept themselves hidden from prying eyes by making camp at the lake's far side. At dusk a pearly glow settled over the city. From the city's ancient mosque, the muezzin called the faithful to the day's final prayer.

As night gathered, fires glowed the entire length of the lake and glimmered along the distant city's walls. Their glow and the sunset burnished the lake to a coppery sheen. Fishermen glided gracefully across this brilliant surface, poling themselves in slender boats as long as the surrounding trees were tall. Jake spent the cool hour watching these fisherfolk, two polers working bow and stern, while from amidships three others fanned out nets, tossing and pulling them in with motions older than written history.

While the evening meal was being prepared, Jake and Pierre brought Omar to the lakeside, and through Jasmyn explained the plan. He heard them out in silence, then stared out over the darkening lake. Finally he said, "For several days it has been clear that your brother is not up to the journey. But I did not feel it my place to speak first."

"It's the only idea we have had," Jake said, speaking for them all. "But if you have a better one, we would like to hear it."

Omar examined him. "How can you be sure that the French are not after him as well?"

"Even if they are, it will be for Patrique and not for us," Jake replied, hoping that what he said was true.

"It is doubtful," Pierre added, "that the traitor could order a hunt for Patrique through official French channels without revealing his plot."

"We are hoping that the people who ordered us to proceed northward will be watching for anything like that," Jake explained.

Omar pondered their words long and hard before the call came to gather for the evening meal. Rising to his feet, the chieftain said, "I can see no danger in this plan that another plan would not also contain, and I have no other idea as sound as this one. We shall think on it further this night and see what the dawn brings before deciding."

Patrique was feeling fit enough to join them for the evening meal, but his eyes glittered feverishly in the firelight. Watching him, Jake knew at some deep level that tonight marked an ending. Come what may, this portion of his journey and his life was over. Jake looked about the campfire, studying each of the faces he had come to know so well, trying to etch the power of the memory and his feelings upon his very soul.

He sat and ate as the others did, dipping into the communal pot using only his right hand, the action totally natural now. He accepted a goatskin, drank, passed it on. He listened to words he could not understand, seated in the dust at the very frontier of civilization, surrounded by men and women who could neither read nor write, and felt himself to be the richest man on earth.

Abruptly Pierre stood, helped Jasmyn to her feet, and motioned for Jake to join them. He raised his hands for silence, then said through her, "I have told this to Omar, but I wish to also speak these words to all the tribe. It is only because of the help you have given that my brother is here and alive

today. The tribe of Al-Masoud has placed upon me a debt
that can never be repaid."

"Hear, hear," Patrique said hoarsely.

"Although much of my time and energy has gone to caring for my brother, still I have learned much from my time
with you," Pierre went on. "One such lesson is that questions are rarely asked about what is considered private or
personal. Still, I think you may like to hear how we came
to be with you."

An appreciative murmur rose around the fire. Pierre
looked at Jake and asked, "Shall you start, or shall I?"

"You're doing fine so far."

Pierre began with the cries of the young Lilliana Goss
through the wires of the detention camp—in mistaking
Pierre for his missing twin Patrique, she had set the whole
saga in motion. Pierre carried them through the search for
his brother in Marseille, took them along on the hot, dusty
train ride to Madrid and Gibraltar, then told how Jake had
saved his life both in a smugglers' cafe and again on a boulevard in Gibraltar.

The tribesmen showed themselves to be a marvelous audience. They drank in the story with the rapt attention of a
people raised on stories, a folk bereft of books and film or
any entertainment save what they made for themselves.

Pierre, too, became caught up in the telling, filling the
spaces created by Jasmyn's translations by using his wiry
body and expressive face to describe the things of which he
spoke. Quietly Jake lowered himself down on his haunches
so that he too could enjoy watching his friend act out the
spectacle of two terrified assassins tied to hospital beds in a
Gibraltar cave, with great Barbary apes glowering and
screaming down at them. Jake took great pleasure in joining their delighted roar of approval.

But the desert people's strongest reactions were saved for
the scenes that took place in Telouet, for here was a place
they knew. When Pierre threw himself into a parody of
Jake's saluting the diminutive official Hareesh Yohari, the
entire camp howled. They silenced only long enough to
hear of how Jasmyn had directed the search to the palace

dungeon. But when Patrique stood on shaky legs to display the festering scars remaining on his wrists and ankles from the dungeon's chains, they roared like a pack of hungry lions. All had seen or heard of Patrique's injuries by then, yet now the story lived for them.

Pierre next described Jake's attempt to pull out the dungeon's window bars by means of ropes attached to the sultan's antique Rolls Royce. At that point, one of the elders became so excited that he sprang to his feet, grasped Pierre's robes, and began shaking the grinning Frenchman back and forth, jabbering at the top of his voice.

Omar himself had to stand and lead the old man back to his place before Pierre could describe the grand finale, which occurred when Jake finally lost his temper and crashed the car into the palace walls. The image of him throwing caution and silence to the wind and using a Rolls Royce as a battering ram against the palace wall had the audience rolling about the fire in helpless convulsions. And they laughed even harder at the notion of hundreds of sleepy traders being transformed into pole vaulters and high divers as a car suddenly flew down an otherwise empty street, before the sultan's own guards saluted Jake and Pierre as they drove through the gates and off to freedom and safety.

Jake watched the people gathered about the fire, saw the hands raise to wipe tears from leathery faces, and knew an astonishing pleasure. With the sharing of their tale, they had entered into the tribe's living history. He stood with the others, content beyond measure that they would now remain long after their paths and their duties had taken them elsewhere.

Chapter Ten

*T*HEY CAME IN silence and in stealth, just after dawn. They chose their moment well, arriving when the camels were being inspected. This was a normal procedure at every longer halt and was a monstrously noisy affair. Whether unloading or loading, feeding or watering, rising to their feet or lowering to their knees, sick or healthy, camels responded to every command with great complaining bellows. In the desert stillness, their bellows were audible for more than two miles. Here in the confines of the caravansary, their noise was deafening.

Jake followed Omar along his slow inspection, watching him give each hoof a careful examination, then talk long and seriously with the tribe's chief drover. They were alone. The rest of the tribe had placed as much distance as possible between them and the camels' cacophony. Occasionally Omar turned and showed something to Jake, but not often. The issues were too technical to be communicated well with hands alone. Jasmyn was busy elsewhere, fashioning Pierre's uniform to Patrique's more slender frame—an important part of their plan. Jake did not mind. Not even the camels could disturb his pleasure at walking and watching and learning.

The Tuareg's arrival caught them all by surprise. One moment, Jake was watching Omar kneel and use his knife to inspect a sensitive swelling on one hoof, while the camel punctuated their work with aggrieved bellows. The next, another knife suddenly jabbed toward Jake's ribs.

Jake's war-honed reactions took instant control. In one lightning motion he spun and grabbed and wrenched forward. Jake's lack of hesitation caught the mercenary by surprise; the Arab was pulled forward and off balance enough for Jake to force the dagger from his grip, sweep one leg out to trip him, and strike the base of his skull with an iron-hard fist.

Jake spun about in time to see Omar leap backward, avoiding the knife thrust of another Tuareg. Omar's hands were empty, his own knife lost somewhere in the dust kicked up by their struggle and the frightened animals. The drover was rolling in the dirt, fighting a third Tuareg while the camels bellowed and danced to avoid stepping on the fighting men. The remainder of the camp was blocked from view by the milling animals and the dust.

"Omar!" As he shouted, Jake tossed the knife he found in the dust at his feet. Omar flashed a swift glance, caught the knife by its haft, blocked the next parry, and shouted something back. Jake caught the tone of warning and spun in time to meet the attack of a fourth Tuareg.

The mercenary snarled a curse as Jake slithered out of the blade's reach and drew his own dagger. The hook-nosed Arab crouched and weaved, the dagger blade before him. Jake willed himself to watch the eyes and not the blade, for it was there that the first signal would come. The mercenary was skilled, however, and used his polished blade to flicker sunlight into Jake's eyes. Jake blinked at the blinding brilliance, saw the Tuareg ready for the pounce, and knew a heartbeat's quavering that he faced a more experienced foe.

Then the camel came to his rescue.

Clearly the animal had endured all the jostling it was willing to take for one day. Whether it was because the Tuareg was a stranger, or simply because he was within closest reach, the camel reached down and gripped the Tuareg's shoulder with its great yellow teeth.

The man howled, dropped his weapon, and struggled to free himself. The camel responded by lifting the man clear of the earth.

Jake sheathed his dagger, stepped forward, and put every ounce of energy he had into one solid blow to the Tuareg's midsection. The camel obliged by choosing the next moment to unceremoniously drop its cargo. Before the Arab could fold, Jake planted both feet in the prescribed manner and hammered a right to the Tuareg's chin. He felt the impact all the way down to his toes. The Tuareg lifted clear of the earth a second time before collapsing in a defeated heap.

Omar shouted a second time. Jake spun, saw that the chieftain was busy tying up his defeated foe. Omar tossed a rope and pointed back to where Jake's first attacker was stirring. Swiftly Jake knelt and bound the man's hands and feet, dragged him over, and tied him and the second Tuareg back to back. The drover hauled his own unconscious adversary over and attached him to the others, as did Omar with the fourth man. Cloths were stuffed in each mouth and the ropes were carefully checked. Omar motioned that the attackers should be left where they sprawled, blocked from view by the animals, until the remainder of the camp had been patrolled. He ordered the drover to stand guard over them, then led Jake back toward the camp.

They skirted the animal paddocks, and the tents came into view beyond a sheaf of towering palms. Something caught Omar's eye. He held up one hand, searched, then crouched and drew Jake down with him. His hand signals were so complex Jake did not understand at first. Again the hands rose to fix an imaginary cap upon his head, then down to straighten an invisible tie. Jake nodded. He was to go put on his uniform. Something was bringing the plan into action long before they had expected.

Jake skirted the outer tents, dropped to his knees at the back of his own, saw Omar rise and carefully dust himself off and straighten his clothes, then march solemnly forward, every inch the tribal chieftain. Jake lifted the back flap and rolled into the tent.

He dragged out his satchel from the tent's back corner, dug down and extracted his uniform. His actions speeded by the rise and fall of voices outside, he undressed and dressed. The uniform was heavily creased from weeks of heat and hard travel, but there was nothing he could do about that. He wiped the dust from his boots, opened the satchel's side pocket and extracted his papers, straightened his jacket, set his cap at the proper angle, then hesitated. He reached down and slid the tribal dagger into his belt, and walked from the tent.

And faltered.

He could not help it. There before him stood a sudden mystery, a Pierre shrunk and yet still the same, a Pierre made fragile by the fever that glittered in his eyes. Jake forced himself forward, nodded at Patrique standing there in Pierre's uniform, and asked as calmly as he could, "What's going on?"

Patrique gestured toward the official standing before him. "This gentleman is here on behalf of the sultan of Raggah," he replied, and Jake could see that he was holding himself erect and calm only with the greatest effort. "They have received word that the Al-Masoud tribe was harboring two thieves. Foreigners."

Jake turned toward the slender man with swarthy skin and darting eyes. His robes were rich, his cloth-topped boots long and curled and decked with silver threads. He also appeared very nervous. Clearly, the situation here in the camp was not at all as he had expected.

Jasmyn stood at his side, quietly translating everything that was said. Jake strived to hide his surprise at her appearance; even though they had discussed it, still it was a shock to see her in a long beige skirt, pumps, blouse, and headkerchief—the only Western clothes she had carried with her. As calmly as he could, Jake shook his head and replied, "Not here. The only foreigners traveling with this tribe were us."

The official spoke, his voice very high and nasal. Jake found himself relaxing. It was hard to be afraid of somebody who sounded as if he were still on the wrong side of puberty. Jasmyn translated, "The official wishes to examine both your papers."

Together they unbuttoned their shirt pockets and proffered their passes. Jasmyn pointed to each line in turn, patiently translated everything that was written there. The official made a pretense of listening, yet all the while his eyes nervously scanned the camp. The trio of swarthy guards flanking the official were equally puzzled and far less secretive in their search of the perimeter. Jake kept his face set but thought to himself, sorry, chumps, your buddies aren't going to make this party.

The official persisted with his charade of questions about who they were, where they had come from, what they were doing with the tribe, how Jasmyn had come to be their official interpreter, and so on, and so forth. But clearly his instructions had included nothing about arresting two Allied officers in uniform, their chests decorated with medals, and their papers all in order.

Reluctantly he handed back Patrique's papers, and Jake permitted himself a full breath. Home free. For the moment.

The official turned to Jake, who already had his hand outstretched, his palm itching, then stopped. A sly glint appeared in the prince's eyes, and Jake felt the band tighten around his chest. The official withdrew the hand holding Jake's papers and spoke again in that high nasal voice. Jasmyn said, "He does not think the sultan has ever had the honor of meeting an American officer before. He wishes to invite you to the palace, where the sultan himself will return your documents and perhaps entertain you for tea."

"What can we do to stop him?"

"Nothing," she said, her melodious voice urging Jake to remain calm. "He is being an Arab, nothing more. He wishes to have the final word and show that he, too, has power."

The prince saw the spark in Jake's eyes and smiled like a well-fed cat. He spoke again, vastly pleased to have this final moment of control. Jasmyn said, "The sultan will be delighted to see you anytime tomorrow afternoon."

Jake yearned to reach over and throttle the whining little voice right out of the prince's head. All he said was, "I'll be there."

Omar stood and watched until the official was out of sight, then said through Jasmyn, "Our choices have just been taken from our grasp. We must take the injured one to safety and then, papers or no, move to safety ourselves." He looked first at Jake, then the others. "You are ready?"

Pierre stepped forward, still dressed in his desert garb. "What happened?"

Swiftly Jake recounted their attack in the camel paddock. "They planned it well. They waited until we were split off from the main camp and attacked only with knives. Swift and silent and almost deadly."

"If they left any friends watching and waiting in reserve, our escape route may already be cut off," Omar pressed. "We must hurry."

Pierre squared his shoulders. "We go."

A tremor passed across Jasmyn's lovely features. She raised a hand toward Pierre, who stepped forward and took her in his arms. He lowered his face close to hers and spoke words meant only for Jasmyn. Tears gathered and cascaded down her cheek as she nodded once, raised her head, and returned a soft and lingering kiss before allowing Pierre to step back, take a shaky breath, and say, "Let us proceed while we still are able."

Chapter Eleven

"*T*HERE IS NO longer any need for subterfuge," Omar said as they walked toward Raggah, their pace set by Patrique. "As soon as we accomplish our task here, we shall leave all our tribe but a chosen few with the M'Barek tribe. They are an honorable folk and can be trusted to treat our people well. Then we shall proceed with all haste across the northern reaches for Melilla."

"If this works," Pierre said quietly.

When the translation was made, Omar shook his head. "We no longer have a choice. It must work."

Small squadrons of Omar's men flanked them as they walked. They carried their weapons with deceptive ease, sauntering along before and after the group, far enough away not to grant a threatening impression to the city's guards, yet close enough to defend at an instant's warning.

Pierre said to Jake, "I had no idea you could handle a knife."

"I can't," Jake replied. "That camel saved my bacon."

"She was merely repaying your earlier kindness," Omar said through Jasmyn.

"My what?"

"Did you not recognize her as one of those you led back to safety across the barren land?"

463

"They all look pretty much the same to me," Jake confessed.

"Then be thankful that the camel was more discerning," Omar replied, humor glinting in his dark eyes. "Nonetheless, I agree with you. The gift of good fortune has shone on you this morning. Let us hope it holds."

The central streets of Raggah were shaded by tall trees whose desert-trained roots reached deep enough to tap the underground water. The lanes opened into great ceremonial plazas, dusty spaces with large central wells lined by palms. All commerce took place under the trees' shade. Whole families gathered upon layers of bright desert carpets, living out their daily lives beneath the ancient trees. All conversation, all trade halted to watch the spectacle of two foreign officers in uniform and the beautiful woman in Western clothing. Only when they had passed beyond view did the desert city life resume.

Farther along, plastered alcoves had been cleverly built to melt into the line of trees, making for a covered market. Here men and women from all the tribes of northern Africa gathered to barter wares. Despite the numerous caravans camped alongside the lake, the display in the town's market was disappointing. Omar watched Jake take note of the paltry wares and through Jasmyn explained, "Here is evidence of the city's corrupt nature. Nowadays, everything of value is traded in secret. Not even the names of the traders are bandied about openly."

The houses were buttressed and fortlike, with thick clay walls and windows too narrow for even a child to crawl through. The central mosque was built like a pyramid, with precious logs used to support its five-story structure. Upon the city's sandy lanes walked wild-looking desert warriors, all armed with ancient rifles slung upside down over one shoulder and grasped by the barrels. The position of the rifles, according to Jasmyn, was a sign that they came in peace.

Water was delivered from house to house in goatskins. There was no electricity, no lights, no advertisements, and no motor vehicles in the central city, for the prince prohibited them all. Jake found the city unnaturally still for its size, as though beaten into submission and held in quiet despair.

The French outpost came into view just in time. Patrique crossed the heat-stricken square on legs that barely had the strength to hold him aloft. His breath rasped noisily, and his features were streaked with sweat. His gaze was blank, unfocused; all his attention was drawn to the struggle of putting one foot in front of the other.

With a single word Omar stopped his men from continuing with them. Silently they slipped into neighboring shadows and vanished from sight.

The outpost stood separate and isolated from its neighboring structures, with the only raised wooden porch Jake had seen in the entire city. A pair of flags hung limply in the dusty heat. A lone Arab soldier in puttees sweltered at guard duty. He eyed them with tired hostility as they approached.

As they arrived at the bottom stair, Omar gave an almost imperceptible motion to Pierre—they were to remain there. Jasmyn saw and understood, and a choked sob forced its way through her locked throat.

"No tears," Pierre murmured. "Be strong for us all, my beloved, and look to when we will be united before everyone, for all our days."

Jasmyn lifted her chin once again, her face set with tragic determination. Without looking Pierre's way, she whispered, "My heart, my prayers, my very reason for living goes with you."

Together they climbed the stairs. On the top step, Patrique faltered and would have gone down had Jake and Jasmyn not gripped his arms and held him upright. The Arab soldier took a hesitant step forward, then turned and shouted into the dark interior.

A bored Frenchman wearing desert uniform and corporal's stripes stepped into view. His eyes widened at the sight of an unknown French officer being half carried toward him. He bolted forward, took Patrique's arm from Jasmyn, and barked something at Jake. Jasmyn replied in a hesitant tremolo, which the corporal clearly took as worry over the officer's state. Patrique moaned a brief reply of his own.

"Tell him we were traveling on official duty through the western Sahara when Major Pierre Servais was stricken with an unknown illness," Jake said, his voice officer-sharp, speaking more to establish himself as an American than because the words were important. "You, as his nurse, must immediately escort him to a military hospital."

The corporal gaped at him as together they eased Patrique down onto the barren office's only bench. Jasmyn continued to speak, her voice desolate with loss. Jake was sorry for her, but at the same time felt that her sadness was the perfect attention grabber. Nobody could have faked the concern she was showing.

"The corporal says that the nearest clinic is at the Foreign Legion fortress in Colombe-Bechar," Jasmyn said.

"How far?"

"If we leave now by transport, we could arrive before nightfall. He will have to radio and obtain permission before we can take the truck."

"Tell him to hurry," Jake said, and bent over Patrique's sweat-drenched form. "You're gonna make it, buddy. Almost home free."

"I'm so very thirsty," Patrique replied.

Jasmyn spoke with the corporal, who went to his desk, poured out the half glass remaining in his water bottle, and carried it over to Patrique. He spoke to Jasmyn, who said to Jake, "He says there is a good tearoom down the side street and across the next square. I could go—"

Jake straightened. "I'll do it."

"But Pierre—"

Jake looked at her hard and spoke very carefully, "The only way we will know if everything is all right with Patrique's being transported to the official French government hospital is if you are here to overhear whatever they say."

Her shoulders slumped in defeat. "You are right. Of course."

He patted her arm, murmured, "Be strong," and was out the door.

Jake bolted down the stairs, motioned for Omar and Pierre to follow him, and headed down the side passage. Once out of sight he said, "Patrique's losing a lot of liquid. We need to get him something to drink. Both of them, for that matter."

"And the plan?"

"Looks like the soldier's bought it. He's radioing for permission to drive him to the hospital at someplace called Colombe-Bechar."

"Colombe-Bechar," Omar repeated, using the Arab pronunciation, then nodding his head vigorously. The destination clearly met with his approval.

The tea house's interior was as grand as the exterior was simple. Arched colonnades gave the great hall a pretense of being separated into a series of interconnected chambers. The pillars were of darker granite, the floor of polished marble slabs, the walls of grand desert carpets and ornate mosaic designs. The sound of dice and slapped backgammon chips accented the lively talk. Hookahs bubbled and sent up pungent clouds of smoke. A central fountain tinkled merrily, spraying out a continual sheen of perfumed water.

Omar ignored the silence and the stares that their appearance caused and imperiously ordered a waiter into swift action. Within minutes a tray was brought bearing heavily sweetened tea and glasses of cooled honey and curds. Jake drained his glass in one thirsty gulp and then reached for his tea. "I want to get back and see if everything is all right."

"Agreed." Pierre licked at his white moustache and took the tray with the extra servings. He said to Omar simply, "Patrique and Jasmyn."

But when Pierre turned for the door, the waiter grasped his arm and began arguing. Omar reached into the leather purse slung from his belt and spoke soothing words. Impatiently Jake stepped back into the sunlight.

As he moved across the square, he felt the bottom drop from his world when a familiar voice hissed, "Yes indeedy, just as was thinking. Is the one destroying Hareesh Yohari's world and home and life."

Jake spun and found himself facing a diminutive figure, hopping from one foot to the other with rage, his head raised to eye level by standing on the well's stone border, both hands gripping an ancient single-shot pistol. From Jake's perspective, the gun looked as big as a cannon. All he could think to say was, "How's business?"

"Business, yes, man now speaking of business. I speaking of business too. Business of missing Rolls Royce motor vehicle. Business of palace wall and escaping prisoner. Business of ruining life of sultan's official chief assistant." He shook the barrel inches from Jake's eyes. "But I am making all correct. Yes. Am bringing head of number one criminal back to sultan, sitting on front of formerly stolen Rolls Royce motor vehicle. Now you are telling me where—"

"Is that who I think it is?"

Hareesh Yohari jumped and spun about. His eyes widened at the sight of Pierre marching toward him, dressed in desert garb and burned to a leathery brown, bearing a gleaming tray with tea and curds. The little official squeaked, "You!"

Then Jake did the only thing that came to mind, which was to bend over and grip Yohari's ankles, lift, and fling the man over the lip of the well. The sultan's former official gave a lingering wail that ended with a resounding splash. Jake straightened up and did not bother to mask his grin. "All in a good day's work."

"Come, my friend," Pierre said. "The tea is growing cold."

They turned the corner to find a dusty jeep stationed in front of the French post, its motor idling noisily. "For once my army has acted with dispatch and efficiency," Pierre proclaimed. "I must write a note of commendation once I am again myself."

Jasmyn appeared at the head of the stairs, Patrique leaning heavily upon her. Her eyes fastened upon Pierre and remained so throughout the maneuver of loading the sick man into the jeep. Yet she said nothing. Her gaze shifted only when the corporal came around the jeep and officiously helped her in. She permitted the man to load her into the back beside Patrique, shook her head to the proffered tea, and handed both glasses to Patrique, who drank greedily. Then her eyes turned to Jake. "Colonel Burnes."

"Yes, ma'am."

"You are to take care of my treasure," she said quietly, her gaze dark with unspoken loss.

"With my life." Jake fumbled over the affection he felt for that beautiful, brave woman. "Everything I've learned here has been because of you."

"No, Colonel," she corrected. "I have helped. But you have learned because you have wanted to. You have not been stopped by the alien surroundings or the hardship or the fatigue. You have given great honor to my mother's people. I am proud of you. As are they."

"Jake," Patrique called hoarsely. "Thank you."

Before Jake could reply, the corporal gunned the motor and wheeled the jeep in a tight circle. Through the rising dust Jasmyn looked back at Pierre, and as a single tear escaped she mouthed the words, *I love you.*

Then she was gone.

Chapter Twelve

*J*AKE FOLLOWED OMAR back to where the tribesmen waited, giving Pierre silent space to compose himself and erase the naked emotions that lay etched upon his features. Already he felt Jasmyn's absence, and not just because of his friend's sorrow. There was a new barrier between Omar and him, one that respect and hand signals could never fully cancel.

Behind them, a hysterical voice began shouting incomprehensible words. They spun about, and spotted a wet and bedraggled Hareesh Yohari emerge from the side passage and limp furiously across the square toward them.

Pierre mused aloud, "Now how did he get out of that well so swiftly?"

A band of desert warriors appeared from the shadows behind Yohari. At the sight of Omar they howled their fury. Omar hissed, "Tuareg."

"That explains it," Jake said.

Omar pressed them forward and ordered his tribesmen into a phalanx blocking the alcove behind them. They turned and fled as the passage erupted into fighting, shouting men.

Omar led them in a twisting, winding pattern down countless, nameless streets. From time to time they would catch wind of voices shouting and calling to unseen fellows, before Omar jinked and sped them off in a different direction.

The chase forced them farther and farther away from the oasis and the tribe and safety. Every time Omar sought to direct them around and back toward the camp, voices barely one street over warned them away.

Jake crouched with the others in a shallow doorway, panting and sweating and feeling like a prey hunted by beaters, driven toward exposure and death.

He opened his mouth to tell Pierre that it was time to separate, to let him and Omar try to draw them off while Pierre escaped with Patrique's testimony on the traitor. He knew it was futile, that his friend would never let others sacrifice themselves so that he could live, yet all the same he had to at least try.

Suddenly the voices of the approaching mercenaries were drowned out by a sound once familiar to Jake, and yet now so alien that for a moment he thought it was thunder.

He craned and searched the empty spaces overhead, when abruptly the sun was blocked from view by a great roaring beast. Before the sky again emptied, Jake was up and racing and shouting behind him, "Come on!"

They sprinted with all the strength they had left, Omar following a pace behind them and shouting fearful words they could neither understand nor spare breath to answer. Jake followed the sound of revving motors out beyond the final border of houses, through the great sand-and-mortar embankment erected as the city's first line of defense, over the first line of dunes, up the second, where he flattened himself into a shallow crevice and drew the others down with a swift motion of his hand.

Cautiously they raised their heads over the summit and looked down at a long, flat stretch of rocky terrain marked only by a series of blackened oil barrels, a dusty shed of corrugated sheeting, and a limp French flag. They scarcely saw any of it. Their attention remained fastened upon the behemoth standing just beneath their perch. Its four great engines idled noisily, impatient to break free from its earthly bonds and fling heavenward once more.

The Lancashire bomber had seen many hundreds of hours of hard wartime service. Bullet holes traced a silvered pattern from wing to tail, the flaps were streaked with oil and ancient grime, one side window was starred and shattered, and two of the wheels were worn down to dangerous white patches. Despite all this, the great plane bore its age and scars with pride, and the engines rumbled with smooth accuracy. It was the sweetest sound Jake had ever heard.

"Beautiful," Pierre murmured, clearly agreeing with him.

The pilot clattered down the back loading ramp, pushing an overloaded trolley and carrying a folded sheaf of papers in his mouth. Behind him came a single Arab guard, pushing a second trolley piled so high with boxes that he had to crane around the side to find his footing. Together they maneuvered their cargo into the rusting warehouse.

"Now's as good as it's going to get," Jake whispered.

Omar hissed, causing them to swivel about on their bellies. A cadre of Tuareg appeared in the embankment's narrow opening, searching the empty desert reaches and arguing fiercely among themselves.

Keeping himself below the lip of the defile, Jake slid the knife from his belt and offered it back to Omar. "I wish you could know what it has meant to travel with you," he whispered.

Omar looked down at the knife for a very long moment, then pushed it back toward Jake.

"I can't," Jake murmured, reaching out once more.

Again Omar pressed the hand back, harder this time, and pointed with his chin toward the waiting plane. Go.

Jake grasped the chieftain's shoulder and held it firmly. Omar returned the gaze and nodded once. He understood.

Pierre reached over and gripped the chieftain's hand. "I owe you much," he whispered. "I will repay. A way will be found."

Omar murmured a reply, the meaning clear.

Jake slithered forward and rolled over the edge, followed by Pierre. Together they scrambled down the dune, raced at a crouch across the open terrain, and pounded up the plane's loading ramp.

Inside, the noise was deafening. The plane's age was visible everywhere, from the rusting struts to the string of bullet holes that provided the interior's only light and ventilation. The hold was mammoth and filthy and rocked continually in time to the droning engines. Boxes and bales were strapped along both sides, and loose padding littered the central gangway.

Jake was still standing there, trying to get his bearings, when voices approached and shouted words indistinguishable over the engines' roar. Panicked into action, he and Pierre ripped up padding, pressed themselves into two empty pockets between the bundled cargo, crouched down, and flung the filthy burlap over their heads.

A pair of boots climbed the metal ramp, shouted something more, then operated a winch that ground and groaned and finally pulled the ramp up tight with a resounding bang. The boots walked forward, passed Jake's hiding place, and headed up into the cockpit.

The engines' roar rose to a new pitch. The plane rattled and groaned and trundled slowly about. The thunder rose even higher, the ground bumped beneath them, then with a gut-wrenching swoop they felt themselves leap from the earth.

Jake eased himself as much as he could in his cramped position and took a couple of easier breaths. Safe.

Then he almost jumped out of his skin when a voice shouted just inches from his ear, "Well if this ain't a sight for sore eyes, I don't know what is."

A boot kicked at his shin, and the Texas twang went on, "You two come on outta there. My copilot's down with the galloping whatsis, and this baby don't fly too well without a firm hand on the tiller."

Chapter Thirteen

"*L*UCKY FOR YOU boys I was blocking the guard-house window," the pilot told them once they had joined him in the cockpit. "That Arab back there woulda probably shot you for renegades. Me, now, I got a naturally curious nature. I see what appears to be an American Army officer skedaddling for my plane with an Arab in them fancy desert robes hot on his tail, why, I figure this is probably one for the books."

He pointed through his window and went on, "That river coming out of the Raggah oasis used to be almost two miles wide. Now it's not much more than a stream. Not much farther on, it just gets swallowed up by the desert. This lake here is the last gathering place for waters that used to be wide as an inland sea."

Jake tried to match his easy tone. "How do you know all this?"

"Oh, you mosey around these parts long enough, you'd be surprised what you learn. So happens I like the desert and the people. Folks around here haven't bothered with the folderol of people back home. Got a lot to teach us, if only we'd unplug our ears and stop thinking of them as backward. They're perfectly adapted to where they live.

Why, you put one of your so-called civilized fellas down here, and they wouldn't last a week."

The pilot eyed Jake. "Which brings me to ask what you're doing here."

"I can't tell you."

"Like that, is it. Well, long as it's not breaking the laws of here or home, I'm not bothered."

"It's perfectly legal," Jake said. "Sort of."

"Sounds like a good desert-type answer to me." He gave them both another up-and-down inspection. "You don't aim on skinning me while I'm driving this crate, are you? So happens I'm right partial to living."

Out of the corner of his eye Jake spotted a worn and tattered Bible crammed in with flight documents. He plucked it out, held it before him, and said, "I give you my word as a Christian that I mean you no harm."

"Well, I guess that's good enough for me." He stuck out a leathery hand. "Frank Towers. Formerly of the United States Army Air Force, currently head of Tower Transport, the only asset of which you're crouching in."

"Jake Burnes. Commander of the garrison at Karlsruhe. And this is Major Pierre Servais, head of the French base at Badenburg."

That brought a start. "You're a Frenchie?"

"I am indeed," Pierre replied, extending his own hand. "I am happy to meet you, Mr. Towers."

"Likewise. You boys musta been out there quite a while, to get as sunburned and sandblasted as you look."

"Quite a while," Jake agreed solemnly.

"Why don't you slide yourself on into the copilot's chair, Colonel. You'd be a durn sight more comfortable, and I won't have to keep craning around to see you."

"Thanks. The name is Jake."

"Pull down that seat in the bulkhead there beside you, Major."

"Pierre."

"Right you are. It'll take both hands, seeing as how it ain't been used since the war. Can't afford a radio man, and even if I could, most of the places I fly don't have a soul on the air I could talk to."

"What are you doing here, if you don't mind my asking?" Jake said.

"A likely question. Joined up in thirty-nine, flew them lend-lease planes 'til we decided to jump into the fighting ourselves. After that, well, I flew just about anything you'd care to name." He eyed Jake in the seat beside him. "That true, what you said about being a Christian?"

"It is."

"This I can confirm," Pierre said gravely. "My friend has taught me not only with words, but with the way he tries to live."

"That's nice. Real nice. Myself, I saw the light after getting shot down around Arnheim. Guess maybe you heard about that. Brother, let me tell you, that was one whale of a mess. Anyway, I managed to crawl back to where it was safe, but I lost a lot of good buddies out there. So I started looking for answers, something that'd make some sense of what I'd been going through." He pointed at the Book in Jake's hand. "Had a buddy start showing me things in there, stuff I'd heard all my life but never bothered to think about before. Been trying to live up to the Master's example ever since."

Frank Towers stretched out his lanky frame as much as the cramped cockpit would allow. "After the fighting was over, I didn't have much to go home to. Then this mission group came by the church I was attending at our air base in England, said they were planting some schools down here and asked if maybe I'd fly out supplies. Craziest thing I ever heard of, but somehow I sorta felt like I was being called to help out. One thing led to another, and now all of a sudden I've got a name down here. Got more and more folks coming by, asking me to take this and that to places I never even heard of before, can't hardly find them on the map first time out."

He gave an expansive grin. "Things've gotten so busy I'm about ready to buy my second plane. Don't suppose either of you boys knows how to fly a crate?"

"Not a chance," Jake said.

"Sorry," Pierre replied.

"No matter. There's a lot of fly-boys out there looking for something that'll keep 'em in the air. It'd be nice to find another believer, though."

Jake swiveled in his seat and gave Pierre a long hard look. The Frenchman's features screwed up momentarily before he nodded slowly.

Jake turned back and said, "Seems to me we should trust you with our story."

"Well, now, there ain't nothing I like much better than a good yarn. 'Specially when we got a full day of flying stretching out in front of us."

"A day?" Pierre exclaimed.

"Where are we going?" Jake asked.

"Oh, guess I didn't tell you." The wide-mouth grin reappeared. "Either of you boys ever had any thought of visiting Malta?"

Chapter Fourteen

"*L*ET ME SEE if I got this straight," Frank Towers said, sipping cold coffee with one hand while the other guided their thundering craft over sparkling blue Mediterranean waters. "You're aiming on stepping off this plane and going straight to the British authorities—"

"Or whatever authorities are in charge," Jake corrected.

"Son, the only folks in charge on Malta are the British, and they ain't near as much in charge as they'd like. But let's leave that for a while." He was enjoying himself immensely. "So you aim on marching straight up to the chief honcho himself and apologizing on account of the fact that one set of papers are traveling across the Sahara with the wrong fella, namely the major's very own long-lost twin brother, who just happens to be wearing his uniform. Meanwhile, the colonel's ID is in some backwater sultan's rear pocket. Then you're gonna spin this tale about an admiral perched at the other end of the Med who thinks you're the cat's pajamas and how you need to borrow one of his boats so you can get to France and save the country."

Slowly Frank shook his head. "Man, are you ever in for a shock."

"It's not a tale," Jake insisted. "It's the truth. All of it."

"Oh, I believe you. Trouble is, I doubt if you'd get past the corporal of the guard without papers, and sure as granny's lost spectacles he ain't gonna risk his stripes on any yarn like that one."

Pierre leaned forward and said, "Enlighten us."

"Right. To begin with, Malta was hit sixteen ways from Sunday in the war. The island's been a British enclave for a donkey's years, and they were using it as the main supply point for the desert war, and then for the invasion of Italy. Perfect place for a supply point, let me tell you. That's why I've set up there. It's the closest you can come to North Africa and still find a taste of home. So where was I?"

"The war," Jake said, staring out the window. Sparkling sunlit water stretched out in every direction as far as he could see. It was breathtakingly beautiful, and yet he could not help but feel as though it did not belong. So much water.

"Right. The Germans bombed it with everything they had, and the Maltese put up with it. They're a tough bunch. Scrappy. They like the British, and they hated the Germans, but now that the war's over, they want to be repaid for all they did by getting their independence. And the British, bless their souls, they'd probably give it to them, give or take another coupla hundred years. Only the Maltese figure they've earned the right to rule themselves now. And they're getting jumpy, if you know what I mean. So here you've got an important naval depot, hundreds of ships, a city that's gone through years of bombing, and people that're fast running out of patience."

"Confusion," Pierre offered. "Chaos."

"You said it. Whole island reminds me of the time a squirrel crawled up the leg of my daddy's overalls."

Malta was a rocky jewel set in the glittering azure of the Mediterranean. The capital, Valletta, was a hodgepodge of structures and styles. Steep-sided hills rising from the water were crammed with buildings from many different eras. A number were in ruins.

"Seems like everybody's conquered Malta at one time or another," Frank Towers told them. "Romans, Greeks, Arabs, Turks, French, British, Italians, even the Holy Roman Empire. Every one of 'em's ended up cussing at the Maltese people's stubbornness and their clannishness. They're proud, these people. Reminds me of folks back home. But their islands were too small to build up a strong army. So they've had to put up with more than their share of foreign tyrants."

Valletta was dominated by the Grand Harbor, and the harbor by a large central spit of land, and the spit by an ancient fortress—or more accurately, a dozen fortresses built like crumbling steps one upon the other. From the air, much of the capital looked the same, with houses and official buildings alike erected upon the ruins of other, older structures.

When Jake commented on that, Towers replied, "I heard a tale the first time I touched down here. Back before the war a Roman bath was discovered directly under Valletta's central fish market. It was so well preserved that archaeologists flocked here from all over the world. Trouble was, these experts found themselves working in a steady rain of fish scales and rotting garbage, on account of the Maltese absolutely refused to move their fish market someplace else. Why should they? Another conqueror, more ruins, who cared?"

The Grand Harbor was a vast rock-lined sea perhaps ten miles wide and laced with numerous inlets, all filled with British ships, both merchant and navy. The waters gleamed gold and copper in the late afternoon sun. Jake said, "I don't think I've ever seen so many warships in one place before."

"This place is no stranger to men of war," the pilot agreed. "Not to war either. Like I said, the Germans bombed it almost every day for three solid years. Sometimes as many as fifty air sorties every day."

"It's a wonder anyone survived."

"You'd be surprised. Like you can see, the main town here was blasted to smithereens, a lot of it, anyway. Except the churches. They're in pretty good shape, overall. Strange how the Germans managed to shoot around the biggest buildings like that. Anyway, most of the islanders lived through it to tell the tale, hunkered down in these big ol' caves. Like I said, they're a stubborn lot, these Maltese. They just plain refused to give in. Worked like the dickens to help the Allies. The king gave them the George Cross. First time an entire people was ever granted such an honor."

They flew inland to the airfield near the village of Luqa. As they entered into their final approach, Towers had Jake and Pierre return to their hiding places in the cargo hold.

They landed with a thud and rolled across an uneven surface. As the brakes squealed and the engines drummed to a halt, Jake bundled the burlap wrapping up and around him. The air ached in the sudden silence.

"Not a peep from either one of you," Towers warned, passing down the hold's central gangway. "I'll be back as soon as I can. If you hear voices, play dead."

The winch creaked noisily as the rear loading platform was lowered. A fresh breeze blew through the hold. Through the burlap Jake smelled fragrances he seemed to recall from another lifetime—flowers, pine, ripening earth, a hint of the sea.

The minutes stretched into endless hours, and Jake fought against the restlessness of cramped and aching muscles. He dozed for a time, jerked awake as voices came within range and then passed by, dozed again.

The light had faded and the evening breeze had turned cool by the time Frank Towers returned. "Okay," he said softly. "Coast is clear."

Jake tossed aside the burlap over his face and scratched his scalp. "What time is it?"

"Almost midnight."

Another heap of burlap groaned, shivered, and fell to reveal a vastly disgruntled Pierre. "Which day?"

"I don't think I can move," Jake said.

"Had to wait until things settled down for the night," Towers said, crouching over a canvas duffel. He pulled out two zip-up flight coveralls and tossed them toward the groaning men. "Slip these on. If anybody stops us, you're new crew I've taken on for the second plane."

With every muscle complaining, Jake stripped and dressed in the airman's one-piece uniform. He rolled up his army dress and tucked it in the canvas sack. "You really think this is necessary?"

"Hard to say. But at least this way your friends in Gibraltar will be able to grease your slide in, if you see what I mean."

"It makes sense," Pierre agreed.

"So what now?" Jake asked.

"You two look dead on your feet," Towers replied. "Some friends of mine run a little guesthouse down the road a ways. Nothing fancy, but the food's good and the beds are clean."

"Sounds perfect," Jake said, suddenly ravenous. "But we don't have any money on us."

"Don't you worry about that just yet, I'll take care of it and you can pay me back later. We'll just get you settled in there for what's left of the night. I've got an idea of how we can move forward, but it's gonna mean an early start tomorrow." Towers grinned at Jake's almost silent moan. "Like they say, Colonel, you can sleep when the war's over."

Chapter Fifteen

*T*HEY WERE UP and out before dawn, rumbling down the steeply sloped terrain in a car that appeared to be held together with spit and baling wire. Jake's single cup of coffee before departure had barely dented his drowsiness. But five minutes into the journey he was as awake as he had ever been in his entire life.

He leaned forward and said, "Do you think maybe you could ask the driver to slow down a little?"

"Wouldn't do a bit of good," Towers replied cheerfully. "Folks around these parts say the Maltese don't drive on the left or the right, but in the shade. And they're taught to drive fast to keep up a steady breeze."

The ancient vehicle raced down the hillside so fast the dawn-tinted vista outside Jake's window was reduced to a pallid blur. Every now and then, tendrils of fog teased their way across the street, obliterating all view of what lay ahead. "How can he see where we're going?"

"Probably can't," Towers said. "But there aren't many roads on this island. He knows every twist and turn by heart."

Jake decided that watching was doing his nerves no good whatsoever, so he turned to his friend. No help there.

Pierre's face was an interesting shade of green. He turned
back to the front. "How can you sit there so unconcerned?"

"Oh, I've found that driving around this island does my
prayer life a powerful lot of good," Towers replied easily.

They crested a final rise, and the city of Valletta came
into view. Below them stretched a web of narrow, hilly
streets, running down to the Grand Harbor and the Mediterranean's glorious blue. "The city was built by the
Knights of St. John after they were kicked out of the Holy
Land by the Ottomans," Towers told them. "The original
Knights of St. John were founded around the year eleven
hundred. They were people who helped Christians visiting
the Holy Land, which wasn't all that easy with the Ottomans in charge. Charles of Spain gave them the island after
the Arabs finally kicked them out of Jerusalem, and they
came here and built the fortress you see down there. They
made Valletta the capital in 1530."

Whenever the narrow lanes reached a level patch, they
opened into great stone-lined squares. Imposing churches
stood surrounded by solid North Africa–type houses. Their
little taxi whizzed through the empty plazas, then plunged
back into rutted ways as pitched and tilting as a roller
coaster track. Signs of war and ruin were everywhere.

"The knights were known as the fighting monks," Towers went on, seemingly oblivious to the taxi's death-defying
speed. "Six hundred of them and four thousand locals
fought and held off an invasion of thirty thousand Ottomans. But with time the knights became richer and forgot
that they were supposed to be brothers to the locals and not
princes. Knight-generals started trying to outshine whatever their predecessors had built, blind to everything but
their own selfish desires for earthly grandeur. The islanders
were forgotten, ignored, and grew poorer. The gulf widened,
and so when the French came at the end of the eighteenth
century, the islanders welcomed them with open arms.
They remained under the French until the British took control during the Napoleonic wars."

The driver turned onto a grand boulevard lined with imposing buildings of state. "The main street of Valletta, Sta de Real," Towers said. "We're almost there now."

They turned onto another nameless alley and stopped before a tiny shop that differed from its neighbors only because the metal outer door had been drawn halfway up and because a crowned symbol over the shuttered window proclaimed that this was a local post office. Frank Towers was already out of the taxi before it had fully halted. He tapped on the door, which was opened by a sleep-touseled older gentleman. The man shook Frank's hand and motioned impatiently for Jake and Pierre to enter.

Once they had slipped into the little shop, the proprietor slid the metal portal back down. He lifted the ancient lantern and led them into the back room, then set the lantern upon a table that was bare save for an ancient telegraph set. He seated himself, coded in, waited, listened at his headset, coded again. The minutes passed in silence. Finally he straightened, looked up at Frank Towers, and nodded once.

"Okay, boys, it's all yours."

Jake looked at him. "What is?"

"You said you had buddies in Gibraltar, didn't you? Okay, now's your chance. Only make it fast. I promised the old gent here we'd be done and gone before he opened for the day."

Jake seated himself, scrunched his head in concentration, then requested a patch-through to the Gibraltar garrison. The minutes dragged until the code sounded. He keyed in, THIS IS COLONEL JAKE BURNES. URGENT I SPEAK IMMEDIATELY WITH COMMANDER TEAVES OR ADMIRAL BINGHAM. TOP PRIORITY.

Again there was an interminable wait. Jake turned and asked for a pad and pencil, which would make the return messages easier to read clearly. Finally the set coded back, TEAVES HERE. REQUEST CONFIRMATION OF WHO IS ON THE LINE.

Jake grinned. Commander Harry Teaves was an American Naval officer assigned garrison duty in Gibraltar, and the man who helped them during their hunt for Patrique.

Jake keyed in, HELLO HARRY. HOW ARE MILLIE AND THE APES?

The response was instantaneous. JAKE, YOU OLD JOKER. KNEW YOU WERE TOO TOUGH TO HOLD DOWN. SORRY TO INFORM YOU RECEIVED REPORT OF YOUR DEMISE SOMEWHERE IN THE BACK OF BEYOND. ASSUME YOU ARE THEREFORE SPEAKING FROM HEAVEN.

Jake said to Pierre, "Somebody's claimed the reward on my head."

"It appears they try to use your papers as evidence," Pierre agreed, squinting to decipher Jake's handwriting. "Pity we must disappoint them."

Jake keyed in, YOU ARE NOT FAR OFF. AM IN MALTA.

There was a moment's pause, then, NO DOUBT A STORY THERE BUT MUST WAIT. SERVAIS WITH YOU?

ONE OF THEM. PATRIQUE TAKEN ILL, SENT TO FRENCH GARRISON HOSPITAL COLOMBE-BECHAR.

SITUATION CRITICAL HERE. URGENT REPEAT URGENT WE RECEIVE INFORMATION ON POSSIBLE TRAITOR.

Reading over his shoulder, Pierre murmured, "It appears, my friend, that your speculation was correct. The stakes were much higher than we thought."

"Shame they're playing with our lives on the table," Jake replied, and keyed in, WE CARRY WRITTEN CONFIRMATION. WHERE DO WE DELIVER?

IMPERATIVE YOU PROCEED TO US EMBASSY IN PARIS. ASK FOR WALTERS. HE IS YOUR FRIEND IN NEED. WAIT ONE. There was a long pause, then, OFFICIAL CONTACT IN MALTA QUESTIONABLE, NEW COMMANDANT, UNKNOWN TO BINGHAM. WE WILL MAKE SEARCH FOR ALLIES, BUT MUST MOVE WITH CAUTION. CAN YOU MAKE IT ON YOUR OWN?

PARIS. YOU DO NOT ASK MUCH, DO YOU. Jake thought a moment, then continued, PATRIQUE SERVAIS AT HOSPITAL ACCOMPANIED BY JASMYN COL-

TRANE. URGENT YOU RESCUE THEM BEFORE TOO LATE.

CONSIDER IT DONE. ANYTHING ELSE?

HOW ABOUT SOME FUNDS?

TRANSFER POSSIBLE. GIVE NAME AND BANK.

Jake asked Towers, "What's your bank here?"

"Midland. Why?"

FRANK TOWERS. MIDLAND BANK. MALTA BRANCH.

WILL DO TODAY. MALTA. HOW ON EARTH?

MEET ME IN PARIS. I WILL TELL YOU ALL ABOUT IT.

ROGER THAT. WILL CONTACT WALTERS MYSELF TODAY. ANY WAY HE CAN GET A MESSAGE BACK TO YOU?

Jake asked and received the post office's address and telegraph code. When he had passed on the information, he finished with, THANKS FOR HELPING HAND.

TOO FEW GOOD MEN AS IT IS. TAKE CARE. WATCH THE OLD NOGGIN. LET ME KNOW IF WE CAN DO MORE. WILL GET BUSY ON THIS END. SEE IF WE CAN RUSTLE UP SOME CAVALRY. TEAVES OUT.

Frank Towers inspected the page of messages over Jake's shoulder and said, "I guess you really are who you say you are."

Jake turned around. "You didn't believe us?"

"Let's just say I was keeping a healthy dose of skepticism right close at hand," Towers replied cheerfully. "There's a lot of tall-talers walking about these days, especially on the routes I'm flying. Anyway, glad I let you boys come along for the ride."

"We are too," Pierre replied. "And we are in your debt. Those are words I am saying quite often these days, but true just the same."

"Speaking of which," Jake said, "you will hopefully be receiving a hefty sum in the next few days."

"Might as well come to me," Towers drawled. "Seeing as how I aim on collecting as much as possible for services rendered."

"You mean you'll help us?" Jake asked, then added, "More than you already have, I mean?"

"I've gotten you this far, might as well see where we end up."

"That's great," Jake said with feeling. "Is there any chance I could send another message to the U.S. Embassy in Paris?"

The old gentleman spoke for the first time, in English starched by an accent Jake had never heard before. "Is unlikely they have direct line," he replied. "Leave message and I will send it myself."

"You can trust ol' Carlos," Towers assured them. "I oughta know. I'm planning on making an honest woman of his daughter."

"Right." Jake seated himself and swiftly composed a message to Consul Walters. He passed over the sheet and asked, "What now?"

"From the sounds of things, your best bet would be to lay low for a spell," Towers replied, looking a question at the old man.

Carlos thought a minute, then replied simply, "Mdina."

"Perfect," Towers said.

"What is that?"

"Old capital. Also known as Notabile. Place is pretty as a picture and about as far off the beaten track as you can get on an island this size. I've got a buddy up there. C'mon, let's go see if he can stash you in some hole for a coupla days."

Chapter Sixteen

$\mathcal{T}$HE AIR WAS freshened by the steady sea breeze, warmed by the brilliant sun, and filled with birdsong and the fragrance of flowers. To their immense relief, Towers secured them transport with a driver willing to drive slower in return for a sizable tip. He kept his speed down, but punctuated his driving with scornful snorts for all fainthearted foreigners. Jake did not mind in the least. Pierre did not seem to hear him at all.

Their more comfortable pace granted Jake the chance to rubberneck. As they drove back through the gradually awakening city, he studied the faces out walking, talking, sweeping, working, filling the cafes, preparing for the day. The streets between the great squares were winding and odoriferous and lined with small shops and tall apartment buildings. The apartments' iron balustrades were often so close overhead that housewives could hand things from one side of the street to the other. The populace was a vivid mixture of races, every face testifying to a melange of Arab and Mediterranean bloodlines. Jake observed, "These people don't look like any I've ever seen before."

Towers nodded his agreement. "Down the centuries, ships from Europe, Africa, and the Orient have dropped anchor here. Countless cultures have left their mark on the land and the people. Yet somehow through it all, the Maltese have remained their own folk." Towers appeared to be enjoying the ride as much as Jake. "The Maltese are strange folks. Never seen much freedom, but they're the most freedom-loving people I've ever known. Can't be more than half a million of them, but they're proud as citizens of the greatest empire on earth. Got to admire people with that kinda spunk."

"There seem to be a lot of churches," Pierre observed.

"Yeah, there's a church for every day of the year, and they're all pretty well used," Towers replied. "Wherever the Maltese go, their God goes with 'em. Their religion is right there in the middle of everything they do. That's another part of the life here that agrees with me."

"I can understand that sentiment perfectly," Pierre murmured, "having seen how they drive."

Towers pointed out his open window at a church they were passing. "This here's the Mosta Church. Three years ago, three bombs landed on the roof during a service. The hall was packed to the gills. Two of the bombs actually bounced off and landed in the courtyard. The other fell through the roof and came to rest in the middle of the congregation. None of the three exploded. Folks call it the Miracle of the Bombs. When you talk to the islanders about the war, this is the first thing they will tell you about. Not about all the bad things that happened, but about their miracle. How can you help but love people like that?"

The hour was proclaimed from churches on almost every street corner they passed. Several were bomb-damaged, and one Jake saw had no roof. But everywhere the people were busy with repairs. A few homes and businesses were decked out with scaffolding, but every church harbored masses of swarming workers. Every church. It touched Jake deeply to see that even their own homes took second place to rebuilding the churches.

When he mentioned it, Towers replied, "Here the churches are not just houses of God. In the local tongue they're called Homes to the Community. Their front veranda and stairs are called the Parish Sitting Room. People come and meet and speak and drink and laugh and court and weave their lives together with each other and with God. When the war ended, the rebuilding started on the churches first, almost without discussion. It was just what had to be done."

They left the city behind and began a series of steep climbs through vineyards and orchards and groves of pine and olive trees. The church and its symbols dominated both town and country. Around almost every curve was a roadside shrine.

High on a hillside beyond Valletta rose an ancient fortress town. "The city of Mdina, former capital of Malta," Towers said proudly. "The town's over two thousand, six hundred years old. Reputed to be one of the finest walled cities in the world."

They crested the final rise, emerged from a carefully tended orchard of fragrant pear trees, and passed under great arched portals. The city's outer walls were more than twenty feet thick.

In the morning light, the ancient limestone buildings shone with the color of champagne, giving the entire city a texture all its own. The taxi entered into ways so narrow there was scarcely room for it to pass without climbing the cobblestone curb.

"Streets in these old towns were built winding and narrow so that invaders had no place to mass their forces and could easily get lost," Towers told them. "Folks like it nowadays because most of the town stays shady even at high noon, and the streets funnel the breeze into almost every house, no matter which direction it blows."

They entered a square dominated by a great rose-tinted church. When the taxi halted, Towers unwound his lanky frame and said, "Might as well get out and stretch your legs. I won't be long."

Jake climbed out, eased his back, and took deep drafts of the fragrant air. The loudest noises were the gentle clip-clop of hoofs and the bells on horse-drawn carriages passing across the square.

At the sound of footsteps treading down the church stairs, Jake turned to find Frank Towers leading a gray-haired priest toward them. "Like you gents to meet Father Ian. He's a Brit, or was, but he's been here long enough to call Malta home. Father, let me introduce Colonel Jake Burnes and Major Pierre Servais, late of Germany and Morocco and goodness knows where else."

"Welcome to the Silent City," Father Ian said, walking forward with outstretched hand. "That is the name this town has carried for over two millennia."

"It sure is quiet," Jake agreed. The priest's grip was firm and cool.

"My friend tells me you are in need of sanctuary."

"If it's no trouble," Jake replied. Sanctuary. He liked the sound of that word.

"No trouble at all. The Cathedral of Saint Paul has been home to wayfaring believers for longer than any of us would care to count." Kindly gray eyes held Jake with a keen gaze. "The place where you stand was reputedly where a man by the name of Publius once had his home. Does that name mean anything to you, Colonel?"

"Please call me Jake." He searched his mind and came up with, "Wasn't he the Roman governor of Malta when Paul was shipwrecked here?"

Father Ian turned and cast a nod back toward Frank Towers. "Very good, very good indeed," he said approvingly. "Frank mentioned that you were a believer. I hope this will add a special flavor to the time you spend here with us."

Towers stepped forward. "I'll be saying my goodbyes here. Got a whole mess of work to do and another shipment due out of here tomorrow morning."

"We can't thank you enough," Pierre said.

"Don't mention it. I'll try to make it back here tonight, just to look in on you boys and make sure you're behaving yourselves." He gave the priest a friendly nod and walked back to the w iting taxi.

"Come." Father Ian gestured toward the church. "Let me show you to your new quarters."

As he led them up the stairs and through the great portico, Father Ian told them, "The apostle Paul was shipwrecked here in A.D. 60 while on his way to Rome. After healing Publius's sick father, Paul declined the governor's hospitality and decided to live with the locals. Many dwelled in the natural caves such as the catacomb under this church. It is said that Paul made his home for a time in the very caves where you will now reside."

The cathedral's interior was vast and domed and ornately decorated, yet the surroundings held no sense of dominating the people. Smiling, chattering crowds filled the aisles and overflowed into the alcoves, joyously occupied with a variety of tasks. "We have a local festival this evening," Father Ian told them. "You will be most welcome to join us, if you like."

He led them to the front of the nave, through a side portal, and down a flight of steep stone stairs. "Malta is a tiny speck of land, set out in the middle of nowhere, really. The island is only seventeen miles by eight. Blink in a bad storm and you'd miss it entirely. Which makes it even the more miraculous, of course, that Paul managed to beach here. Literally one wave pushing them farther to one direction or the other, and they would have missed landfall entirely and starved or drowned before ever reaching Africa."

The catacombs were enormous, extending out in every direction, a vast series of interconnected caves the size of great halls. Many of the walls were decorated with ancient holy pictures. The electric lighting overhead was one of the few signs of modernity Jake saw.

"Paul had been arrested for spreading a strange new religion in the eastern provinces and had been placed on a ship bound for Rome," Father Ian went on. "In Cyprus he tried to convince the captain to hold over for the spring, as the autumn storm season was already well underway. But the captain decided to go on. The ship was hit by a violent storm and blown hundreds and hundreds of miles off course."

The second chamber they passed through held a great rectory table and perhaps forty or fifty high-backed chairs.

Cooking smells wafted in from a side alcove, reminding Jake that it had been a while since he had eaten.

"When Paul and Luke left after their enforced stay, Luke wrote about the regret they felt upon departure, the friendliness of the people, and the many gifts granted them by these simple folk. As a result of this one man, the entire island nation came to believe. And this faith of theirs was not an easy course, let me tell you. After the Roman Empire dissolved about A.D. 500, there was a dark time here. Very dark indeed. The Arabs came and ruled for over eight hundred years. Some of the princes and sultans were good men, others cruel beyond our wildest imaginations. The churches fled underground and hid themselves in caves like the ones here. Finally the Knights of Saint John arrived and the modern era of Maltese history began."

Father Ian stopped before an ancient wooden door. "One of you may take this cell, another the next one along. They are simple quarters, but I hope you will be comfortable. Many of your neighbors observe the rule of silence, so we ask that you reserve your conversations for the dining hall." He smiled warmly. "From the looks of you, I would imagine you both could use some food and rest. We will be serving our midday meal in about half an hour. Please don't hesitate to come find me if there is anything further you require."

Jake spent the day eating and catching up on what felt like weeks without enough rest. The hours passed uncounted, as the caves had neither clocks nor natural lighting. His cell was utterly bare save for a bed, a washstand, and a simple crucifix hung upon the wall. When the light was extinguished the cell was quiet and dark as a tomb, yet filled with a sense of comfort and peace. Jake felt as though he were surrounded by centuries of prayer.

Then, to his utter astonishment, the peace was shattered by a series of booming explosions. He bolted from his bed, rushed out into the hallway, and confronted a rumpled Pierre, who demanded sleepily, "Are we under attack?"

"I thought somebody told me the war was over," Jake replied.

They raced up the catacomb stairs and entered pandemonium. The church was filled with incense and song and revelry. Above their heads the church bells had begun a bonging chorus.

They pushed their way outside into the night, only to find the entire square filled with shouting, dancing, laughing people. Fireworks flashed and banged high overhead, the obvious source of the explosions. A smiling Father Ian appeared at their side and explained, "Almost every weekend throughout the summer, one of the local parishes celebrates a saint's feast day."

There were bands and bunting and singing and feasting and many expressions of great good cheer among the celebrants. Statues were paraded about. Flowers woven into intricate garlands crowned the brows of some of the most beautiful young girls Jake had ever seen.

"If there's one thing these islanders know how to do, it is enjoy their faith," the priest shouted above the din. "I miss this whenever I return to England. People seem so somber there whenever faith is mentioned. It is almost as though they have been told that you cannot be joyful and religious at the same time. What rubbish! We are *commanded* to be joyful. Look at these people. See their smiles, their dancing, their laughter? They endured as much as any people during the war. I scarcely know any family who did not suffer the loss of at least one loved one. And yet look at them! They are *joyful*.

"That is why I have decided to make Malta my home. Not just to serve them, but to learn from them. Twenty years I have been here on this island, and still I am learning from them the lesson of joyful worship."

Bells sounded continually, and incense wafted upward in great, white, fragrant clouds. There were fireworks and choirs and processions of lay people praying and singing and throwing scented water over the throngs.

"This is not just a carnival," Father Ian told them. "This is a time of religious thanksgiving. They give thanks for what has happened in the past year. They spend almost two hours praying for the coming year—for health and happiness and prosperity and growth, never forgetting that last item. Then the festival begins. This is part of their enjoyment of being Christians and servants of God on this lovely island."

The priest smiled and turned toward the merry throng with a gesture of affection. "These, my adopted people are a people of celebration. They rejoice in their faith. They see it not in terms of commandments and do nots, but in terms of victory. They celebrate their freedom from death. And now more than ever."

It was well after midnight when Frank Towers appeared at the table where they sat surrounded by drink and food and joyful celebration. He eased himself down, grabbed a chicken leg off a passing platter, took an enormous bite, and waved a yellow paper toward Jake. "This came in a couple of hours ago."

Jake unfolded the flimsy page and read, CANNOT CONFIRM A WALTERS ON EMBASSY STAFF. DO NOT TRY FURTHER COMMUNICATIONS. LINE NOT SECURE.

Jake read it a second time, passed it over to Pierre, and watched as his friend grimaced mightily at the words. "This is not good news."

Frank Towers shrugged his unconcern. "Doesn't deny this Walters fellow is there either, you notice that?"

"What are you saying?"

"Seems to me they're playing it cagey, like maybe they have to, given the circumstances."

Jake struggled to push the noisy festivities out of his mind and concentrate. "So somebody may have intercepted my communication and knows where we are."

"Maybe," Towers conceded. "On the island at least. But look at it this way. There ain't a soul outside of here that knows where you are except me and Father Ian. And there ain't anybody here that knows *who* you are except for us. The good father's got enough secrets to his name to sink this island if he had a mind to. You're as safe here as any-where."

Jake felt himself relaxing. "What do you suggest we do?"

"Lay low for a while. Both of you look like you could use a year's sleep. I'll be back in three, maybe four days. Soon as I'm back, we'll meet up and work out the next step."

Towers rose to his feet. "Spend a little time on your knees, why don't you? I ain't never found a better place to work through the impossibles in life."

Chapter Seventeen

*J*AKE WAS SO lost in reverie that he did not notice
Father Ian until the priest had settled down on the pew
beside him. "How are you doing, Colonel?"

"Jake, please."

"Jake, then. No, do not answer that. There is no need. I
have watched you these past three days and seen how you
seem to drink in the peace here. It shines from your face."
Kindly gray eyes rested on him. "I can therefore see how
you are."

Jake looked about the splendid ornamentation of the ancient church. "It *is* peaceful here," he agreed. "I've had the
feeling I can sort of stop off and lay everything down. Take
a little time out from the world."

He hesitated, then confessed, "I've been thinking a lot
about a lady I care for. Her work has her back in America,
too far away for my liking. Then there's the war; it keeps
popping up in my mind. It's almost like this is the first
time I've had to really think things through since it all
happened. And the desert."

"Yes, your friend has told me a little of what took place
during your recent adventures." The priest's voice was
gently probing, inviting. "Is there anything you would like
to speak with me about?"

It seemed to him then that Jake had been waiting for this question, hoping for it on some level far below that of conscious thought.

"So much happened back there," Jake replied, "and still what I think about most is the silence. At the time, it felt like I was surrounded by noise almost constantly. But the desert's quiet was sort of waiting, always there, whenever the noise stopped, and I could just enter into it."

His eyes searched beyond the church's confines for the memories of treasured dawns, then he went on, "Even here, I find myself missing that special silence."

The priest asked gently, "Do you feel yourself called toward the contemplative life, Jake?"

"I—" Jake struggled to search his heart. "No. I want the silence. I am learning here how important it's become to me. But I don't have the sense that this is where I belong." He turned a troubled gaze toward the priest. "Still, the thought of leaving here and losing all touch with the silence really bothers me."

Father Ian rose from the pew. "Would you care to join me for a little walk? I find some problems can be better resolved when I am moving."

They left the church, walked across the square and down a narrow lane. Father Ian opened a stout iron-studded gate, which revealed a narrow tunnel through the city wall. "This was known as Death's Gate and was once the way earlier inhabitants departed the city for the last time."

Beyond the ancient cemetery stretched a glorious vista of trees and flowers and rock and sea. From their position high on the hill, the entire world appeared ringed by endless blue. A refreshing sea breeze took the bite from the day's heat.

"You may find this surprising to hear coming from a priest who has felt called to a life upon this tiny island," Father Ian told Jake as they walked. "But the Scriptures tell us clearly that true faith does not mean retreating from the world. True faith means confronting whatever the world offers us and seeking God in the midst of it. To do that, however, we must also find a way to move apart from the world, to know God in the quiet.

"In the very first pages of the gospel of Mark, we are told that Jesus went away at dawn and went to a lonely place. We find such references throughout the Scriptures, where in the midst of movement and activity He sought out a time of stillness and silence. All those people would be seeking to hear Him and touch Him and be near Him, and He would withdraw to be alone with the Father.

"In my own studies, I find that there is almost nothing predictable about Christ's teachings. Seldom did He do what was expected. One predictable pattern of His ministry, however, was this regular retreat into solitude, the seeking of a quiet place."

He led Jake over to a bench set upon a rocky precipice. The cliff dropped down to orchards and a tiny village and the sea. Jake settled himself down beside Father Ian, looked out, and felt as though the entire world were there on display for him.

"You as a Christian are called to be led by the Holy Spirit," Father Ian went on. "But unless you make regular room for the quiet, it will not be God who leads you, but people. And pressure. And fears. And the world. Mind you, all these must be attended to. But they should not drive and motivate you."

"I'm not sure I'm strong enough to keep that balance," Jake confessed.

"Of course not," Father Ian agreed. "No one is. Remember, Jake, it is through our weakness that the Lord's power is fully revealed. Here, let me offer you one key that may help you. It is not important that the Lord release you from the events and the circumstances that are causing you all of these pressures. What is important is that you allow Him to release you from the pressure itself."

The priest set his hands on his knees and rocked back and forth. "One of the most difficult burdens I bear is the need to examine people who come to me declaring that they have felt called to a contemplative life. You see, Jake, most people come because they seek to run away from something. But a monk's cell is no escape. Oh no. Far from it. The world can never be totally put aside. What is most troubling to all men is not what they find outside themselves, but rather what they confront within their own hearts and minds."

Butterflies and hummingbirds speckled the rocky promontory with their living rainbows of color, feeding off flowers that seemed to grow from the rock itself. Jake watched them dance lightly upon the wind and felt the priest's words settle in deep. "Then what am I supposed to do?"

"Build an island of quiet within yourself. Remember how, even during the intense pressure of Christ's own life of ministry, He retreated to places of calm and knew moments of sweet release."

Father Ian looked at him with the gentle knowledge of one who had learned the lesson for himself. "The desert gave you a time of quiet, of space, of limitless horizons. You must learn to recognize this as a constant need and seek to carry it with you. Wherever you are, whatever life confronts you with, maintain these moments of solitude. Create a desert within yourself. Hold in your heart this quiet place, where you may retreat and commune with the Father."

Chapter Eighteen

JAKE CAME TO full alert without knowing exactly why.

He reached for his watch and saw it was still a half hour to the breakfast bell. But something had altered. He felt some subtle shift of the atmosphere that registered on his war-honed senses.

Which was why he was up and dressed when footsteps sounded in the hall outside his cell. Jake stepped to the door, hesitated, wondered what it was that left him feeling the air was as charged as before a thunderstorm.

There was a gentle scratching at this door and a man's voice whispered, "Jake?"

"Frank?"

"Yeah, it's me. Open up."

Jake pulled the door back to reveal Frank Towers grinning broadly. "Now if you ain't a sight for sore eyes. Hope I didn't disturb your beauty sleep."

"I was awake. What's going on?"

"A whole mess of stuff, that's what." He extended a flimsy yellow sheet. "This came for you a couple of hours ago."

Jake accepted the paper and read, TEAVES HERE. SORRY TO BE BEARER OF FURTHER BAD NEWS. SERVAIS

BROTHERS DECLARED OUTLAWS BY FRENCH GOV-
ERNMENT. REWARD ON THEIR HEADS. ALSO BUSY
THROWING DIRT ON YOUR GOOD NAME, NEWS OF
YOUR DEMISE NOTWITHSTANDING. BINGHAM PUB-
LICLY CRITICIZED FOR HARBORING FUGITIVES. BIG
STINK. SOMEBODY MUST BE SWEATING. YOUR AR-
RIVAL IN PARIS MOST CRITICAL. TAKE GREAT CARE.

Jake looked up and observed, "You're incredibly cheerful
for somebody out in the middle of the night with news like
this."

If anything the grin broadened. "I've got my reasons."

"So what do we do now?"

"That's all been worked out." At the sound of footsteps
tapping down the stone hallway, Towers chuckled. "But
before we jump into that, I got somebody here you might
like to give a big howdy."

Frank stepped back, drawing Jake with him. Jake looked
down the corridor to where a smaller figure stood silhouetted by the dim light. Jake felt the hairs on the nape of his
neck stand upright.

An achingly familiar voice said softly, "Hello, soldier."

His body was frozen to the spot. He whispered, "Sally?"

Then she was running and flinging herself into his arms
and holding him tight, so tight, so very tight, her face nes-
tled against his chest and her arms squeezing him with a
force that registered deep inside, down in the heart's
caverns that had remained empty since her departure. He
raised numb arms, touched her back, her neck, her hair,
lowered his face and drank in the incredibly special fragrance of her. Sally.

The door behind him creaked open. Pierre gasped, then
said softly, "Am I dreaming?"

If I am, Jake thought, I don't ever want to wake up, not
ever. But the power of speech escaped him just then. He
was holding her. She was there in his arms. Sally.

"Stopped by to pay my respects to my fiancée. Her family
lives above the shop where you sent the cable," Towers
offered, enjoying himself immensely. "And what do you
know, but there waiting for me was this lovely lady. Been

waiting out there for a good part of the night, hoping some-body might be able to tell her where to find the fellow who sent that message.

Pierre asked for him, "How is this possible?"

"Before we start into all that," Towers replied cheerfully, "maybe we better mosey on back upstairs. We stay here, somebody's bound to come out and have themselves a surefire fit. Can't be more than sixteen dozen rules we're breaking, having y'all wrapped around each other down here."

With a trembling gasp Sally released her hold, grasped his hand, slipped her other arm through his own, leaned on his shoulder, and slowly shook her head back and forth, wiping her eyes over and over on his sleeve. Only then did he realize she was crying.

Together they walked back through the caverns and up the stairs, never for an instant relinquishing their hold upon each other. They walked down the church and through the great portals and entered a world glorying in the splendor of an awakening dawn.

On the church's front steps Jake reveled in another long embrace, then repeated Pierre's question. "How did you get here?"

She breathed deep and sniffled hard and gathered herself as much as she was able. "Flying in wasn't a problem," she said, her voice still shaky. "Getting you out will be another thing entirely."

"Whole island is buzzing," Towers confirmed brightly. "I've been back less than three hours, and already I've had two people come up and offer to share the reward if I can help them find a pair of renegades recently imported from Morocco."

"Renegades," Jake repeated, and handed Pierre the cable he was still holding.

"Reward," Pierre murmured, reading and shaking his head.

"From what my daddy-in-law-to-be told me," Towers went on, "they got spies and smugglers and all kindsa slimy critters crawling outta the woodwork, all looking for you two. Local police are having themselves a field day, trying to figure out what's going on."

Jake looked down at Sally. "But why, I mean, how—"

"I got tired of writing up reports in triplicate when all I could think of was a certain colonel back in Germany," Sally replied. "I pleaded a case of the never-get-overs, and the general let me go. But when I arrived in Karlsruhe, I heard all kinds of tales about lost brothers and traitors and chases halfway around the world. Were they true?"

"Probably. Some of them, anyway," Jake replied dumbly. Sally. He looked down at the hand still gripped by both of hers. It really was her.

"They were true," Pierre replied for him. "All of them and more. Your Jake is a hero."

"That's not what they were calling you in Paris," she replied, but her gaze was deep and full and only for him.

"Paris," he echoed.

"That's where General Clark sent me. He was the one who filled me in, at least as much as he could. It seems a mysterious letter from Morocco popped up at our Paris embassy."

"Jasmyn's letter?" Jake exclaimed. "Her letter got through?"

Sally nodded. "The embassy heard through Clark's staff that I was back in Germany and got me on the phone and read as much of it to me as I would let them, then I traveled to France and read the rest of it myself. Jasmyn never did manage to explain how she happened to be along on this adventure."

"Long story," Jake said. Her smoky gray eyes were even more beautiful than he remembered.

"Jasmyn is my fiancée," Pierre explained.

"That's what she said." Sally's gaze remained fastened upon Jake. "She called you a hero, too, Jake."

"True," Pierre repeated. "All true."

Down at the base of the stairs someone cleared his throat. Sally glanced behind them, but Jake could not tear his gaze away from her. She turned back, and a look of yearning tenderness filled her eyes and her face. She clung to him once again, with a fierceness that warmed his very bones. "Oh, Jake," she whispered. "When Clark told me the rumors about . . . I wanted the earth to open up and swallow me."

"Miss Anders, ma'am," murmured a voice behind them.

Reluctantly she released Jake and stepped back. "I'm afraid we've got company."

A pair of clear-eyed, blank-faced young men climbed lightly up the church stairs. Their stances were so rigid that even in their civilian garb they looked like picture-book officers. And tough. With one glance Jake knew the pair were as hard as they came.

The first one said, "I'm Lieutenant Akers, sir. This is Lieutenant Slade."

"Gentlemen."

"We're sort of assigned as watchdogs to you and Major Servais, sir."

Pierre demanded, "Do we need watching?"

"Call us guides if you'd rather, sir. Or escorts. We really don't care. Titles don't mean a whole lot in this business."

"I see," Jake said, confused. "And what business are you in?"

"That's not for us to say, sir. I suggest you hold those questions for when we get to Paris."

"If we get there," Pierre muttered.

"When, sir," Akers corrected. "Our job is to make sure it's when and not if."

Sally explained, "They need you back there, Jake, and fast. Things have become very serious."

Akers asked, "Major Servais, I am to inform you that your brother was recovered successfully from Colombe-Bechar and is now settled into the garrison hospital on Gibraltar. They got him out just in time, from the looks of things. Big stink about that one, too. Seems Commander Teaves forgot to inform anybody about the little flight he made down to Africa along with a squad of Royal Marines."

"How is he?"

"Not good, I'm afraid. Too weak to talk much. Which is why we need to get you back to Paris with the evidence.

You're the only one who's got the information to set things straight. But the doctors say they think the infection was caught in time and that he has a good chance of making it intact."

Pierre showed his concern only with a deepening of the creases of his face. "And the woman with him?"

"Yessir. She's okay." Akers permitted himself a small smile. "Miss Coltrane is some classy dame, sir."

"They sent me along to make sure you were really who you said you were," Sally explained. "After I twisted their arms a little."

Jake smiled at her and asked, "When are we supposed to move out?"

"Now, sir. If you're ready."

"Now?" Visions of a lingering reunion faded swiftly.

"Time for all that later," Sally said softly, understanding him perfectly. "I promise."

"We were going to try and bring in a transport tomorrow, find some way to sneak you on board," Akers said. "But Captain Towers here has agreed to fly us out this morning, soon as we can stop by Valletta and get off a coded message to Paris."

"Spies and traitors and pretty ladies and sunrise rendezvous," Towers said, and laughed out loud. "I wouldn't have missed this for all the tea in China."

Jake asked, "So what's the plan?"

Towers swung his grin toward Jake. "Believe me, you don't want to know a second sooner than you have to."

"What's that supposed to mean?"

"You'll find out soon enough," Towers promised.

"But—"

"I'm telling you," Towers insisted. "Don't ask."

"Time to be moving out, sir," Akers pressed. "Now."

Chapter Nineteen

*T*HEY STOPPED ONCE for refueling at the U.S. military base on Sardinia. They evidently were expected, as they were directed to a quiet corner of the airfield and left utterly alone, save for the fuel truck and a jeep of military police parked beneath the plane's nose.

Jake peered through the pilot's window at the white-helmeted MPs studiously ignoring the plane and asked no one in particular, "What gives?"

"You are strictly persona non grata, sir," Akers replied.

"Monsieur le Ministre Clairmont has panicked," Pierre surmised.

"I wouldn't know anything about that, sir," Akers said. "They just told me to get, and we got."

"You're bound to know something," Jake pressed.

"Not really, sir. Only whatever it is, it's *big*."

The habitually silent Lieutenant Slade added, "Never seen the like of the comings and goings here. Haven't spotted so much brass in one place since we left Washington."

"What were you doing in Washington?" Jake demanded.

"Long story, sir," Slade replied, his features returning to poker-faced blankness.

"All we know," Akers went on, changing the subject, "is that we have to get you back to Paris without talking to *any* official. No police, no customs, no military, not even a postman."

"But why?" Jake asked.

"Sir, if you don't know, then I don't guess anybody on this plane does. All I can say is that you and the major here are a pair of walking powder kegs."

"And just how," Pierre wanted to know, "do you intend on bringing us into Paris without some form of clearance?"

"You're headed back into that 'don't ask' territory I was telling you about," Towers warned. "Okay, folks, the fuel truck's done and those Happy Harrys in the jeep are giving us the go sign. Not a moment too soon, either. So just get back to your places and settle down for the ride."

They flew on through the sunset and into the night. Pierre gathered with Towers and Akers and Slade in the cockpit, granting Jake and Sally a semblance of privacy back in the cavernous hold.

Their seats were formed from dusty burlap sacking and canvas straps. The hold was drafty and smelled of oil and dirt and previous cargoes. The ancient plane creaked and groaned and bucked and roared.

Jake had never felt happier or more comfortable in his entire life.

It was far too noisy for conversation, save the occasional few words spoken loudly and directly into the other's ear. Words about loving and missing and wanting. The hold was dark save for a single dimly glowing lamp that granted just enough light for them to see each other's eyes if they drew up close, which was how they remained. All else was said with looks and embraces and lips.

Too soon the hold echoed with shouts and movements. Reluctantly Jake released her and rose to his feet, pulling Sally along with him. They walked up to where the others gathered at the back of the cockpit. "What's up?"

Towers turned from his controls and grinned. "You remember that part I said you didn't want to know about? Well, it's done arrived."

"Here, sir," Akers said, thrusting a bulky knapsack toward Jake. "You need to put this on."

Jake looked down at the bundle. "What is this?"

"Showtime, old son," Towers said gaily.

"This is a parachute," Jake said. "What do I need a parachute for?"

"Makes the drop a lot easier to take," Towers replied. "Especially the last part."

Sally moved up close to him. "You wouldn't make me go out there by myself, now would you? Not in the dark."

He looked down at her. "You knew about this?"

"Right from the start, sir," Akers confirmed. "The brass spent a good half hour describing a night drop to her, trying to convince her to give them something they could use to confirm that you were who you said you were. But she wouldn't budge." He looked at Sally and shook his head. "Looks like you and Major Servais both got more than your share of luck in the dame category."

"It wasn't luck," Sally said, her eyes resting on Jake.

"Anything you say, ma'am." Akers adjusted his own chute and said, "Better get a move on, sir. We're at two minutes and counting."

A creak and roar and rush of wind announced the winching down of the back ramp. Pierre moved up to Jake and shouted, "Have you ever jumped before?"

"Not since basic training."

"That's more than I have had. Any advice?"

"Bend your knees before you hit, and stay out of the trees."

"How am I to see trees at night?"

"That's the part I never figured out." Jake turned toward the grinning Towers. "I suppose I should thank you."

"Wait until you're safe and sound and send me a postcard." Towers stuck out his hand. "Good luck, old son."

"You're a true friend, Frank."

"I suppose somebody's paid me a nicer compliment somewhere along the line, but I don't remember when." Towers had a grip as hard as iron. "I'll be praying for you, Jake."

"One minute, sir," Akers pressed. "Chute up."

Jake's fingers fumbled with unfamiliar straps and catches. He watched Akers tighten Sally's rig and followed his example. Together with the others he walked back toward the cold clear night that shone through the aft opening and felt his heart rate surge. He found Sally's hand nestling in his own, glanced at Pierre, found himself trading an idiot's grin.

"Hook on, everybody!" Akers called and connected Sally's clip to the overhead wire. As Jake followed suit, Akers yelled above the roaring slipstream, "Slade goes first, I go last. Five seconds between each person. Ready?"

Sally reached up and planted a final kiss firmly on Jake's lips. She shouted something that the wind whipped away. But the look in her eyes was crystal clear.

"Go! Go!"

Chapter Twenty

*T*HE INSTANT OF free-fall before his chute opened seemed to go on and on forever. Then there was a great whomping tug on his shoulders, and his view of the stars was suddenly cut off by a huge circular envelope that glowed pale and beautiful in the faint illumination. Jake took a look around, spotted two other chutes within range, hoped one of them was Sally, resisted the urge to call to her.

The ground rushed up impossibly fast, dark and foreboding. Jake found his heart rate surging to an impossibly high pace, his breath coming in explosive little gasps. Shreds of distant training echoed around in his panicking brain. Choose a point, bleed air, stay loose, try to take up a coiled position like a spring ready to bounce.

Then all thought froze, the ground charged up, his feet struck, and he rolled and rolled and bumped and finally stopped. Jake lay completely wrapped up in the cords and the silk, gasping hard, his heart thundering in his ears. He took stock. Everything hurt. His feet and legs and back and arms and shoulders and head. Everything. But he could feel his toes; he had read somewhere that was a good sign. And his fingers moved. He checked his thighs, found nothing out of the ordinary. And then his breathing eased, and suddenly he found himself laughing.

"Colonel Burnes, is that you, sir?"

"That was great," Jake said. "Just don't ask me to do it again, okay?"

"Anything you say, sir. Hang on and let me cut you loose."

"Where's Sally?"

"Slade's seeing to her."

"And Pierre?"

"Landed like a pro, sir," Akers replied, his voice registering both shock and approval. "By the time I got to him he was already stowing his chute."

Another set of footsteps approached, and Pierre said, "Is that a shroud for the dearly departed colonel, or is he merely having a rest, I wonder."

"Show-off," Jake muttered.

"Perhaps you and I could get together again when this is over," Pierre offered, "and I could give you a few lessons."

"Not on your life." The ropes loosened, and Jake managed to clear the chute from his face. He looked up at a broadly smiling Pierre and asked, "How did you do it?"

"To be perfectly honest, I have no idea. One minute I was up and flying, the next I was standing in this glorious field under this beautiful sky."

"Beginner's luck," Akers said, sawing through the final rope. "Okay, sir. You're clear."

Jake kicked his legs free, scrambled to his feet, and looked over to where another chute lay spread out in the moonlight about a hundred feet away. Something about the scene caught in his throat. He raced over.

Jake fell to his knees beside where Sally sat, with Slade crouching by her legs. "What's the matter?"

"Nothing," Sally snapped, but even in the dim light he could see she was in pain.

"Ankle," Slade said. "Doesn't appear too serious, though. Just a twist or maybe a minor sprain."

"Maybe we should leave you here with the others, ma'am," Akers said, coming up alongside.

"Not a chance," Sally said. "Jake, make them listen to reason. I didn't come this far to miss out on the grand finale."

Jake looked up at Akers. "What others?"

Pierre hissed, crouched, and pointed at the trees bordering their field. Jake squinted, saw a series of shadows separate and began walking toward them. He was reaching to scoop up Sally when Akers stopped him with, "It's okay, sir. They're some of ours." He straightened and whistled softly. Again.

A slender figure broke away and raced ahead of the others. A familiar voice called out, "Pierre?"

"Jasmyn!" Pierre leapt to his feet and bolted toward her. They came together and embraced and their two shadows became one.

"Like I said, sir," Akers said approvingly. "That's some dame."

Chapter Twenty-one

"WE DID NOT FIGHT and sacrifice for our freedom to see it taken away from within."

The gruff-voiced elder was the only one of the group crammed into the back of the ancient transport van who spoke any English. Yet the intensity with which the others listened to his words left no room for doubt that they all felt the same.

"We have always known there were those among us who would climb upon the backs of their countrymen, ever hungry for more land, more money, more titles, more power." The elder passed on the flagon without even seeing what moved through his hands. "The tradition of *La Résistance* is as old as France herself. We have ever had to fight the forces of greed and tyranny. It is the way."

The way. Jake fed hungrily on the fresh-baked bread and crumbly farmer's cheese and ripe early summer apples, taking great bites from each in turn while he pondered what the old man was saying. The way. He listened and heard not only the words, but the same connecting thread he had found in the desert reaches, a world and more away from this rattling van rumbling through the night toward Paris.

Men and women would be ever faced with choices. Their values and actions formed both who they were and the world in which they lived. And those who chose the path of honor would ever be challenged by the fierce crosswinds of those who sought to live for self alone.

Jake suddenly saw that he would be called to stand and defend all he saw as precious—his faith, his land, his way of life. But all he said was, "It is good of you to help us."

"It is an honor to serve with Mademoiselle Coltrane and the brother of Patrique Servais. Even here in the north we have heard of their work. Friends of theirs are friends of ours." Dark eyes glinted beneath brows frosted with the winter winds of age. "And while there is still strength left in this old body, ever will I stand ready to do battle for my beloved country."

"Let us hope it does not come to that," Pierre murmured, his eyes resting upon Jasmyn.

They were all dressed in worker's blue denim, the traditional uniform of the countless denizens who labored at menial tasks throughout all France. Sally and Jake sat squeezed together at the back of the jouncing wheezing van, one of many bringing day laborers into early-morning Paris.

A hiss of warning from the front seat silenced further conversation as they approached the police checkpoint marking the city's outskirts. A pair of blue-caped men opened the back doors, requested papers, inspected each face in turn. Jake glanced at Sally and saw a face smudged and lined with exhaustion and pain, her hair tucked up into her denim cap. Indeed they all looked exhausted, their features matching those of people bored and sleepy and disgruntled over an uncomfortable daily routine.

The policemen handed back their papers, slammed the rear doors, and with a belch of smoke the ancient van trundled on toward Paris.

When the city finally came into view, Pierre wrenched his gaze from Jasmyn's face to watch the skyline through the smudged back windows. "It seems as though my Paris has returned to an earlier age."

"Your Paris?" Jake looked at him. "I thought your family was from Marseille."

Pierre cast him a haughty glance. "All Frenchmen may claim Paris as their own. It is part of our birthright."

The city did appear to have slipped back into a bygone era. Many of the buses and transports were horse-drawn affairs, rattling along on rickety wooden spindle-wheels and being chased by high-backed jalopies that passed with bleats from side-mounted brass horns and winks from the polished lanterns serving as headlights. There were so many of these dilapidated vehicles that the occasional modern car seemed out of place.

"Paris belongs not just to the Parisians," Pierre went on. "Paris belongs to all France. Paris is the crown worn by all Frenchmen. One comes to Paris to escape from the provincial life. One returns to the provinces to escape from Paris."

"You realize," Jake said, exhilarated by the feeling that it was all drawing down to the wire, "you're making absolutely no sense whatsoever."

"That's because you're not French," Pierre said smugly. "There are some things that can be understood only by one of our—"

"Persuasion?" Jake offered.

"Sensibilities," Pierre corrected.

"You're saying I don't belong?"

"Oh no," Pierre replied, only half mocking. "The fact that you are in love, my friend, makes you welcome here. For all those who love, Paris is their second home. Even when they are not here, Paris remains their second home."

Jake turned his gaze back to the window. The River Seine sparkled and beckoned in the early-morning sunlight. Elms and chestnuts lining the riverbanks spread banners of leafy welcome over their passage. In the distance, the Eiffel Tower rose straight and proud into the glorious blue sky.

"Paris is an enormous experience," Pierre said to the window. Jasmyn watched him with a fond smile of approval brightening her tired features. "It is a city to be seen and touched and tasted and breathed. It is a city made for sunlight, for walking, for laughing, for love."

"I'm all for that." Jake looked down at Sally and felt his heart grow wings at the joy of it all. "You doing okay?"

"You don't need to keep asking me that every five minutes," she replied, but she graced him with a from-the-heart look.

"Heads up, everybody," warned Akers from his seat at the front. "We're beginning the final approach."

They joined the hodgepodge of bicycles and trucks and horse-drawn wagons and buses and cars jamming into a great circular plaza adorned by a lofty Egyptian monolith. "Place de la Concorde," Pierre said. "The new American Embassy is just ahead of us, beside the Hotel du Crillon."

A hiss from the front seat silenced them as the van rumbled around the square and pulled up in front of great iron gates. A cordon of blue-caped policemen flanked a pair of striped barriers. Together with the others, Jake climbed from the van and handed his papers over for a second inspection. He watched the policeman examine the forged documents with his head down and his heart in his throat. But the policeman was tired and bored and had no interest in harassing the morning cleaning crew, especially when their papers bore the official embassy stamp. He shoved the papers back into Jake's hands and waved for the barrier to be raised. Jake walked forward, resisting the urge to offer Sally a helping hand. She walked on beside him with a barely discernible limp, her face set in grimly determined lines.

Once through the first barrier, they came face-to-face with a phalanx of Marines, backed up by a master sergeant with the jaw of an ox and eyes of agate. He cast one lightning glance at Akers and gave the soft order, "Pass 'em all. Now."

They were in.

Chapter Twenty-two

THE EMBASSY STILL bore remnants of elegance from its former existence as a ducal residence. They walked up the cobblestone path, through the great double doors, and were immediately surrounded by shouting, scurrying activity.

"Colonel Burnes. Here, sir, over this way. You too, Major Servais."

Jake struggled against the arms pulling him forward. "But Sally—"

The young staffer wore a severe dark suit and a white shirt so starched it looked almost blue. "Sir, there's no time. The minister is due here in less than twenty minutes."

Jake wrenched his arm free and halted traffic by simply refusing to budge. "You just hold your horses, mister."

"But sir—"

"Quiet," Jake snapped. He turned back to the denim-clad group standing in the foyer. He searched out the old man who spoke English and told him, "We could not have done this without you."

"Is it true what Mademoiselle Coltrane says?" the elder demanded. "Your evidence will be enough to end this traitor's quest for power?"

Pierre stepped forward and promised solemnly, "We are going to bury him. Just as he has tried to do to me, my friends, my fiancée, and my brother. His name will be wiped from the pages of history."

"Then it was our duty to help." The elder straightened as much as his years would allow. He raised his work-hardened hand into a salute. Jake and Pierre came to attention and snapped off a reply. "Go with God, messieurs."

Jake turned back to the gaping official and stated flatly, "Miss Anders and Miss Coltrane are to accompany us wherever we are going."

The young man sputtered, "But the ambassador explicitly said—"

"That is an order, mister," Jake snapped.

The young man wilted. "Yessir. This way, gentlemen, ladies."

They were led down a series of halls, up stairs, down another hall, past doorways and empty offices. Jake supported Sally with one arm around her waist and kept his pace to a comfortable speed.

Pierre asked, "Is it not a bit early in the day for you to be having official visitors from the president's cabinet?"

"It was the only time he had available." The staffer was gradually recovering his poise. "The ambassador had to personally request this meeting to get him to come at all. We, ah, that is, the ambassador—"

"I told Clairmont I had news of the greatest importance in regards to two renegade officers," finished a craggy man of strength and height and distinguished features. He walked forward with arm outstretched. "John Halley, United States Ambassador to France."

"Jake Burnes," he said, releasing Sally in order to accept the firm handshake.

"A pleasure, Colonel, and I mean that sincerely." He turned to Sally and said, "Have you hurt yourself, Miss Anders?"

"It's nothing," Sally replied.

"Ankle," Lieutenant Akers said from behind them. "Twisted it on landing, sir."

"Well, don't say I didn't warn you. Shall I help you to a chair?"

"I can manage, Mister Ambassador. But thank you."

"Not at all. Welcome back." He turned on a courtly smile and finished, "And good work."

He turned to Pierre and extended his hand once more. "And you must be Major Servais."

"Yes, Mister Ambassador. May I present—"

"Miss Coltrane needs no introduction." The dark-suited gentleman possessed a lofty charm. He gave a stiff little bow and said, "It is seldom that my day is graced by two such beautiful and courageous women. Your country owes you a great deal, Miss Coltrane."

"Thank you, Mister Ambassador," Jasmyn said quietly, her regal air only slightly diminished by the denim work suit she was wearing. "But it is these two officers who are the real heroes."

A second gray-haired gentleman appeared in the doorway and stated in a clipped British accent, "Yes, well, now that the niceties have been observed, perhaps we can get down to business."

"Of course." Ambassador Halley motioned toward the second gentleman and said, "May I introduce Sir Charles Rollins, His Majesty's envoy to Paris?"

"Charmed, I am sure." His inspection of their scruffy forms dripped disapproval. With an impatient gesture he plucked an engraved watch from his vest pocket and sighed. "Well, I suppose we don't have the time now to send them off someplace to wash and change into something more appropriate."

"I seriously doubt that the minister will give much thought to their appearance," the ambassador replied gravely. "Especially after he hears what I have to say."

"No, perhaps not." The British envoy snapped his watch closed and peered at Pierre from beneath bushy brows. "Major Servais, do I understand that you carry with you a written testimony of your brother's findings?"

"I do," Pierre replied. "In detail."

"May I see it, please?"

"Of course." Pierre extracted a rumpled and folded sheaf of papers. "They are in French, I am afraid."

"No matter," the envoy said, drawing out a pair of reading spectacles. The gathering was silent for a long moment until the envoy finally lifted his eyes and nodded once. "These will do rather nicely."

"I did not doubt it for an instant," Ambassador Halley replied.

"No, of course not. Still, it is best to be certain before confronting a member of the president's cabinet with an accusation of high treason." Sir Charles permitted himself a frosty smile. "All of you are to be congratulated. Minister Clairmont has proven himself to be a dedicated foe to our efforts to create a unified and strengthened Europe." He turned his gaze toward the American ambassador. "I don't suppose there is any reason not to share the news with them, is there?"

"If anyone deserves to hear it, they do," Ambassador Halley replied, and gestured through the doorway. "Why don't we all go in and sit down. Bill, see if you can rustle up some coffee and sandwiches."

"Right away, sir," the young official said.

The ambassador turned to where Akers and Slade stood in silent patience. "You gentlemen are a credit to your service. I imagine you will want to report in to Mr. Walters. I will be speaking with you later."

"Thank you, sir." With a friendly nod toward Jake and another at Sally, they turned and walked down the hall.

"Come in, all of you." They entered a grand salon redesigned as a small conference room. Beyond the oval table was a setting of brocade sofas and chairs gathered about a low coffee table. Once everyone was seated, Ambassador Halley said, "Why don't you carry on, Sir Charles."

"Delighted." The portly gentleman leaned forward and said, "As we speak, our governments are actively engaged in establishing a new and unified military force intended to combat future threats to our freedom and our peace. We hope that this force will be sufficiently strong to stop such disastrous armed conflicts from ever happening again. Nip such troubles in the bud, as it were."

"We intend to call it NATO," Ambassador Halley explained. "The North Atlantic Treaty Organization."

"Yes, and our efforts are being stymied at every turn by a certain Minister Clairmont," Sir Charles huffed, "who has rallied about him every isolationist, Communist, and troublemaker in France."

"He is a power-mad menace," Ambassador Halley agreed. "But this very same power has made him virtually impossible to dislodge. That's why your information has become so vital."

"Exactly," Sir Charles agreed. "Bring Clairmont down, and we behead the behemoth. Then NATO shall emerge from the drawing boards into reality, and Europe shall be taken one step closer to lasting peace."

"So you see, gentlemen," Ambassador Halley concluded, "the information in your charge had much more weight than the discrediting of just one man for wartime treason."

"Indeed, yes," Sir Charles agreed adamantly. "And this also explains why he was able to draw such widespread support when it appeared you had managed to escape the grasp of his minions in Morocco. Clairmont and his supporters saw their entire house of cards begin to tremble in the sudden winds of change."

The young official appeared in the doorway. "Excuse me, Mister Ambassador, Sir Charles. Minister Clairmont is here."

Instantly the two gentlemen were on their feet, raising the others with a single warning glance. "Show the gentleman in, please."

The first thing Jake noticed were the lips. They were pale and fleshy and formless, as was all of the man. He moved with the boneless grace of a jellyfish. His broad girth was encased in hand-tailored finery, yet nothing could disguise the loose-fleshed flaccidity of a dedicated glutton. With every mincing step on his overpolished shoes, his entire body quivered.

"I do hope there truly is an emergency, Ambassador," he said petulantly. His voice was not high, but rather lacked any tone whatsoever. "It was most inconvenient to make time for this, especially with your insisting that we meet here and not in my own offices."

"I assure you, Minister, that these circumstances fit the word emergency perfectly."

He sniffed his disdain and turned to the British envoy. "I do not recall being informed that you would be joining us today, Sir Charles."

"I took it upon myself to come, Minister, I do hope you will excuse the intrusion. Given the gravity of this situation, I thought both our governments should be represented."

The minister raised a contemptuous eyebrow at the denim-suited four and sniffed a second time. "Don't tell me you have discovered a ring of thieves among your cleaning staff."

The look on Pierre's face turned so murderous that the minister took an involuntary step back. Jake reached one hand over and touched Pierre lightly on the back. He watched his friend force himself back to the relaxed calm of a hungry tiger.

The minister noticed it as well. Nervously he said, "Perhaps we should have security join us for this discussion."

"Minister Clairmont, may I introduce Jasmyn Coltrane, formerly of the French Resistance in Marseille. This is Sally Anders, of my own government's administrative staff."

"Ladies," he murmured in his quietly rasping voice. He cast an uncertain glance up and down their rumpled forms. "If this is your idea of a joke, Ambassador, I assure you I am not amused."

"And this," Ambassador Halley continued with evident relish, "is Major Pierre Servais, commandant of the French garrison at Badenburg. The other gentleman is none other than Colonel Jake Burnes, head of the American military base at Karlsruhe."

The thick folds encasing the minister's small eyes widened noticeably. A tremor began upon those pale fleshy lips and passed through his entire body. He tried to speak, but could utter no sound. His corpulent body gradually folded in upon itself, and he collapsed into the chair behind him.

"Let us make ourselves perfectly clear," Sir Charles said crisply. "Nothing would give me greater pleasure than to turn the information that these gentlemen have brought with them over to the newspapers. I would truly delight in watching you be publicly destroyed."

Another tremor passed through the spineless frame, and the pale lips emitted a faint groan.

"However," Sir Charles went on, "our governments have decreed otherwise. We are gathered here to offer you an alternative. You will today call a press conference and declare your total and unequivocal support for NATO. A week from now, you will retire from all public offices. In return for these actions, we will withhold all evidence and allow you to pass from public view with your good name intact."

A visible rage swept through Pierre. Again Jake reached over and gave his friend a warning tap.

The minister raised his eyes in mute appeal. "There is absolutely no room for maneuvering or negotiation," Ambassador Halley stated in a hard voice. "Take it or leave it."

The corpulent shoulders slumped in abject defeat. "I have no choice," he murmured.

"Indeed not." Sir Charles turned to Ambassador Halley. "Perhaps our esteemed visitors might be excused while we go over the details."

"Good idea." Ambassador Halley turned to Jake and said, "I've reserved four rooms at the Hotel du Crillon next door. Rest up and have a look around, why don't you. We'll get together again once this matter has died down."

"We don't have any papers," Jake confessed. "Or money."

"And there is the matter of a price on our heads," Pierre said, his gaze not budging from the minister's bald pate, his fury barely contained.

"My assistant will see to your registration. And as to the matter of the warrants for your arrest," Ambassador Halley said, his own cold loathing showing through as he glanced down at the deflated minister, "I'm sure they will be cleared up in a matter of hours."

Jake shook the offered hands, took a firm grasp of Pierre's arm, and led them all toward where the young official stood waiting in the doorway. Farther down the hall, he pulled Pierre to one side. "I was afraid you were going to lose it there for a minute."

"I cannot believe they expect me to let this matter simply fade away," Pierre hissed. "I will not allow it. The life of my brother has been threatened."

"Not to mention our own," Jake added, grinning broadly.

"And my family's honor is at stake," Pierre continued, then looked sharply at his friend. "I see nothing whatsoever that is the least bit humorous about this affair."

"Think for a minute," Jake said, still smiling. "Did they order you to remain bound by this agreement? Or your brother to stay quiet?"

Pierre's eyes narrowed. "What are you saying?"

"Give them their time in the spotlight," Jake replied. "Let them get this NATO agreement down on paper. Who's going to stop you from going to the papers yourself in a couple of months?"

Pierre stood and digested this for a long moment before the furrows rose in a smile that creased his face from chin to forehead. "My friend, the weight of the world has just dropped from my shoulders."

Jake clapped him on the shoulders and steered him around. "Come on, buddy. The ladies are waiting."

Chapter Twenty-three

SCARCELY HAD THEY entered the elegant hotel lobby when a gray-suited gentleman approached. "Colonel Burnes, my name is Walters."

"Ah," Pierre said. "The man who was not there."

Mr. Walters kept his gaze on Jake. "I was wondering if I could have a minute of your time."

"I was sort of looking forward to having a bath and putting my feet up for a while," Jake replied.

"This won't take long. Please."

Jake looked at Sally and said, "Why don't you go on up to your room? I'll be along directly."

"Thank you so much." Mr. Walters guided him over to a quiet corner and gestured him into a seat. "Can I offer you something?"

"I'll wait for the others, thanks."

"Then I'll come right to the point." Mr. Walters was a trim, mild man whose appearance was so nondescript he almost went unnoticed. Yet there was a tensile strength to his voice, and his gaze was rapier keen. "I hope you will excuse me for not joining you for your little session with the minister. I vastly prefer others to take the limelight. Such things tend to get in the way of those in my profession. I trust everything went according to plan?"

"As far as I could tell," Jake replied. "Are you a spy?"

"I prefer to consider myself an agent in the service of my country. You are familiar with the Office of Strategic Services?"

"The OSS? Who isn't?"

"We are in the process of disbanding. Our mission, that of helping to win the war, has been accomplished." The gaze bit deep, and the crisply articulating voice did not require volume to hold Jake's attention. "But other conflicts are arising, Colonel Burnes. Other dangers loom on the horizon, threatening both our nation and our way of life."

"Just what are you getting at?"

"We need men like you," Walters responded frankly. "Men who show such a combination of traits as you have during the past few weeks—leadership, the ability to think on one's feet, the capacity to land in alien surroundings and both build allies and accomplish the impossible, absolute trustworthiness in adverse circumstances, and much else."

"I have been living on luck," Jake replied flatly.

"Luck plays a great part in the success of our business," he replied. "We try to prepare ourselves as well as possible, and then choose people who have the proven capacity to make their own luck."

Jake felt like he was being blindsided. "You are asking me to give up command of the Karlsruhe base?"

"Is that the life you would prefer for yourself, Colonel? Riding a desk in Germany, bound by all the rules and regulations of a peacetime army?" Slowly Mr. Walters shook his head. "I think not. You are a man who feeds upon adventure. And that is exactly what I am offering. Along with the opportunity to serve your country in ways that best suit the kind of man you are."

Adventure. Jake felt his heart surge at the call. "Where would I be based?"

"Anywhere the need arises." Mr. Walters rose to his feet. "I think we have said enough for one day. Why don't you think on it, Colonel, and get back to me in a day or so."

Chapter Twenty-four

*T*HE NEXT FEW days were filled with the wonder of Sally, the glory of Paris, and the delight of being in love.

The streets of the city teemed with life, but people seemed in no hurry to go anywhere. Simply to be there, to sit and stroll and watch and window-shop, was enough. Thin faces framed bright eyes that peered at everything with great intensity, eager to drink it all in, store it up, refill the heart and mind after the long empty war years.

They took the clattering lift up to the top of the Eiffel Tower, climbed the circular stairs in the Arc de Triomphe, held hands walking down the Champs-Elysees, sat for hours over simple meals. They took a horse carriage along the Bois de Boulogne. They leaned over the back railings of overcrowded buses, allowing the other passengers to push them up together, and relished being in a city where kissing in public was a natural part of life. They lazed in sidewalk cafes for uncounted hours, replete with the day's joy. They walked along the Seine, watched the fishermen and the artists and the other lovers, and felt that here indeed was a haven where love was meant to be renewed.

Paris was a city of love, of passion, of memories, of hope for better tomorrows. The peace and tranquility, the excitement and verve, the beauty and the despair, the fashion and the poverty—it all meant so much more to Jake because he shared it with Sally.

It was there on the banks of the Seine, the third morning after their arrival, that Jake led Sally away from Pierre and Jasmyn and the painters and the fishermen, down to where a bench awaited them, poised beside the river's edge and sheltered by two ancient chestnuts.

Sally seemed to know it was an important moment. Her wide eyes were focused upon him, and for once her customary wit had fled to reveal a woman-child who appeared as nervous and solemn as Jake felt.

Jake turned to her and grasped both of her hands as he had planned to do, his heart hammering with the fear and the joy and fullness of the moment. He looked deep into those beautiful smoky eyes and asked with all the love and gentle force he could muster, "I love you, Sally Anders. With all my heart. Will you marry me?"